1600
99 BB

Cognitive Growth and Development

Essays in Memory of Herbert G. Birch

Edited by

MORTON BORTNER PH.D.

*Professor of Psychology and Education
and Director of Clinical Training,
Ferkauf Graduate School,
Yeshiva University, New York*

BRUNNER/MAZEL, *Publishers* • New York

Library of Congress Cataloging in Publication Data

Main entry under title:
Cognitive growth and development.
    "Publications, Herbert G. Birch": p.
    Includes bibliographies and index.

    1. Cognition—Addresses, essays, lectures.   2. Cognition in children—Addresses,
essays, lectures.   3. Neuropsychology—Addresses, essays, lectures.   4. Birch, Her-
bert George, 1918-1973.   I. Birch, Herbert George, 1918-1973.   II. Bortner,
Morton.   [DNLM: 1. Cognition—In infancy and childhood.   2. Perception—
In infancy and childhood.   3. Child development. WS105.5.C7 C676]
BF311.C5517   153.4   78-12036

ISBN 0-87630-183-9

Published by
BRUNNER/MAZEL, INC.
19 Union Square West, New York, N. Y. 10003

Preface

This volume is dedicated to the memory of Herbert G. Birch, who was a moving force in the field of psychology. I would like to begin this preface by making some comments about the scientific importance of Birch's work. I will then conclude with some personal notes on Birch's life and influence on his colleagues.

A Scientific Appreciation

To the best of my knowledge no one has contributed more broadly to the solution of problems of mental retardation than Herbert G. Birch. He long ago recognized that an increase in our ability both to prevent retardation and to help retarded children depended upon an increase, both quantitatively and qualitatively, in our understanding of the laws of normal behavioral development and of the influences, both physiological and environmental, that could contribute to a disruption or disorganization of this normal path. The scope of his work reflects this attitude, and embraces such diverse problems as the epidemiology of mental retardation, the obstetrical and social antecedents of defective development, the relation of malnutrition to intellectual functioning, the behavioral organization of the newborn, the detailed study of brain-damaged children, the nature of reading disability, the examination of the developmental course of integration among the separate sense systems, the nature of temperament, the development of cognition, and the relevance of comparative psychology and its methods for the study of mental retardation.

His competence in a variety of areas based upon both graduate training in psychology and medicine, with special talents in developmental neurology, behavioral development, comparative psychology and nutrition, resulted in a broad and penetrating approach utilizing clinical, experimental, observational and epidemiological methods. His work helped greatly in the delineation of behavioral organization and development in normal and aberrantly functioning children and reflected an interest in both the intrinsic features of behavioral organization and the environmental circumstances which may affect this system during the course of its development. His special concern was with those deviations that result in subnormal intellectual functioning, and with the consequences for behavior that stem from either central nervous system damage or exposure to environmental risk that endangers the integrity of development.

These concerns resulted in a series of publications, sometimes done on a collaborative basis with younger investigators who gained by their exposure to his thinking, and who were thereby trained as research cadre.

FIELD STUDIES

Birch was highly ingenious in defining problems for community investigations and in identifying uniquely valuable settings for field studies which contribute fundamentally to our understanding of factors which contribute to mental retardation. These studies have taken place in Scotland, Guatemala, Mexico and Jamaica. Each of the settings was selected because of its particular value as a place in which a different opportunity existed for enhancing our understanding of causes for mental retardation. The particular problems and findings in each of these settings are briefly summarized in the following paragraphs.

Obstetrics, Social Status and Retardation. Aberdeen, Scotland is unique as a community in which a stable population has been obstetrically supervised by a singe obstetrical research service under the direction of Sir Dugald Baird since 1947. In this community it was therefore possible to study the total population of children and link the presence of intellectual subnormality and school failure with the events surrounding the pregnancy and delivery of which the child is the product. The community is also one in which the social circumstances of different segments of the population are clearly definable. Consequently, in this setting it was possible to examine the interaction between social circumstances and obstetrical events in the production of mental handicap. The volume *Mental Subnormality in the Community: A Clinical and Epidemiologic Study* reports one portion of the results of these studies and clearly is destined to be a classic in the field. Additional work reported in journals also attests to the value of the setting for defining causes for educational failure; taken as a whole, this study provides a firm foundation upon which to build a biosocial conception of defective development.

Malnutrition and Mental Development. In Guatemala, Mexico and Jamaica, Birch and his collaborators focused on the risk which malnutrition in infancy and early childhood creates for faulty intellectual growth. His studies in Guatemala with Cravioto pointed to the lags in intersensory information processing which attach to chronic malnutrition. His continuing studies in Mexico with the same co-investigator contributed to our understanding of the ecology of both malnutrition and intellectual backwardness. In both Mexico and Jamaica he conducted follow-up studies of seriously malnourished infants and their intact siblings which further clarified the role of malnutrition in mental retardation.

Concept and Theory. These field investigations caused Birch to become broadly concerned with the multiple ways in which malnutrition may affect mental development on an intergenerational basis. This led him to an overall concern with the problem of social and biological disadvantage. His thoughts on this question appeared in a book *Disadvantaged Children: Health, Nutrition and School Failure,* a unique integration of basic knowledge in public health, obstetrics, growth, sociology, comparative psychology, history, social policy, and nutrition, which establishes a sound conceptual basis for understanding the sources of mental retardation in a biologic and social perspective.

Studies of the Newborn

Birch's studies of the newborn are concerned with both normal neonates and neonates who have been subjected to a variety of conditions of risk. The major intent of these studies was to define what constitutes effective stimulation for the neonate, and to do so by determining the manner in which he processes information and patterns his behavior. These interests led to studies of lateralization and studies which examined hierarchical relations of sense systems in newborn infants. In order to pursue these objectives, these studies identified sources of effective stimulation and behavioral indicators which reliably and stably permitted one to determine whether or not an applied stimulus was effective in producing a definable and reliable response in the young organism. Having identified such indicators, he was then able to study the relationship between the infant's physiologic condition at birth and the direction and magnitude of laterally differentiated behaviors. The results of these studies have suggested a positive relation between physiologic intactness at birth and the extent to which infants exhibit clear lateral differentiation in the organization of behavior.

Through the use of these indicators, he was able to examine the hierarchical organization of sense systems in the newborn infant, as well as differences in the infant's responsiveness to teloreceptor (auditory) and proximoceptor (somesthetic) inputs. In studying this problem he used differential habituation rates to the stimuli as the basis for determining the hierarchical position of sense modalities. It was found that teloreceptor inputs are more rapidly habituated and that upon repetition of presentation these types of stimuli soon become relatively ineffective in eliciting a response. In contrast, somesthetic stimulation appears to be markedly resistant to habituation and the infant persists in his responsiveness to such stimulation even after many repetitions of the presentation.

These studies have provided a clearer understanding of the neurologic and behavioral dynamics of early infancy. They have shown that sensitive examinations may be of considerable help in defining abnormalities in infants subject to birth insults. In addition, they have provided methods and indicators which, as they are applied, will permit us to know the aspects of the world of stimulation to which the newborn responds. As a consequence, they are fundamental both for the science of child development and for the very early diagnosis of behavioral abnormality.

Studies of Temperament

In collaboration with Alexander Thomas and Stella Chess, Birch spent almost 20 years in the longitudinal study of temperament and its development in children. These studies were begun because of their conviction that our emphasis on the "what" and "how well" of behavior was being carried out without sufficient attention being paid to the "how" of behavioral organization. It appeared to him that this neglect made it impossible to understand behavioral individuality and the contributions which the child's own behavioral style, as reflected in his activity level, mood, distractibility, persistence, sensory threshold and malleability, made to his own development.

In the course of these studies, it was shown that a child's temperament is definable in the first months of his life and is a persistent contributor to his developmental course. The stability of temperament, as well as its relation to child care, learning, social functioning and behavior disorders, has been examined in the investigations conducted by Thomas, Chess and Birch. More recently, certain of the techniques for the evaluation of temperament have been applied to problems in the development, course and management of mentally retarded and brain-damaged children. The work has been most fully summarized in three books: *Behavioral Individuality in Early Childhood, Your Child Is a Person,* and *Temperament and Behavioral Disorders in Children.*

These studies were later extended to a consideration of differences and similarities in temperamental organization in different social and ethnic groups.

Cognitive Development

Central to his investigations in this area is the study of perceptual development. The underlying view is that the development of inter-sensory organization constitutes one of the primary developmental processes in childhood, and that it represents a sensitive indicator of organization or disorganization of central nervous system functioning. A disordering of the interrelations among the separate sense systems may represent a fundamental defect contributing to wide ranging deficiencies and defects in adaptive behavioral competence in children.

Much of his work was directed at the development of methods for the examination of intersensory functioning and perceptually based motor functioning in children and with the establishment of reliable baseline indicators for behavioral assessment of normal and deviant children. He and his colleagues developed methods for studying modality interrelations in sensory functioning, as well as for analyzing hierarchical relations among the sensory systems, intersensory equivalences and the relation of intersensory organization and of perceptual competence to the development of voluntary motor control. Work in the interrelationships between the development of intersensory organization and the ability of the child to direct his action on the basis of a visual model is summarized in his monograph (with Lefford) on *Visual Discrimination, Intersensory Integration and Voluntary Motor Control.*

Deviant patterns of intersensory organization have been demonstrated in a number of groups of children who are deviant in their development and include cerebral palsied children, children with reading disabilities, mentally subnormal children and children with psychiatric disturbances. Many of his views in this area are summarized in the edited book *Brain Damage in Children* and in the monographs and articles written in collaboration with Lefford, Belmont, and Bortner.

In addition, Birch and his colleagues became engaged in other fundamental studies of cognitive functioning. In a continuing series of longitudinal, cross-ethnic investigations, he was concerned with cognitive
style as it is reflected in characteristic responses to demands for intellectual work in middle-class white and Puerto Rican working-class children. This work was reported in a monograph and indicates that as
early as three years of age children in disadvantaged groups already
exhibit markedly divergent patterns of function which affect intellectual
growth. The strategies used in this study have been adopted by workers
in other countries as a prototype for their own investigations.

Other studies in cognition have dealt with the patterning of intellectual functioning in normal, retarded, brain-damaged and emotionally
disturbed children. These studies have contributed to a clearer delineation of the particular areas of competence and incompetence which
characterize subgroups of handicapped children. This knowledge lays a
firmer basis for educational planning and suggests mechanisms of different kinds which may underlie defective behavior.

Birch also dealt with conceptual, theoretical and methodologic issues
in cognitive growth. He and his colleagues emphasized the important
distinction between cognitive capacity and cognitive performance. They
have pointed to ways in which the modification of the child's performance set and conditions for work affect the availability of his possessed
capacities. These considerations must lead to a re-evaluation of views on
cognitive development and suggest a basis for effective pedagogy.

Neurological and Behavioral Organization in Older and Brain-damaged Adults

As a student of development and as an evolutionary theorist, Birch
long believed that a considerable amount of insight with respect to the
processes and mechanisms of normal brain development could be obtained through the study of behavioral deterioration in older and
brain-damaged adults. As a consequence, he and his associates conducted
a series of studies of neurobehavioral organization in older persons with
brain damage which deal with alterations in sensory and perceptual functioning. These studies analyzed the organization of sense systems, the
manner in which sensory information was utilized in the organization
of action, and the manner in which the sense systems related to one
another. They were concerned with the general problem of arousal and
its relation to afferent organization and involved the investigation of
autonomic responsiveness, stability and instability. They led to the

conclusion that in both normal and brain-damaged elderly adults certain alterations in the mechanisms of excitation-inhibition occurred and that these changes appeared to underlie the organization of behavior in these persons.

Investigations of mechanisms of nervous system excitability in normal and brain-damaged elderly adults, using behavioral indicators, were based on the view that: 1) afferent organization is the main determinant of action in all individuals; 2) the effective environment is different for normal and for brain-damaged individuals and that these differences in effective environment and information processing in brain-damaged individuals provide clues regarding the development of afferent organization; and 3) normally and abnormally functioning mechanisms of afferent organization may be fruitfully viewed in terms of a changing balance between excitatory and inhibitory processes in the nervous system. Investigations of functional patterns were therefore based upon the study of excitation-inhibition balance within and between afferent systems in the normal nervous system and the analysis of changes in such balance which occur as a consequence of damage to the brain.

One series of studies (using the auditory time-error technique) led to the view that damage to the nervous system results in increased inertia in nervous system functioning which is reflected in: 1) an increase in the time required by the damaged system to process information; and 2) an increase in the time required by it to recover from the effects of preceding stimulation. Studies of the mechanisms underlying extinction were undertaken, and they confirmed and elaborated upon the inertia hypothesis. Results of such studies suggested that stimulation of the affected side of a patient having unilateral cerebral damage leads to a slower rate in the development of response by the affected hemisphere than by the intact hemisphere. This difference in rate results in the earlier attainment of an effective level of organization on the intact side and the suppression of the more slowly developing process on the damaged side.

The studies also suggested that certain basic mechanisms of arousal and inhibition are the same in both the normal and damaged brain except for differences in the latency of response. These studies supported the view that inhibition in the normal adult nervous system is the product of differential timing of activation which occurs as a consequence of the application of multiple stimuli and of the selective interference of the organization of one input by another.

These investigations of older persons suggest strongly that the developmental mechanisms of two aspects of brain function require intensive study. The first of these is the process of inhibition which when disturbed results in fundamental disorganization of behavior. It appears possible that higher order behavioral development depends upon effective inhibition, the laws for the development of which are only poorly understood. The second is the patterning of interhemispheric relationships, an area we are only beginning to explore.

Some Personal Notes

Shortly after Herbert G. Birch's death in 1973 a number of his colleagues and collaborators met on several occasions to discuss ways in which his life and work could be honored. One of the decisions that came out of these meetings was that a memorial volume be published.* Such a book was to contain original contributions by some reasonable number of his friends and colleagues. We soon realized that a collection of papers from the variety of areas that interested him would have required another Birch to integrate and synthesize. No one present felt equal to such a task. It became necessary, therefore, to find a theme that suggested his breadth, and yet at the same time would address itself to an identifiable constituency in psychology and/or medicine. Such a theme, we believed, was *cognition*, which cuts across many boundaries both within and between psychology and medicine. The work reported in the present volume, therefore, is representative of only one facet of Birch's incredible range. The contributors to this volume are necessarily a small sample of the large army of researchers around the world who were attracted to and worked or consulted with him.

One way to estimate the extensiveness of Birch's collaborations and influence is to look at his publications. The complete listing of his journal articles, monographs and books are included in an Appendix to this volume for the readers' convenience and edification. This listing was kindly supplied by Mrs. Ida Hafner. No volume dedicated to the memory of Birch would be complete without mentioning the support that he received from this extraordinary woman, who was his secretary, administrative assistant, confidante, and right hand. Even he would not have done as good work as he did without her help. His writings, if taken alone, however, would lead to an underestimate of his influence, since there were scores of professionals, clinicians, and researchers who consulted with him without necessarily publishing with him.

---

* In addition to this book, a school has been named in his honor. All royalties accruing from the sale of the present volume have been pre-assigned to the Herbert G. Birch School for Exceptional Children, Inc., New York.

Birch was a highly productive man. What were the sources of his productivity? I only know that he was driven. I do not pretend to know what drove him, and I sincerely doubt that he himself knew. Although I will not presume to describe his personal qualities in any detail, I will mention some outstanding qualities for the record.

He was at home in the physical and biological sciences, in history and the social sciences, in languages, literature and music. As a young man he had been an athlete, a carpenter, a bartender and a musician. He built his house in the country with his own hands. He never lost an argument, needed very little sleep and probably exaggerated just a bit.

He was by training a psychologist and a physician, and yet nothing very much like any psychologist or physician I've met before or since. He brought to each of these two roles, which he integrated in the interest of scientific research, the wisdom which one usually associates with a lifetime of scholarship and study, and which for most of us encompasses not more than one or two domains of knowledge. His knowledge, however, encompassed comparative, developmental and physiological psychology, neurophysiology, neurology, pediatrics, nutrition and heaven only knows what else.

He was a man of prodigious knowledge, skills, personal warmth and strength, and social concern. Various eulogies have referred to him as a man of genius. They said his life was an exhortation to us all. These statements are undoubtedly correct but they are insufficient. He was primarily an *advocate for the disadvantaged of the world*. He used his knowledge and persuasive skills for them. Indeed, it was in this sense that he was the personification of science and ethics in the service of man.

He was a *life force*. This expression comes closest to conveying a certain essence about him which had an extraordinary effect on those around him. His presence enriched their personal and professional lives. I am sorry for those who did not know him. When he died, the bell tolled for all of us, and we were diminished by his leaving. If I had to characterize him most succinctly, I would choose to call him a *gift*. We cannot complain that he left so soon. We were lucky to have had him at all.

M.B.

Contents

Introduction

The present volume follows convention and places the chapters into convenient categories of Perceptual Processes, Intellectual Processes, and Complex Processes and Complex Behaviors.

Chapters 1 to 6 are attempts to develop special theories of perception. Since they all have a biological orientation they can probably best be described as developmental and neuropsychological theories. In this first section McGuinness and Pribram review research on early appearing sex differences and conclude that males as early as four to five months of age respond to objects more than do females. By puberty they internalize these inclinations and are able to solve visual-spatial problems by nonverbal transformations. These abilities in interaction with keen visual acuity and increasing physical strength lead to superiority in exploratory and manipulative action. In contrast, females of similar age show a preference for faces over objects. They are more sensitive to certain aspects of auditory input, especially to changes in intensity and to localization of sound. They go on to develop a relatively stronger interest in people. The authors relate these findings to a theory of brain organization which hypothesizes greater flexibility in females in hemispheric function which in turn derives from hormonally induced differences in the arousal mechanism.

McGuire and Turkewitz discuss Schneirla's approach-withdrawal theory, and concentrate on the intensity hypothesis which describes a relationship between the nature of an organism's response and the intensity of stimulation. Low intensity evokes approach and high intensity evokes withdrawal. Thus, a basis is suggested for the organization of behavior at early stages of development in all animals. At higher phyletic levels these intensity-determined behavior patterns, characteristic only of early stages of development, provide the foundation upon which later, higher level functioning rests. Mechanisms are suggested by which transitions occur from intensity-determined patterns to more complex levels of responding.

Benton reminds us of the variety of abilities which underlie the task of finger recognition. He goes on to ask about the relationship between poor finger recognition and educational achievement. He distinguishes between *concurrent* and *predictive* relationships and concludes that only the latter are supported by research. Why should the abilities involved in finger recognition foreshadow the success with which children master reading and arithmetic? Benton hypothesizes that the finger recognition task requires competence in a number of cognitive-perceptual areas, including the ability to utilize pictorial representations as a guide to action, to translate tactile information into visual terms, and to utilize verbal labels.

Braine reviews current thinking on the development of orientation perception and suggests an alternative view with supporting evidence. The prevailing view explains developmental progress by referring to the low salience of orientation as a discriminative cue and the gradual learning to attend. Errors, therefore, are due to defective attention to relevant dimensional cues. Braine argues against this attentional hypothesis. She goes on to propose that identification occurs when the features of a shape are processed in serial order, beginning with a focal feature at the top and continuing in a downward direction. She reports a series of experiments in which it is demonstrated that in young children shapes are identified according to hierarchically organized stages of development. The interesting conclusion to be derived from this developmental theory of orientation perception is that orientation errors in the reproduction of designs by brain damaged individuals are not simply errors—rather, they may be seen as reflecting different levels of organization in the processing of information that correspond to levels of human development.

Bakker reviews the literature on auditory and visual asymmetry, i.e., right or left sided superiority, in relation to reading ability. Reading ability may be psycholinguistically differentiated according to whether the perceptual elements (early reading) or meaning (advanced reading) is being stressed. The left hemisphere, because of its association with the semantic aspects of language development subserves advanced reading. According to Bakker's theory, right hemispheric representation of language, because of its association with the perceptual features of the text, subserves early reading. Hence, the theory predicts different laterality-reading relationships at different stages of the learning to read process.

Belmont is interested in neuropsychological processes underlying perceptual and perceptual-motor functioning in brain-damaged adults. He reviews studies dealing with the increased time required by the damaged nervous system to process information. In this connection, he reports a program of research with older, right CVA patients in which he utilized the time error technique. In normals, as the time interval between tones is increased the response shifts from judgments that the second tone is softer to judgments that it is louder. In brain-damaged patients this state of affairs is maintained but requires a longer time to evolve. What are the behavioral consequences of the fact that the intact hemisphere of the brain processes information in advance of the affected hemisphere? Belmont suggests that stimuli presented successively may be experienced as simultaneous. Also, that when stimuli are presented simultaneously (as in the face-hand test) the result is the suppression of one of the stimuli. Such interference phenomena may underlie observed deficiencies in perception and awareness, and the organization of action.

Chapters 6 to 9 of Section II on *Intellectual Processes* constitute a cohesive section insofar as all are concerned with influences, adverse and otherwise, on the development of intelligence, and with methodological issues that emerge in describing the relationship between such influences and intellectual performance.

Tizard joins the battle over the relative contribution of genes and environment to the vague constellation of capacities and competencies that we call intelligence. It is his belief (and one which I know was shared by Birch) that the current controversy owes its renewed interest to political rather than scientific concerns. He argues against Jensen's methods and conclusions and advances the view that the whole current debate about heritability is based on the untenable assumption that inferences about *within*-group differences can be used to explain differences *between* groups.

Bortner believes that the diagnostic term "brain damage" subsumes a diversity of cognitive disabilities. Since a variety of entities may underlie this obscurantist label, there is the methodological issue of how to define "heterogeneity." He describes three research strategies for the study of cognitive patterning and concludes that distinct subgroups among children diagnosed as brain damaged do in fact exist. In addition, in exploring the variety of neurological signs that characterize brain-damaged children, he reports a positive relationship between number of soft signs of CNS impairment and level of intellectual functioning.

Issues related to birth order and family size were examined by Lillian

Belmont who reports that both are associated with intellectual competence, school success and psychiatric status. The finding of a downward
gradient as birth order increased was consistent. Her findings relate
birth order to school failure, as well as to psychiatric disturbance.

Stein and Susser report on the relation of early nutrition and mental
development. The association between maternal undernutrition and low
birthweight and retarded development in the infant was the theoretical
background against which the Stein and Susser study took place. The
famine in the Netherlands during the years 1944-1945 provided the
unhappy laboratory for studying the effects of reduced nutrition in
mothers on their offspring who had thereby suffered nutritional deprivation at specified times in intrauterine life. They were able to document
the untoward effects of the famine on fertility, mental performance,
outcome of pregnancy, infant mortality, health status and obesity.

Chapters 10 to 12 deal with a variety of *Complex Processes and Complex Behaviors* which do not lend easily to any single useful categorization, but in each of which cognitive performance, in a confounded
sense, plays a central role. Although it is true that Thomas and Chess
are primarily discussing the emergence and development of temperament, they are also describing a bridge between cognition and affect.
Rutter is also constructing bridges between cognitive and affective behavior in the area of psychopathology. Thus, the chapters of Thomas
and Chess and Rutter can be read as a refutation of that aspect of
Kant which so schematically separated cognition from affect.

Thomas and Chess summarize their well-known longitudinal study in
which they report that the behavior of children can be classified into
various categories of temperament. These temperamental characteristics
play an important role in the interaction between child and environment
during the course of his development. The child's temperament influences the responses of significant others which in turn act back on the
child in a mutually reciprocal interaction. Implications for effective
schooling are drawn and it is suggested that success in academic achievement may, in part, reflect the extent to which certain of the above described affective tendencies are accommodated. Thus, the arbitrary
separation of temperament and cognition is bridged.

Rutter summarizes a decade's research on the defining characteristics
of autistic children. First, he confirms that the entity is meaningful in
that it can be differentiated from other psychiatric conditions. The three
major bases on which such differentiation occurs are interpersonal incapacity, language handicap, and ritualistic phenomena such as repetitive and stereotyped play patterns. The family interactions of these

children were found to have no etiological significance. Biological correlates were equally unimpressive. More striking are Rutter's own findings based on twin studies that some kind of cognitive disorder is genetically transmitted. In fact, it is cognitive defect that appears to be central to Rutter's view of autism; this defect subsumes difficulties in language and the interpersonal handicap is secondary.

Whiteman reviews the literature dealing with Piaget's theory of moral realism and the distinction between subjective and objective responsibility. Consequences are, of course, judged in relation to intent, and this is a developmental phenomenon, with young children showing an increasing capacity with age to judge the intent of the actor. However, the nature of intent is, itself, complex and Whiteman points out the need to make distinctions within this broad category.

Contributors

DIRK J. BAKKER, PH.D.
Head, Department of Developmental and Experimental Neuropsychology, Paedologisch Institut, Koningslaan, Amsterdam, The Netherlands

IRA BELMONT, PH.D.
Professor of Psychology, Yeshiva University, New York

LILLIAN BELMONT, PH.D.
Research Scientist V (Epidemiology), New York State Psychiatric Institute; Senior Research Associate, Division of Epidemiology, School of Public Health, Columbia University, New York

ARTHUR BENTON, PH.D.
Professor of Neurology and Psychology, University of Iowa, Iowa City

MORTON BORTNER, PH.D.
Professor of Psychology and Education and Director of Clinical Training, Department of Psychology, Ferkauf Graduate School, Yeshiva University, New York

LILA GHENT BRAINE, PH.D.
Professor and Chair, Department of Psychology, Barnard College, Columbia University, New York

STELLA CHESS, M.D.
Professor of Child Psychiatry and Director of Child and Adolescent Services, New York University Medical Center, New York

DIANE McGUINNESS, Ph.D.
Lecturer, Department of Psychology, University of California. Santa Cruz, California

IRIS McGUIRE, Ph.D.
Research Fellow, Department of Pediatrics, Rose F. Kennedy Center, Albert Einstein College of Medicine, Yeshiva University, New York

KARL H. PRIBRAM, M.D.
Professor of Neuroscience, Departments of Psychology, Psychiatry and Behavioral Sciences, Stanford University, Stanford

MICHAEL RUTTER, M.D.
Professor of Child Psychiatry, Institute of Psychiatry, London

MERVYN SUSSER, M.B., B.Ch., F.R.C.P. (E)
Professor and Head, Division of Epidemiology, Columbia University School of Public Health, New York

ZENA STEIN, M.A., M.B., B.Ch.
Director, Epidemiology of Mental Retardation Research Unit, New York State Psychiatric Institute, and Professor of Public Health (Epidemiology), Columbia University School of Public Health, New York

ALEXANDER THOMAS, M.D.
Professor of Psychiatry, New York University Medical Center, New York

JACK TIZARD, Ph.D.
Research Professor of Child Development, Institute of Education, University of London and Director, Thomas Coram Research Unit, London

GERALD TURKEWITZ, Ph.D.
Professor, Department of Psychology, Hunter College, City University of New York, and Visiting Associate Professor, Department of Pediatrics, Rose F. Kennedy Center, Albert Einstein College of Medicine, Yeshiva University, New York

MARTIN WHITEMAN, Ph.D.
Professor of Clinical Psychology, School of Social Work, Columbia University, New York

COGNITIVE GROWTH AND DEVELOPMENT

Essays in Memory of Herbert G. Birch

Section I

PERCEPTUAL PROCESSES

1

The Origins of Sensory Bias in the Development of Gender Differences in Perception and Cognition

DIANE MCGUINNESS *and*
KARL H. PRIBRAM

INTRODUCTION

A chapter relating sex differences and neurophysiology may seem out of place in a volume dedicated to Herbert Birch, as he was involved in neither field of investigation. Nevertheless, as with any pioneer, his ideas and endeavors have had a significant impact on many areas apparently unrelated to his own fields of study. This impact has been critical for one of us (DM) in the formulation of certain theoretical proposals which attempt to chart the development of perceptual and cognitive differences between the sexes and to relate this to brain function.

The essence of living organisms is that they adapt to their environment. This adaptation is always regulated by biological constraints. One aspect of the process of adaptive biology has been highlighted in a pioneering study in human development by Thomas, Chess and Birch (1969). Applying ethological techniques in a longitudinal framework, these researchers were able to show that biologically endowed temperamental and behavioral characteristics endure from infancy to adulthood. The healthy psychological development of the individual was seen to be determined by the *interaction* of specific combinations of traits and the way parents and society responded to them. For example, a child with a slow tempo, who needed time to adapt to change in his environment, could be handled with patience and forbearance. If, however, such a child was pressured or rushed, the ensuing stress could lead to a gross sense of inferiority and neurotic symptoms. These findings are particularly relevant to an assessment of the development of differences between the sexes. The critical problem is to establish which inherent capacities are the most or least modifiable.

Birch's research has also added insight into another important area in the study of sex differences. This deals with the question of how certain perceptual and motor skills become integrated to give rise to the qualitatively different abilities found in males and females. Modality preferences seem evident and lead to the suggestion that cross-modal integration may be different between males and females. This relates not only to the primary sensory modalities but also to the integration of the image of an act with its subsequent visual-motor feedback. Birch's initial involvement with problems of cross-modal function have been detailed in an excellent review by Freides (1974), in which he charts the development of the field from the original work of Birch and Belmont (1964). In his assessment of the literature, Freides is led to ask the following questions:

> Is it possible that modality preference (verbalizers versus visualizers) interacts with informational demands to determine the pattern of differentiation or integration at higher levels of cognitive processing? Do genetic factors or early childhood experiences differentially bias or organize modality preferences? The questions do not appear to have been asked in this way, so the data are not available (pp. 302-303).

These are precisely the questions that one of us has been asking (McGuinness, 1976a). That the answers appear elusive may in large part be due to the fact that almost all the studies on cross-modal functioning have ignored sex differences, or have selected subjects in such a way that sex differences are obscured or eliminated. For example, as most females are good readers, and most remedial reading classes contain largely males, a selected population of either all good or all bad readers includes an abnormal sample of male or female subjects.

This chapter takes up the questions posed by Freides and will go on to suggest that the answers are in the affirmative. By assessing the problem in terms of sex differences it can be seen that both genetic and environmental factors do bias modality preferences and that these preferences lead in turn to differences in efficiency for certain cognitive skills. Used in this fashion, the study of sex differences in some circumstances can substitute for more time-consuming longitudinal techniques.

As the sexes differ noticeably and consistently in certain cognitive abilities, the fundamental question is whether or not they also differ in more basic sensory capacities which may contribute to the higher-order function, and if so, does this occur in a consistent manner? For instance, a high degree of discriminative ability in the auditory mode would scarcely be expected to bear much relationship to visual-spatial skill, but could conceivably be involved in the perception of speech.

If we succeed in presenting a convincing case for basic sensory differences between the sexes, we are also faced with the awkward but fascinating question of how similar brain tissue and functional anatomy can give rise to such differences. We propose in the final section a model of brain function in which specific processing facilities are based on the integration of brain *systems*. This is in contrast to current theories which attribute differences in cognitive skills to isolated regions of brain tissue.

The chapter is organized in the following manner: The next section reviews the literature relevant to establishing that basic sensory differences between the sexes do exist and that they can be detected at early ages. This section also includes information on the differences in response patterns between the sexes. In the final section these data are used to present a theory of attention which illustrates the way in which attention to sensory information can act as a bias on the developing system. This section also details the data that support a "systems" theory of brain integration, and contrasts this approach to current simple hemisphere dominance hypotheses.

SEX DIFFERENCES IN PERCEPTION AND COGNITION: A REVIEW

Sex Differences in Sensory Capacities and
Response Characteristics

Sex differences in sensory capacity and response characteristics provide some of the most important evidence on the development of perceptual differences. It is difficult to argue that basic sensitivities or responsivities over which the subject has little control are the products of subtle differences in reinforcement due to environmental contingencies. If there is evidence for consistent differences in sensory capacity and responsivity between the sexes throughout life, then it is conceivable that these differences may contribute to other more complex central processes.

Sensory capacity in infancy

In the very young infant, neither the ear nor the eye is functional at any level approaching that of the child or adult (Spears & Hohle, 1967). Thus, the possibility for individual variation in the rate of development is great and sex differences are, therefore, difficult to demonstrate. Tactile sensitivity appears somewhat greater in females in some studies (Lipsitt & Levy, 1959; Bell & Costello, 1964; Wolff, 1969), but negative findings appear in others. Lipsitt and Levy (1959) report a failure to replicate, and Gullicksen and Crowell (1964) could find no sex differences. Data on the neonate for the auditory and visual modalities show little effect of sex (Engel et al., 1968; Eisenberg, 1972; Korner, 1970, 1971; Korner & Thomas, 1970), which suggests, in view of the differences found subsequently, that these modalities in the neonate are not sufficiently developed to provide much useful information. Reviews by Korner (1973) and by Maccoby and Jacklin (1974) essentially confirm this.

There is, nonetheless, a consistent trend in a number of studies investigating neonates and infants up to the age of about four months (Friedman et al., 1970; Greenberg, 1971; Greenberg & O'Donnell, 1972; Collins et al., 1972). When measuring fixation to either checkerboards, stripes, or dots of increasing complexity (diminishing size), females are generally found to fixate the larger or the simpler of the stimuli. Males tend to rapidly habituate to the larger simpler input, while females often habituate more rapidly to the most complex input. As it has been clearly demonstrated that this effect is age dependent, with older children spending more time in fixation of the more complex input, this paradigm seems to be tapping an acuity mechanism (Greenberg & Weizmann, 1971; Greenberg & O'Donnell, 1972). The results from several of these studies suggest that females may have poorer acuity than males, and that the reason they habituate quickly to a fine grained checkerboard or fine stripes is because they appear as a uniform surface. One exception to this result was found in a study by Greenberg and Weizmann (1971) where girls showed more appropriate differential responses to checkerboards of three sizes. Nevertheless, the boys produced more rapid habituation in most stimulus conditions. These findings accord with the significantly superior visual acuity found in males at later ages.

Sensory capacity in the child and adult

Taste. Apart from the finding that females tend to prefer greater concentrations of sugar or saccharin to males (see Maccoby & Jacklin,

1974), the only available information on taste differences and sensitivities between the sexes comes from a well-controlled study by Bailey and Nichols in 1888. They tested 82 males and 46 females of college age to determine thresholds for taste sensation across a number of categories. Their initial interest was the relationship among taste sensitivities to different substances, but they were surprised to find consistent sex differences in each case. The mean scores for males and females for the different thresholds are presented in Table 1. No statistics were performed on these data, but the trend is clearly present, with females most sensitive.

TABLE 1

Sex Differences in Taste

*The number of parts of water to one part of
substance for detection threshold*

	Quinine	Sugar	Acid	Alkali	Salt
Males	392,000	199	2,080	98	2,240
Females	456,000	204	3,280	126	1,980

N — 128 from Bailey & Nichols (1888)

Smell. Nichols and Bailey (1886) again provide evidence on sex differences in sensitivity to smell. Here the trend is reversed, with males considerably more sensitive. Their sample of subjects was 17 male and 17 female college students in the first study and 27 males and 21 females in the second. The data have been collated from the two experiments and are presented in Table 2.

Nichols and Bailey's findings were replicated on 50 adults by Otto-lenghi in Italy in 1888. Ottolenghi included a control for smoking. Unfortunately, no further studies are available on either taste or smell to corroborate these very interesting results.

Touch. The trend favoring females in tactile threshold in the neonate is convincingly demonstrated in children and continues into adulthood where the evidence shows overwhelming sensitivity in the fingers and hands of females (Jastrow, 1892; Axelrod, 1959; Weinstein & Sersen, 1961; Ippolitov, 1972). Often there is no overlap between male and female scores. It seems, therefore, reasonable to suggest that greater levels of sensitivity in females will contribute to their superior ability in tests of finger dexterity, which will be discussed in the next section.

Table 2

Sex Differences in Smell

Combined data from two studies indicating the number of parts of water to one part substance for detection threshold

	Oil of Cloves	Nitrate of Amyl	Garlic	Bromine	Cyanide	Prussic Acid	Oil of Lemon	Oil of Wintergreen
Males	88,218	783,870	57,927	49,254	109,140	112,000	280,000	600,000
Females	50,667	311,330	43,900	16,244	9,002	18,000	116,000	311,000

Total N = 82 from Nichols & Bailey (1886).

Audition. In the auditory mode, studies on threshold for sound have consistently demonstrated superior hearing for high frequencies in females from childhood onwards. The sex difference increases with higher frequencies and with age (Corso, 1959; Eagles et al., 1963; Hull et al., 1971; McGuinness, 1972). Corso's findings are particularly relevant, as he could find no evidence that sex differences were in any way attributable to specific envirnmental factors. After eliminating all subject who had even remote experience with environmental noise, or any history of hearing difficulties, the sex differences remained and were, if anything, more pronounced than those found in the total sample.

The most important and consistent difference between the sexes in auditory sensitivity is found in tests involving response to intensity. Since we will be presenting a theoretical position based on such differences in sensitivity and leading to the development of speech and the reaction to inflection, the evidence will be considered in some detail. Females are intolerant of loud levels of sound both in childhood (Elliott, 1971) and adulthood (Corah & Boffa, 1970; McGuinness, 1972). The data from the experiment by McGuinness are presented in Figure 1, which illustrates the level at which adults adjust the volume of sound until it is perceived as barely "too loud." The mean scores across all frequencies were 75 db for the women and 83 db for the males. As loudness doubles

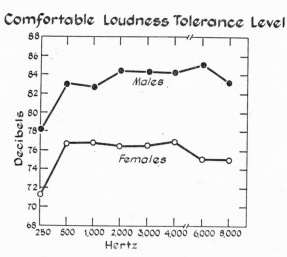

FIGURE 1: Levels of volume set by 25 males and 25 females to the criterion of just "too loud." College age sample. From McGuinness, 1972.

subjectively at about 9-10 db, the findings suggest that by about the level of 85 db, females will hear the volume of any sound as twice as loud as males.

Sensitivity to volume is also found in other tasks. Zaner et al. (1968) report that when children aged 4 to 8 years were asked to judge which aspect of an auditory stimulus was varying, girls were significantly more able to distinguish between changes in intensity. The sexes did not differ in their ability to notice changes in frequency, duration, or number of signals. Also, when Shuter (1964) factor analyzed her results on 200 male and female students of above-average musical ability, a broad general factor of musical ability was found. An appreciation of intensity changes was included in the factor for women, but was entirely absent for men. Shuter also found no sex differences in pitch discrimination between the sexes, a finding which has been replicated (McGuinness, 1972).

Women's sensitivity to sound intensity also occurs during sleep. Wilson and Zung (1966) instructed subjects to waken at the sound of two specific stimuli and to remain asleep during all other noises. EEG was monitored throughout. The sexes behaved similarly in the instructed condition: All awakened, but significantly more EEG activation occurred in females to the noises that subjects were told to ignore. A further study, in which subjects were unaware of the response they were producing, showed that women habituated more slowly on an autonomic measure of digital blood flow to a series of repeated tones (McGuinness, 1973). Slower habituation appears to be reflected by intolerance of auditory repetition in females (McGuinness, 1972).

In the study by McGuinness (1972), it was demonstrated that efficiency in hearing is not continuous across a range of tasks. No correlations could be found among tests of threshold, intensity judgment, pitch discrimination, and tolerance of repetition. This suggests that the total auditory experience is the result of "multiplexing" a number of unrelated sensitivities (Spinelli & Pribram, 1967; Lindsay, 1970). Of the tasks investigated, only pitch discrimination showed any effect of training, improving linearly with the amount of time spent in musical study. As training had no effect on any of the other tasks, it was suggested that these sensitivities are inherently stable and unchanging.

Vision. Sensory capacity in the visual modality also differs between men and women; in this instance the male is more efficient in conditions of light and females more sensitive in the dark. The ability of males in photopic visual acuity has a well documented history. Carter in 1892 calculated the sex difference ratio with respect to the population at large and 10,000 patients seen by him for ophthalmological treatment. Greater defects in all types of acuity disorder were demonstrated in females 6% more often than should normally occur. His conclusion was that this was due to defective eye muscles. Normative surveys carried out in Sweden (Key, reported in Ellis, 1896) and in America and England by West (1892) and Warner (1893) show that at all ages except at 5 years, girls had more minor visual defects, generally myopia and hyperopia. In Key's report on 14,000 children aged 10-11, over three times as many girls as boys were found to be myopic. All of these authors, however, report a greater number of serious defects in male vision and more blindness; however, with respect to the general population, these are uncommon.

More recent and better controlled studies have produced identical results indicating male superiority in both static and dynamic visual acuity (Roberts, 1964; Burg & Hulbert, 1961; Burg, 1966; McGuinness, 1976b). However, all these studies are on teenage to adult populations. The early work suggesting defects in younger females has not yet been replicated. Skoff and Pollack (1969) could find no sex differences in Vernier acuity for either colored or black and white targets in 96 boys and girls ages 7-14.

In general, comparable data to those presented on the auditory mode are lacking. Only one study is available (McGuinness, 1976b) in which a number of visual tasks were investigated and compared. The study looked at sex differences in young adults in threshold, intensity judgment, acuity, and short-term iconic store. Here, the sex difference in judgment of intensity was the reverse of the finding in audition, with males significantly more sensitive to brightness. However, females were consistently more sensitive in tests performed in the dark, adapting more rapidly and to lower threshold levels than the men (Figure 2). In the visual persistence test (iconic memory), females showed significantly longer visual holding than the males, but only in the dark. The difference disappeared entirely after light adaptation. As in the auditory study, no correlations were found between the tasks, with the one striking exception of photopic acuity and scotopic dark adaptation. This only occurred when the sexes were assessed separately, but was highly significant in both cases.

Other visual phenomena have yielded sex differences. In a continuation of the persistence experiment above, McGuinness and Lewis (1976) investigated sex differences in young adults in response to a Ganzfeld (a field of uniform saturation) and to an after-image produced by a black cross silhouetted against a white photoflood. Men had longer dura-

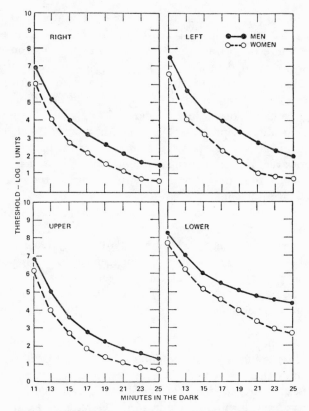

FIGURE 2: Dark adaptation curves for four field positions tested at 20 degrees of visual angle in 30 adult males and females matched for visual acuity. From McGuinness, 1976b.

tions of visual experience in both cases. This was particularly significant in the Ganzfeld experiment. Also, in this study men were consistently more liable to report large fluctuations in the disappearance and reappearance of color, often experiencing the perception of a number of colors not actually in the visual field. None of these effects was commonly observed by the women.

The finding that men have longer after-images corresponds to a similar result in a study by Brownfield (1965). McGuinness and Lewis also investigated sex differences in the phenomenon called the "flight of colors," which is a common effect in an after-image experience. Subjects were asked to report colors at fixed intervals. Table 3 illustrates the frequency distribution for the various colors reported. One hundred percent of the women, as opposed to 50% of the men, reported colors in the pink-red or low frequency spectrum domain. This was highly significant. It is interesting that the greater sensitivity to red was also shown in the Ganzfeld study, in which women, but not men, held the perception of red significantly longer than green.

TABLE 3

Frequency Table Showing the Number of Subjects Reporting
Colors in the After-Image Experiment

	Violet	Blue	Blue/Green	Green	Yellow	Orange	Red/Pink
M	8	11	4	9	10	1	10
F	4	13	7	4	11	1	20

From McGuinness and Lewis, 1976.

In tests where illusions are demonstrated, sex differences are also found. Boys are more susceptible to experiencing rapid reversals in a reversible figures test (see Garai & Scheinfeld, 1968). A further study (Immergluck & Mearini, 1969) on children aged 9, 11, and 13 showed that boys had higher reversal rates over all ages. The authors note that in a previous study on adults a high correlation was found for rate of reversals and performance on the Rod and Frame Test, which suggests that rapid reversals may have some connection to visual-spatial skills. This will be discussed later.

On other tests of visual illusions sex differences are not so stable. Pohl and Caldwell (1968) found that women had lower thresholds for the Phi phenomenon, the apparent movement of two alternatively lit figures. Females also tend to show less susceptibility to the autokinetic effect, where a stationary light appears to move in the dark (Voth, 1941; Chaplin, 1955; McKitrick, 1965). However, in later studies (Aranoff, 1973; Simpson & Vaught, 1973), these findings were not replicated. It is possible that many of these results could be related to the superior performance of females in the dark as shown above. When dark adaptation and room light conditions are not precisely controlled, sex differences may be exaggerated.

In summary, the evidence on sensory capacity shows that females are more sensitive to all modalities at threshold, with the possible exception of smell, and that they possess a certain advantage in some aspects of tactile and auditory processing. Men have superior visual acuity and greater sensitivity to light. The findings are supported largely by studies on an adult population. This is particularly true of tests on vision, which is rather surprising. There are at present no normative data to support the findings on children carried out at the turn of the century, though the data available are in the predicted direction. Until more developmental studies are performed, the firm evidence on consistent sex differences across the whole age range seems to be that on tactile thresholds and sensitivity to high frequencies and loudness in the auditory modality.

Responses in infancy

In early infancy males tend to be awake for longer periods than females (Moss, 1967; Sander & Cassel, 1973). Male activity is considerably stimulated by the mother who spends more time in direct physical contact with her son (Moss, 1967; Lewis, 1972). Maternal activity has been found to correlate with increased exploratory activity in later childhood (Rubenstein, 1967), which has been demonstrated to be the province of males, particularly at ages 3-6 years (see Maccoby & Jacklin, 1974).

Studies which have investigated overall activity levels, including both gross and discreet actions, often find that no differences can be demonstrated between the sexes (Maccoby & Jacklin, 1973). However, differences do arise when types of response are investigated. As children develop, response differences begin to reflect intended action. Responses are organized to a purpose and, as will be demonstrated, this purpose is to achieve an understanding and control of the environment.

By nursery school age, males are more apt to engage in rough and tumble play and in aggressive acts (Sherman, 1971; Smith & Connolly, 1972). Findings by Goldberg and Lewis (1969) show that boys of one year are more attracted to the unusual and spend more time in play with objects other than toys, while devising novel ways of using them. Girls' activity is generally directed to play which is highly suitable to the toy.

When the total amount of vocalizations are assessed, sex differences fail to emerge, but again the *types* of vocalizations subsequently employed by each sex are noticeably different. In the rate of early babbling, males and females are similar (Moss, 1967; Lewis, 1972), but it has frequently been observed that over time a much higher rate of vocal interchange develops between mothers and daughters (Goldberg & Lewis, 1969; McCall, 1972; Messer & Lewis, 1972). Lewis' study (1972) suggests that this occurs because of a complex interaction between the vocal behavior of the infant and the behavior of the mother. First it was noted by Lewis that girls receive much less physical attention from the mother, which supports the findings by Moss (1967) noted above, and that girls appear to be comforted by "distal" stimulation, like speech and singing. Males, by contrast, require physical comfort. However, the infants do not differ in the amount of vocalization they produce, and Lewis found that mothers actually reinforce more of the male vocalizations than those of the female. When he looked at his data in terms of how vocalizing by the infant initiated a response from the mother, he found that 50% of male vocalizations elicited a response. but that only 37% of female vocalizations were reinforced. However, 67% of female vocalizations were *in response to* maternal behavior, despite the lower level of reinforcement for these responses. Certainly mothers do not appear to speak more "effectively" to one or the other sex. In a complex series of experiments, Phillips (1973) could find no difference whatsoever in the number and complexity of words per utterance to male and female infants aged 8, 18, and 28 months.

In general, there is little support for the idea that the language facility, both in amount and quality, in females could be produced by the reinforcing behavior of the mother. Lewis' study might even suggest the opposite. The relevant issue is the function of vocalization to the female. Girls use vocalizations to *communicate*, to acquire information about their environment "distally" and they also appear to respond to the emotional inflection in speech, which will be discussed later. The use to which vocalizations are employed by the sexes are illustrated in Table 4 where Smith and Connolly (1972) show that boys make more noises, whereas girls use more speech. Utilization of vocal ability in verbal communication may result in findings at later ages (McCarthy, 1930; Harms & Spiker, 1959; Hull et al., 1971; Oetzel, 1967) that girls have greater clarity and quality of speech throughout childhood. This finding is strongly paralleled by girls' ability to sing in tune. Male monotones outnumber females by about 6 to 1 (Bentley, 1968; Roberts, 1972).

TABLE 4

Distribution of Vocalizations as a Function of Age and Sex

	Vocalizations		Talk to Child		Play Noise	
	Boys	Girls	Boys	Girls	Boys	Girls
3:9-4:9 years	82.9	82.4	47.0	65.6	27.7	7.6
2:9-3:9 years	52.8	54.9	24.3	36.7	19.8	8.2
Combined means	67.9	68.7	31.8	46.0	23.8	7.9

From Smith and Connolly (1972)

Sensory-motor integration in the child and adult

Garai and Scheinfeld (1968) have categorized the sex differences in response characteristics as perceptual-motor tasks, which favor males, and as clerical skills, which favor females. Others (Tyler, 1965; Hutt, 1972) have also accepted these distinctions without considering the part played by purely sensory or response characteristics. Two basic findings emerge when only response parameters are considered. Males are superior from mid-childhood onward in speed of reaction time. Because their ability largely parallels muscular development, causing an improvement over girls at about 10-11 years, reaching its asymptote at about 18 years and remaining stable throughout life (Noble et al., 1964; Simon, 1967; Fairweather & Hutt, 1972), it seems reasonable to assume that speed of response might be related to increasing muscle mass and force.

By contrast, females excel in manual dexterity involving discrete movements of the fingers and fine coordination. Using a test of finger dexterity, a peg-board task where subjects have to shift a peg along a series of holes as rapidly as possible, Annett (1970) found that females were superior over all ages tested (3½-15 years), using a sample of 219 subjects. Superiority for females at all ages in most tests of manual dexterity, particularly of fine motor skills, has been well documented (see Tyler, 1965).

It does appear, therefore, that males excel in speed of gross motor outflow, while females excel in speed of discrete and finely controlled motor responses.

When information must be processed before a response is made, the speed of output is then determined by both the type of information and the type of response required. When the information is in the form of a visual display, and the response requires large muscle units, males excel to an overwhelming degree. Cook and Shepard (1958) found that boys are superior when operating a lever to change direction of a spot of light at ages 5, 10 and 20 years. In a similar task where subjects had to displace a green disc to coincide with a red ring that appeared in 1 of 49 positions, boys and men, aged 5-70 years, consistently scored more correct matches over all ages. Ammons et al. (1955) also report that, in tracking tasks, boys' performance begins to diverge noticeably from the girls' at about 11-12 years and thereafter is consistently superior. In two further studies on adults (Noble & Hays, 1965; Shepard et al., 1962), males were found to be greatly superior in producing rapidly timed movements to visual displays. It has been suggested by Harris

(1976) that there is a spatial component in these tasks. This will be considered in the section on cognitive processes.

When information is in the form of symbolic or semantic material, and the response required demands attention to detail, females are superior. Tasks such as typing, cancellation tests, and others categorized as "clerical" (Garai & Scheinfeld, 1968) are always performed more efficiently by women (Tyler, 1965). The WISC and the WAIS coding and digit substitution tests are also consistently performed best by females.

It is possible that males and females utilize different types of environmental information preferentially, and in addition to this we note here that where gross differences arise, the response to the task is also relevant. The tasks which favor females generally require small and reasonably well-coordinated movement, while those which favor males incorporate larger motor processes. In order to disentangle stimulus effects from response effects, a female-typical response should be paired with a male-specific input, or vice versa.

The nearest approach to this type of experiment is that of Fairweather and Hutt (1972), where they varied information in bits in a choice reaction time test. These authors found that at ages 5-7 years, girls were faster in simple reaction time, a cross-over effect occurred where sexes were matched at about 8-9 years, and from then on boys were superior. However, when information was increased (choice reaction time), the girls were found to be superior at all ages and this difference increased as the information load (in bits) was increased. In their adult sample the difference largely disappeared, although no details of the size and age of this sample were given. Since we know that men are faster in simple reaction time, this finding would mean that females process information faster across all ages.

When assessing the types of tasks that favor women, such as clerical skills, it is important to recognize that certain of these tasks are, in fact, tests of choice reaction time. An example par excellence is typing, where information from a written or printed sheet is rapidly transferred by pressing the appropriate keys. Speed of typing reflects both manual dexterity and speed of information processing. As yet there are no conclusions as to what is involved in rapid information processing. It could be that attention span in females is somewhat greater than in males, and in our view this concept is interchangeable with some type of intermediate or short-term memory system. Holding a number of items in store simply refers to the amount of information one can *attend* to at any one time. We will therefore proceed to review the relevant literature on attention.

Sex Differences in Attention

In 1890 William James presented an extensive systematization of attentional characteristics in which he discussed the evidence for involuntary (reflex) and voluntary (selective) processes. Recently this type of analysis has been extended to present a comprehensive model of attention based upon both behavioral and physiological data (Pribram & McGuinness, 1975). Three basic attentional systems are considered in the model: *reflex attention* or arousal; *vigilant readiness* or activation; and *effort in which the input is coded to produce a change in a neuronal model.* These three systems have different sequences and organizations when different types of attention are operating. Thus a range is possible from open and unfocused attention during selection to a situation in which reflex arousal is inhibited to allow for the complex transformations essential in a reasoning task. Flexibility and inhibitory control are part of the developmental process in the young child.

In the quest for the organizing forces producing sex differences in perception, the emphasis in this section is on the development of these attentional systems in the infant, and how infants differ in stimulus preference. It appears, from the data, that at ages where infants have not as yet been affected by selective reinforcement, they nevertheless show an interest in certain stimulus characteristics and not others. Types of stimulus information are more salient to one sex than the other and, as will be shown, this salience relates to channel efficiency and subsequently to the way in which the developing child seeks to control and interpret his environment.

The data presented on infant attention are selected to illustrate the *common trends* in the literature. It must be emphasized that, when measuring attention in infants, their undeveloped control makes it difficult to replicate consistently. Thus it is in searching for commonalities that we can progress. As is often the case, the data which contribute towards this inductive process are not always those data the experimenter intended to produce, or even those he wished to emphasize.

One of the most consistent trends observed in a number of studies is that females are particularly attentive to certain types of auditory cues, and they appear to attend to the emotional and meaningful properties of sound. Simner (1971) found that 1-week-old females distinguished noticeably between the sound of an infant's cry and white noise played at the same volume. Although Simner could not replicate these findings entirely, the trends are consistent, and females were also found to be significantly more stable in their crying responses over time than males.

Watson (1969) investigated 14-week-old infants and found that girls could be trained to maintain visual fixation of a white circle when a tone was used as reinforcement, but not when a line drawing of a face was employed. Boys performed better with visual reinforcement. However, it must be noted that Ramey and Watson (1972) could not replicate this result.

In a comprehensive study, Kagan and Lewis (1965) found that 24-week-old girls responded more to music (complex input) on measures of motor and autonomic changes, whereas boys reacted more to tones (a simple repetitive input). In the same infants at 13 months, girls consistently reacted to verbal input with *high* inflection and a significant positive correlation was found for the girls who had high attention levels to music in the first experiment and who at 13 months paid most attention to the verbal input with the maximum uncertainty, illustrating that they noticed its novelty. It is possible that the reaction to high levels of inflection relates to the females' sensitivity to intensity differences illustrated in the preceding section. Girls were also found to vocalize more to auditory input than boys.

Bernstein and Jacklin (1973) found a significant effect favoring females in infants 3½ months of age. Females were more attentive to both social and non-social sounds. This result was replicated in a study by Cohen (1973) on infants 5 and 8 months old. He found that females looked significantly more at a sound source than males. There is also evidence in young children aged 1 year that loud frightening sounds are less effective with males than females, and particularly so at lower volumes (Maccoby & Jacklin, 1973).

The evidence on visual attention suggests that the sexes respond preferentially to two different categories of visual input, and that this has little to do with maturational factors affecting visual acuity (Fagan, 1972). Faces are a powerful stimulus for both sexes. However, from about 4 months, females show more interest and discriminability than males, whether exposed to masks of faces, photographs or line drawings (Lewis et al., 1966; Lewis, 1969; Fagan, 1972). Girls are able to distinguish between realistic and unrealistic line drawings and vocalize appropriately to the most realistic (Lewis, 1969) and are able to discriminate between photographs of two very similar faces (Fagan, 1972). Boys did not show this ability on any of the tasks using photographs.

By contrast, where sex differences are found, males from 4-6 months onwards respond preferentially to blinking lights, geometric patterns, colored photographs of objects and three-dimensional objects (Myers & Cantor, 1967; McCall & Kagan, 1970; Pancratz & Cohen, 1970; Cohen et al., 1971; Kagan & Lewis, 1965; Cornell & Strauss, 1973). Boys had faster habituation (showing rapid coding) to non-social stimuli, and particularly produced consistent orienting responses to novel objects. This is an interesting contrast to the slower habituation of males to faces found in a study by Lewis (1969). Boys do not appear to differentiate between faces and objects in the amount of vocalizations they produce. In the Kagan and Lewis study, boys vocalized significantly more to the blinking light presentation, and findings by McCall and Kagan (1967) support the interpretation that in boys vocalization is part of a spontaneous motor outflow reflecting *interest*. In this study infants aged 4 months were shown a series of random patterns. When males exhibited a heart rate deceleration to a stimulus, indicating vigilant attention, this was almost always accompanied by vocalization. No such relationship was found for girls. These same sex differences in smiling responses to objects and to faces have been noted in some of the studies above, with the sexes not differing in the amount of smiling, but the males smiling equally at objects and faces, and females smiling only at faces.

These findings can be interpreted to suggest that girls give more appropriate and discriminating responses to social or socially affective stimuli—a reaction which is sighly stable in females, but not in males. This is also supported by the finding of Moss and Robson (1968) that girls' visual behavior is related to the amount of social interaction with the mother. Social responses were also present in the boys but not nearly to the same degree. Boys appear responsive to novel stimuli when it is non-social in character and especially when it is brightly colored or three-dimensional (McCall & Kagan, 1970; Pancratz & Cohen, 1970; Cornell & Strauss, 1973). Further work of Mitchell and Brandt (1970) shows a similar sex difference in looking and social behavior in the rhesus monkey.

Subtle differences in timing of responses found between the sexes reveal differences between the informational and meaningful properties of the stimulus. Information relates to the amount of uncertainty which is reduced by any particular input, while meaning is related to intention (Pribram, 1976). Any input that ultimately produces an intentional motor response rather than an unintentional one can be said to be meaningful. To clarify this point it was noted that frequently vocalizations and smiling responses for boys were unintentional or reflex motor responses. Heart rate deceleration and vocalization were found to correlate for boys, while heart rate deceleration and movement arrest correlate for girls (McCall & Kagan, 1967; Kagan & Lewis, 1965). Also, in a study by McCall (1972), boys were found to produce smiling responses to novel input, while this reaction was not predictable for girls. Girls specifically smile and vocalize when stimuli are presented that are most likely to smile and vocalize back. This suggests that they distinguish stimuli, including a realistic face from an unrealistic one, on the basis of their functional significance or *meaningfulness,* and not only on the basis of their novelty, and that they relate their behavior appropriately. These findings provide convincing evidence that females are aware of the social and non-social implications of stimuli and that their response output is utilized intentionally for the purpose of communication. Boys' intentions are revealed by gross motor and manipulative action, as discussed below.

Studies on attention during childhood have concentrated exclusively on the response to novelty. However, the interpretation of this term is often misleading. In fact, all children in these experiments respond to the novel input; they notice its occurrence. It is rather what they choose *to do* about it that distinguishes their behavior. Another misconception is that only objects are novel. This sometimes leads to the inference that because boys are significantly more likely to show approaches to novel toys (Smock & Holt, 1962; Mendel, 1965; Hutt, 1970), they are more sensitive to novelty *per se,* as well as being more imaginative in devising ways of playing with the novel toys than girls.

Yet *people* can also be novel. In an observational study of newcomers entering a play group, McGrew (1972) reports that girls as young as 3 years of age responded to new children with affection, interest and comforting actions and verbalizations. The "novel" interlopers were initially ignored by the boys and were excluded from their games.

The object-social distinction between males and females appears pervasive throughout all age groups, but this dichotomy tends to be blurred when social interaction is investigated. Maccoby and Jacklin (1974) review the evidence and conclude that greater social orientation cannot be clearly demonstrated in females. What their review does suggest, however, is that people *mean* different things to males and females. People appear to be assessed by males more on the basis of their function or utility (can they play games or build a tree house?) than on the basis of their personal characteristics. Thus boys can often appear more social because they are group oriented, while females are found to seek out more intimate personal relationships. However, females do appear to be more interested in people, and certainly males show more interest in objects.

This distinction is clearly brought out in a study on adults using binocular rivalry by McGuinness and Symonds (in press). When photographs of objects were paired with photographs of people and presented stereoscopically, one to each eye, females spent significantly more time reporting people than objects, while males reported the opposite. Since it has frequently been observed that the effect of a disparate stereoscopic display is to produce attention to the most meaningful input (Bagby, 1957; Engel, 1956; Kleiven & Rommetveit, 1970), these results confirm the suggestion in the literature that males are more object oriented while females are more social.

An understanding of the quality of this difference can be provided by evidence from an early study by Jastrow (1891). High school and college students were asked to form word associations to a list of words. Jastrow categorized these associations and found that males and females were remarkably different in their associative processes. Table 5 sets out the sequence of word association categories in order of the most to the least frequently employed.

One of the most interesting findings was that the typical male response to an object is to provide its *action,* a response which did not occur in females. Instead, females responded to objects by naming their quality. This illustrates that objects interest males because of what they *do.* The female supplies the descriptive code which is most communicable. Also relevant to this distinction is the finding that males provide part association to a whole, whereas females provide whole associations to parts. Again, this is indicative of the inferred action stimulated by the word. Reducing objects to parts implies a manipulative tendency. Associating wholes to parts improves memory (chunking or categorization) and aids the communicative processes.

TABLE 5

Sex Differences in Categories of Word Associations
from Most to Least Common

Males
1. Homophone
2. Whole ⟶ part
3. Object ⟶ activity
4. Activity ⟶ object
5. Category

Females
1. Part ⟶ whole
2. Object ⟶ quality
3. Quality ⟶ object
4. Unclassifiable—Ambiguous or remote

From Jastrow (1891)

Sex Differences in Cognitive Competencies

So far the literature reviewed in this chapter has provided evidence for consistent trends and biases between the sexes. The evidence on tactile sensitivity and manual dexterity for females shows how sensory information and response efficiency are integrated. Similarly, in the infant studies, the potency of social stimuli for females and non-social stimuli for males finds its mutual counterpart in subsequent behavior. The argument that these differences arise because of differential reinforcement is difficult to support when the following questions are posed: Why do males, who receive more affection and direct physical contact with their mothers, prefer objects to people? If female speech is supposed to be fostered by maternal behavior, how does the male response repertoire escape this influence? There are no adequate answers to these questions unless certain processes are assumed to be biased by differences in neural structures present in early life. In what fashion do these biases affect cognitive functioning?

Although space does not permit an extensive coverage of the evidence on differences in cognitive ability between the sexes, certain factors discussed in this section are relevant to the conclusions drawn in the final section. Two points are of interest. First, our view of a communicative female and a manipulative male will be expanded by new evidence on sex differences in other cognitive processes besides the classic linguistic and visual-spatial distinctions, such as memory, imagery, social intelligence and problem solving. These findings make up the content of this section. Secondly, to clarify the problem of how cognition is defined an excerpt from the paper "The Neurology of Thinking" (Pribram, 1959) illustrates that in cognitive processing two basic functions are involved: One deals with the programs that partition inputs into sets (categorization) and the second with a mechanism that evaluates outcomes (intention).

> This distinction allows greater precision in the description of attitudinal factors: those related to differentiation can be redefined as a capacity to acquire information—to search through a large number of possible inputs (especially negative instances); those related to intention can be redefined as the capacity to choose one outcome (a positive instance) in the face of a large number of possible outcomes (Pribram, 1959, p. 282).

Cognitive processing often depends upon the dovetailing of these two modes of thought—the capacity to define sets and subsets of information and the capacity to choose efficiently and wisely between actions related to them. We have made the point throughout this presentation that, due to certain sensory and response biases inherent in males and females, their capacities of differentiation and their intentions will be dissimilar. Thus we infer that primary perceptual processes and perceptual-motor integration are the building blocks of any cognitive system and that attentional controls furnish the programs or subroutines that determine the architecture of that system. Reasoning, or high-level cognition, occurs when the anticipation of the outcome is matched against the accuracy of categorization.

In characterizing the sexes as exhibiting dissimilar intentions, we have suggested that the male is biased to express his intention in action, and the female in communication. If this distinction is valid, it should be maintained at the cognitive level in two ways: First, the higher level skills pertaining to intentional behavior should function along similar output dimensions, and second, the information or knowledge available to the individual will be processed or "captured" by different categorical systems. A manipulative animal presumably would code the product of his actions and would be alert to information that allowed for sufficient scope for his manipulative tendencies. One would anticipate that visual images, particularly images in depth, would receive special attention. A communicative animal needs to receive and transmit all signs and symbols held in common by her species and to relay expressive movement. A further requirement is that she *remember* the information long enough to transmit it to another.

Clearly, we cannot maintain that the sexes are exclusively adapted to two entirely different modes of thought. We suggest merely that there is a difference of degree. It is not that the female is inactive, but that her activity is directed toward more communicative aims. The male also communicates, but as Jastrow's experiment on word association has shown, the male linguistic code has been biased toward action. Bearing these distinctions in mind, we set out briefly in this section a summary of the known data on sex differences in cognitive ability. In most cases the skill involved is more accurately subsumed under higher-level categorizations: in few others the ability is reflected in the efficiency of intended action when multiple outcomes are possible. In only two instances—verbal reasoning and problem solving—does the complex interaction of differentiation and intention occur to produce behavior that is perhaps most truly "cognitive."

Special abilities in females

Verbal and Auditory Skills. It was mentioned earlier that females aged 1-5 years are more proficient in linguistic skills, especially the earlier onset of speech, and length of utterance. Perhaps the most notable distinction between the sexes at this early age is the use of speech by females for specifically communicative purposes. This was clearly brought out by the data of Smith and Connolly in Table 4. The early aptitude of females is fully documented in the review by Maccoby and Jacklin (1974).

However, this early advantage tends to fade during middle childhood. Again the reader is referred to Maccoby and Jacklin for a review of these studies. In particular, vocabulary tests fail to produce sex differences, though females retain a marginal advantage in overall language ability such as fluency, comprehension, verbal reasoning, and flexibility in handling verbal symbols (anagrams). Their superiority is mainly evident in large sample surveys, though they do perform outstandingly well in tests of reading skill. It is well known that remedial reading classes contain significantly higher proportions of males (Ounsted & Taylor, 1972; Maccoby & Jacklin, 1974).

In adolescence and adulthood, females once again clearly emerge as the superior sex and Maccoby and Jacklin suggest that this may be due to different phases of development. While this must remain a possibility, we would suggest that environmental factors may also be critical. First, as early schooling places greatest emphasis on verbal skills, these pressures could markedly improve male performance. Later, the insistence in maintaining static age groups in most schools may handicap females and retard progress. Thus the natural ability of the female is partially checked to emerge later when more complex verbal skills are needed. When subjects are introduced that are more specifically related to masculine aptitudes, like higher mathematics and science, females would again begin to demonstrate their linguistic advantage. Support for this view is given by the findings of the Stanford Research Institute survey on deprived families. Here females in middle childhood were noticeably ahead on all linguistic measures (see Maccoby & Jacklin, 1974). These results indicate, by negative inference, that a *good* environment can reduce the natural differences between the sexes in language ability. To anticipate a later discussion, we would like to point out that early emphasis on spatial-motor skills might produce a similar remedial effect for females.

Recently, behavioral data from McGuinness' laboratory have suggested that there are two components of a biasing process which facilitates language development. The first is involuntary attention to a specific mode, and the second is a further bias to the most competent subsystem within that mode. From our evidence it appears that what is noticed or attended to by females in the auditory domain is a range of specifically *linguistic* cues. It will be recalled that *no* sex differences have been found in other auditory skills such as pitch discrimination, rhythmic aptitude, harmonic analysis, and so forth.

Two studies were carried out. The first (Biggs, unpublished) produced overwhelming evidence that females process verbal stimuli faster and more accurately than males. Biggs presented words just below threshold followed immediately by a masking stimulus. Subjects had to respond to the stimulus by naming the word and then by making various categories of inference about the word. The analyses focused upon the "subliminal" stimuli. The few correct replies were discarded as data. There were two major findings. For both sexes, *meaning* was processed more accurately than any other characteristics of the stimulus, such as identification of parts of speech (verb or noun), number of syllables (1 or 2), and upper or lower case characters. Subjects of both sexes performed well above chance when asked to provide an associative category and to rate words on Osgood's dimensions of evaluation and potency. The second result was that on every measure females were noticeably superior to males, with males performing at chance on the tasks requiring judgments of the physical characteristics of the stimulus. It must be noted that the sexes did not differ significantly in flash rate threshold, so one sex did not have an advantage in stimulus availability.

Biggs concludes from her data that word recognition is a sequential process in which meaning is extracted first, followed by the physical characteristics of the stimulus and finally by recognition and naming of the word in conscious awareness. She suggests that the sex differences occur because the sequence is accelerated in females. It is possible, however, that more parallel processing or attentional capacity is available to the females for linguistic material, though their scores on the various tasks followed the same linear trend as the males'.

In a suprathreshold experiment (McGuinness & Courtney, unpublished), male and female college students were tested in their speed and accuracy for both visual and auditory search. Subjects were asked to press a key to either a letter or a sound (A, or ā, I or ī) in words presented visually and verbally. There was a further condition of distraction (auditory or visual) versus no distraction. Allowing for the faster simple reaction times found universally in males of this age, on the order of 50 milliseconds, males and females were equal in time to locate a letter or a sound in a word presented visually. In the auditory conditions females were superior. Also, the error scores for males in both auditory tasks were 2 to 3 times greater. In keeping with the findings on auditory and visual sensitivity, males were found to be more distracted by visual stimuli (a series of complex random patterns) while processing auditory information. Females were not differentially affected by the distractors.

Both studies provide direct evidence that selective attention and, subsequently, cognitive processes are primed by neural competence. Males and females receive equal amounts of all types of auditory information from birth onwards, and one must conclude that the differences in processing capacity must be derived from innate competencies.

In concluding this section, we would like to emphasize that female skill in language reflects each aspect of the cognitive skills, in anticipating outcomes (intention), and also in the complex interaction of the two by virtue of their superior performance in tests of verbal reasoning (Herzberg & Lepkin, 1954; Lindzey & Goldberg, 1953).

Memory. Jastrow in 1891 carried out a word association test on large numbers of high school and college students. The results of the categories employed in association are reported in Table 5. Jastrow also asked that subjects return 48 hours later whence they were told to provide a list, unprompted, of all the words they had supplied during the test. Females scored a mean of 58%, males 40% correct. When the subjects were supplied with the cue word, the sex difference disappeared.

Recent work confirms these earlier findings showing females superior in most forms of visual and verbal memory. In tests of verbal recall presented both visually and aurally, Zahorsky (1969) found that in children, aged 8, 11, and 14, girls were superior at all ages in both modes of presentation. This result was similar to findings produced by Mittler and Ward (1970) and by Duggan (1950), who tested verbal and object recall in 14-16 year olds. Superior recall is also found in adult females for categorized and uncategorized items (Randhawa, 1972) and for visual and verbal information with both low and high imagery contents (Ernest & Paivio, 1971). Ernest and Paivio also report a female superiority in a subsequent test of incidental memory for which the subject was unprepared. Here female superiority increases particularly for the high imagery items. This result has been replicated in a study measuring recall for an array of several colored photographs in both adults and students by Marks (1973). Maccoby and Jacklin (1974) report that females are particularly superior in verbal recall.

In view of the results cited on social facility in females, memory for socially relevant information ought to be superior in females. Witryol and Kaess (1957) tested 170 students in three tests of social memory, which involved remembering names and faces either from photographs or in realistic group situations. The girls' scores were significantly higher than the boys' on all three tests. In an even more realistic approach, Bahrick et al. (1975) tested social memory for face recognition and matching names and faces in students who had graduated from high school across a wide range of years. Women were found to be superior at remembering both the faces and the names of former classmates.

The data indicate that when the subject is instructed to remember the items, females are superior, but more importantly, even when not instructed females remain superior. This was demonstrated in the Jastrow study, and by Ernest and Paivio (1971). A test of incidental recall was also carried out in our laboratory (Chaplin, unpublished data) on school children, aged 16-18 years. Subjects were asked to rate lists of words or pictures projected onto a screen. Females were found to recall more of the words in all conditions, and improve noticeably when compared to males over subsequent recall trials.

Social. Guilford in 1967 outlined his factor theory of intelligence. While we do not wish to debate the merits of factor analysis, we do agree that his category of "behavioral intelligence" is important as well as neglected. Part of intellectual ability includes appropriate and efficient responses to social cues. Guilford defines this as the ability to extract information about the intentions, wishes and aims of the other person. Behavioral intelligence is therefore a higher-order *empathy*. Unfortunately, there are few studies that investigate this problem directly. As has already been noted, girls as young as 3 years respond appropriately to children in need (McGrew, 1972) and Hutt (1972) reports on the females' greater cooperative spirit. The Witryol and Kaess study shows that girls remember socially relevant stimuli more than boys. This has been strongly confirmed by Bahrick et al. (1975).

Goodenough (1957) has found that sensitivity to persons occurs in girls at 2-4 years. Girls included more persons in their drawings, while boys scarcely drew people. Also, girls were found to verbalize more about people in a test designed to elicit verbalization from abstract stimuli. Ninety-two percent of the girls talked about people as opposed to 38% of the boys. Oetzel (1967) lists 21 studies in which girls and women were reported to have a significantly greater interest in people and social matters than males.

However, while one might expect that a greater *interest* in people would bring about more intelligent behavior with respect to empathetic understanding, this remains an undocumented field. The most concrete support comes from studies which show that females use significantly more complex psychological categories or constructs in describing others than males (Livesley & Bromley, 1973; Little, 1968; Yarrow & Campbell, 1963).

Special abilities in males

Spatial-Mechanical. The superiority of males in visual-spatial ability is well documented and need not be discussed extensively (Guilford, 1967; Tyler, 1965; Garai & Scheinfeld, 1968; Hutt, 1972; Buffery & Gray, 1972; Maccoby & Jacklin, 1974; Harris, 1976). Barratt (1955) reported that men had higher scores on all 10 of Thurstone's spatial tests, and were significantly superior on 8. Hutt (1972) has compiled a table for the main findings over several studies using the WAIS and WISC subtests. Males are more often superior on the object assembly test and, to a lesser degree, in block design and picture completion. Spatial ability is also highly related to mechanical ability, as measured by mazes, puzzle boxes, and assembly of small objects. In the Bennett mechanical comprehension test, a highly significant sex difference is found in favor of boys and men. Only one girl in 20 exceeded the male average (Bennett & Cruickshank, 1942). Males also experience considerably less disorientation in real space (La Grone, 1969). An extensive review of the tasks at which males excel is presented by Harris (1976). In general, their superiority is confined to abilities which relate to perception of objects in space.

A particular aspect of spatial ability at which males excel seems to be the capacity to rotate or isolate visual images into new planes and combinations. It is often observed that the solution to a mechanical problem is more readily resolved by looking rather than by continuous trial-and-error manipulations. However, if the theoretical views of Piaget (see Flavell, 1963) are correct, schemata are internalized only after a great deal of exploratory and manipulative behavior. The salience for males of novel objects and their exploratory tendencies have been noted earlier. It is possible that early manipulation will give rise to a high degree of three-dimensional spatial imagery.

In studies of "cognitive style," Witkin et al. (1962) have investigated certain performances in males and females designed to reflect "independence" or "dependence" on the field. Males fall into the "independent category. The most reliable of Witkin's tests has been the Rod and Frame Test, in which the subject is asked to set a rod to the vertical when it is surrounded by a tilted frame. As the Rod and Frame correlates and forms a factor with block design, picture completion and object assembly on the WISC (Witkin's own data), then it seems reasonable to conclude that the Rod and Frame Test is measuring certain aspects of spatial ability and that performance on the Rod and Frame Test has little to do with being "analytic," "global," or "independent" of the field as Witkin would suggest.

It is thus undeniable that men excel in the area of mechanical-spatial ability and that this can be demonstrated on a number of tasks. What is unacceptable to us and to others (Sherman, 1967; Bock & Kolakowski, 1973) is the assumption that performance on such tasks as the Rod and Frame Test is indicative of some higher-order capacity for analytic thought.

Another question arising from an assessment of visual-spatial differences between the sexes relates to the relative importance of genetic and environmental components. Young children do not exhibit the differences to any large extent and the advantage for males does not occur until mid-childhood or later (Witkin et al., 1962; Garai & Scheinfeld, 1968; Maccoby & Jacklin, 1974). A developmental change appears to occur due to either environmental or genetic factors. Recent findings (Berman, 1974) show that boys exhibit poorer spatial ability than normal in certain stressful environments, particularly where the father is absent. Thus environmental factors are implicated but the evidence for a genetic component is becoming more convincing (see Bock & Kolakowski, 1973). Harris (1976) summarizes the data for the genetic viewpoint, showing that there is evidence for a recessive gene on the X chromosome, but goes on to suggest that the genetic influence is primed by androgen. In the absence of certain minimum levels of circulating male hormones, spatial ability fails to develop, even when the genetic disposition is such that spatial skills should be high, as in the case of Turner's syndrome.

There is the additional evidence that certain spatial tasks, such as mechanical aptitude, aimed throwing, and, to a lesser extent, tracking speed and accuracy, are superior in males from quite early ages, as noted earlier. It is conceivable that, if a genetic basis for spatial ability exists, it is initially expressed in exploratory and manipulative behavior. It has never been demonstrated whether the more sophisticated cognitive tasks requiring spatial-rotational skills are related to earlier ability to perform in simpler mechanical tasks. If such a relationship were found, it would support the genetic theory, and would suggest that this genetic visual-spatial advantage could be developed by training.

Thus the later development of abilities in visual rotation of objects, maze learning, map reading and sense of direction could either evolve from differential learning or be accelerated by genetic releasing mechanisms controlling male hormones—or both. Data from Berman on the effect of stress on boys' spatial ability (but not girls') could be interpreted to implicate both genetic and environmental factors: the stress producing a reduction in androgens through the link with the pituitary adrenal axis which controls cortico-steroids, and/or the effect produced by a female dominated environment.

Mathematical. While there is no difference between the sexes in mathematical ability until early teens (see Maccoby & Jacklin, 1974) it appears that, while males improve over females at this time, girls' mathematical ability actually *declines* from ages 11-15 with respect to their previous performance (Ross & Simpson, 1971). The available evidence would indicate that this is not entirely due to the emphasis in schools on mathematical ability being a "boys'" subject. The data suggest, however, that mathematical superiority in males occurs as the problems dealt with increase in their emphasis on spatial properties. Bock and Kolakowski (1973) note that spatial ability correlates with school geometry $(r = .57)$ and quantitative thinking $(r = .69)$, as well as with drafting, shop mechanics and watch repair. Werdelin (1961) studied performance on school tests of geometry on 143 male-female pairs matched for age, social class, reasoning, verbal and number abilities. He concluded that the inferior female skill is due to spatial factors. Sherman (1967) reviews some of the evidence on this problem and warns against grouping studies on problem-solving and mathematical ability without first assessing the spatial component involved in the problem.

Curiosity and Problem-Solving. The studies cited earlier on boys' distractibility by novel objects and their exploratory behavior suggest that "curiosity" may be the best summary term to reflect these behaviors, as it implies both awareness and activity. There is now fairly convincing evidence that this characteristic of curiosity in boys (but not in girls) leads to success in certain types of problem-solving tasks, usually those which require visual or manipulative solutions. Greenberger et al. (1971) found that problem-solving ability in boys was highly correlated to two tests of curiosity, while in girls the correlation was to verbal ability. These results and the confirming results of Kreitler et al. (1974) strongly suggest that where problem-solving involves the manipulation of objects and the ability to break set, to try a range of approaches, boys will be superior. That boys excel in problems which involve restructuring is now well documented (Garai & Scheinfeld, 1968; Hutt, 1972; Maccoby & Jacklin, 1974).

Thus it can be seen over all these abilities in which males excel that there are specific skills in categorizing spatial relations and in framing appropriate intentions on the basis of successful manipulations. At later ages, this allows a high degree of three-dimensional visual imagery and produces success in reasoning tasks which require the interplay of action in relation to space.

Conclusions

The essential findings are these: Males respond to objects more than females, and most noticeably those which are geometric, brightly colored or three-dimensional. Novel visual input produces a range of responses which extends from spontaneous vocalizations in infancy to direct contact, manipulation and investigation in childhood. Boys generally appear more active and impulsive, and eventually are able to solve restructuring problems with greater alacrity. From years of early experience in contact with physical objects, they ultimately learn what can be done with objects and object relations. By puberty much of this ability is internalized and visual-spatial problems can be solved without manipulation by silent nonverbal transformations. Nevertheless, males consistently are attracted by objects, and enjoy the challenge of coming to grips with the physical environment.

Are these abilities a result of cultural influence, or do they arise from the young male infant's initial fascination with objects? There is no doubt that an interaction occurs, but mechanical ability must be derived from some early interest. The data show that this interest is predominantly found in males and that it is manifested as early as 4-5 months of age, before the infant can be selectively influenced by the tangible physical properties of his environment. Further, from early teens onwards, males possess keen visual acuity and fast efficient responses which correspond to their increasing physical strength. All of these attributes lend themselves to an all around superiority in exploratory and *manipulative action*.

The nearest one can come to describing a central trait for females is to subsume many of their skills under the heading of *communication*, though this does not capture the range of female capacities. The data on the youngest age group show that, in females, the auditory system is at first predominant. As was seen earlier, before visual discrimination is developed, females listen and respond meaningfully to a range of auditory inputs, whether in the form of an infant's cry, adult speech, or to music. By the age of 4-5 months they show a preference for faces over objects, and by 5 months are able to distinguish not only one person from another, but also photographs of people. Females also show a specific response pattern to auditory and visual information that captures their interest. Their motor activity slows, along with heart rate deceleration (Kagan & Lewis, 1965), and they smile and vocalize to social stimuli, whether their own mothers, or photographs of representations of socially meaningful stimuli. From these early and highly consistent behaviors, females continue through life to be more sensitive to certain categories of auditory input, in particular intensity changes and localization of sound (Pishkin & Blanchard, 1964; Pishkin & Shurley, 1965; Schaie et al., 1964), and to develop a strong interest in people and social situations. During this developing period they also display consistent superiority in handling speech and singing, at all levels of perception and production.

Apart from these findings, females also show greater tactile sensitivity from early childhood; this is later expressed in fine digital coordination which finds its outlet in delicate handwork and musical performance. It is assumed that fine motor control is a predominant contributory factor to "grace," as exhibited in the dance. Finally, females show ability in remembering verbal, visual and social information and display a greater degree of visual imagery than males. The data suggest that they can process more information initially (see Fairweather & Hutt, 1972) and respond with flexible selective programs more efficiently than males.

NEURAL SYSTEMS AND SEX DIFFERENCES

Introduction

The data reviewed in this chapter have been organized under the headings of cognitive, attentional and sensory-motor performance. In the introductory remarks to the attention and cognition sections we pointed out that it is difficult to disentangle the effects of sensory-motor constraints on control functions such as attention, or on higher-order processing involving the cognitive capacities of reasoning and abstraction. In this final section, we hope to make a case for the development of a brain organization distinguished on the basis of simple effector, i.e., motor and endocrine differentiation between the sexes. First, however, we will review the current neurophysiological theories which take as their starting point the *cognitive* dimension exclusively.

Cognitive Explanations Based on Brain Asymmetries

Almost without exception, physiological theories of sex differences in perceptual and cognitive skills concentrate on the linguistic-spatial dis-

tinction between the sexes, and attempt to correlate these functions with
the evidence that the left posterior hemisphere controls language in
almost all right-handed and most left-handed people, while the right
posterior hemisphere subserves certain spatial processes. These data are
reviewed by Sperry (1974) and by Buffery and Gray (1972).

Levy (1971) proposes the most straightforward theory that females
are left, and males are right hemisphere dominant. Buffery and Gray
(1972) suggest that males show more equivalence between hemispheres,
are more bilateral, while females are left hemisphere dominant; more
recently the remaining possibility has been presented by Harris (1976)
who interprets the data as indicating that the female is more bilateral
for language specifically, and the male more asymmetric.

All of these theories share the common opinion that cognitive ability
is pre-wired, and that the structures of the brain *initiate* the function,
providing no gross deprivation has occurred. This view must at least in
part be accurate, in that, unless brain tissue were competent to subserve
and initiate language and other functions, these would not develop. It
is a somewhat different question whether sex differences can be explained by genetically determined structural differences in *cortex* between the hemispheres: The substrates for all cognitive processes may
well be present initially in both sexes, and differences may become developed through differential *use*. There are also crucial data which make
the logic of a strict left-right dichotomy untenable, and force the conclusion that a new approach is essential.

The first difficulty with the three theories outlined above is that they
all tend to cite identical anatomical evidence on structural asymmetries
in adult and fetal brains, selectively interpreted to support each of the
contradictory theories (see Geschwind & Levitsky, 1968; Carmon & Gombos, 1970; Matsubara, 1960). One of the most frequently cited is an investigation of 200 fetal and adult brains by Wada et al. (1975). The only
sex difference to emerge was that females more often had an enlarged
"Wernicke's" area in the *right* hemisphere. When the right hemisphere
difference appeared, it was usually accompanied by a similar enlarge-
ment on the left. The converse was not the case. This evidence could be
taken as support of a female brain which is bilateral for speech (Harris,
1976), thus making the female less at risk for language ability following
left hemisphere trauma. The evidence could also be interpreted to
explain the female's relatively superior ability in face recognition
(Fagan, 1972; Bahrick et al., 1975), as it appears that the homologue of
Wernicke's area in the right hemisphere is precisely the region that,
following trauma, produces a loss in the ability to recognize faces

(Hécaen 1962; de Renzi & Spinnler, 1966). This example shows the difficulties of adopting this approach.

There is also damaging evidence to cortical theories when a volume of literature on sex differences in brain weight ratios is assessed. Sex differences in brain ratios were reported on hundreds of brains by top anatomists of the Victorian period. These findings, which have been summarized by Ellis (1896), are given in Table 6.

The general findings are that the frontal lobes in females have a

TABLE 6

Summary of Data on Brain Region Ratios to Total Cerebrum.
Collated from Data Presented by Ellis 1896

Frontal Lobes	*No. of Brains*	*Larger In*
Broca	360	Females
Clapham	450	No difference
Eberstaller	270	Females
Cunningham	Not specified	" (including infants)
Parietal Region		
Broca	Not given	Males
Meynert	"	"
Rudinger	"	"
Crichton-Browne	"	"
Tigges	"	"
Occipital Cortex		
Broca	Not given	No difference
Crichton-Browne	"	Females
Basal Ganglia		
Crichton-Browne	Not given	Females
Martin	"	"
Tigges	"	"
Cerebellum (Ratio to Cerebrum, Medulla & Axial Portions)		
Gall & Cuvier	Not given	Females
Broca	360	"
Rey	Using Broca data	" *plus* all centers below cerebrum
Boyd	188	"

small but consistently higher ratio to the remainder of the cerebrum, whereas the reverse is true of the parietal region, with males showing larger ratios in *both* hemispheres. One of the most noticeable sex differences is the greater ratio of basal ganglia and cerebellum to the cerebrum in women. There is always a temptation to infer that *size* of structure confers superiority, but Ellis warns against this, and supports his argument by listing the professions of the males and females who had the largest recorded brains. These range from Turgenev the novelist to an imbecile. The logical outcome of the classification given in Table 6 would be the suggestion that females are frontal lobe dominated and males are posterior creatures. This should (according to current dogma) give the males superiority in *both* language and spatial skill, particularly as lateralization seems more evident in posterior systems, but this is negated by further evidence that certain male abilities—object-assembly, rotation of forms, etc.—are also frontal lobe functions.

However, the most damaging evidence to any cortical "specialist" attitude is the simple fact that many of the so-called right hemisphere functions are superior in *women*. It has always seemed a puzzle to us that models of brain function in men and women have been postulated using only two pieces of information about differences in cognitive skills. The sexes differ in more than two abilities, as has been demonstrated throughout this paper. To illustrate this Table 7 has been compiled of all the available data from clinical patients with known brain damage, from studies on dichotic tasks, and from laterality experiments (Milner & Teuber, 1968; Milner, 1974; Buffery & Gray, 1972; Bogen & Gordon, 1971; Luria, 1966; Teuber, 1974; Hécaen, 1962; Sperry, 1974).

An inspection of the table reveals that perceptual-motor abilities which distinguish the sexes are to be found in nearly all parts of the brain—front-back, left-right, etc. These findings suggest that in order to arrive at some conclusions as to whether sex differences in performance can be explained by differences in functional location, subtler questions will be necessary. It can be seen that none of the hemisphere dominance theories can be maintained in the face of the evidence reviewed in the preceding sections and the findings reported on functional asymmetry. For example, all three theories would have to predict superior musical ability in males, whereas little has been demonstrated (Shuter, 1968). The only well documented sex differences in musical aptitude—singing in tune, and sensitivity to dynamic changes—are female specific abilities. Also, all theories would have to predict a male superiority in the following abilities: visual memory, imagery, face recognition, and drawing. When sex differences do occur in these aptitudes they generally show

TABLE 7

Perceptual Functions Affected by Lesions of Different Regions of the Brain

M indicates tasks at which males are generally superior
F indicates tasks where females are superior
N is where no difference is found

RIGHT HEMISPHERE

Right Temporal Lobe		Right Parietal Lobe	
Vision			
Memory for Abstract Pictures		Memory for Objects	N
Geometric Figures	M	Drawing Figures	F
Incongruous Figures		Memory for Numbers	N
Maze Learning	M	Visual-spatial Tasks	M
		.... Location in Space M	
		.... Recognition of Faces F	
Audition			
Singing in Tune	F		
Tonal Memory (equivocal)			
Timbre: Perception of Tone Quality			
Musical Appreciation			
Dynamics and phrasing	F		

LEFT HEMISPHERE

Left Temporal Lobe		Left Parietal Lobe	
Audition			
Sound Localization	F	Naming Objects	F
Phonemic Coding	F	Categorization of Objects	
Word Memory	F	Concept Formation	
Verbal Sequences	F	Memory for Numbers	N

BILATERAL REPRESENTATION

Bilateral Temporal

Rhythmic Memory	N
Pitch Discrimination	N
Recognition of Bird Song	

Bilateral Frontal

Vision		Audition	
Figural Reversals	M	Programming Verbal Output	F
Spatial Figures:		Verbal and Tonal Memory	F
Gottschaldt Figures	M		
Poppelreuter's Figures	M		
3-D Object Recognition & Assembly	M		

females superior (Zahorsky, 1969; Randhawa, 1972; Goodenough, 1957; Fagan, 1972; Ernest & Paivio, 1971; Marks, 1973; Bahrick et al., 1975). The Buffery and Gray hypothesis (1972) suggests that because males are more bilateral this makes them superior at spatial tasks, while Harris (1976) argues for the opposite point of view, that the female's bilateral organization makes her *less* efficient at spatial tasks because she is using both hemispheres for language. However, neither explanation can answer the findings that females are superior at functions subserved by *both* hemispheres and little interference seems to occur as a result. There seems to be enough compatibility for sharing between a number of functions, and these can operate easily between both hemispheres.

The hemisphere dominance theories reviewed above not only ignore several well demonstrated "cognitive" differences between the sexes, none of which can be accommodated by any one explanation, but also fail to consider the contribution of any of the basic sensory or motor differences reviewed in this chapter. It is important, therefore, to return to the discussions concerning the meaning of cognitive functioning. Earlier, we defined cognition as a process whereby the capacity to make accurate categorizations was joined with the ability to evaluate outcomes or make accurate decisions. In the first case, *perceptual* skill is required, and in the second, *behavioral* skill forms a necessary prelude to eventual prediction.

Likewise, the control mechanisms which regulate attention during a task are crucial to appropriate cognitive functioning and appear to operate more fluently when sensory-motor aptitudes are high. As more information, both in the input and output domains, becomes coded and efficiently ordered (chunked), higher level processing (cognition) can be more readily achieved. William James (1890) has observed that genius arises not because of any capacity to bring a wandering attention back to the task (an imbecile can be obsessively attentive) but because the genius gains ever new and interesting insights (new combinations) from the same stimulation, which in turn maintains his attention.

Thus, we suggest that a more productive attitude in terms of understanding sex differences in brain organization is to focus on simpler elements. The critical issue is whether sensory-motor differences prime control systems regulating such processes as attention, or whether the control mechanisms themselves are the source of the major distinction between the sexes.

The Intensive Dimension and Protocritic Processes

When a question involving *either-or* is posed in connection with a psychological or a neurophysiological process, the answer is almost inevitably paradoxical. Both alternatives are true and yet not true. This occurs first of all because of the impossibility of delineating biological mechanisms which are truly independent of one another. This dilemma, so clearly reflected in the attempts to tease apart nature and nurture, is also present when investigating both macro and micro structure of the brain. The brain is a mirror of the total organism/environment interaction.

Therefore, it is not surprising to find that attention is a function of both a control regulation *and* the organization due to intrinsic competence of sensory-motor systems. As an example, one cannot attend to visual stimuli if one is blind, but one cannot regulate attention to *any* modality if control systems are absent or malfunctioning. In short, our problem in attempting to specify the neurophysiological substrates for sex differences in higher-order processing becomes the problem of determining what portion of these differences is due to differences in the regulatory mechanisms or to differences in intrinsic sensory competences, or to their interaction.

A clue is available in evidence that has often been ignored in neurophysiology. This evidence suggests that the intensive dimension of experience is regulated by neural systems initially separate from those that process local sign (the patterning of spatial and temporal configurations). Henry Head (1920) distinguished such separate systems in the peripheral nervous system and christened them as epicritic (local sign) and protopathic (because the intensive dimension appeared undifferentiated when nerve regeneration first took place after sectioning). However, the intensive dimension of somatosensory stimulation, especially of the pain and temperature modalities, is processed in distinct systems in the spinal cord, and, as has been recently demonstrated (Chin et al., 1976), through the brainstem into the forebrain. The term protocritic is, therefore, a more appropriate partner for epicritic since both systems operate in normal, not just pathological, states.

Of interest here is the fact that the protocritic brain systems which process the intensive dimension of experience and behavior engage the very same systems (limbic and basal ganglia) that have been shown by other techniques to function in the control of attention (Pribram & McGuinness, 1975). We can, therefore, rephrase our initial question and ask whether the observed sex differences that have been reviewed in this chapter can be accounted for by differences in the protocritic—i.e., intensive and quantitative—dimension of sensory-motor function.

There is strong psychological evidence in support of the hypothesis that the locus of sex differences lies in the intensive dimension of sensory-motor processes. An analysis of the data on sensory psychophysical experiments comparing the sexes reveals that the most consistent differences are found in performances utilizing stimuli which can be scaled quantitatively. This category of stimuli has been discussed by Stevens (1961), who distinguishes a *prothetic* dimension from one that is *metathetic*. Metathetically experienced stimuli are arranged spatially and give rise to qualitative differences (similar to Head's definition of epicritic) that can only be scaled nominally and ordinally. Prothetically experienced stimuli give rise to a quantitative (protocritic) dimension that obeys the power law—a ratio scale. Our central thesis is that differences in sensitivity to the intensive or quantitative dimension of a stimulus (produced by the amplitude of the signal) result in an early (even in utero) modality bias. As intensity is a central factor in producing arousal which allows a stimulus to be registered in the nervous system (Sokolov, 1963; Berlyne, 1970; Pribram & McGuinness, 1975), a more intense signal in one channel will produce a greater amount of arousal which becomes coupled to that input. This develops the competence of that channel by enhancing complexity (information processing capacity) through experience.

Experimental studies using Stevens' scaling technique with regard to sex differences have not yet begun. But, in assessing comfort levels, McGuinness (1972, 1973, 1976a) found different sensitivities for males and females in the visual and auditory modes. This is not the only sex-related distinction that arises. Threshold, also a quantitative dimension, is found to be highly sex-determined in all modalities. However, sex differences in subjective comfort (related to the power slope) and threshold are not correlated (McGuinness, 1972, 1976b). Since threshold is the non-linear portion of what ultimately becomes a linear power function, the two become dissociated, as Stevens (1961) has indicated. Thus, at least two independent processes are operating to determine the quantitative dimension: One regulates threshold, the other subjective magnitude. The question, therefore, arises whether the protocritic neural systems regulate both threshold and experienced magnitude or whether the protocritic systems are responsible only for the magnitude estimation functions. The answer to this question is the topic of current research.

On the motor side of sensory-motor processing, males and females also exhibit rather different patterns of behavior. Males with their ordinarily larger muscle masses, respond with more robust, vigorous and holistic movements. In females, the fine motor system is more efficient. These differences lead to others—such as the fact that males' more active movements in space require precise judgments of speed and depth, while the females' fine movements necessitate precise timing of sequentially ordered acts. Further, in order to mobilize robust and vigorous movements of the extremities, the axial musculature of males must be held in relatively fixed postures. Females, freed from such rigidities, move their axial muscles more fluidly and develop their fine-motor midline systems—e.g., the tongue and vocal cords.

Much more research is required to categorize these differences in terms of brain mechanisms, but a few clues are available. Control over gross postural set is a function of the basal ganglia which, as noted above, are intimately involved in protocritic processes. If we assume that gross postural set is especially sensitive to spatial stimuli, this would account for a greater integration of visual cues into an action. Visually guided motor behavior can be characterized as "movement with objects," which is the male mode of action, as opposed to that of the female, which is typically "movement without objects."

"Movement without objects" appears related to linguistic aptitude. Kimura (1976), in a series of studies using populations of brain-damaged subjects, discovered a gross deficit in manual motor function in left but not right lesioned patients. Slowing of motor control was highly correlated with severity of aphasia. The deficit lay in the inability of subjects to make the transition from one movement to another and not in the sequencing per se. Ordering remained intact, but left hemisphere lesioned subjects took longer to execute each movement, often perseverating. This difficulty is reminiscent of monkeys with motor cortex removals (Pribram et al., 1955-56) and stutterers (more often males) who repeat the same phoneme again and again. Thus, fluency, not sequential ordering, is seen to be impaired by left hemisphere motor cortex lesions.

Both the female's fluency and the male's skill with objects (and their images) are epicritic processes. But, as we have noted, perceptual and mechanical skills with objects derive from protocritic origins in the development of the basal ganglia. In a similar fashion, fluency depends initially on another protocritic system which centers on the amygdala, a basal ganglion-like structure which forms part of the limbic forebrain. Protocritic processes involving the amygdala regulate arousal (as measured by the orienting reaction) and thus the transition from one act to another. And the amygdala is one of the major brain locations sensitive to the action of sex hormones. But more of this in a moment.

Research has not as yet been performed to test the hypothesis that the sex-related differences in motor function are due to some difference in a quantitative dimension. But, as suggested above, a few leads are available. The large *vs.* fine motor system distinction is, after all, a quantitative one and can, therefore, by way of feedback, directly influence the prothetic, protocritic processing mechanisms of the brain which in turn may modify the development of epicritic functions.

Sex Differences in Core Brain Systems and Their Influence on the Development of Sensory-Motor Processing

To determine whether or not there are neurophysiological or neurochemical differences in neural organization of protocritic processes which could account for sex differences in experience and behavior, it is useful to begin with an assessment of non-human primates. One can assume that here sex differences are largely acultural, particularly when they are observed in all non-human primate species. When hormonal or endocrine involvement is found in such fundamental behaviors as aggression or nurturance, the question is raised as to whether the more subtle distinctions between the sexes discussed throughout this paper could have a similar basis.

Sexual dimorphism in primates is one of the most noticeable characteristics of the species. Sex differences are observed in size and intra-group aggression as well as in the more obvious differences in mating behavior and child rearing which are also common to other species. In all primate societies the division of labor by gender creates a highly stable social system, the dominant males controlling territorial boundaries and maintaining order among lesser males by containing and preventing their aggression, the females tending the young and forming alliances with other females (see Eaton, 1976). Human primates follow this same pattern so remarkably that it is not difficult to argue for biological bases for the type of social order that channels aggression to guard the territory which in turn maintains an equable environment for the young.

The critical question arises: Do these pervasive differences which undoubtedly reflect differences in hormonal regulation by sub-cortical brain systems lead to differences in attention and cognition because of innate biases on sensory-motor systems, *or* does the behavioral interaction with the environment produced by these sub-cortical differences subsequently alter cortical structures by producing differential sensory input? This question may be rephrased: Do perceptual and cognitive gender differences arise *solely* because of *intrinsic* brain properties, or through an *extrinsic behavior/environment interaction* producing sensory-motor modification?

Our thesis will be that innate sex differences can be shown to occur in some of the structures that subserve protocritic processes (as discussed above) and that these differences differentially bias sensory-motor *behavior*. Different *behaviors*, in turn, alter the anatomical structure of other portions of the developing brain—portions which control epicritic processes. Thus, specific behaviors tend to engage one sensory modality rather than another, by virtue of the nature of the action: e.g., gross movements tend to engage the visual system because of radical alterations in the appearance of the visual environment, while the fine movements activate touch via dexterity and auditory sensitivity via the mechanisms for speech.

The problem lies in determining which protocritic core-brain mechanisms prime this process. We might begin with portions of the hypothalamus (a core-brain control system) which is functionally dissimilar in male and female brains. The circulatory system of normal males and females contains proportions of all sex hormones. However, recently it was shown by Fox (1975) that cells of the preoptic hypothalamic region of the brain contain macromolecules which bind either androgen or estrogen alone or proportions of both androgens and estrogens, the estrogen generally acting as an androgen inhibitor. Fox concludes that both androgens and estrogens are important to both sexes and states:

> We propose that the brain receptor mechanisms for "sex steroid" hormones function by direct detection of the relative concentrations of androgen and estrogen rather than by independent detection of the absolute levels of the respective hormones.

Studies on the development of behavioral patterns which arise from hormonal activation have also demonstrated that specific hormone binding *ratios* are essential during critical periods to give rise to sex-specific behaviors. Hormone ratios, therefore, mobilize systems which are in fact available in both sexes, but can remain dormant. By priming a dormant system with the appropriate hormone concentration, male behavior can be elicited from females and vice versa (see Strand, 1975).

In addition to the preoptic hypothalamic cells, receptor sites for sex hormones are concentrated largely in the amygdala, which is the forebrain focus for the brain systems that control arousal (see Morrell et al., 1975). As noted earlier, Pribram and McGuinness (1975), in an extensive review, discerned three major systems that control attention: an *arousal* system that organizes phasic responses to input (based on a "Stop" or "Interrupt" satiety mechanism); an *activation* system that organizes the tonic readinesses or sensory-motor sets of the organism (based on a "Go" or "Initiate" appetitive mechanism); and an *effort* system that coordinates arousal and activation. The forebrain focus for each of these systems is anatomically distinct: amygdala for phasic arousal, basal ganglia for readiness, and hippocampus for effort. Neurochemically the systems are also clearly distinct: As noted above, the arousal system contains (among other sensitivities such as those for serotonin and for norepinephrine) receptors sensitive to the ratio of sex steroid hormones; the activation system is characteristically dopaminergic; and the effort system is centered on receptor sensitivity to adrenal cortical steroids. This last system has recently become of special interest because it is regulated centrally, i.e., within the brain, as well as peripherally (at the adrenal cortex) by the amount of circulating adreno-cortico-trophic hormone (ACTH), a polypeptide secreted by the pituitary gland. Adrenal cortical steroids related chemically to the steroids androgen and estrogen are known to enhance transmission in the sensory input systems: Henkin (1970) has demonstrated that thresholds for taste, smell and hearing are significantly lower and that suprathreshold discrimination is abnormal in patients with Addison's disease in which the absence of normal adrenal function prevents the secretion of corticosteroids. Conversely, in the past several years, ACTH and other closely related polypeptides have been shown to act as a ligand for morphine, i.e., they bind the receptor sites that engage morphine to produce analgesia and enhance comfort. In fact, there is good evidence that organisms, including man, ordinarily secrete a polypeptide which protects against pain and effort—a substance named encephalin whose active portion is called endorphin (see review by Pribram, 1977).

Another line of evidence on anatomical substrates for primary sensory differences has been demonstrated in animal studies that auditory preferences over visual, and vice versa, are largely eliminated by tectal and pretectal lesions (in placements not too far removed from the site of action of morphine and encephalin), but not at higher levels (Jane et al., 1962; Thompson et al., 1963). In the Jane et al. study neither cortical nor thalamic ablations, nor lesions of 90% of the auditory fibers leading from the colliculi, eliminated cats' preference for a low intensity sound over a bright flashing light—while a restricted lesion in the inferior colliculus abolished this prepotency effect. Thompson et al. discovered a pathway in which visually (but not auditory) conditioned responses could be decoupled. They propose that pretectal sites are involved in visual-motor integration (brightness discrimination was not affected).

Also relevant, although somewhat more remote phylogenetically, is the finding that sex hormone receptor sites have been discovered in the nucleus intercollicularis in birds (see Morrell et al., 1975). Both auto-radiographic and behavioral data indicate that this testosterone activated region is essential to the production of song. While this comparison be-tween birds and mammals may be spurious, it does point to the possi-bility that auditory/visual and vocal mechanisms which do distinguish the sexes may have an anatomical substrate in the chemically sensitive brainstem region around the tectum.

Thus, it is clear that hormones have a powerful central nervous system effect on altering sensory sensitivities and, consequently, behavior. The question arises whether the neural systems centered on the preoptic hypothalamus and amygdala, which contain the sex hormone receptor sites, can account for *all* the sex differences in sensory-motor perform-ances—and therefore secondarily for the sex differences in attention and cognition—that we have reviewed here.

The answer to this question devolves on the possibility of demonstrat-ing that sex differences result from differences in the mechanisms of arousal, since we have shown the amygdala to be the center of the forebrain regulatory mechanisms for arousal. We defined arousal in terms of the orienting reaction: a phasic, i.e., short-lived response to sensory input which habituates rapidly. The orienting reaction ordi-narily involves the visceroautonomic response system and after amyg-dalectomy the visceroautonomic components of orienting are no longer sensitive to repetitions of the input (they either fail to occur at all or fail to habituate), while the behavioral components invaribaly fail to habituate. We interpreted these findings as showing that the arousal system ordinarily modulates the organism's sensitivities to recurring sensory inputs—i.e., the arousal system is responsible for modulating reactions (orienting and habituation) to the intensive dimensions of sensory stimulation.

But the arousal system interacts with another—the readiness system which is centered on the basal ganglia—and the coordination of arousal with readiness centers on the hippocampal circuit and takes effort. The fact that there are sex differences in peripheral motor function (males tend to act robustly, while females tend to interact with the environ-ment via their fine muscle systems) must influence the development of the readiness system, which becomes progressively more competent in providing the muscular sets which enable these acts.

Thus, differences between the sexes in arousal and in readiness can be expected on the basis of their physiological differences in both types of effector mechanisms—their different relative concentrations of sex hormones and their different organization of muscle competences. As noted above, these differences are fed back into the central nervous system, differentially organizing those parts of the brain which are involved in processing the intensive aspects of sensory experience. Our hypothesis, therefore, should take into account sex differences in both arousal and readiness, and perhaps even in the relation between the two as expressed in effort.

From Protocritic Control to Cortical Organization

The cortical terminus of the arousal, readiness and effort systems is the anterior portion of the frontal lobe; the protocritic systems have a cortical representation in the frontal extremity of the brain just as the sensory projections to specific thalamic regions are re-represented at cortical sites in the posterior part of the brain. Part of our understanding of sex differences in the organization of protocritic processes stems, therefore, from the way in which the frontal lobes function.

Goldman et al. (1974) have discovered sizeable sex differences in the rate of development of frontal lobe function in non-human primates. Resections of the orbital frontal cortex (that portion which is especially related to the limbic forebrain) were found to impair male monkeys in infancy (2½-15 months) on tasks involving object reversal, delayed response and delayed alternation. Females were uninfluenced by frontal lesions until 2 years of age, when both sexes were affected similarly. Goldman's data run counter to the proposal (Hutt, 1972; Buffrey & Gray, 1972) that the human male is, in general, developmentally retarded both physically and intellectually.

Goldman's data can, however, account for the observation that an assortment of male abilities that develop early because of their dependence on gross muscular control are noticeably affected by frontal lesions. These abilities are usually classed as visual-spatial aptitudes and Table 7 reviews the evidence that frontal lobe function is implicated in the performance of tasks that tap these aptitudes. After frontal lesions, the pattern of figure reversal (e.g., with Necker cubes) is disturbed, with normal baselines either exceeded or reduced. Object assembly is significantly impaired and various spatial-mechanical tasks similarly affected. Goldman's data suggest that the earlier maturation of their arousal-readiness coordination (the effort) mechanism gives males an advantage in behavior depending on spatial-mechanical relationships.

This early advantage could transform the characteristic mode of male behavior which, as we have seen, is holistic and robust to something essentially discrete (object thrown, struck or turned). This transformation would come about by the early coordinated interaction of the two systems we have been discussing: a readiness mechanism makes possible the tracking of a stimulus and an arousal mechanism that stops the tracking when the outcome of the movement matches the visual-spatial input that initiated it. To learn to do this efficiently produces a process in which simultaneous use of both hemispheres is essential: a left hemisphere motor outflow (including frontal eye field activity) and right hemisphere visual analysis. Two hemispheres work in parallel and the protocritic systems and frontal lobe function to integrate the process.

Yen (unpublished Ph.D. thesis) tested a large number of subjects of both sexes on a battery of spatial-mechanical tasks. The results showed that right-handed males were significantly superior to left-handed males. This suggests that for the male, visual-spatial skill is greater when the two hemispheres do not compete in processing. In males, an image of the performance appears to be constructed in the left hemisphere motor system, and at the same time, the visual feedback is separately monitored by the right hemisphere. Such a trade-off in hemispheric function is irrelevant to females who attempt to solve spatial problems *verbally*. In the Yen study, no difference was found for handedness in females, who consistently performed more poorly than the left-handed males. Behavioral data support this view.

Perseveration and deficits in ordering behavior are also produced by frontal lobe lesions (see Pribram, 1971). The later maturation of frontal cortex and perhaps the protocritic processes as a whole in the female may bias her towards more frontal lobe involvement in the temporal than the spatial domain. Thus, the female, who tends to fluidity which develops gradually towards a dominance of linguistic analyses, has another hemisphere available for visual imagery. Because the two processes do *not* engage similar systems, but operate independently, this allows the female to shift flexibly from one to the other. Such flexibility in control is a demonstrated function involving the mature frontal lobe (Pribram et al., 1964) and is the basis for proper sequencing of behavior. The data of McGuinness and Courtney (unpublished) reported earlier indicate that the primary male deficit in the perception and translation of speech to written language is an ability to transfer rapidly from an auditory image to its visual counterpart. Once shifted to an auditory mode, they cannot readily engage a visual representation.

Support for the view that females have the capacity to shift flexibly between hemispheres is provided by studies on control of alpha rhythm. Davidson et al. (1976) report significant differences between the sexes in alpha rhythm control during biofeedback. Females are highly asymmetric at rest, but show a significantly greater ability to enhance or diminish alpha power in one or the other hemisphere independently, as well as an ability equal to males to maintain a symmetric bilateral integration of either alpha-ON or alpha-OFF.

A further investigation (Tucker, 1976) showed that the balance of alpha power between the hemispheres is unrelated to females' success in a variety of tasks ranging from verbal to spatial. Males were more efficient at the spatial tasks during greater right hemisphere desynchrony, while left hemisphere desynchrony was correlated to verbal performance. These data, in effect, suggest that when males are operating in the auditory-motor mode they are effectively locked out of a visual-motor mode.

Conclusion

Thus, the relationship between sex differences and hemisphere specialization need no longer be so bewildering. A flood of data has shown beyond doubt that such a relationship exists. Still, the origin of the relationship on any reasonable physiological basis has remained a mystery. Our proposal can be phrased in terms of two hypotheses which rest on plausible consequences of clearly demonstrated sex differences: 1) The demonstrated hormonal sex differences in the arousal mechanism (amygdala-frontal) predispose females to greater flexibility in the control of hemispheric function so that they excel in tasks demanding ordered flexible shifts between hemispheric functions. When no such competition between functions is involved, males demonstrate superiority. 2) Because of a more massive musculature, the male readiness (basal ganglia-frontal) system predisposes to spatial-mechanical (object) aptitude which then engages the visual mode. By contrast, the female, because of her finer muscular organization, becomes more proficient in auditory-verbal (fluent, communicative) performance.

These two hypotheses can readily be tested both at the neuropsychological and neurophysiological level. We doubt that they will account for all the biologically based differences in experience and behavior that distinguish the sexes—but at least they provide a starting point for understanding the *mechanism* by which the distinctions are produced.

We believe that sex differences in cognitive processes are derived from early biases produced by these two demonstrated distinctions in effector function. The theory could account for the slow development of those sensory-motor skills which have best contributed to the enormous success of the species Homo sapiens. The theory also leaves room for adaptive change in both neural structure and behavioral function when demands on skills change with changing cultures.

REFERENCES

AMMONS, R. B., ALPRIN, S. I., and AMMONS, C. H. Rotary pursuit performance as related to sex and age of pre-adult subjects. *Journal of Experimental Psychology*, 1955, 49, 127-133.

ANNETT, M. The growth of manual preference and speed. *British Journal of Psychology*, 1970, 61, 545-558.

ARANOFF, D. Relationship between immobilization and autokinetic movement. *Perceptual and Motor Skills*, 1973, 36, 411-414.

AXELROD, S. *Effects of Early Blindness. Performance of Blind and Sighted Children on Tactile and Auditory Tasks.* New York: American Foundation for the Blind, 1959.

BAGBY, J. W. A cross-cultural study of perceptual predominance in binocular rivalry. *Journal of Abnormal and Social Psychology*, 1957, 54.

BAHRICK, H. P., BAHRICK, P. O., and WITTLINGER, R. P. Fifty years of memory for names and faces: A cross-sectional approach. *Journal of Experimental Psychology (General)*, 1975, 104, 54-75.

BAILEY, E. H. S. and NICHOLS, E. L. On the delicacy of the sense of taste. *Science*, 1888, p. 145.

BARRATT, E. S. The space-visualization factors related to temperament traits. *Journal of Psychology*, 1955, 39, 279-287.

BELL, R. Q. and COSTELLO, N. S. Three tests for sex differences in tactile sensitivity in the newborn. *Biologia Neonatorum*, 1964, 7, 335-347.

BENNETT, G. K. and CRUIKSHANK, R. M. Sex differences in the understanding of mechanical problems. *Journal of Applied Psychology*, 1942, 26, 121-127.

BENTLEY, A. *Monotones.* London: Novello & Co., 1968.

BERLYNE, D. E. Attention as a problem in behavior. In: D. I. Mostofsky (Ed.), *Attention: Contemporary Theory and Analysis.* New York: Appleton Century Crofts, 1970.

BERMAN, L. R. Sex differences in intellectual development: Are boys more vulnerable. *Reports of Psychol. Lab.* University of Stockholm, 1974, #417.

BERNSTEIN, R. C. and JACKLIN, C. N. The 3½ month-old infant: Stability of behavior, sex differences and longitudinal findings. Unpublished Masters Thesis, 1973.

BIRCH, H. G. and BELMONT, L. Auditory-visual integration in normal and retarded readers. *American Journal of Orthopsychiatry*, 1964, 34, 852-861.

BOCK, R. D. and KOLAKOWSKI, D. Further evidence of sex-linked major-gene influence on human spatial visualizing ability. *The American Journal of Human Genetics*, 1973, 25, 1-14.

BOGEN, J. E. and GORDON, H. W. Musical tests for functional lateralization with intra-carotid amobarbital. *Nature*, 1971, 230, 524.

BROWNFIELD, M. K. Sex and stimulus time differences in after image durations. *Perceptual and Motor Skills*, 1965, 21, 446.

BUFFERY, A. W. H. and GRAY, J. A. Sex differences in the development of spatial and linguistic skills. In: C. Ounsted and D. C. Taylor (Eds.), *Gender Differences: Their Ontogeny and Significance.* Edinburgh: Churchill Livingstone, 1972.

BURG, A. Visual acuity as measured by dynamic and static tests: A comparative evaluation. *Journal of Applied Psychology*, 1966, 50, 460-466.

BURG, A. and HULBERT, S. Dynamic visual acuity as related to age, sex, and static acuity. *Journal of Applied Psychology*, 1961, 45, 111-116.

CARMON, A. and GOMBOS, G. M. A physiological vascular correlate of hand preference: Possible implications with respect to hemisphere cerebral dominance. *Neuropsychologia*, 1970, 8, 119-128.

CARTER, R. B. An analysis of ten thousand cases of disease or disturbance of the eyes, seen in private practice. *Lancet*, October 1892.

CHAPLIN, J. P. Sex differences in the perception of autokinetic movement. *Journal of General Psychology*, 1955, 52, 149-155.

CHIN, J. H., PRIBRAM, K. H., DRAKE, K., and GREENE, L. O., JR. Disruption of temperature discrimination during limbic forebrain stimulation in monkeys. *Neuropsychologia,* 1976, 14, 293-310.

COHEN, L. B., GELBER, E. R., and LAZAR, M. A. Infant habituation and generalization to differing degrees of stimulus novelty. *Journal of Experimental Child Psychology,* 1971, 11, 379-89.

COHEN, S. E. Infant attentional behavior to face-voice incongruity. Paper presented at meeting of Society for Research in Child Development. Philadelphia, 1973.

COLLINS, D., KESSEN, W., and HAITH, M. Note on an attempt to replicate a relation between stimulus unpredictability and infant attention. *Journal of Experimental Child Psychology,* 1972, 13, 1-8.

COOK, T. W. and SHEPARD, A. H. Performance on several control-display relationships as a function of age and sex. *Perceptual and Motor Skills,* 1958, 8, 339-345.

CORAH, N. L. and BOFFA, J. Perceived control, self observation and response to aversive stimuli. *Journal of Personality and Social Psychology,* 1970, 16, 1-4.

CORNELL, E. H. and STRAUSS, M. S. Infants' responsiveness to compounds of habituated visual stimuli. *Developmental Psychology,* 1973, 2, 73-78.

CORSO, J. F. Age and sex differences in thresholds. *Journal of the Acoustical Society of America,* 1959, 31, 498-507.

DAVIDSON, R. J., SCHWARTZ, G. E., PUGASH, E., and BROMFIELD, E. Sex differences in patterns of EEG Asymmetry. *Biological Psychology,* 1976, 4, 119-138.

DE RENZI, E. and SPINNLER, H. Visual recognition in patients with unilateral cerebral disease. *Journal of Nervous and Mental Diseases,* 1966, 142, 515-525.

DUGGAN, L. An experiment on immediate recall in secondary school children. *British Journal of Psychology,* 1950, 40, 149-154.

EAGLES, E. L., WISHIK, S. M., DOEFLER, L. G., MELNICK, W., and LEVINE, H. S. *Hearing sensitivity and related factors in children.* Pittsburg: University of Pittsburg Press, 1963.

EATON, G. G. The social order of Japanese Macaques. *Scientific American,* 1976, 235, 97-106.

EISENBERG, R. Unpublished data reviewed by Korner, 1971, 1972.

ELLIOTT, C. D. Noise tolerance and extraversion in children. *British Journal of Psychology,* 1971, 62, 325-330.

ELLIS, H. *Man and Woman: A Study of Human Secondary Sexual Characteristics.* London: Walter Scott, Ltd., 1896 and 1930 (6th Ed.).

ENGEL, E. The role of content in binocular resolution. *Amer. J. Psych.,* 1956, 69.

ENGEL, R., CROWELL, C., and NISHIJIMA, S. Visual and auditory response latencies in neonates. In: *Facilitation Volume in Honour of C. C. de Silva.* Ceylon: Kularatue and Company, 1968.

ERNEST, C. H. and PAIVIO, A. Imagery and sex differences in incidental recall. *British Journal of Psychology,* 1971, 62, 67-72.

FAGAN, J. F. Infants' recognition memory for faces. *Journal of Experimental Child Psychology,* 1972, 14, 453-476.

FAIRWEATHER, H. and HUTT, S. J. Sex differences in a perceptual motor skill in children. In: C. Ounsted and D. C. Taylor (Eds.), *Gender Differences: Their Ontogeny and Significance.* Edinburgh: Churchill Livingstone, 1972.

FLAVELL, J. H. *The Developmental Psychology of Jean Piaget.* Toronto: D. Van Nostrand Co. Inc., 1963.

FOX, T. O. Androgen and estrogen-binding macromolecules in developing mouse brain: Biochemical and genetic evidence. *Proceedings of the National Academy of Sciences, U.S.A.,* 1975, 72, 4303-4307.

FREIDES, D. Human information processing and sensory modality. Cross modal functions, information complexity, memory and deficit. *Psychol. Bull.,* 1974, 81, 284-310.

FRIEDMAN, S., NAGY, A. N., and CARPENTER, G. C. Newborn attention: Differential decrement to visual stimuli. *J. Exp. Child Psychol.*, 1970, 10, 44-51.

GARAI, J. E. and SCHEINFELD, A. Sex differences in mental and behavioral traits. *Genetic Psychological Monographs*, 1968, 77, 169-299.

GESCHWIND, N. and LEVITSKY, W. Human brain: Left-right asymmetrics in temporal speech region. *Science*, 1968, 161, 186-187.

GOLDBERG, S. and LEWIS, M. Play behaviour in the year old infant: Early sex differences. *Child Development*, 1969, 40, 21-31.

GOLDMAN, P. S., CRAWFORD, H. T., STOKES, L. P., GALKIN, T. W., and ROSVOLD, H. E. Sex-dependent behavioural effects of cerebral cortical lesions in the developing Rhesus monkey. *Science*, 1974, 186, 540-542.

GOODENOUGH, E. W. Interest in persons as an aspect of sex differences in the early years. *Genetic Psychological Monographs*, 1957, 55, 287-323.

GREENBERG, D. J. Accelerating visual complexity levels in the human infant. *Child Devel.*, 1971, 42, 905-918.

GREENBERG, D. J. and O'DONNELL, W. J. Infancy and the optimal level of stimulation. *Child Devel.*, 1972, 43, 639-645.

GREENBERG, D. J. and WEIZMANN, F. The measurement of visual attention in infants: A comparison of two methodologies. *J. Exp. Child Psych.*, 1971, 11, 234-243.

GREENBERGER, E., O'CONNOR, J., and SORENSEN, A. Personality, cognitive and academic correlates of problem-solving flexibility. *Developmental Psychology*, 1971, 4, 416-424.

GUILFORD, J. P. *The Nature of Human Intelligence*. New York: McGraw-Hill, 1967.

GULLICKSEN, G. R. and CROWELL, D. H. Neonatal habituation to electroactual stimulation. *Journal of Experimental Child Psychology*, 1964, 1, 388-396.

HARMS, I. E. and SPIKER, C. C. Factors associated with the performance of young children on intelligence scales and tests of speech development. *Journal of Genetic Psychology*, 1959, 94, 3-22.

HARRIS, L. J. Sex differences in spatial ability: Possible environmental, genetic and neurological factors. In: M. Kinsbourne (Ed.), *Hemispheric Asymmetrics of Function*. Cambridge, England: Cambridge University Press, 1976.

HEAD, H. *Studies in Neurology*. Oxford: Oxford Medical Publications, 1920.

HÉCAEN, H. Clinical symptomatology in right and left hemisphere lesions. In: V. G. Mountcastle (Ed.), *Interhemispheric Relations and Cerebral Dominance*. Baltimore: John Hopkins, 1962.

HENKIN, R. I. The neuroendocrine control of perception. In: D. A. Hamburg, K. H. Pribram, and A. T. Stunkard (Eds.), *Perception and Its Disorders*. Baltimore: Williams and Wilkins, 1970, 123-138.

HERZBERG, F. and LEPKIN, M. A. A study of sex differences on the primary mental abilities test. *Educational and Psychological Measurement*, 1954, 14, 687-689.

HULL, F. M., MIELKE, P. W., TIMMONS, R. J., and WILLEFORD, J. A. The national speech and hearing survey: Preliminary results. *ASHA*, 1971, 3, 501-509.

HUTT, C. Curiosity in young children. *Science Journal*, 1970, 6, 68-72.

HUTT, C. Neuroendocrinological behavior and intellectual aspects of sexual differentiation in human development. In: C. Ounsted and D. C. Taylor (Eds.), *Gender Differences: Their Ontogeny and Significance*. Edinburgh: Churchill Livingstone, 1972.

IMMERGLUCK, L. and MEARINI, M. C. Age and sex differences in response to embedded figures and reversible figures. *Journal of Experimental Child Psychology*, 1969, 8, 210-221.

IPPOLITOV, F. V. Interanalyser differences in the sensitivity-strength parameter for vision, hearing and cutaneous modalities. In: V. D. Nebylitsyn and J. A. Gray (Eds.), *Biological Bases of Individual Behavior*. London: 1972, 43-61.

JAMES, W. *Principles of Psychology*. London: Routledge and Kegan Paul, 1890.

JANE, J. A., MASTERTON, R. B., and DIAMOND, I. T. The function of the tectum for attention to auditory stimuli in the cat. *Journal of Comparative Neurology*, 1962, 125, 165-191.

JASTROW, (not known). A statistical study of memory and association. *Educational Review*, 1891, December.

JASTROW, (not known). Studies from the laboratory of experimental psychology of the University of Wisconsin. *Am. J. Psychol.*, 1892, April.

KAGAN, J. and LEWIS, M. Studies of attention in the human infant. *Merrill-Palmer Quarterly*, 1965, 11, 95-127.

KIMURA, D. Motor functions in the left hemisphere. Paper delivered at the 21st International Congress, Paris, 1976.

KLEIVEN, J. and ROMMETVEIT, R. Meaning and frequency in a binocular rivalry situation. *Scand. J. Psych.*, 1970, 2.

KORNER, A. F. Visual alertness in neonates: Individual differences and their correlates. *Perceptual and Motor Skills*, 1970, 31, 499-509.

KORNER, A. F. Individual differences at birth: Implications for early experience and later development. *American Journal of Orthopsychiatry*, 1971, 41, 608-619.

KORNER, A. F. Sex differences in newborns with special references to differences in the organization of oral behavior. *Journal of Child Psychology*, 1973, 14, 19-29.

KORNER, A. F. and THOMAS, E. B. Visual alertness in neonates as evoked by maternal care. *Journal of Experimental Child Psychology*, 1970, 10, 67-68.

KREITLER, S., KREITLER, H., and ZIGLER, E. Cognitive orientation and curiosity. *British Journal of Psychology*, 1974, 65, 43-52.

LA GRONE, C. W. Sex and personality differences in relation to feeling for direction. *Journal of General Psychology*, 1969, 81, 23-33.

LEVY, J. Lateral specialization of the human brain: Behavioral manifestations and possible evolutionary basis. Paper presented at 32nd Annual Biology Colloquium. Oregon State University 1971.

LEWIS, M. Infants' responses to facial stimuli during the first year of life. *Developmental Psychology*, 1969, 1, 75-86.

LEWIS, M. State as an infant-environment interaction: An analysis of mother-infant interaction as a function of sex. *Merrill-Palmer Quarterly*, 1972, 18, 95-121.

LEWIS, M., KAGAN, J., and KALAFAT, J. Patterns of fixation in the young infant. *Child Development*, 1966, 37, 331-341.

LINDSAY, P. H. Multichannel processing in perception. In: D. I. Mostofsky (Ed.), *Attention: Contemporary Theory and Analysis*. New York: Appleton Century Crofts, 1970.

LINDZEY, G. and GOLDBERG, M. Motivational differences between males and females as measured by the TAT. *Journal of Personality*, 1953, 22, 101-117.

LIPSITT, L. P. and LEVY, N. Electroactual thresholds in the neonate. *Child Development*, 1959, 30, 547-554.

LITTLE, B. R. Factors affecting the use of psychological versus non-psychological constructs on the Repetory Test. *Bulletin of the British Psychological Society*, 1968, 21, 34.

LIVESLEY, W. J. and BROMLEY, D. G. *Person Perception in Childhood and Adolescence*. London: Wiley & Sons, 1973.

LURIA, A. R. *Higher Cortical Functions in Man*. London: Tavistock, 1966.

MACCOBY, E. E. and JACKLIN, C. N. *The Psychology of Sex Differences*. Stanford: Stanford University Press, 1974.

MACCOBY, E. E. and JACKLIN, C. N. Stress, activity and proximity seeking: Sex differences in the year old child. *Child Development*, 1973, 44, 34-47.

MARKS, D. F. Visual imagery differences in the recall of pictures. *British Journal of Psychology*, 1973, 64, 17-24.

MATSUBARA, T. An observation on cerebral phlebograms with special reference to changes in superficial veins. *Nagoya Journal of Medical Science*, 1960, 23, 86-94.

McCALL, R. B. Smiling and vocalization in infants as indices of perceptual cognitive processes. *Merrill-Palmer Quarterly*, 1972, 18.

McCALL, R. B. and KAGAN, J. Attention in the infant: Effects of complexity, contour perimeter and familiarity. *Child Development*, 1967, 38, 939-952.

McCALL, R. B. and KAGAN, J. Individual differences in the infant's distribution of attention to stimulus discrepancy. *Development Psychology*, 1970, 2, 90-98.

McCARTHY, D. Language development of the preschool child. *Institute of Child Welfare Monograph No. 4*. Minneapolis: University of Minnesota Press, 1930.

McGREW, W. C. Aspects of social development in nursery school children with emphasis on introduction to the group. In: E. Blurton-Jones (Ed.), *Ethological Studies of Child Behavior*. London: Cambridge University Press, 1972, pp. 129-156.

McGUINNESS, D. Hearing: Individual differences in perceiving. *Perception*, 1972, 1, 465-473.

McGUINNESS, D. Cardiovascular responses during habituation and mental activity in anxious men and women. *Biological Psychology*, 1973, 1, 115-123.

McGUINNESS, D. Perceptual and cognitive differences between the sexes. In: B. Lloyd and J. Archer. *Explorations in Sex Differences*. New York: Academic Press, 1976a.

McGUINNESS, D. Away from a unisex psychology: Individual differences in visual perception. *Perception*, 1976b, 5, 279-294.

McGUINNESS, D. and LEWIS, I. Sex differences in visual persistence: Experiments on the Ganzfeld and the after image. *Perception*, 1976, 5, 295-301.

McGUINNESS, D. and SYMONDS, J. Sex differences in choice behavior: The object-person dimension. *Perception* (in press).

McKITTRICK, K. G. Bodily activity and perceptual activity. *Percept. and Mot. Skills*, 1965, 20, 1109-12.

MENDEL, G. Children's preference for differing degrees of novelty. *Child Development*, 1965, 35, 452-465.

MESSER, S. B. and LEWIS, M. Social class and sex differences in the attachment and play behaviour of the year old infant. *Merrill-Palmer Quarterly*, 1972, 18, 295-300.

MILNER, B. Hemisphere specialization: Scope and limits. In: F. O. Schmitt and F. G. Worden (Eds.), *The Neurosciences Third Study Program*. Cambridge, Mass.: MIT Press, 1974.

MILNER, B. and TEUBER, H.-L. Alteration of perception and memory in man: Reflection on Methods. In: L. Weiskrantz (Ed.), *Analysis of Behavior Change*. New York: Harper & Row, 1968.

MITCHELL, G. and BRANDT, E. M. Behavioural differences related to experience of mother and sex of infant in the Rhesus monkey. *Development Psychology*, 1970, 3, 149.

MITTLER, P. and WARD, J. The use of the Illinois test of psycholinguistic abilities on British four-year old children: A normative and factorial study. *British Journal of Educational Psychology*, 1970, 40, 43-54.

MORRELL, J. I., KELLEY, D. B. and PFAFF, D. W. Sex steroid binding in the brains of vertebrates. In: K. M. Knigge, D. E. Scott, H. Robayashi, Kiura-shi and S. Ishi (Eds.), *Brain-Endocrine Interaction II*. Basel: Karger, A. G., 1975.

MOSS, H. A. Sex, age and state as determinants of mother-infant interaction. *Merrill-Palmer Quarterly*, 1967, 13, 19-35.

MOSS, H. A. and ROBSON, K. S. Maternal influences and early social visual behaviour. *Child Development*, 1968, 39, 401-408.

MYERS, W. J. and CANTOR, G. N. Observing and cardiac responses of human infants to visual stimuli. *Journal of Experimental Child Psychology*, 1967, 5, 16-25.

NICHOLS, E. L. and BAILEY, E. H. S. Letter in *Nature*, 1886, 25th November.

NOBLE, C. E., BAKER, B. L., and JONES, T. A. Age and sex parameters in psychomotor learning. *Perceptual and Motor Skills*, 1964, 19, 934-945.

NOBLE, C. E. and HAYS, J. R. Discrimination reaction performance as a function of anxiety and sex parameters. *Perceptual and Motor Skills*, 1965, 23, 1267-1278.

OETZEL, R. M. Annotated bibliography. In: E. Maccoby (Ed.), *The Development of Sex Differences*. London: Tavistock Publications, 1967.

OTTOLENGHI (not known). L'Olfatto nei Criminali. *Archivio di Psichiatria*, 1888, 9, Fasc. 5.

OUNSTED, C. and TAYLOR, D. C. *Gender Differences: Their Ontogeny and Significance*. Edinburgh: Churchill Livingstone, 1972.

PANCRATZ, C. N. and COHEN, L. B. Recovery of habituation in infants. *Journal of Experimental Child Psychology*, 1970, 9, 208-216.

PHILLIPS, J. R. Syntax and vocabulary of mothers speech to young children. Age and sex comparisons. *Child Development*, 1973, 44, 182-185.

PISHKIN, V. and BLANCHARD, R. Auditory concept identification as a function of subject, sex and stimulus dimensions. *Psychonomic Science*, 1964, 1, 177-178.

PISHKIN, V. and SHURLEY, J. T. Auditory dimensions and irrelevant information in concept identification of males and females. *Perceptual and Motor Skills*, 1965, 20, 673-683.

POHL, W. and CALDWELL, W. E. Towards an analysis of a function deficit. *Journal of General Psychology*, 1968, 79, 241-255.

PRIBRAM, K. H. On the neurology of thinking. *Behav. Sci.*, 1959, 4, 265-284.

PRIBRAM, K. H. *Languages of the Brain*. Englewood Cliffs, N.J.: Prentice-Hall, 1971.

PRIBRAM, K. H. Self-consciousness and intentionality. In: G. E. Schwartz and D. Shapiro (Eds), *Consciousness and Self-Regulation*, Vol. 1. New York: Plenum Publishing Corporation, 1976.

PRIBRAM, K. H. Peptides and protocritic processes. In: L. H. Miller and C. L. Sandman (Eds.), *The Neuropeptides*, 1977.

PRIBRAM, K. H., AHUMADA, A., HARTOG, J., and ROOS, L. A progress report on the neurological process disturbed by frontal lesions in primates. In: I. M. Warren and K. Akert (Eds.), *The Frontal Granular Cortex and Behavior*. New York: McGraw-Hill Book Company, Inc., 1964, pp. 28-55.

PRIBRAM, K. H., KRUGER, L., ROBINSON, F., and BERMAN, A. J. The effects of precentral lesions on the behavior of monkeys. *Yale J. Biol. and Med.*, 1955-56, 28, 428-443.

PRIBRAM, K. H. and McGUINNESS, D. Arousal, activation and effort in the control of attention. *Psychology Review* (1975), 82, 116-149.

RAMEY, C. T. and WATSON, J. S. Nonsocial reinforcement of infant's vocalizations. *Devel. Psychol.*, 1972, 6, 538.

RANDHAWA, B. S. A case for the uses of multivariate analysis in concept grouping, dominance level, and sex, as related to verbal recall. *Multivariate Behavior Research*, 1972, 7, 193-201.

ROBERTS, E. Poor pitch singing. Ph.D. dissertation. Liverpool University, 1972.

ROBERTS, J. Binocular visual acuity of adults. Washington: U.S. Department of Health, Education and Welfare, 1964.

ROSS, J. M. and SIMPSON, H. R. The national survey of health and development: 1. Educational attainment. *British Journal of Educational Psychology*, 1971, 41, 49-61.

RUBENSTEIN, J. Maternal attentiveness and subsequent exploratory behavior in the infant. *Child Development*, 1967, 38, 1089-1100.

SANDER, L. W. and CASSEL, T. Z. An empirical approach to the study of interactive regulation in the infant-caretaking system and its role in early development. Paper presented at the meetings of the Society for Research in Child Development, Philadelphia, 1973.

SCHAIE, K. W., BALTES, P., and STROTHER, C. R. A study of auditory sensitivity in advanced age. *Journal of Gerontology*, 1964, 19, 453-457.

SHEPHARD, A. H., ABBEY, D. S., and HUMPHRIES, M. Age and sex in relation to perceptual-motor performance on several control display relations on the TCC. *Perceptual and Motor Skills*, 1962, 14, 103-118.

SHERMAN, J. Problem of sex differences in space perception and aspects of intellectual functioning. *Psychology Review,* 1967, 74, 290-299.

SHERMAN, J. *On the Psychology of Women: A Survey of Empirical Studies.* Springfield, Illinois: Thomas, 1971.

SHUTER, R. P. G. An investigation of hereditary and environmental factors in musical ability. Ph.D. dissertation. University of London, 1964.

SHUTER, R. *The Psychology of Music.* London: Methuen, 1968.

SIMNER, M. L. Newborn's response to the cry of another infant. *Developmental Psychology,* 1971, 5, 136-150.

SIMON, J. R. Choice reaction time as a function of auditory S-R correspondence, age and sex. *Ergonomics,* 1967, 10, 659-664.

SIMPSON, W. E. and VAUGHT, G. M. Visual and auditory autokinesis. *Perceptual and Motor Skills,* 1973, 36, 1199-1206.

SKOFF, E. and POLLACK, R. H. Visual acuity in children as a function of hue. *Perception and Psychophysics,* 1969, 6, 244-246.

SMITH, P. K. and CONNOLLY, K. Patterns of play and social interaction in pre-school children. In: N. Blurton-Jones (Ed.), *Ethological Studies of Child Behavior.* Cambridge: Cambridge University Press, 1972.

SMOCK, C. D. and HOLT, B. G. Children's reaction to novelty: An experimental study of curiosity motivation. *Child Development,* 1962, 33, 631-642.

SOKOLOV, E. N. Higher nervous function, the orienting reflex. *Annual Review of Physiology,* 1963, 25, 545-580.

SPEARS, W. C. and HOHLE, R. H. Sensory and perceptual processes in infants. In: Y. Brackbill (Ed.), *Infancy and Early Childhood.* London: Collier MacMillan, 1967.

SPERRY, R. W. Lateral specialization in the surgically separated hemispheres. In: F. O. Schmitt and E. G. Worden (Eds.), *The Neurosciences: Third Study Program.* Cambridge, Mass.: MIT Press, 1974.

SPINELLI, D. N. and PRIBRAM, K. H. Changes in visual recovery function and unit activity produced by frontal cortex stimulation. *Elec. Clin. Neurophysiol.,* 1967, 22, 143-149.

STEVENS, S. S. In: W. Rosenblith (Ed.), *Sensory Communication.* Cambridge: MIT Press, 1961.

STRAND, F. L. The influence of hormones on the nervous system. *Bioscience,* 1975, 25, 568-577.

TEUBER, H. L. Why two brains? In: F. O. Schmitt and E. G. Worden (Eds.), *The Neurosciences: Third Study Program.* Cambridge, Mass: MIT Press, 1974.

THOMPSON, R., LESSE, H., and RICH, I. Dissociation of visual and auditory habits following pretectal lesions in rats and cats. *Journal of Comparative Neurology,* 1963, 121, 161-171.

THOMAS, A., CHESS, S., and BIRCH, H. G. *Temperament and Behaviour Disorders in Children.* New York: New York University Press, 1969.

TUCKER, D. M. Sex differences in hemispheric specialization for synthetic visuospatial functions. *Neuropsychologia,* 1976, 14, 447-454.

TYLER, L. *The Psychology of Human Differences.* New York: Appleton Century Crofts, 1965.

VOTH, A. C. Individual differences in the autokinetic phenomenon. *Journal of Experimental Psychology,* 1941, 24, 306-322.

WADA, J. A., CLARK, R., and HAMM, A. Asymmetry of temporal and frontal speech zones in 100 adult and 100 infant brains. *A.M.A. Archives of Neurology,* 1975.

WARNER, F. (No title available). *British Medical Journal,* March 1893.

WATSON, J. S. Operant conditioning of visual fixation in infants under visual and auditory reinforcement. *Development. Psychology,* 1969, 1, 508-516.

WEINSTEIN, S. and SERSEN, E. A. Tactual sensitivity as a function of handedness and laterality. *Journal of Comparative and Physiological Psychology,* 1961, 54, 665-669.

WERDELIN, I. *Geometric Ability and the Space Factors in Boys and Girls.* Sweden: University of Lund, 1961.

WEST, I. *American J. of Psychol.*, August 1892.

WILSON, W. P. and ZUNG, W. K. Attention, discrimination and arousal during sleep. *Archives of General Psychiatry*, 1966, 15, 523-528.

WITKIN, H. A., DYK, R. B., FATERSON, H. F., GOODENOUGH, D. R., and KARP, S. A. *Psychological Differentiation.* New York: Wiley & Sons, 1962.

WITRYOL, S. L. and KAESS, W. A. Sex differences in social memory tasks. *Journal of Abnormal and Social Psychology*, 1957, 54, 343-346.

WOLFF, P. H. The natural history of crying and other vocalizations in early infancy. In: B. M. Foss (Ed.), *Determinants of Infant Behavior*, Vol. 3. London: Methuen, 1969, pp. 113-138.

YARROW, M. R. and CAMPBELL, D. J. Person perception in children. *Merrill-Palmer Quarterly*, 1963, 9, 57-72.

YEN, W. M. Sex-linked major gene influences on human spatial abilities. *Dissertation Abstracts*, 1974, 34B, 566-567.

ZAHORSKY, T. Short-term memory in children as a specific function of different sensory modalities. *Psychologia a Patapsychologia Dietata*, 1969, 4.

ZANER, A. R., LEVEE, R. F., and GUNTA, R. R. The development of auditory perceptual skills as a function of maturation. *Journal of Auditory Research*, 1968, 8, 313-322.

2

Approach-Withdrawal Theory and the Study of Infant Development

IRIS MCGUIRE *and* GERALD TURKEWITZ

Schneirla (1959, 1965) has offered a comparative theory of behavior which has major implications for our understanding of development. Despite the broad scope of this theory, which has been applied to the study of a variety of developmental processes in animals as diverse as amoeba and chimpanzee, it has not received much attention from investigators of human development. The purpose of this paper is to introduce *approach-withdrawal theory* to investigators of human development and to examine its usefulness for suggesting testable hypotheses about infant development. It is not our purpose to present a comprehensive review of the literature in relation to approach-withdrawal theory; rather, particular examples will be selected to illustrate various tenets of the theory, and several types of infant studies will be discussed according to an approach-withdrawal interpretation of their findings.

The three main concepts of approach-withdrawal theory are what we shall term the *maturation-experience principle,* the *levels concept* and the *approach-withdrawal (A/W) intensity hypothesis.* This chapter will focus on the A/W intensity hypothesis. However, the maturation-experience principle and the levels concept will first be discussed briefly, because they provide a foundation necessary for understanding the A/W intensity hypothesis, and because all three concepts are inextricably interwoven in the theory.

We thank Gilbert Gottlieb, Warren G. Hall, Jay Rosenblatt and Holly Ruff for their thoughtful criticisms of an earlier draft of the manuscript.

Portions of this paper were written while the first author was receiving support from NIH Training Grant T32HD07053 in Human Developmental Biology at Albert Einstein College of Medicine.

THE MATURATION-EXPERIENCE PRINCIPLE

The maturation-experience principle emphasizes the interrelatedness of structure and function throughout both phylogenetic and ontogenetic development. Without minimizing the contribution of genes to development, the effects that "function" can have on the development of structure and on the development of subsequent function are stressed. Approach-withdrawal theory defines *maturation* as the contribution to development made by tissue growth and differentiation, with the realization that during development, especially in the rapidly progressing initial stages, such structural changes are influenced by the milieu in which they occur. *Experience* includes all aspects of stimulation, both external and internal, and "trace effects" from prior stages of development. Maturation and experience are not viewed as separate systems that interact with each other; rather they are viewed as fused systems with no real line of demarcation between them. As the inseparability of maturation and experience has been treated at length elsewhere (Gottlieb, 1976; Kuo, 1967; Lehrman, 1953, 1970; Schneirla, 1956) it will not be discussed further here.

THE CONCEPT OF LEVELS OF FUNCTIONAL ORGANIZATION

The concept of levels of functional organization provides a framework for describing and comparing the psychological capacities of organisms at different phylogenetic and ontogenetic stages of development. Within this framework, behavior patterns are analyzed in terms of the way in which their organization enables the organism to adjust to environmental change. A behavioral organization that permits a wider range of responses to changing conditions is considered to be higher level than one that restricts an organism's range of responses. Since behavior patterns are ranked in terms of plasticity, rather than in terms of complexity or adaptive value, a behavior pattern that is highly complex and has great adaptive value for a species in a particular environmental niche would not be considered high level if it were not readily modifiable as conditions changed. Because they are more variable, centrally controlled behaviors are generally considered to be higher level than peripherally controlled ones, and volitional behaviors are considered higher level than reflexive ones.

Since the levels concept calls attention to processes and mechanisms underlying behavior, rather than to the result of the behavior, it leads to an appreciation of the possibility that a common outcome, e.g., feeding, may be the result of patterns of behavior that are organized differently in different organisms. As Birch (1971, p. 508) pointed out, "when dealing with process or behavior patterns that have a general phenomenal similarity, one has to be concerned with the possibility that what is similar at a phenomenal level is, indeed, different as to mechanism. . . ." The concept of levels emphasizes the need to search for qualitative differences in behavior, an emphasis that guards against the seductiveness of labeling behaviors in terms of their outcome (e.g., aggression, hunger, instinct), instead of examining underlying causes. By encouraging examination of possible differences in the bases for behavior at different ontogenetic and phylogenetic stages of development, use of the levels approach also helps to curb tendencies toward endowing humans with attributes of other animals, endowing other animals with human capacities and endowing infants with adult capacities (Birch & Turkewitz, 1966). This approach thus differs fundamentally from Skinnerian behaviorism, Lorenzian ethology, and recent cognitive views of development (e.g., Bruner, 1970; Bower, 1974) in which monomorphic constructs are used to categorize behaviors occurring in diverse animal forms or in organisms of different ages.

It should be noted that this approach, which stresses process, rather than outcome, facilitates detection of fundamental differences in behavior patterns which otherwise appear to be similar. Such differences can be found when comparing the behavior of individuals at different stages of development, as well as when comparing behavior in different species. In each case, the criterion for assessing level of organization is plasticity of adjustment, with greater plasticity indicating higher level.

An example of the way that a levels approach can facilitate analysis of developmental changes in behavioral organization comes from a recent series of experiments by Hall and Rosenblatt (1977), in which different mechanisms underlying the suckling behavior of rat pups at different ages were identified. In this study, pulses of milk were delivered periodically through surgically-inserted cannulas whenever the pups suckled. The results indicated that control of feeding behavior in 5-day-old pups was markedly different from that of older animals. When milk was made freely available, 5-day-old pups continued to ingest milk until they fell off the nipple "struggling for air" and turning blue, with milk "spilling out of the mouth and nares." Activating them by handling and cleaning led to resumption of nursing when they were placed near a nipple. Such resumptions of feeding would occur regardless of stomach loading, even when attachment was hindered by the size of their swollen abdomens, and further ingestion was not possible. At 10 days of age, pups pushed themselves off the nipple when milk began to spill out of their mouths, with no evidence of respiratory distress. At 20 days of age, pups left the nipple even though they were physically capable of further ingestion, resulting in more moderate intake than observed in younger pups.

These findings indicate that when milk is made freely and frequently available, infant rats do not control their intake, and ingestion ceases only when milk overflow and respiratory distress cause the pup to leave the nipple. In the normal situation, suckling appears to be mother-initiated rather than pup-initiated (Rosenblatt, 1965) and the amount of milk let down by the lactating female determines the amount that will be ingested. Pups gradually develop the capacity to control their intake, and by about 20 days of age display patterns of ingestion that suggest more central control of feeding. It should be noted that, in the typical situation, regulation of feeding by younger and older pups is not readily distinguishable. It is only when greater demands for modification of behavior are made (as when frequency of milk delivery is increased) that the organizational differences in behavior become apparent.

As in infant rats, suckling in infant humans may not initially be directly dependent upon nutritional state. During early neonatal stages, the stimuli that facilitate the elicitation of suckling need not be related to food, and treatments such as pinching a toe or pricking with a pin (Jensen, 1932) lead to resumption of suckling even after the infant appears to be "satiated." In addition, food-deprived infants at this stage of development can be quieted by rocking, singing them a lullaby, etc., as well as by feeding. Suckling at this stage appears to be reflexive and related to a general level of excitation which can be brought about in many different ways (from internal stimulation associated with food deprivation to an open diaper pin) and which can be reduced in many ways. As early as the first few weeks of life, however, changes in the basis for suckling occur, and there is evidence of non-reflexive suckling. For example, when placed in a feeding posture, older infants may make anticipatory sucking movements if they are food-deprived, but not under other conditions of excitation. These infants' sucking responses also seem in other ways to be more directly related to food. For example, when food-deprived, older infants may stop crying only when they see food on the way, while younger infants may be quieted by means other than feeding. While feeding behavior is never solely determined by nutritional state, it appears that during early neonatal development the effect that nutritional state has on feeding behavior becomes more specific, with transitions from general-intensity-determined reflexive responses to responses that are specific to feeding situations.

THE APPROACH-WITHDRAWAL INTENSITY HYPOTHESIS

The A/W intensity hypothesis is useful, together with the levels concept, since it provides a basis for identifying the lowest level of organization for adaptive functioning, and thus provides a starting point for the comparative analysis of behavior at different phylogenetic and ontogenetic stages. This hypothesis suggests a basis upon which behavior is organized at early stages of development in all animals, and throughout the entire life history of animals only at low phyletic levels. It states that there is a direct relationship between the kind of response an organism makes and the intensity of stimulation that the organism receives, such that low intensities of stimulation tend to evoke approach-type reactions, while high intensities tend to evoke withdrawal-type reactions. It should be noted that approach-withdrawal theory, as distinct from the A/W intensity hypothesis, suggests that, at later stages of development, approach and withdrawal responses are more properly considered seeking and avoidance because they reflect a higher level of organization. Thus, different hypotheses regarding motivation and initiation of behavior will be required to account for such behaviors.

In general, approach-type responses orient the animal toward an external source of stimulation. Often, but not necessarily, these responses serve to decrease the distance between the subject and the source of stimulation. Approach-type responses are governed by the arousal of A-processes, which are classified as either tonic or phasic. Tonic A-processes are, in general, energy-conserving mechanisms necessary for the continued development, survival and well-being of the organism. At higher phyletic levels, e.g. in vertebrates, such mechanisms correspond to the functions controlled by the parasympathetic branch of the autonomic nervous system, including patterns of regular respiration, heart rate and blood pressure, as well as digestive and other visceral, vegetative functions. Tonic A-processes may also serve a reinforcing function, providing a facilitative background for the development of phasic A-processes. Phasic A-processes are episodic, rather than continuous, and underlie overt approach actions such as food-getting. Examples of responses governed by A-processes, and consequently considered to be approach responses, are phasic responses such as nestling movements, pleasure calls and pecking by precocial birds, the head lunge response of lizards, gaping and imprinting in altricial birds, and tonic responses such as cardiac deceleration, lowering of blood pressure, digestion, etc. Examples of approach responses in human infants include phasic responses such as looking toward, turning toward, limb extension, smiling, etc. and tonic responses such as motor quieting, cardiac deceleration, etc.

Withdrawal-type responses, in general, orient an animal away from a source of stimulation and often serve to increase the distance between the subject and the source of stimulation. Such responses are governed by the arousal of W-processes, which are energy-expending, interruptive processes corresponding to the functions of the sympathetic branch of the autonomic nervous system. Tonic W-processes govern responses such as rapid breathing, increased blood pressure, suppression of digestion, etc. Phasic responses include actions such as turning the head away or displacement of the entire body away from the source of stimulation, depending upon the intensity of stimulation and the context in which it occurs. Examples of tonic withdrawal responses in human infants include general motor tension and cardiac acceleration. Phasic withdrawal responses include down-turning of the mouth, looking away, turning away, limb flexion, and crying.

It is central to approach-withdrawal theory that W-processes have higher thresholds than A-processes, responding only to high magnitudes of effective stimulus input. Thus the A- and W-systems may often involve the same structures, but in functionally different ways. In addition, the kinds of phasic responses observed will depend upon the stimulus situation. For example, an approach response of a precocial bird to a weak external stimulus might be a peck, in the feeding situation, or locomotion toward the stimulus if it is gradually moving away. The same animal's withdrawal response to a high-intensity stimulus might be turning the head away, or walking away. Approach and withdrawal responses are thus not classified as such according to how much of the animal's body moves toward or away from a stimulus source; nor are they to be conceived of as physically equal and opposite. Rather they are functionally antagonistic responses that are the result of activation of different systems in response to different levels of intensity of stimulation.

This relationship between stimulus intensity and the nature of responses has different developmental consequences at different phyletic levels. At lower levels (e.g., in amoeba) the relationship between intensity of stimulation and response direction shows no ontogenetic change, remaining direct and mechanical through the lifetime of the organism. Thus, in the amoeba, mild stimulation in the form of weak light, heat, chemical concentration or tactile stimulation has a direct effect on the physical characteristics of the protoplasm, the area on which the stimulus falls becoming more fluid than the rest of the animal's protoplasm, resulting in protoplasmic flow in the direction of the source of stimulation. With more intense stimulation, the process is reversed, and the flow is in the opposite direction. The amoeba never reaches a higher level of organization of its behavior.

At higher phyletic levels (e.g., in vertebrates) behavior which is primarily intensity-determined is characteristic only at early stages of development. However, such behavior patterns are hypothesized to provide the foundation upon which later, higher-level functioning develops. The suggestion is that early intensity-determined approach behavior may lead to seeking behavior which is goal-oriented and plastic, as opposed to lower-level approach behavior which is stimulus-directed and stereotyped. Similarly, withdrawal behavior which is intensity-determined at early stages may lead, at later stages of development, to its higher-level counterpart, avoidance behavior. Later in this paper we will suggest possible mechanisms by which transitions from intensity-determined to more complexly determined responses occur in human infants. At this time, however, it is sufficient to note that the analysis of early intensity-determined patterns is important for understanding development in organisms that achieve higher levels of functioning, because such responses may provide the foundation for higher-level responding.

EFFECTIVE STIMULUS INTENSITY

In order to appropriately apply the A/W intensity hypothesis, it is necessary to distinguish betwen objective and effective intensity. Objective intensity refers to those characteristics of a stimulus which can be measured independently of the organism upon which they impinge. Effective intensity is dependent upon the objective stimulus intensity and the characteristics of the organism. As such, it is determined by all the following factors: 1) the state of the organism (e.g., whether aroused or quiescent), including the state of the receptors (e.g., whether light or dark adapted); 2) the nature of the receptors (i.e., their stimulus filtering properties, e.g., rods vs. cones); and 3) the objective, external, physical stimulus characteristics. Effective intensity is thus considered to be the result of both external and internal factors. "Effectiveness" depends upon whether or not resulting stimulation is sufficient to reach either the A-system or the W-system thresholds. Because effective intensity at any given time is the result of the first two factors described above, as well as all the characteristics of the external stimulus, there is no a priori way of predicting whether any particular stimulus will be effective in eliciting approach or withdrawal. This has been a point of misunderstanding on the part of several critics of approach-withdrawal theory. Hailman (1970, p. 151), for example, insists upon "restricting attention to only the physical stimulus," and then complains that the meaning of A-stimulus is unclear.

Clearly, an objective, physical stimulus could be of "high intensity and decreasing simultaneously" (Hailman, 1970, p. 151). But, as pointed out above, objective intensity is only one of the factors to be considered in determining whether a particular stimulus will be effective in eliciting approach or withdrawal. For example, a bright light (high objective intensity) which is gradually decreasing in intensity might lead to an approach response by a light-adapted animal or a withdrawal response by the same animal when dark-adapted. If it is rapidly changing in intensity, it might lead to withdrawal whether the animal is light- or dark-adapted, if the sudden change results in input sufficient to reach the W-system threshold. Receptor thresholds, internal state, and objective intensity must all be considered before predictions can be made.

Hailman (1970) has also suggested that the concept of effective intensity is incapable of negation because it is inherently circular: "any stimulus that elicits approach can be said to be of low intensity, and there is no possibility of finding a behavioral system that does not fit the theory" (p. 151). Later in this paper, several studies of behavior in human infants which have used the concept of effective intensity without circularity will be presented. At this time, however, the general logic behind such experiments will be examined in order to show that the notion of effective intensity need not, in fact, be circular.

There are at least two methods for examining the relationship between effective intensity and responses. In one method, state is kept constant, while objective intensity of stimulation is varied. As mild but increasing amounts of stimulation are presented to subjects that have been equated for state, approach responses should be observed when stimulation reaches the A-system threshold. Approach responses should then be observed until a level of stimulation above the W-system threshold is introduced. There should then be withdrawal responses to this and any other stimuli that are objectively more intense. Figure 1 illustrates the proposed relationship between stimulus intensity and responses when organismic factors are held constant. Although it is not possible to predict where on the curve a particular stimulus would fall, consistent approach responses to any stimulus more intense than that which first

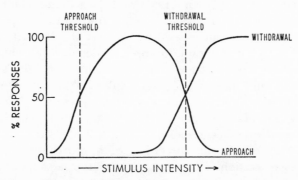

FIGURE 1. The relationship between approach and withdrawal responses over a wide range of stimulus intensity. Approach responses begin at low intensities of stimulation, reach maximum frequency at moderate intensities, and decline in frequency as stimulus intensity increases. Withdrawal responses begin to appear at moderately high levels of stimulus intensity. At the withdrawal threshold, approach and withdrawal responses occur at about equal frequency. Further increases in intensity lead to increases in withdrawal response frequency until, at very high levels of intensity, only withdrawal responses are observed. It should be noted that these are *response* curves, intended to reflect the differential distribution of approach and withdrawal responses over a wide range of stimulus intensity. Because the functions of the A- and W-systems are mutually exclusive (e.g., heart rate acceleration and deceleration cannot occur simultaneously), a model representing A- and W-*processes* would necessarily differ from the one presented here. In such a model, A-processes would reach a peak at moderate levels of intensity, and then terminate as W-processes took over at higher levels of intensity. From: McGuire, I. and Turkewitz, G., 1978.

evoked consistent withdrawal would be sufficient to refute the intensity hypothesis.

An alternative method for examining the intensity hypothesis would be to hold objective intensity of stimulation constant, and vary the condition of the organism. Exposure to light, for example, could be varied so that different subjects were adapted to different levels of light. Subsequent differences in these subjects' responses to the same objective intensity of light could then be observed. It would be expected that dark-adapted animals of the same species and age would withdraw from the same stimulus which light-adapted animals approached.

The A/W intensity hypothesis and the associated concept of effective intensity are not simple concepts, and in the original formulations (Schneirla, 1959, 1965) they were presented in a way that led to some confusion and misinterpretation. For example, the important restriction—that the relationship between effective intensity and response direction is meant to apply only to behavior at very early stages of development—although mentioned, was not emphasized. Thus, several experimenters, e.g., Pfaffman (1961) and Jaeger and Hailman (1973) incorrectly used data obtained without consideration of phyletic level and stage of development as evidence against the intensity hypothesis. Since this hypothesis is meant to apply throughout the entire lifetime only at the lowest phyletic level, findings such as Pfaffman's (1961) for adult humans and Jaeger and Hailman's (1973) for adult annurids provide interesting information about intensity-response relationships at advanced stages of development, but they do not test the intensity hypothesis, which predicts response direction only at early developmental stages. In fact, correct interpretation of approach-withdrawal theory leads to the expectation of more complex relationships between stimulus and response at later developmental stages, an expectation that is not refuted by Pfaffman's and Jaeger and Hailman's data.

In addition to the limitation of the theory's testability only at early stages of development (the theory does not contain specific hypotheses about the determination of behavior at later stages), there are other important limitations which should be discussed. One is related to the a priori specification of "early stage of development." While this is an empirical question that can only be answered by careful investigation of the particular animal under consideration, complications arise because sensory and sensorimotor systems develop at different rates, so that identification of low-level, intensity-determined patterns of response in one system cannot be generalized to other systems without experimental verification. That is, it is quite possible that at a particular age in a particular subject, one system (e.g., the auditory-motor) may have reached a higher level of organization than another system (e.g., the visual-motor), which may still operate at a lower level of organization. Thus, if negative results are found for any one system, they may always be attributed to that system's having reached a later stage of development. In other words, results that do not seem to support the intensity hypothesis may be explained on the grounds that behavior was not examined at an "early enough" stage of development.

Another limitation of the theory stems from its inherent complexity. Approach-withdrawal theory, with its emphasis on the complex interrelationships among factors that must be considered in order to understand behavior, can be exceedingly cumbersome to apply. This is not to say that an appreciation of the complexities of real events should be sacrificed in order to present a simpler model that is more easily applied. However, in many cases the theory lends itself to application only with great difficulty and, in some situations, it may even be methodologically untestable. For example, failure to get withdrawal responses neither supports nor refutes the theory, since failure to obtain withdrawal can be attributed to failure to present sufficiently intense stimuli. In practice, certain kinds of stimulation cannot be presented at intensities high enough to achieve withdrawal. For example, sugar is not held in high enough concentrations in saliva; certain odors continue to act as attractants when presented in the highest concentrations possible. Because approach responses to stimuli *established to be above the withdrawal threshold* provide the only evidence that negates the theory, it is not easy to see how the theory can be applied in some areas of investigation. Nonetheless, it is applicable in many situations, and it often provides a more parsimonious description of behavior at early developmental stages than has been previously offered.

APPROACH-WITHDRAWAL THEORY AND STUDIES OF EARLY HUMAN INFANCY

Despite the limitations discussed, approach-withdrawal theory has provided testable hypotheses about the nature of responsiveness at early stages of development that have guided several investigations of behavioral organization in human infants. Turkewitz, Fleischer, Moreau, Birch and Levy (1966) examined the relationship between feeding condition and flexor/extensor movements in newborn infants. Their hypothesis was that state (as manipulated by varying time since feeding) would be an important factor in determining infants' directional responses to ambient stimulation from the environment. Specifically, they suggested that before feeding, heightened internal stimulation (e.g., from stomach contractions) in combination with ambient external stimulation would provide a total level of stimulation sufficient to reach the W-system threshold and elicit finger flexion (withdrawal) responses; after feeding, reduced internal stimulation would result in a lower total level of stimulation, so that ambient stimuli of the same objective intensity would be effectively less intense, eliciting finger extension (approach) responses. Flexion was considered a withdrawal-type response because flexor responses generally serve to increase the distance between the subject and external source of stimulation; extension was considered an approach-type response because extension generally serves to decrease that distance. It had also been suggested (Sherrington, 1906, cited by Schneirla, 1959) that flexion is the dominant muscle response in vertebrates under conditions of intense stimulation, while extension is the dominant response under conditions of mild stimulation. The results clearly supported the hypothesis, with infants displaying more flexion than extension before feeding and more extension than flexion after feeding. These findings indicate that feeding condition can alter the effective intensity of stimuli which are of equal objective intensity and that response direction may be a function of the effective intensity of stimulation, with approach to weak and withdrawal from strong sources of stimulation.

To further explore the relationship between response direction and effective intensity of stimulation in infants, McGuire and Turkewitz (1978) examined the relationship between visual stimulus intensity and finger movement direction. In this study, infants of different ages were equated for state as far as possible by having them well-fed, well-rested, dry, quiet and alert during testing. Trials on which the infant's state did not meet these criteria were excluded from the analysis. Visual stimulus intensity was varied by manipulating the distance, size and brightness of a slowly rotating red cone. The cone could be near or far, large or small, bright or dim, with eight possible combinations presented in random sequence for 5-second trials, repeated until half an hour elapsed, or the infant became fussy. The direction of the infants' first finger movement on each trial was recorded. It was hypothesized that younger infants (10 to 15 weeks old) would make finger extension (approach) responses to the least intense combination (far-small-dim) and finger flexion (withdrawal) responses to the most intense combination (near-large-bright). In support of this hypothesis, the younger infants extended their fingers significantly less and flexed them significantly more as stimulus intensity increased. In accord with an hypothesized shift away from intensity-based responding at later ages, no clear relationship between stimulus intensity and response direction was seen in the older (20-25 week old) infants.

It should be noted that, despite their directionality, the flexion and extension responses of the younger infants in the studies described above are hypothesized to be the result of arousal of A- and W-processes brought about by supra-threshold levels of stimulation, and need not be thought of as responses aimed at the stimuli. An infant may, for example, extend a hand toward an object that effectively arouses A-processes, but the hand is not extended in order to get it closer to the object. Rather, the decrease in distance between hand and object is a consequence of the A-system's characteristic mode of responding with motor extension to mild sources of stimulation. Although these movements are viewed as intensity-based, automatic, reflex-like responses, they are considered to play an important part in the transition to intentional reaching and grasping, which will be discussed later.

Bi-directional responses as a function of stimulus intensity have also been found for the auditory system. Hammer and Turkewitz (1975) looked at eye movements in newborns in response to laterally presented white noise stimuli. Based upon prior findings (Turkewitz, Birch et al., 1966) that the right ear has a lower threshold than the left, it was hypothesized that the same objective stimulus would be effectively more intense when presented to the infant's right than when presented to the left. The A/W intensity hypothesis predicted that there would be towards-turning to effectively weak and away-turning from effectively strong stimuli. It was clearly supported by the finding that there was significantly more towards-turning when a 90 db noise was presented to the left ear and significantly more away-turning when the same stimulus was presented to the right ear.

Before interpreting the data from studies in other laboratories, it is necessary to review the nature of the relationship between stimulus intensity and response direction that the approach-withdrawal intensity hypothesis predicts. According to the theory, the relationship between intensity of stimulation and response should be a complex function, as shown in Figure 1, with approach responses increasing as intensity reaches the A-system threshold, and decreasing as intensity reaches the W-system threshold. Withdrawal responses should occur as the W-system threshold is reached, and should be observed in response to all stimuli of greater intensity. It is important to note that this function would be observed only over a wide range of intensities for a particular stimulus. When only a limited range of intensities is presented, either increases or decreases in approach responses might be related to increasing stimulus intensity, and withdrawal responses might or might not be seen. For example, if the stimuli chosen were all on the low end of the range, only increases in approach would be observed as intensity increased. If all stimuli were from the middle of the stimulus range, a monotonic decrease in approach responses and a monotonic increase in withdrawal responses would be observed. At the high end of the stimulus range, only withdrawal responses would be observed. It is only when the full range of stimulus intensities is presented that one would anticipate an inverted U-shaped function for approach responses and an ogive for withdrawal responses, as shown in Figure 1, with withdrawal responses increasing at the point at which approach responses decrease. All the response patterns described above would be consistent with the approach-withdrawal intensity hypothesis. However, any pattern in which increases in approach followed decreases, as intensity increased, would be clearly inconsistent with the hypothesis. With this clarification in mind, we now turn to studies of infant behavior which, although not generated by approach-withdrawal theory, provide data that are consistent with it.

In a number of studies of infant visual attention, investigators have varied a particular attribute of stimulation and found effects of this variation on infants' looking behavior. Although these investigators have not generally considered their stimulus conditions in terms of stimulus intensity, it is possible to do so. Thus, variations in stimulus attributes, such as contour density, number of elements, size of elements, and number of angles, in addition to brightness, can each be considered to affect stimulus intensity, when a broad definition of intensity, such as we have offered, is used. In this view, intensity is defined in terms of the amount of neural activity that a stimulus provokes. In the absence of a direct measure of neural activity, it is assumed that stimuli with greater contour density, greater number of elements, larger elements, more angles or higher level of brightness result in more neural activity than stimuli with less contour density, fewer elements, smaller elements, fewer angles, etc. Using this concept of general intensity, it is possible to interpret the results of several different studies as consistent with expectations from A/W theory. For example, in a study of visual orientation behavior in newborn infants, Hershenson (1964) obtained an inverted U-shaped relationship between the brightness of patches of light and infant orientation. He found that newborns looked more towards patches of intermediate brightness than they did to either brighter or dimmer patches of light. Similarly, Cohen (1969) found that infants exposed to patterns of lights that changed at different frequencies looked longest when the amount of change was intermediate, with less looking at either more or less frequently changing patterns of lights. Hershenson, Munsinger and Kessen (1965) found that newborns looked longest at patterns with intermediate numbers of angles, looking less at patterns with fewer or more angles. In each of these experiments, an inverted U-shaped function was obtained between looking behavior and what can be considered stimulus intensity, with looking behavior increasing for weak stimuli and decreasing for stimuli that were more intense. This kind of relationship between stimulus intensity and response pattern has also been observed by Karmel (1969a) and Karmel, Hoffman and Fegy (1974), who found that both looking behavior and the amplitude of visually-evoked cortical potentials can be described as an inverted U-shaped function of the contour density of stimuli to which infants are exposed. They found that infants looked longest (and had higher amplitude evoked potentials) at intermediate levels of contour per unit area, with less looking (and lower amplitude evoked potentials) when the contour density of visual patterns was either increased or decreased. McCall and Kagan (1967) obtained an inverted U-shaped relationship between fixation time and length of contour in 4-month-olds, and Volkmann and Dobson (1976) got an inverted U-shaped functional relationship between rate of movement across the visual field and ocular fixation in 1-, 2-, and 3-month-olds. Thus, responses to aspects of stimulation such as brightness, amount of change, number of angles, length of contour, contour density and rate of movement have each been found to follow curves which A/W theory would have predicted.

Because the results of the studies we have just described can also be used to support an optimal level theory of stimulation in infancy, it is necessary to discuss an important difference between optimal level theory and approach-withdrawal theory: Approach-withdrawal theory is biphasic, proposing two functionally opposed systems that have a specific relationship to stimulus intensity and to each other, while optimal level theory is concerned with response systems considered separately. In the above studies, both theories would predict the kinds of response curves that were obtained. However, approach-withdrawal theory would predict that, in addition to a decrease in attentional (approach) responses with increasing stimulus intensity, there should be an increase in withdrawal responses, such as looking *away*. Unfortunately, although it is conceptually easy to separate looking-toward from looking-away, it does not seem possible to operationally separate the two in a visual attention study, when duration of looking is the only response measured. In such a study, there are problems in trying to distinguish between not responding and looking away. That is, if the infant does not look at a particular stimulus, he might simply be not responding, or he might be looking away. In addition, looking-toward and looking-away are reciprocally related when duration of looking is the only measure, i.e., the infant must look toward before he can look away, and the more time he spends looking away, the less time he can spend looking toward.

Because of problems like these, it seems that, in order to test the A/W intensity hypothesis for infant visual responses, it may be necessary to add another response measure which is clearly specifiable with regard to direction. For example, recording either heart rate or finger movements in addition to visual fixation time might make it possible to separate not responding from looking away. In such an experiment, it would be expected from the A/W hypothesis that heart rate deceleration (and finger extension) would accompany looking-toward (approach), no change in heart rate or finger movement direction would accompany not looking (no response), and heart rate acceleration (and finger flexion) would accompany looking away (withdrawal).

Another way of examining the A/W intensity hypothesis with regard to the visual response system is to focus on identification of the basis upon which responses are made, rather than examining the bidirectional aspects of responding. In this approach, an attempt is made to separate responsiveness to the quantitative aspects of stimulation from responsiveness to qualitative aspects. In one such study, Ruff and Turkewitz (1975) examined developmental changes in the effectiveness of stimulus intensity as a determiner of infant visual attention. They showed infants from 6 to 24 weeks old pairs of bulls-eyes and striped patterns of different sizes so that there were two patterns of two different sizes on each trial. Their hypothesis was that as infants got older, stimulus intensity (as determined by the size of the stimuli) would decrease in its effectiveness as a determiner of looking behavior and the effectiveness of pattern would increase. In support of this hypothesis, they found that infants under 10 weeks responded primarily on the basis of size, looking more at the larger member of a pair of stimuli, regardless of its pattern. In older infants, however, the bulls-eye was preferred regardless of its size and the size of the striped pattern with which it was paired.

To further assess developmental changes in the importance of stimulus intensity for determining visual attention in infants, stimulus intensity was again compared to pattern. Ruff (1976) showed infants 10, 17 and 25 weeks of age pairs of stimuli that were equated for intensity (area, contour length, contour density, number of segments, black to white ratio and general configuration) but differed in pattern detail, being composed of either angles or straight lines. As anticipated, the intensity hypothesis was supported by the behavior of the 10-week-olds, who looked equally at the stimuli of each pair. The two older groups showed significantly more looking at the angled stimuli, supporting the suggestion that, as infants develop, intensity has less of an effect upon visual attention and pattern has more of an effect.

LEVELS IN THE DEVELOPMENT OF PERCEPTUAL
FUNCTIONING IN INFANCY

In recent years, increasingly sophisticated methods of assessing infant functioning have led to the discovery of the neonate's refined discrimination of various stimulus properties such as described earlier. Thus, it has become impossible to accept James' (1910) description of the perceptual world of the infant as chaotic and undifferentiated. However, the impressive array of discriminative abilities that neonates show has led some authors to the conclusion that neonatal perceptual functioning is essentially adult-like, except that a degree of sharpening occurs during development. Although there is little doubt that infants do discriminate subtle differences in size, brightness, contour, angularity, etc., of stimuli, the basis for such differential responding remains open to question. In the following discussion of infant discrimination, we will use approach-withdrawal theory to provide an alternative to the view that neonatal discriminative behavior is similar to adult perceptual functioning. We will take the position that early neonatal functioning is essentially non-perceptual, and we will distinguish between perceptual and non-perceptual functioning by examining the basis upon which discriminative responses occur. In our view, perception is supported by higher-order cortical functioning which permits processing of the qualitative as well as the quantitative differences among stimuli. Non-perceptual functioning is limited to the processing of only quantitative aspects of stimulation and may be subcortically mediated. In examining discriminative behavior, we will first look for evidence that discrimination is determined by processing of quantitative factors exclusively (e.g., intensity), and this level of functioning will be classified as non-perceptual. If differences in intensity cannot account for the discrimination, higher-level processing is taking place and the behavior will be considered perceptual. Although it is possible to classify all discriminative behavior as perceptual, and then distinguish between higher and lower levels of perception in terms of whether quantitative or qualitative differences among stimuli are processed, we prefer to reserve the term perception for higher-level processing of qualitative differences among stimuli, because the differences in responding to quantitative and qualitative aspects of stimuli seem more important than do the similarities. With these clarifications in mind, we now turn to examination of studies of perceptual functioning in infants.

In our view, the case for early perceptual functioning seems to rest, to a considerable extent, upon a failure to distinguish between withdrawal and avoidance responses, as well as between approach and seeking behaviors, as representing different levels of organization. Many investigators have not, for example, separated withdrawal responses, which in our view are non-perceptual, from avoidance responses, which reflect perceptual processing. Interpretations of behavior in which non-perceptual and perceptual bases of responding have been confused come from two main types of studies—studies of infants' responses to stimuli which change real or apparent position in space, and studies of infants' responses on a visual cliff.

In the first type of study, Ball and Tronick (1971) observed what they considered to be integrated defense movements in 2- to 11-week-old infants who were shown a visual pattern that expanded when projected on a screen, providing, to an adult observer, the illusion of a rapidly approaching object. Whether an infant's experience in this situation is comparable to an adult's is, however, questionable. Infants in this situation are reported to have responded to the stimuli by moving their heads backward and away from the screen and bringing their arms up toward their faces, responses which the authors considered to be integrated defense movements, presumably consequent on the infants' anticipation of collision. In a similar experiment, Bower, Broughton and Moore (1971) described what they considered to be a 3-component avoidance response (eye-widening, moving the head back, and interposing the hands between face and object) in infants as young as 6 days old, who were exposed to a variety of approaching objects.

Yonas, Bechtold, Frankel, Gordon, McRoberts, Norcia and Sternfels (1977) offer an interpretation of Ball and Tronick's (1971) and Bower et al.'s (1971) findings which is consistent with A/W theory. Yonas et al. suggest that the responses observed when infants are presented an optically expanding pattern are not defensive reactions, but orienting or tracking responses that are accompanied by postural changes. In their view, the infant's head would be expected to go up and back as the upper contours of the stimulus moved upward in the visual field. "As the head rotates backward, the infant may lose balance and his arms may come up as part of a postural reflex" (p. 97). To test their hypothesis, they presented infants from 1 to 9 months old optical patterns specifying collision, noncollision and a nonexpanding rising contour. The responses measured were heart rate, blinking, head rotation and withdrawal, fussing and tracking. The results indicated that blinking responses were absent in the youngest group (1-2 month olds), began to appear at 4-6 months, and were consistently present at 8-9 months. In the younger infants there was no difference among the three conditions for any of the responses, except head rotation. Although the amount of head rotation was significantly greater in the collision than in the miss condition, it was even greater in the condition with rising contour and no expansion, a finding that supports the suggestion that the infants were indeed tracking rather than avoiding.

To further examine the tracking hypothesis, Yonas et al. (1977) presented collision and non-collision patterns to 1-to-2-month-olds in such a way that the upper contours of the patterns remained at eye level. The results indicated no differences in blinking, head withdrawal, arm movement, fussing, or head rotation. The only difference was that there was more tracking of the miss than of the collision condition. The same pattern of results was found for a real object presented on a collision or a non-collision course. In conflict with Bower et al.'s (1971) finding of greater magnitude of avoidance and fussing when a real object was used, Yonas et al. (1977) found no fussing, and no differences between the 2 conditions in head rotation, withdrawal, blinking or arm movement responses. Again, there was greater tracking of the object on the non-collision course, than when the object was on a collision course.

Yonas et al.'s findings suggest that infants' responses to optically expanding patterns may be neither avoidance nor withdrawal responses, but approach movements elicited by the effective intensities of the stimuli presented. Their finding that there was more tracking of the non-symmetrically expanding pattern (non-collision) than of the symmetrical (collision) pattern is interpretable within the framework of A/W theory because of the differences in stimulation which such stimuli provide. Because of the concentric arrangement of excitatory and inhibitory receptor fields (Kuffler, 1953), symmetrically and asymmetrically expanding stimuli would provide different amounts of stimulation, providing a basis for differential tracking.

Interpretational differences also come from a study by Bower, Broughton and Moore (1970) in which infants less than a month old were considered to show evidence of object perception, based upon their responses to virtual images of objects (3-dimensional, non-substantial images, like holograms) which were advanced toward the infants. In this study, the infants were preselected for their tolerance of wearing polaroid goggles which were necessary for providing the illusion of three-dimensionality. Infants who wore the goggles for several minutes without crying were included in the experimental group. A control group did not wear goggles and were shown tangible 3-dimensional objects. Increased crying in the experimental group was attributed to their frustration when their hands passed through the virtual images, and their expectations of tangible objects were violated. The fact that only the experimental group wore goggles was dismissed as unimportant because these infants had been preselected for goggle-tolerance. We would suggest, however, that although goggle-wearing was insufficient to elicit withdrawal responses before testing, there might have been a summative effect of gggle-wearing and stimulation from the approaching stimuli, sufficient to elicit crying during testing. That is, stimulation from wearing goggles, combined with stimulation from the advancing images, might have been intense enough to reach the W-system threshold and elicit the crying responses observed. Ths, stimulation intensity, rather than object perception or expectation, is sufficient to account for the results obtained.

Examination of infants' responses on a visual cliff (Walk & Gibson, 1961) provides another area for which A/W theory offers an interpretation of data which differs from that of other investigators. Previous interpretations of behavior on the visual cliff have been based on the view that the organisms involved have been avoiding an apparent cliff, presumably because of perception of depth and fear of falling. Because differences in depth always entail concomitant differences in stimulus intensity (as a function of retinal size, angle, motion parallax, etc.), both the perceptual and non-perceptual hypothesis about infant responsiveness result in the same prediction about behavior when only depth is varied. However, when other aspects of stimulation are also varied, differential responding to the two sides of the apparatus (which may in this case be equally deep) is not readily understood in terms of avoidance of depth or fear of falling, but can be understood in terms of approach and withdrawal based on the intensity of stimulation coming from each side of the apparatus. In support of this intensity hypothesis, Simner (1967) found that chicks would approach either the shallow or deep sides of a visual cliff, depending upon the size of the squares of which the surface patterns were composed. Walk and Waters (1974) found that both the texture of the surfaces of the two sides and motion parallax influence the preferences of chicks and rats; while Karmel (1969b) found that the contour density of patterns to which rats and chicks were exposed determined their responses on the visual cliff. Together, these findings suggest that, at early stages of development, it is not a perceptual process (e.g., depth perception or fear of falling) that leads to differential responding on the visual cliff, but a lower-level, non-perceptual process in which differences in effective intensity of stimulation (that can be achieved in many ways) elicit differential approach and withdrawal patterns of responding.

This interpretation of stimulus intensity, rather than perception of depth, as the determiner of early responses on the visual cliff is also supported by a study of the behavior of human infants who could not yet crawl (Campos et al., 1970). It was hypothesized that such infants, when placed on the deep side of the visual cliff, would show cardiac acceleration (a "defensive" response), and when placed on the shallow side, would show cardiac deceleration (an "orienting" response). The results were that, when placed on the deep side, the infants showed cardiac deceleration, and when placed on the shallow side, cardiac acceleration. There was also more looking down on the deep side than on the shallow, as well as less fussiness and crying, resulting in "a total picture . . . on the deep side . . . of motor quieting . . . these criteria characterize quieting rather than fear" (p. 197). Even though the responses were in a direction other than expected, the authors interpreted the results as "consistent with the view that infants perceive depth at the ages tested" calling the responses "non-specific orienting responses" that indicate discrimination of depth (p. 197). Rather than considering these findings evidence of depth perception or other perceptual processing, we would consider the obtained responses to be the result of differential intensity of stimulation provided on the two sides of the apparatus. If such responses were due to stimulus intensity, rather than perception of depth and associated emotional responses, we would expect the same kind of differential responding to patterns presented at different distances *in front* of the infants. Again, differences in responding in this situation would be difficult to attribute to "fear" or other perceptual processing.

As illustrated above, approach-withdrawal theory suggests that infants' behavior in different situations (responding to rapidly approaching objects and responding on a visual cliff) need not be attributed to higher-order perceptual processing. Rather, responses in these situations can be understood as reflex-like reactions to the effective intensities of stimulation which the situations provide. Consideration of the A/W hypothesis regarding infant behavior also has important implications for the way in which "stimulation" is conceptualized. If it is the intensity, not the quality, of stimulation that determines the nature of responses, then stimuli which are objectively different may be effectively equivalent. That is, stimuli of different modalities and stimuli of different dimensions within a modality may have the same effect upon response direction if they result in equal intensities of stimulation. Furthermore, if total intensity determines the behavioral result, then various sources of stimulation may have additive effects. This view suggests that the search for dimensions of stimulation to which infants are responsive may be misdirected. Changes in behavior which follow changes in a particular stimulus dimension, at early stages of development, do not necessarily indicate processing of the qualitative, perceptual characteristics of that dimension. In fact, when more than one dimension has been manipulated, data suggest the summation of effects from several dimensions. Thus, in the McGuire and Turkewitz (1978) study of finger movements discussed earlier, the size, distance and brightness of a cone contributed to its total effective intensity and the determination of response direction. When intensity was ranked according to the number of dimensions with high values, finger extension decreased as a function of intensity and finger flexion increased. Other studies also suggest summation of effects from various dimensions. Fantz and Fagan (1975) found that size and number of elements in a pattern were both effective in the determination of fixation time for infants 45 to 60 weeks post-menstrual age. There was an interaction between these variables and age, with preferences based on size decreasing, and those based on number of elements increasing, as age increased. Greenberg and Blue (1975) assessed the effects of number of elements in a pattern and contour density, and found that, in 2- and 4-month-olds, these dimensions had to be varied simultaneously in order to get an effect of age on visual fixation. Similarly, McCarvill and Karmel (1976) found a luminosity-dependent shift in contour density preferences in the looking behaviors of younger (9-week-old) but not older (13-week-old) infants. If these dimensions had been considered contributors to stimulus intensity, rather than as dimensions unique in their effectiveness, then effects of the kind reported would have been expected. In addition, disagreements about the unique importance of the various dimensions (e.g., Karmel, 1974; Fantz & Fagan, 1975; Greenberg & Blue, 1975) would be resolved by the view that all these dimensions are contributors to intensity, and thus influence responses by influencing intensity. If infants are, in fact, responsive to stimulus intensity, in experiments set up so that only contour density varies, contour density will appear to be uniquely important; experiments set up to test the effect of size will find size uniquely effective. However, the results reported above suggest that the various dimensions have combined effects on intensity, and each dimension is effective in terms of its contribution to overall intensity rather than in terms of its unique characteristics.

The Transition from Lower to Higher Levels of Organization

Since the A/W intensity hypothesis is not intended as an explanation of behavior at later stages of development (when higher levels of organization characterize behavior), the theory becomes developmental in its concern for understanding the way in which transitions from lower to higher levels of organization occur, so that seeking and avoiding behaviors develop at later developmental stages.

In the previous discussion, we indicated that, according to approach-withdrawal theory, it is the effective intensity of stimulation that determines a young organism's response, regardless of the manner in which that effective intensity is achieved. Thus, at early stages, various dimensions of visual stimulation are viewed as interchangeable and having summative effects upon total stimulus intensity. Although the above discussion stressed the implications of this view for an analysis of discrimination between stimulus dimensions within a modality, this approach is also pertinent for analysis of the relationship between modalities. According to A/W theory, even when they impinge on different sensory systems, stimuli will be equivalent to the extent that they provide effectively equal intensities of stimulation. Such intermodality equivalence is not only an important determinant of early behavior, but also provides a possible basis for the transition from lower to higher levels of organization.

The intensity-based equivalence of stimuli in different modalities is hypothesized to enable an integrated behavior pattern in response to stimulation in one modality to occur in response to stimulation in another modality. For example, Kuo (1932) has suggested that pecking behavior in the embryonic chick is initially organized under the tactile and proprioceptive stimulational constraints and opportunities of a shell-enclosed environment, together with the specific characteristics of the chick's morphology and physiology.* Schneirla (1965) suggested that this integrated pattern of pecking behavior can be elicited in the visually naive chick after hatching by visual stimuli of the same effective intensity as the tactile and proprioceptive stimuli which elicited the pecking response before hatching.

The striking consistency in the order in which sensory systems become functional during the development of a variety of birds and mammals has been documented by Gottlieb (1971), who describes the development of sensory systems as following a sequence of emergence of function in which audition and vision follow the tactile, chemical and proprioceptive senses. This sequence is consistent with Birch's (1962) hypothesis that there is a developmental shift from early proximoceptor dominance of functioning to later teloreceptor dominance. In this view, intensity-based intermodal equivalence may account for highly organized responses to stimuli on their initial presentation, making it possible for stimulational experience in one modality to affect the development and organization of responses to stimuli in other modalities. Evidence that infants' tactile experience with objects affects their visually guided be-

---

* Hamburger (1971) and Hamburger, Wenger and Oppenheim's (1966) failure to find evidence of an effect of deafferentation on spontaneous movements in click embryos is irrelevant to this discussion, since the issue is not whether behavior can occur independently of input, but rather the importance of sensory stimulation for the development of an organized pattern of behavior.

havior comes from a study by Gottfried, Rose and Bridger (1977), in which infants who mouthed objects without seeing them subsequently looked at and reached more often for novel than for familiar (previously mouthed) objects, when these objects were presented visually for the first time.

Similarities in infants' responses to stimuli in different modalities have been documented by observers since Pratt, Nelson and Sun (1930) reported that infants often made the same responses to stimuli of several different modalities. Such findings can be understood if stimuli in different modalities are considered to be interchangeable in terms of their effective intensity. For example, the studies of finger movements in infants discussed earlier indicated that finger movements such as flexion and extension occur in response to effectively intense levels of interoceptive (Turkewitz, Fleischer et al., 1966), auditory (Turkewitz et al., 1971) and visual (McGuire & Turkewitz, 1978) stimulation. It is possible that infants' finger movements in response to auditory and visual stimuli are dependent upon the equivalence of effective intensity that these stimuli had with tactile and proprioceptive stimuli that controlled these movements in utero.

Intensity-based responses may also provide a basis for the transition to responses that are no longer based upon stimulus intensity, when such responses result in opportunities for temporal contiguity of input from different modalities, so that integration of multimodal input can take place. Thus, early intensity-determined extension of the fingers, which may result in getting the hand out into the visual field, may provide a first step in the establishment of associations between the seen and the felt hand. The importance of such associations for the development of eye-hand coordination has been demonstrated by Held and Bauer (1967) and Held and Hein (1958) for behavior such as visually-guided reaching. In addition, these movements may facilitate the development of object perception. Piaget (1952) has suggested that object perception is based upon the association and integration of multimodal inputs from the same object. Reflex-like extensions of the fingers, which decrease the distance between the hand and an object, make contact between them more likely, increasing opportunities for tactile and visual experience to take place simultaneously.

Another example of the way in which low-level, intensity-determined responses may have important consequences for the development of object perception comes from examination of eye-turning behavior in infancy. It has been observed that the newborn infant turns its eyes in the direction of a sound (Wertheimer, 1961; Turkewitz, Birch et al.,

1966). Although this behavior has been interpreted as "seeking" or search-ing for the stimulus (Wertheimer, 1961), we believe that the behavior can be more appropriately viewed as an approach response to weak stimulation. This preference for considering the behavior *approach* rather than *seeking* is based upon the facts that 1) turning away is observed when the effective intensity of the sound is increased (Hammer & Turke-witz, 1975), and 2) the response occurs with the eyes closed and in the dark, as well as with the eyes open in the light (Mendelsohn & Haith, 1976; Turkewitz, Birch et al., 1966). Although initially reflexly deter-mined,* these movements of the eyes may serve an important function for the subsequent perceptual development of the infant. Intensity-based eye-turning in the direction of a sound source may promote the develop-ment of object perception by increasing the likelihood that the infant will simultaneously experience the auditory and visual components of the stimulus object. Thus, opportunities for association and integration between the two aspects of stimulation emanating from the same object would be increased, and the development of object perception would be facilitated.

CONCLUSION

In conclusion, we have attempted to show how various aspects of approach-withdrawal theory can be applied in order to gain a better understanding of human development. This approach provides a way of organizing a vast body of information and suggests hypotheses worthy of investigation. By emphasizing the significance of differences as well as similarities in behavior at different stages, it calls our attention to distinctions between trivial and essential changes that take place during development. It should be clear that approach-withdrawal theory does not present a picture of early behavior as chaotic and undifferentiated; nor does it represent early behavior as an approximation of adult be-havior. Rather, the behavior of the neonate is viewed as organized from the very beginning, albeit differently organized from that of the adult. While this view places emphasis on the identification of low-level func-tioning at early stages, it is not intended to promote a reductionistic

---

* Mendelsohn and Haith (1976) argue that directional eye-turning responses to auditory stimuli represent search patterns and are not to be considered reflex re-sponses because they occur over longer time periods than would be expected for reflexes. It should be noted, however, that the auditory stimulus which Mendelsohn and Haith (1976) used was a spoken paragraph which can be considered to consist of multiple stimuli. Thus the responses they recorded might have been sequential reflex responses.

explanation of behavior. As organisms progress in their development, behavior is considered to undergo changes in organization which make it necessary to use methods of analysis and explanatory concepts appropriate for the particular level under examination.

REFERENCES

BALL, W. and TRONICK, E. Infant responses to impending collision: Optical and real. *Science,* 1971, 171, 818-820.

BIRCH, H. G. Dyslexia and the maturation of visual function. In: J. Money (Ed.), *Reading Disability.* Baltimore: Johns Hopkins University Press, 1962.

BIRCH, H. G. Levels, categories, and methodological assumptions in the study of behavioral development. In: E. Tobach, L. R. Aronson and E. Shaw (Eds.), *The Biopsychology of Development.* New York: Academic Press, 1971

BIRCH, H. G. and TURKEWITZ, G. Research perspectives in studying the perceptual world of infants. In: *Perceptual Development: Its Relation to Theories of Intelligence and Cognition.* Institute for Juvenile Research, Chicago, 1966.

BOWER, T. G. R. *Development in Infancy.* San Francisco: Freeman, 1974.

BOWER, T. G. R., BROUGHTON, J. M., and MOORE, M. K. Demonstration of intention in the reaching behavior of neonate infants. *Nature,* 1970, 228, 679-680.

BOWER, T. G. R., BROUGHTON, J. M., and MOORE, M. K. Infant responses to approaching objects: An indicator response to distal variables. *Perception and Psychophysics,* 1971, 9, 193-196.

BRUNER, J. S. The growth and structure of skill. In: K. J. Connolly (Ed.), *Mechanisms of Motor Skill Development.* New York: Academic Press, 1970.

CAMPOS, J. J., LANGER, A., and KROWITZ, A. Cardiac response on the visual cliff in prelocomotor human infants. *Science,* 1970, 170, 196-7.

COHEN, L. B. Observing responses, visual preferences and habituation to visual stimuli in infants. *Journal of Experimental Child Psychology,* 1969, 7, 419-22.

FANTZ, R. L. and FAGAN, J. F., III. Visual attention to size and number of pattern details by term and preterm infants during the first six months. *Child Development,* 1975, 46, 3-18.

GOTTFRIED, A. W., ROSE, S. A., and BRIDGER, W. H. Cross-modal transfer in human infants. *Child Development,* 1977, 48, 118-123.

GOTTLIEB, G. Ontogenesis of sensory function in birds and mammals. In: E. Tobach, L. R. Aronson, and E. Shaw (Eds.), *The Biopsychology of Development.* New York: Academic Press, 1971.

GOTTLIEB, G. The roles of experience in the development of behavior and the nervous system. In: G. Gottlieb (Ed.), *Neural and Behavioral Specificity, Studies on the Development of Behavior and the Nervous System,* Volume 3. New York: Academic Press, 1976.

GREENBERG, D. J. and BLUE, S. Z. Visual complexity in infancy: Contour or numerosity? *Child Development,* 1975, 46, 357-363.

HAILMAN, J. P. Comments on the coding of releasing stimuli. In: L. R. Aronson, E. Tobach, D. S. Lehrman, and J. Rosenblatt (Eds.), *Development and Evolution of Behavior.* San Francisco: Freeman, 1970.

HALL, W. G. and ROSENBLATT, J. Suckling behavior and intake control in the developing rat pup. *Journal of Comparative and Physiological Psychology,* 1977, 91 (6), 1233-1247.

HAMBURGER, V. Development of embryonic motility. In: E. Tobach, L. R. Aronson, and E. Shaw (Eds.), *The Biopsychology of Development.* New York: Academic Press, 1971.

HAMBURGER, V., WENGER, E., and OPPENHEIM, R. Motility in the chick embryo in the absence of sensory input. *Journal of Experimental Zoology*, 1966, 162, 171-204.

HAMMER, M. and TURKEWITZ, G. Relationship between effective intensity of auditory stimulation and directional eye turns in the human newborn. *Animal Behavior*, 1975, 23 (2) , 287-290.

HELD, R. and BAUER, J. A., JR. Visually-guided reaching in infant monkeys after restricted rearing. *Science*, 1967, 155, 718-720.

HELD, R. and HEIN, A. Adaptation of disarranged hand-eye coordination contingent upon reafferent stimulation. *Perceptual and Motor Skills*, 1958, 8, 83-86.

HERSHENSON, M. Visual discrimination in the human newborn. *Journal of Comparative and Physiological Psychology*, 1964, 67, 326-36.

HERSHENSON, M., MUNSINGER, H., and KESSEN, W. Preference for shapes of intermediate variability in the newborn human. *Science*, 1965, 147, 630-631.

JAEGER, R. G. and HAILMAN, J. P. Effects of intensity on the phototactic responses of adult *anuran* amphibians: A comparative survey. *Zeitscrift fur Tierpsycologie*, 1973, 33, 352-407.

JAMES, W. *Principles of Psychology*. New York: Holt, 1910.

JENSEN, K. Differential reactions to taste and temperature stimuli in newborn infants. *Genetic Psychology Monographs*, 1932, 12, 361-479.

KARMEL, B. Z. The effect of age, complexity and amount of contour on pattern preferences in human infants. *Journal of Experimental Child Psychology*, 1969a, 7, 339-354.

KARMEL, B. Z. Complexity, amounts of contour and visually-dependent behavior in hooded rats, domestic chicks and human infants. *Journal of Comparative and Physiological Psychology*, 1969b, 69, 649-657.

KARMEL, B. Z. Contour effects and pattern preferences in infants: A reply to Greenberg and O'Donnell (1972). *Child Deveolpment*, 1974, 45, 196-199.

KARMEL, B. Z., HOFFMAN, R. F., and FEGY, M. J. Processing of contour information by human infants evidenced by pattern-dependent evoked potentials. *Child Development*, 1974, 45, 39-48.

KUFFLER, S. W. Discharge patterns and functional organization of mammalian retina. *Journal of Neurophysiology*, 1953, 16, 37-68.

KUO, Z.-Y. Ontogeny of embryonic behavior in *Aves*. II. The mechanical factors in the various stages leading to hatching. *Journal of Experimental Zoology*, 1932, 61, 395-430.

KUO, Z.-Y. Ontogeny of vertebrate behavior in *Aves*. III. The structure and environmental factors in embryonic behavior. *Journal of Comparative Psychology*, 1932, 13, 245-272.

KUO, Z.-Y. *The Dynamics of Behavior Development: An Epigenetic View*. New York: Random House, 1967.

LEHRMAN, D. S. A critique of Konrad Lorenz's theory of instinctive behavior. *Quarterly Review of Biology*, 1953, 28, 337-363.

LEHRMAN, D. S. Semantic and conceptual issues in the nature-nurture problem. In: L. R. Aronson, E. Tobach, D. S. Lehrman and J. Rosenblatt, (Eds.) , *Development and Evolution of Behavior*. San Francisco: Freeman, 1970.

McCALL, R. B. and KAGAN, J. Attention in the infant: Effects of complexity, contour, perimeter and familiarity. *Child Development*, 1967, 38, 939-952.

McCARVILL, S. L. and KARMEL, B. Z. A neural activity interpretation of luminance effects on infant pattern preferences. *Journal of Experimental Child Psychology*, 1976, 22, 363-374.

McGUIRE, I. and TURKEWITZ, G. Visually-elicited finger movements in infants. *Child Development*, 1978, 49, 362-370.

MENDELSOHN, M. J. and HAITH, M. M. The relation between audition and vision in the human newborn. *Monographs of the Society for Research in Child Development*, 1976, 41 (4) , Serial No. 167.

PFAFFMAN, C. The sensory and motivating properties of the sense of taste. In: M. R. Jones (Ed.), *Current Theory and Research on Motivation*, Vol. 9. Lincoln: University of Nebraska Press, 1961.

PIAGET, J. *The Origins of Intelligence in Children*. M. Cook (trans.), New York: International Universities Press, 1952.

PRATT, K. C., NELSON, A. K., and SUN, K. H. The behavior of the newborn infant. *Ohio State University Study, Contrib. Psychol.*, 1930, No. 10.

ROSENBLATT, J. S. The basis of synchrony in the behavioral interaction between mother and her offspring in the laboratory rat. In: B. M. Foss (Ed.), *Determinants of Infant Behavior III*. London: Methuen, 1965.

RUFF, H. A. Developmental changes in infants' attention to pattern detail. *Perceptual and Motor Skills*, 1976, 43, 351-358.

RUFF, H. A. and TURKEWITZ, G. Developmental changes in the effectiveness of stimulus intensity on infant visual attention. *Developmental Psychology*, 1975, 2 (6) , 705-710.

SCHNEIRLA, T. C. (1956). Interrelationships of the "innate" and the "acquired" in instinctive behavior. In: L. R. Aronson, E. Tobach, D. S. Lehrman, and J. Rosenblatt (Eds.), *Selected Writings of T. C. Schneirla*. San Francisco: Freeman, 1972.

SCHNEIRLA, T. C. (1959). An evolutionary and developmental theory of biphasic processes underlying approach and withdrawal. In: L. R. Aronson, E. Tobach, D. S. Lehrman, and J. Rosenblatt (Eds.), *Selected Writings of T. C. Schneirla*. San Francisco: Freeman, 1972.

SCHNEIRLA, T. C. (1965). Aspects of stimulation and organization in approach-withdrawal processes underlying vertebrate behavior development. In: L. R. Aronson, E. Tobach, D. S. Lehrman and J. Rosenblatt (Eds.) , *Selected Writings of T. C. Schneirla*. San Francisco: Freeman, 1972.

SIMNER, M. L. Age changes in preferences for visual patterned stimulation in newly hatched chicks. *Proceedings of the 75th Annual Convention of the American Psychological Association*, 1967, 2, 107-108.

TURKEWITZ, G., BIRCH, H., MOREAU, T., LEVY, L., and CORNWELL, A. Effect of intensity of auditory stimulation on directional eye movements in the human newborn. *Animal Behavior*, 1966, 14, 93-101.

TURKEWITZ, G., FLEISCHER, S., MOREAU, T., BIRCH, H., and LEVY, L. Relationship between feeding condition and organization of flexor-extensor movements in the human neonate. *Journal of Comparative and Physiological Psychology*, 1966, 61 (3) , 461-463.

TURKEWITZ, G., MOREAU, T., BIRCH, H., and DAVIS, L. Relationship among responses in the human newborn: The non-association and non-equivalence among different indicators of responsiveness. *Psychophysiology*, 1971, 7 (2) , 233-247.

VOLKMANN, F. C. and DOBSON, M. V. Infant responses of ocular fixation to moving visual stimuli. *Journal of Experimental Child Psychology*, 1976, 22, 86-89.

WALK, R. J. and GIBSON, E. J. A comparative and analytical study of visual depth perception. *Psychological Monographs*, 1961, 75 (15) , No. 519.

WALK, R. J. and WATERS, C. P. Importance of texture-density preferences and motion parallax for visual depth discrimination in rats and chicks. *Journal of Comparative and Physiological Psychology*, 1974, 86 (2), 309-315.

WERTHEIMER, M. Psychomotor coordination of auditory and visual space at birth. *Science*, 1961, 134, 1692.

YONAS, A., BECHTOLD, A. G., FRANKEL, D., GORDON, F. R., McROBERTS, G., NORCIA, A., and STERNFELS, S. Development of sensitivity to information for impending collision. *Perception and Psychophysics*, 1977, 21 (2) , 97-104.

3

The Neuropsychological Significance
of Finger Recognition

ARTHUR BENTON

One of the topics that engaged the attention of Herbert Birch in the course of his studies of normal and deviant children was the development of the ability to recognize one's fingers and the question of the possible neuropsychological significance of this ability. With his co-workers, Arthur Lefford and George Green, he conducted a large scale investigation of the performances of preschool children on diverse finger localization tasks designed to make specific demands on visual information processing, tactile information processing, the capacity to integrate visual and tactile information and the capacity to utilize representational information to guide behavior.

The findings of the study (Lefford, Birch & Green, 1974) indicated that there was a rather clearly defined course of development of finger recognition over the age range of 3 to 6 years. Younger preschool children showed some capacity to localize their fingers on the basis of visual or tactile information, or a combination of the two, but they were unable to transfer information from one sensory modality to the other or utilize a pictorial representation of the hand in making localizations. Older preschool children did show some capacity for intersensory transfer of information but were quite deficient in localizing stimulation on a model of the hand. The latter capacity evidently is acquired only at a later age, a finding in consonance with earlier work on the performances of school-age children (Benton, 1955, 1959).

Thus the analysis of the behavior of the preschool children on finger recognition tasks in terms of intrasensory differentiation, intersensory

85

integration and the capacity to utilize a pictorial representation illuminated the developmental course of finger localization and showed how this type of performance could be utilized as an index of cognitive development. In the discussion section of the report of this study, it is suggested that, since fine manual activity and awareness of the fingers are universal human traits, the assessment of finger recognition capacity may be a useful technique in cross-cultural studies of cognitive development. A second practical implication of the findings is also mentioned. Analysis of finger recognition performance "may be of particular potential value for the early identification of children at later risk of school failure."

On the face of it, the capacity to discriminate among one's fingers and disturbances in that capacity on either a developmental or acquired basis would appear to be an unlikely phenomenon to select for systematic study. However, as we have seen, Birch was able to utilize it as a model to study certain cognitive processes that are important components of mental development. In doing this he was following the example set some 50 years earlier by the Viennese neurologist, Josef Gerstmann. When Gerstmann encountered a patient who showed a seemingly inexplicable failure to name or recognize both her own fingers and those of the examiner, he had the acumen to see that her disability might be more than a medical curiosity. He called the disability "finger agnosia," which was an unfortunate choice of terms for a number of reasons. It extended the concept of agnosia beyond its defined meaning of a perceptual-associational disorder within a single sensory modality. In Gerstmann's defense, it must be said that he was not the only sinner in this respect. During the 1920s and 1930s, German neurologists showed a remarkable proclivity for inventing numerous types of "agnosia" such as "simultanagnosia," "physiognomical agnosia," "time agnosia" and even "clock agnosia," thereby transforming failure on particular tasks into basic disabilities (cf., Poeck, 1969). Furthermore, as has been pointed out many times (e.g., Schilder, 1931; Benton, 1959; Ettlinger, 1963; Critchley, 1966), "finger agnosia" implies the existence of a unitary "finger sense" or faculty of finger recognition when in fact it is only a collective term for different types of defective performance, as Birch showed in his study of preschool children.

Two developments followed Gerstmann's early reports. First, his observation was quickly confirmed and defective identification of the fingers became a recognized symptom of brain disease. Secondly, he linked finger agnosia with three other deficits—right-left disorientation, agraphia and acalculia—to form the syndrome that bears his name and he alleged that this distinctive combination of deficits occurred as a consequence of focal disease in the left parieto-occipital region.

FORMS OF FINGER RECOGNITION

Since finger recognition is a collective term covering a range of performances, evaluation of its neuropsychological significance requires that these performances be specified. Schilder (1931) was the first to appreciate this point and he proposed a classification of types of defect in finger recognition and praxis, as shown in Table 1. Schilder emphasized that each defect could occur independently of the others and he believed that each corresponded to a specific lesional localization: the inability to localize one's fingers on verbal command to a lesion in the territory of the angular gyrus of the dominant hemisphere, as postulated by Gerstmann; "visual finger agnosia" to a more posteriorly situated occipital lobe lesion; "finger aphasia," or impairment in naming the fingers, to involvement of Wernicke's area; the apractic disorders to a lesion in the region of the supramarginal gyrus.

TABLE 1

Forms of Defective Finger Recognition

1. Inability to identify one's own fingers ("finger agnosia" of Gerstmann)
2. Inability to identify examiner's fingers ("visual finger agnosia")
3. Inability to name fingers ("finger aphasia")
4. Inability to move individual fingers on command ("apraxia of finger choice")
5. Inability to imitate finger postures ("constructive finger apraxia")

From Schilder (1931)

Later investigators went further in indicating the necessity for precise operational definition of finger recognition performance in terms of stimulus characteristics, response requirements and task complexity. Benton (1959) differentiated finger recognition performances along a number of dimensions, e.g., whether the stimulus was verbal or nonverbal, visual or tactile, single or multiple, whether a verbal response was or was not required, and whether impairment, when it occurred, was shown on one or both hands. Similarly, Ettlinger (1963), in a study of patients with parietal lobe disease, employed no less than 12 tests, some requiring a naming response and others an nonverbal localizing response, some requiring the patient to identify his own fingers and others requiring identification on a model or on the examiner's hands, and still others calling for finger movements.

That these distinctions are not merely logical exercises but do in fact have differential neuropsychological significance has been demonstrated beyond doubt. It is a commonplace observation that many aphasic patients fail finger naming tests but do succeed in identifying their fingers when they can make a nonverbal localizing response. In these cases, the failure in finger naming is usually an expression of a general naming difficulty and to call it "finger agnosia" or "finger aphasia" is superfluous. In this connection, it may be recalled that Schilder placed the crucial lesion for defective finger naming not in the posterior parietal territory favored by Gerstmann for "finger agnosia" but in Wernicke's area. Aphasic patients with receptive language impairment will not only not be able to name their fingers but often also fail to identify their fingers when the names are supplied by the examiner; yet they will be able to make correct manual localizations to tactile stimulation. Here again the factor of language impairment is primary and usually nothing is gained by attaching a special value to the failure to understand the names of fingers in contrast to the names of other objects. There are patients, some with general mental impairment and others with visual-perceptive difficulties, who identify their own fingers quite well but who (like the preschool children of Lefford, Birch and Green) cannot identify fingers on a schematic representation of the hand. If it suits the purposes of one author, he will call this performance failure "finger agnosia" while another author, respecting Gerstmann's definition of the disability as entailing failure to name or recognize one's own fingers as well as those of other persons, will deny that this is a "true" finger agnosia. Finally, a distinction must be made between unilateral and bilateral disturbances of finger recognition. As Head (1920) suggested many decades ago and as Gainotti and Tiacci (1973) have demonstrated, defective localization of tactile stimulation of the fingers on one side of the body in patients with brain disease is a sensitive index of disease of the contralateral cerebral hemisphere. Thus its significance is quite different from bilateral defects in verbal finger identification or specific failure to make localizations on a two-dimensional representation of the hand.

In summary, "finger agnosia" means very little because it means so much, covering as it does diverse performances differing in nature, scope and complexity. Uncritical use of the term has been responsible for much of the confusion and controversy surrounding the Gerstmann syndrome and its meaning. Obviously it would serve the cause of clear thinking if the term were abandoned in favor of more specific designations. But terminology, once established, has a life of its own, and even those who do not believe in the existence of a unitary "finger sense" or a unitary disability called "finger agnosia" still use these terms—but only, as Critchley (1966) once wrote, "under protest."

DEVELOPMENTAL ASPECTS

As has been noted, Lefford, Birch and Green (1974) charted the developmental course of certain aspects of finger recognition in preschool children and found that performance level at different ages was determined by specific stimulus characteristics and response requirements. Some of their results are summarized in Table 2, which shows the proportion of children at three different ages who performed satisfactorily on certain tasks. Inspection of the table indicates that it is much more difficult for a young child to localize finger stimulation on a pictorial model of the hand than on his own hand. For each stimulus-condition (visual-tactile, visual, tactile), the proportion of children performing satisfactorily when they have to make their localizations on a model is decidedly lower than when they localize stimulation on their own hand. For example, virtually all 4-year-olds can localize visually perceived finger stimuli on their hands but about half of them are unable to localize the same type of stimulation on a representation of the hand. The table also shows that the localization of tactile stimulation is much more difficult than the identification of fingers subjected to visual or to combined visual-tactile stimulation. This holds for all ages and for localiza-

TABLE 2

Percentages of Children Succeeding on
Finger Localization Tasks

Task	3 Yrs.	Age Level 4 Yrs.	5 Yrs.
A. Visual-Tactile Localization on Self	73%	93%	99%
B. Visual Localization on Self	63	98	99
C. Tactile Localization on Self	24	63	72
D. Visual-Tactile Localization on Model	15	45	82
E. Visual Localization on Model	20	54	82
F. Tactile Localization on Model	11	28	52

Data from Lefford, Birch & Green (1974)

tion both on the child's own hand and on a schematic representation of the hand.

That tactile information processing, and particularly its translation into visual terms, is relatively difficult for children is shown by my own normative observations on school-age children (Benton, 1955, 1959). Because of differences in the mode of analysis of the data, my findings and those of Lefford, Birch and Green are not directly comparable. But, in essence, my observations can be considered to be an upward extension of theirs.

Three tasks were presented to the child: 1) with his hand visible to him, he had to identify single fingers touched by the examiner; 2) with his hand hidden from his view, he again had to identify single fingers touched by the examiner; 3) with his hand hidden from his view, he had to identify pairs of fingers simultaneously touched by the examiner. An outline drawing of the stimulated hand, with the thumb and fingers numbered from 1 to 5 and on which he could make his localizations, was placed before the child. In adopting this arrangement, I was primarily concerned with giving the child latitude to make a nonverbal response, if he wished to do so. Thus, with the drawing before him, he could call out the number of the stimulated finger or point to it. Or, if he preferred, he could ignore the drawing and identify the finger by name. At the time, it did not occur to me that the distinction between localization on one's own fingers and localization on a model might be important, as Lefford, Birch and Green showed some 20 years later.

The arrangement for assessing finger localization to tactile stimulation without the benefit of visual cues is as follows. At a table adjusted to the child's size, the child inserts his/her hand, palm up, under a small box which acts as a visual shield while the examiner touches the tip of a finger with the sharpened end of a pencil. The child is then free to make his/her localization by pointing to the stimulated finger on the drawing or calling its number or identifying it by name.

Table 3 shows the relative success in localizing the fingers under the three conditions of stimulation in children ranging in age from 6 to 9 years. Clearly, each type of finger localization shows a progressive development with age. And it is equally clear that the processing of tactile information and its localization in visual space poses a more formidable task to the child than does the processing of combined tactile-visual information. At each age level, the percentage of correct localizations to tactile stimulation is lower than to tactile-visual stimulation. For example, 9-year-old children perform at a practically perfect level in localizing single fingers under the tactile-visual condition but at least some of them make an appreciable number of errors under the tactile condition. That complexity of stimulation is a determinant of performance level is obvious. Most 6-year-old children are unable to localize two simultaneously stimulated fingers and the task poses great difficulty for many 9-year-olds.

Wake (1956, 1957; summarized in Benton, 1959) utilized the same test battery to extend these normative observations through age 12, with the results shown in Table 4. For comparative purposes, my findings on both children and normal adults are included in the table. It will be seen that there is a steady increment in total score through the age of 12 years, which is no doubt determined essentially by increasing success in localizing simultaneously stimulated pairs of fingers. But, even at the age of 12 years, level of performance is still below that of normal adults.

TABLE 3

Performances of Children on Finger Localization Tasks

Task	Percentage of Correct Responses Age Level			
	6 Yrs.	7 Yrs.	8 Yrs.	9 Yrs.
A. Visual-Tactile Stimulation: Single Finger	88%	97%	98%	99%
B. Tactile Stimulation: Single Finger	67	82	88	93
C. Tactile Stimulation: Two Fingers	37	43	55	63

Data from Benton (1959)

TABLE 4

Age and Finger Recognition Performance

Age	Mean Percentage of Correct Response	
	Wake	Benton
6 Years	76%	70%
7	84	80
8	89	85
9	91	89
10	93	—
11	94 (93.8)	—
12	94 (94.4)	—
18+	—	98

Data from Wake (1956, 1957); Benton (1959)

Thus one deals with a series of performances that evidently call on cognitive skills which develop all through childhood and which reach maturity some time after the age of 12 years. The analysis of Lefford, Birch and Green (1975) identified some of these skills: intrasensory discrimination, as in making localizations on the basis of visual or combined visual-tactile information; intersensory integration, as in making localizations in visual space on the basis of tactile information alone; and visual-spatial representational thinking, as in making localizations on an external schematic model in place of one's own hand.

A number of considerations of an anatomical and clinical nature suggest that still another cognitive process is involved, at least in the more complex forms of finger identification, namely, the verbal encoding of sensory information as a means of mediating the localizing response. This suggestion is supported by the findings of Stone and Robinson (1968) who studied verbal and nonverbal finger localization in a group of 7-year-old children. The children localized tactile stimulation of single fingers (20 trials) and pairs of fingers (40 trials) on a model of the hands. Each child performed under four different conditions: 1) calling the number of the stimulated fingers on a *numbered* model of the hand; 2) pointing to the stimulated fingers on a *numbered* model of the hand; 3) calling the number of the stimulated fingers on an *unnumbered* model of the hand; 4) pointing to the stimulated fingers on an *unnumbered* model of the hand.

Thus the child made a manual localizing response under two conditions and a verbal response under the same two conditions. The question at issue was whether a difference in level of performance under the verbal and nonverbal response requirements would be shown. If this form of finger localization is a purely nonverbal process, then direct manual localization should be superior to verbal localization since the latter entails a supplementary overt verbal response. On the other hand, if the localization does involve a verbal encoding process, then verbal localization should be superior to manual localization, since the latter entails a supplementary motor response.

The results of the study of Stone and Robinson are shown in Table 5. It will be seen that verbal localization was slightly superior to manual localization with both types of models and that this modest within-subjects difference is statistically significant. Whether the model was numbered or not had no main effect on level of performance nor did the verbal cue provided by the numbers have a specific influence on the accuracy of verbal naming.

Lindgren (1975) has confirmed these findings of Stone and Robinson.

TABLE 5

Performance Level and Mode of Response

	Model With Numbers		Model Without Numbers	
	Manual R	Verbal R	Manual R	Verbal R
Mean No. Correct Responses	56.7	58.4	55.3	58.8
Accuracy	71%	73%	69%	74%

Analysis of Variance

Source of Variation	F	
Mode of Response	5.65	(p < .05)
Type of Model	< 1.00	
Mode of Response X Type of Model	< 1.00	

Data from Stone & Robinson (1968)

In his study, 6-year-old children localized single and double tactile stimulation of a model of the hand by pointing and by calling the numbers of the touched fingers. He found that there was no difference in accuracy in localizing single fingers when the child pointed or called the numbers, both tasks being performed with a relatively high level of success. However, the accuracy of localization of double stimulation was significantly higher under the verbal response condition as compared to pointing. On the other hand, Satz and Friel (1973), working with 5-year-old children, found that localization of single finger stimulation when they pointed to the touched finger was more accurate than when they called its number. Double finger stimulation was not assessed in this study.

A reasonable conclusion is that a number of cognitive processes are called into play in localizing the fingers, the relative importance of each process depending upon the characteristics of the presented task and perhaps the age of the child. In addition to the sensory-discriminative, sensory-integrative and perceptual-representational processes emphasized by Lefford, Birch and Green, a verbal coding process appears to be a significant mediator of performance on more complex tasks.

A further point should be made. Finger recognition capacity in young school children is related not only to their chronological age, as we have seen, but also to their intelligence level, as estimated by their WISC Verbal Scale IQs. Within the age range of 6 to 9 years, children of superior intelligence perform above the expected level for their age although somewhat below the level that would be predicted from their mental age. But evidently the influence of intelligence level wanes with increasing age because this relationship is not apparent in the case of adults. Studying a group of 40 normal adults, Benton (1959) found that the 7 subjects with IQs of 80-89 performed as well as did the remaining subjects with IQs ranging from 90 to 128. In the light of the suggestion of Lefford, Birch and Green (1974) that finger recognition tasks would seem to be particularly suited for cross-cultural studies, it is worth noting that the same absence of a relationship between finger recognition capacity and intelligence level holds for normal Chinese adults. Kao and Li (1939) found no significant association between the two variables in subjects whose IQs ranged from 80 to 139.

However, it must be emphasized that this absence of a relationship between finger localization capacity and intelligence level in adults holds only for those with IQs of 80 or higher. There is substantial evidence from the studies of Benton (1959), Fitzhugh, Fitzhugh and Reitan (1962) and Matthews and Folk (1964) that finger localization capacity is positively related to IQ in retarded adults. In passing, it may be noted that the observations of Kao and Li (1939) on Chinese subjects point to the same conclusion, for they encountered many instances of defective finger recognition in adults with IQs below 80. Moreover, the importance of the perceptual-spatial component in at least some finger localization tasks is highlighted by the demonstration of Matthews, Folk and Zerfas (1966) that there is a closer relationship between finger localization and Wechsler Performance Scale IQ than Verbal Scale IQ in retardates. Poeck and Orgass (1969) have demonstrated the same pattern of relationships, at least for finger localization tasks not requiring an overt verbal response, in patients with brain disease.

CLINICAL AND EDUCATIONAL CORRELATES

Given these background data, the question of whether the finger localization performances of children have clinical or educational significance may be addressed. To do this one must return to the syndrome formulated by Gerstmann which linked "finger agnosia" with right-left disorientation, impairment in writing and impairment in calculation to form a coherent unity with a distinctive neurological significance. Since the latter two deficits involve acquired scholastic skills, the appearance of the syndrome on the neurological scene prompted investigative work with children to determine whether defective finger localization and right-left orientation might be associated with specific learning disabilities. Strauss and Werner (1938) were the first to report an empirical study dealing with the relationship between finger recognition and arithmetic achievement in mentally retarded boys. Subsequent studies concerned themselves with the relationship of finger recognition to not only arithmetic skills but also reading achievement. At the same time, some clinicians advanced the concept of a "developmental" or "congenital" Gerstmann syndrome that included reading disability as a prominent feature as well as the elements of the syndrome as originally described.

The main trends of the substantial body of literature on this topic will be summarized. In the interests of clarity, the relationship of finger localization capacity to arithmetic achievement will be considered separately from its relationship to reading achievement. Further, a distinction will be made between the question of whether there is a *concurrent* association between finger localization capacity and arithmetic and reading skills in the school-age child and the question of whether finger localization capacity in the preschool child is *predictive* of future progress in learning arithmetic and reading skills in the school years. The latter is, of course, the question that Lefford, Birch and Green raised, i.e., whether assessment of finger localization capacity can aid in identifying the preschool child who is at risk for later school failure.

Arithmetic achievement will be considered first. Although Strauss and Werner (1938) in their pioneer study of retarded boys concluded that there was an "obvious" association between finger localization capacity and arithmetic achievement, their analysis of the findings is, in fact, so obscure that it is impossible to determine how they reached that conclusion. Nevertheless, their hypothesis was provocative enough to encourage further exploration, and Benton, Hutcheon and Seymour (1951) decided to study the question in both normal children and mildly retarded adolescents. Their findings were essentially negative. In neither group was a relationship between the two variables, as estimated by correlation coefficients, evident. When attention was focused on the extreme cases, i.e., subjects with extremely poor finger localization scores or, conversely, those with extremely poor arithmetic achievement, there was again no evidence of an association. For example, 3 of the 23 retarded boys showed clearly defective finger localization capacity, their performance levels being some distance below the distributions of scores of the other 20 retardates and of the 22 normal children. Yet the relative arithmetic achievement of each of the 3 subjects was close to the group median. Conversely, 2 retarded boys with mental ages of about 11 years and fair levels of reading achievement showed a very poor development of arithmetic skills. One showed rather poor finger localization while the other scored above the group median. A later study by

Matthews and Folk (1964) also failed to find evidence for a specific relationship between finger localization and arithmetic ability in retardates.

In retrospect, these negative findings are not surprising in the light of what is now known about the Gerstmann syndrome in adult patients. The weight of evidence suggests that the syndrome is, in fact, an artificial combination of deficits, arbitrarily selected for study, and in no way different in nature from a dozen other combinations of deficits involving linguistic, constructional, perceptual and orientational functions that might be formed, if one chose to do so. It has been shown that impairment in finger recognition is no more closely related to impairment in calculation than it is to defects in reading, constructional praxis and visual memory that are not elements of the syndrome (Benton, 1961). Its alleged specific neurological significance, namely, that it appears as a consequence of focal disease in the region of the angular gyrus of the dominant hemisphere, was effectively negated by the searching clinicopathological study of Heimburger, DeMyer and Reitan (1964). Working with a large case material, they identified 23 patients who showed the full Gerstmann syndrome. In every case, the lesion was a massive one generally involving a broad territory including the supramarginal gyrus, the angular gyrus and the superior temporal gyrus of the dominant hemisphere. In no case was the lesion restricted to the angular gyrus alone. And in no case did the complete syndrome appear without associated defects such as aphasia or constructional apraxia. In the opinion of Heimburger, DeMyer and Reitan, the latter defects were "an integral part of the total picture of nervous disability" shown by the patients and not merely ancillary or accidental manifestations.

A substantial number of empirical studies have been concerned with the question of the relationship of finger recognition to reading achievement, a type of performance not included in the original Gerstmann syndrome. For the most part, the results have been negative, but there are some inconsistencies. Rabinovitch and his co-workers (1954) found only one instance of defective finger recognition in a group of 20 dyslexic children. Negative results have also been reported by Drew (1956), Clements and Peters (1962), Brewer (1966) and Lyle (1969). Yet Sparrow and Satz (1970) did find dyslexic children to be inferior in finger recognition to normal readers, the difference being more marked for younger age groups, suggesting that there may be a developmental delay in finger recognition in at least some dyslexic children. Croxen and Lytton (1971) also found that poor readers had somewhat lower finger localization scores than good readers.

That the relationship between the two variables is not simple or direct is suggested by the studies of Kinsbourne and Warrington (1963a, b). Defective finger recognition was observed in retarded readers who showed a WISC pattern characterized by a higher Verbal Scale IQ than Performance Scale IQ. Retarded readers with the more usual WISC pattern of a lower Verbal Scale than Performance Scale IQ showed normal finger recognition. Moreover, the group of children with defective finger recognition showed a number of unusual features in addition to their atypical WISC pattern. Most of them were girls while, as is well known, dyslexia is preeminently a disorder of males. Most of them had IQs under 80 and were retarded in reading only in relation to their relatively high Verbal Scale IQs. Finally, most of the children in this group showed independent signs of brain disease. The possibility that lateral pattern (rather than absolute level) of finger recognition performance may be related to reading achievement has been suggested by Reed (1967).

These observations suggest that the relationship between defective finger localization and dyslexia is a rather tenuous one and that concurrence of the two types of disability is likely to occur within a setting of multi-faceted impairment referable to brain disease. In this respect, we must note that impairment in finger recognition, independently of reading disability, is a behavioral index of brain damage in children. Clawson (1962) found that a remarkably high proportion of non-defective children with brain damage performed poorly on finger localization tasks. Holroyd and Wright (1965) also found an association between defective finger localization and neurological signs of brain damage in children seen in a clinic setting.

Interpretation of these inconsistent findings regarding the concurrence of defective finger recognition and reading disability may be aided by considering the question of whether finger recognition capacity in preschool children has predictive significance for their subsequent reading ability. There is evidence that, as Lefford, Birch and Green (1974) surmised, this is the case. Satz and his co-workers (Satz & Friel, 1973, 1974; Satz, Friel & Rudegeair, 1974) investigated the prognostic value of a battery of 16 tests assessing a variety of verbal and nonverbal skills in kindergarten children by comparing the test performances with the reading achievement of the children at the end of the first and second grades. Finger localization ranked among the very best predictors of subsequent reading achievement. But, interestingly, finger localization capacity, when assessed again in the second grade children, was not correlated with reading achievement. Apparently the particular finger recognition tasks given to the kindergarten children made demands on cognitive functions that play a role in the initial learning of reading. By the end of the second grade they are no longer playing this crucial role as the cognitive functions measured by these particular finger localization tasks mature in the poor readers. The meaning of this shift in the nature of the association between the two variables can be assessed only when one knows the degree to which the reading retardation observed in the second grade is permanent or transitory.

Lindgren (1975), also working with kindergarten children, has confirmed these results of Satz and his co-workers. He found that the performance of the children on a comprehensive battery of finger recognition tests predicted reading achievement at the end of the first grade, the correlation coefficient between the two measures being .55. However, finger localization score was also a significant predictor of end-of-first-grade arithmetic achievement, the correlation coefficient between the two measures being .47. Hence the specificity of the relationship between finger recognition and subsequent reading achievement is called into question.

Thus, these recent predictive studies have generated more interesting results than did the earlier studies of finger recognition and scholastic achievement in children of school age. What can be made of these findings which substantiate Birch's suggestion that assessment of finger recognition performance may help to identify the preschool child at risk for later school failure? What is there about finger recognition that should endow it with predictive significance for subsequent achievement in reading and arithmetic?

Gerstmann (1940) considered that an intact and well-differentiated body image was a necessary precondition for finger recognition and he ascribed finger agnosia to a limited disintegration of the body image, primarily involving the fingers, the most differentiated part of the image. Thus finger agnosia, in his view, was essentially a higher-level perceptual disorder involving the different sensory components of the body image and the spatial relations among the parts of the image. A disorder of the body schema could also explain impairment in differentiating the left and right sides of one's body. Since finger agnosia involved motoric as well as perceptive components (we recall that Schilder described two types of finger apraxia), it could also be invoked to explain why a disorder of writing was a part of the syndrome. Finally, loss of the ability to calculate could be related to the use of the fingers in counting. Our decimal system and arithmetic terminology (as reflected in the term "digit") testify to the significance of the 10 fingers in the genesis of calculation.

Although Gerstmann's account made very good reading, many neurologists (e.g., Lange, 1930, 1933; Conrad, 1932; Stengel, 1944) preferred the more mundane conception that the failure to differentiate among one's fingers, as well as the other components of the syndrome, were only specific expressions of a more general disability in spatial thinking. Impressed by the close association of impaired finger localization to both aphasic disorder and general mental impairment, Benton (1959) advanced a different hypothesis, namely, that it was due to a defect in conceptual-symbolic thinking.

Can these different conceptions of the *Grundstörung* underlying failure in finger recognition be reconciled? The studies of Poeck and Orgass (1966, 1969) and Gainotti, Cianchetti and Tiacci (1972) indicate that no single hypothesis can accommodate the facts; yet each possesses some validity. In patients with unilateral brain disease, the correlates of impaired finger localization depend in part upon the side of the lesion. In this connection, it must be noted that, contrary to general belief, finger agnosia is encountered as frequently in patients with right hemisphere lesions as in those with lesions of the left hemisphere (Gianotti, Ciachetti & Tiacci, 1972). In patients with either left or right hemisphere disease, finger agnosia is correlated with the presence of general mental impairment; additionally, in patients with left hemisphere disease, it is correlated with the presence of aphasic disorder.

These results are in accord with the view that impairment in symbolic thinking plays a significant role in defective finger localization. However, a close look at the findings indicates that linguistic or symbolic impairment cannot account fully for the occurrence of finger agnosia because, as will be seen, many patients with receptive language impairment perform quite adequately on finger localization tasks, particularly if they are of a nonverbal nature.

Table 6 summarizes some results in a study that compared finger localization (and other performances) in patients with and without receptive language impairment (Sauguet, Benton & Hécaen, 1971). None of these patients showed severe general mental impairment or confusion. The group labeled "RH" consisted of patients with right hemisphere disease, none of whom was aphasic. The group labeled "LH-NA" consisted of patients with left hemisphere disease, none of whom showed significant impairment in receptive language as assessed by objective tests. Some of these patients showed expressive speech defects but their language understanding was intact. In contrast, the group labeled

Table 6

Finger Agnosia in Aphasic and Non-Aphasic Patients

Relative Frequency of Defective Preformance

Finger Recognition Test	RA	GROUP LH-NA	LH-A
1. Naming	10%	14%	67%
2. Identification by Name	3	11	62
3. Identification by Number	—	—	33
4. Nonverbal Finger Localiaztion	3	—	19
5. Interdigital Object Identification	—	—	33

RH = Right hemisphere disease; non-aphasic
LH-NA = Left hemisphere disease; non-aphasic or only expressive speech impairment
LH-A = Left hemisphere disease; aphasic with both receptive and expressive speech impairment.
Data from Sauguet, Benton & Hécaen (1971)

"LH-A" consisted of patients with left hemisphere disease who showed both expressive and receptive speech impairment.

It is evident from the figures in Table 6 that only the patients with receptive language defect show an impressive frequency of failure on the finger recognition tests. Non-aphasic patients, as well as those with only expressive language defect, do not show defects in finger recognition. To this extent, it may be concluded that finger agnosia is associated with defects in symbolic thinking, as reflected in defects in language understanding. But the point which has to be made is that many patients with receptive language impairment do *not* show finger agnosia, the relative proportion varying with the particular finger recognition task. With verbal tasks, the proportion is relatively small. With nonverbal tasks, the proportion is much higher.

Thus it must be conceded that receptive language impairment is not a sufficient condition for the occurrence of finger agnosia although it seems to be a necessary condition, at least in patients who are not deteriorated or confused. Conceivably, receptive language disorder interacts with another factor to produce finger agnosia. Benton (1959) advanced the hypothesis that finger agnosia in patients with left hemisphere lesions resulted from "a combination of a disturbance of the body schema with an impairment in symbolic comprehension." Selecki and Herron (1965) proposed a similar hypothesis in their construct of the "verbal body image" representing an amalgam of somatosensory processes and symbolic functions. Disturbances in the image come about as a result of combined somatosensory and aphasic deficit. This view has received some degree of empirical support from the finding of Gainotti, Cianchetti and Tiacci that finger agnosia in patients with left hemisphere lesions shows a significant positive association with the presence of contralateral somatosensory defect. In contrast, there is no association between finger agnosia and contralateral sensory defect in patients with right hemisphere disease, the significant correlate in this group being general mental impairment.

What do these observations on adult patients suggest with respect to the reason why finger recognition capacity in the preschool child has been found to have predictive significance for subsequent achievement in reading and arithmetic? The probable reason is that these task performances make demands on a number of functions or capacities—the integrity and adequate differentiation of the body schema, the capacity to utilize a pictorial representation as a guide to action, the capacity to translate tactile information into visual terms and the capacity to utilize implicit verbal labels in mediating thought. All of these functions are in a state of rapid development during the later preschool years and it may be assumed that their status as a child enters the first grade has a determining influence on his progress as he tries to master the operations of counting, of matching quantitative and verbal symbols to pictorial representations, and of establishing connections between sight and sound in reading. Relative immaturity in any one or more of these functions, for example, in the differentiation of the finger schema, in intersensory integrative capacity or in applying somatosensory information to an external visual representation, will not necessarily make the acquisition of counting and calculating skills or the development of sight-sound associations impossible. But such immaturity may well operate to retard the *rate* of learning these skills and associations so that a child's achievement at the end of the first or second grade will compare unfavorably with his peers. On this view, defective finger recognition is more likely to be predictive of transient difficulty in learning to read and to calculate than of the persistent and severe disability covered by the clinical condition of developmental dyslexia or the rarer condition of specific arithmetic disability. Whether this is actually the case remains to be determined by empirical study. The absence of concurrent relationships between finger recognition and reading or arithmetic achievement in school children suggests that this view may be correct.

No doubt there are other tests and tasks of a more conventional type that assess most, if not all, of the cognitive functions called into play by finger recognition performances. The one distinctive feature of finger recognition is, of course, the body schema component. How important this particular component is and the relative usefulness of finger recognition, as compared to other assessment procedures, for diverse purposes of identification and prediction in adults and children are questions that further analytic research can be expected to resolve. What is so intriguing is that this somatosensory performance, which is seemingly so simple, should have such wide-ranging neuropsychological implications.

REFERENCES

BENTON, A. L. Development of finger-localization capacity in school children. *Child Development*, 1955, 26, 225-230.

BENTON, A. L. *Right-left Discrimination and Finger Localization: Development and Pathology*. New York: Hoeber-Harper, 1959.

BENTON, A. L. The fiction of the "Gerstmann syndrome." *Journal of Neurology, Neurosurgery and Psychiatry*, 1961, 24, 176-181.

BENTON, A. L., HUTCHEON, J. F., and SEYMOUR, E. Arithmetic ability, finger-localization capacity and right-left discrimination in normal and defective children. *American Journal of Orthopsychiatry*, 1951, 21, 756-766.

BREWER, W. F. Finger localization and reading disability. M. A. Thesis, University of Iowa, 1966.

CLAWSON, A. Relationship of psychological tests to cerebral disorders in children. *Psychological Reports*, 1962, 10, 187-190.

CLEMENTS, S. D. and PETERS, J. E. Minimal brain dysfunctions in the school-age child. *Archives of General Psychiatry*, 1962, 6, 185-197.

CONRAD, K. Versuch einer psychologischen Analyse des Parietalsyndroms. *Monatsschrift für Psychiatrie und Neurologie*, 1932, 84, 28-97.

CRITCHLEY, M. The enigma of Gerstmann's syndrome. *Brain*, 1966, 89, 183-198.

CROXEN, M. E. and LYTTON, H. Reading disability and difficulties in finger localization and right-left discrimination. *Developmental Psychology*, 1971, 5, 256-262.

DREW, A. L. A neurological appraisal of familial congenital word-blindness. *Brain*, 1956, 79, 440-460.

ETTLINGER, G. Defective identification of fingers. *Neuropsychologia*, 1963, 1, 39-45.

FITZHUGH, L. C., FITZHUGH, K. B., and REITAN, R. M. Sensorimotor deficits of brain-damaged Ss in relation to intellectual level. *Perceptual and Motor Skills*, 1962, 15, 603-608.

GAINOTTI, G., CIANCHETTI, C., and TIACCI, C. The influence of hemispheric side of lesion on nonverbal tasks of finger localization. *Cortex*, 1972, 8, 364-381.

GAINOTTI, G. and TIACCI, C. The unilateral forms of finger agnosia. *Confinia Neurologica*, 1973, 35, 271-284.

GERSTMANN, J. Syndrome of finger agnosia, disorientation for right and left, agraphia and acalculia. *Archives of Neurology and Psychiatry*, 1940, 44, 398-408.

HEAD, H. *Studies in Neurology*. London: Hodder & Stoughton, 1920.

HEIMBURGER, R. F., DeMYER, W., and REITAN, R. M. Implications of Gerstmann's syndrome. *Journal of Neurology, Neurosurgery and Psychiatry*, 1964, 27, 52-57.

HOLROYD, J. and WRIGHT, F. Neurological implications of WISC verbal-performance discrepancies in a psychiatric setting. *Journal of Consulting Psychology*, 1965, 29, 206-212.

KAO, C. C. and LI, M. Y. Tests of finger orientation. In: R. S. Lyman (Ed.), *Neuropsychiatry in China*. Peking: Henri Vetch, 1939.

KINSBOURNE, M. and WARRINGTON, E. K. Developmental factors in reading and writing backwardness. *British Journal of Psychology*, 1963, 54, 145-156. (a)

KINSBOURNE, M. and WARRINGTON, E. K. The developmental Gerstmann syndrome. *Archives of Neurology*, 1963, 8, 490-501. (b)

LANGE, J. *Fingeragnosie und Agraphie*. *Monatsschrift für Psychiatrie und Neurologie*, 1930, 76, 129-188.

LANGE, J. Probleme der Fingeragnosie. *Zeitschrift für die gesamte Neurologie und Psychiatrie*, 1933, 147, 594-610.

LEFFORD, A., BIRCH, H. G., and GREEN, G. The perceptual and cognitive bases for finger localization and selective finger movement in preschool children. *Child Development*, 1974, 45, 335-343.

LINDGREN, S. D. The early identification of children at risk for reading disabilities. M. A. Thesis, University of Iowa, 1975.

LYLE, J. G. Reading retardation and reversal tendency. *Child Development*, 1969, 40, 833-843.

MATTHEWS, C. G. and FOLK, E. D. Finger localization, intelligence, and arithmetic in mentally retarded subjects. *American Journal of Mental Deficiency*, 1964, 69, 107-113.

MATTHEWS, C. G., FOLK, E. D., and ZERFAS, P. G. Lateralized finger localization deficits and differential Wechsler-Bellevue results in retardates. *American Journal of Mental Deficiency*, 1966, 70, 695-702.

POECK, K. Modern trends in neuropsychology. In: A. L. Benton (Ed.), *Contributions to Clinical Neuropsychology*. Chicago: Aldine, 1969.

POECK, K. and ORGASS, B. Gerstmann's syndrome and aphasia. *Cortex*, 1966, 2, 421-437.

POECK, K. and ORGASS, B. An experimental investigation of finger agnosia. *Neurology*, 1969, 19, 801-807.

RABINOVITCH, R. D., DREW, A. L., DEJONG, R., INGRAM, W., and WITHEY, L. A. A research approach to reading retardation. *Proceedings, Association for Research in Nervous and Mental Diseases*, 1954, 34, 363-396.

REED, J. C. Lateralized finger agnosia and reading achievement at ages 6 and 10. *Child Development*, 1967, 38, 213-220.

SATZ, P. and FRIEL, J. Some predictive antecedents of specific learning disability. In: P. Satz and J. Ross (Eds.), *The Disabled Learner*. Rotterdam: Rotterdam University Press, 1973.

SATZ, P. and FRIEL, J. Some predictive antecedents of specific reading disability: A preliminary two-year follow-up. *Journal of Learning Disabilities*, 1974, 7, 437-444.

SATZ, P., FRIEL, J., and RUDEGEAIR, F. Differential changes in the acquisition of developmental skills in children who later became dyslexic: A three year follow-up. In: D. G. Stein, J. J. Rosen, and N. Butter (Eds.), *Plasticity and Recovery of Function in the Central Nervous System*. New York: Academic Press, 1974.

SAUGUET, J., BENTON, A. L., and HÉCAEN, H. Disturbances of the body schema in relation to language impairment and hemispheric locus of lesion. *Journal of Neurology, Neurosurgery and Psychiatry*, 1971, 34, 496-501.

SCHILDER, P. Fingeragnosie, Fingerapraxie, Fingeraphasie. *Nervenartz*, 1931, 4, 625-629.

SELECKI, B. R. and HERRON, J. T. Disturbances of the verbal body image: A particular syndrome of sensory aphasia. *Journal of Nervous and Mental Disease*, 1965, 141, 42-52.

SPARROW, S. and SATZ, P. Dyslexia, laterality and neuropsychological development. In: D. J. Bakker and P. Satz (Eds.), *Specific Reading Disability*. Rotterdam: University of Rotterdam Press, 1970.

STENGEL, E. Loss of spatial orientation, constructional apraxia and Gerstmann's syndrome. *Journal of Mental Science*, 1944, 90, 753-760.

STONE, F. B. and ROBINSON, D. The effect of response mode on finger localization errors. *Cortex*, 1968, 4, 233-244.

STRAUSS, A. and WERNER, H. Deficiency in the finger schema in relation to arithmetic disability (finger agnosia and acalculia). *American Journal of Orthopsychiatry*, 1938, 8, 719-724.

WAKE, F. R. *Finger Localization in Canadian School Children.* Paper presented at meeting of The Canadian Psychological Association, Ottawa, June 1956.

WAKE, F. R. *Finger Localization Scores in Defective Children.* Paper presented at meeting of The Canadian Psychological Association, Ontario, June 1957.

4

Early Stages in the Perception of Orientation

LILA GHENT BRAINE

A discussion of the development of orientation perception seems particularly appropriate in a volume dedicated to Herbert Birch because the topic, like Birch's interests, encompasses issues both in pathology and in normal development. Brain-injured adults have been described as making orientation errors in the reproduction of shapes (e.g., Royer & Holland, 1975), and children with a variety of different pathologies have also been observed to copy shapes in rotated positions (Bender, 1952). It was these observations from pathology that stimulated my own interest in the problem, and led to the exploration of how orientation perception develops. In the first part of this paper, I shall review briefly some difficulties with current thinking on the development of orientation perception, and shall suggest an alternative way of viewing the problem. The second part will present evidence in support of this alternative view, followed by a short discussion of some of its implications.

TRADITIONAL VIEWS

In his thorough review of perceptual development in 1960, Wohlwill summarized the available material on orientation perception, and con-

The preparation of this paper was supported, in part, by NIH Grant #1 RO1 HD09513-01 to the author. There are many people without whom this work would not have been done, and I would like to thank: a) the toddlers and their parents who so patiently endured our efforts to study orientation perception in very young children; b) the staffs of the Greenwich House Day Care Center and the First Presbyterian Church Nursery School for their gracious cooperation; c) Maryl Gearheart for her sensitive and arduous work with the toddlers, and Patricia Bauer for her splendid work with the 3-year-old children.

cluded that children were unresponsive to the orientation of shapes. During the next 10 years, it became clear that this conclusion was wrong with respect to two kinds of data. First, the idea that young children can recognize disoriented pictures as easily as upright pictures (because children sometimes look at upside-down pictures) has not been supported by direct test; preschool children have even greater difficulty than older children in recognizing non-upright pictures of various sorts (Brooks & Goldstein, 1963; Ghent, 1960; Hunton, 1955). Second, studies using a variety of different methods have found that young children can distinguish and match at least some orientations of shapes (e.g., Ghent, 1961; Gibson et al., 1962; Wohlwill & Wiener, 1964). It is these latter studies that have provided the basis for the current view of orientation perception in children.

Essentially, the prevailing view explains most of the developmental data as due to the low salience of orientation as a discriminative cue for young children, with a gradual learning to attend to orientation as a significant attribute of two-dimensional shapes. In the preschool child's ordinary experience with objects in three-dimensional space, the name or identity of an object does not change with changes in orientation. The orientation of two-dimensional shapes becomes an important attribute of shape as the child begins to draw and to work with letter shapes. From this point of view, any errors that a child makes are due, fundamentally, to deficient attentiveness, either to the relevant dimension or to the appropriate value on the dimension. Despite the seductive plausibility of this line of thought, there are a number of reasons why this view is inadequate.

First, several studies have found that the dimension of orientation can be responded to at a surprisingly young age. Infants between the ages of 3-6 months respond differentially to a figure and its 180° inversion both in a habituation paradigm (Fagan, 1972; McGurk, 1970, 1972a) and in a task measuring affective responsiveness to a face (Watson, 1966). Church (1970) noted that toddlers a little over a year of age go through a period of spontaneously "correcting" the orientation of three-dimensional objects, both realistic and geometric. Some years ago, Hunton (1955) observed that even children as young as 18 months turned non-upright pictures of objects to the upright. These observations on children of 18 months or less make it clear that orientation can be responded to without much opportunity for learning that this dimension is a significant attribute of shapes. (However, all these observations deal with contrasts between upright and non-upright, a point I shall return to later.)

A second line of evidence against a simple attentional hypothesis is that orientation judgments do not change only in accuracy with age, but also in the cues used for making the judgment. Some years ago, Piaget and Inhelder (1956) proposed that young children respond to topological features of objects at an early stage and to Euclidean features at a later stage. This position is supported by Pufall and Shaw's (1973) analysis of the errors made in reproducing the orientation of a toy animal in a spatial array and by Olson's (1970, e.g., p. 183) analysis of the reproduction of the diagonal, which emphasizes the role of topological cues in the performatory domains. Somewhat in the same spirit, Bryant (1974) accounts for many aspects of children's orientation matches on the grounds that children match in terms of whether the items are in-line or out-of-line, or parallel or nonparallel; they do not judge an item in relation to the spatial framework as a whole. Barroso and I (1974) have made a comparable analysis of the effect of alignment on children's orientation matches, suggesting that the very young child matches analogous parts of figures to each other (e.g., tops with tops, thus accounting for many so-called "mirror-image" errors).

As a third point, there is no evidence that a low salience of orientation can explain the pattern of correct responses and errors made by preschool children on orientation tasks, despite the evidence (McGurk, 1972b) that orientation does have low salience for young children. McGurk presented children of 3-5 years with a standard shape and variants that differed from the standard in orientation, in color, in size, or in a combination of these, and the children judged the relative similarity of the variants to the standard. The results were striking—the orientation variants were hardly seen as different from the standard (although these orientation differences had already been shown to be discriminable), whereas the color and size variants were clearly seen as different from the standard. However, the relevance of these findings for understanding children's difficulties with orientation tasks is unclear. In the absence of a comparable study with older people, we do not know whether the low salience of orientation is characteristic of preschool children, or whether it also appears in older age groups who show no difficulty with orientation problems. A second, more serious issue, is that the orientations investigated by McGurk (upright vs. upside down and upright vs. sideways) are the very orientation differences which children attend to in problem-solving tasks without special training (e.g., Rudel & Teuber, 1963). (The orientation differences which children do not attend to spontaneously have yet to be tested with the McGurk paradigm.) Although McGurk's data are usually cited to support the view that the low salience of orientation can account for young children's difficulties with orientation problems, the opposite argument can be made. That is, McGurk's data indicate that a low salience of orientation is irrelevant to the ability to use, as a discriminative cue, the orientation differences between upright and upside down, or between upright and sideways.

A final argument against an attention hypothesis is that simply drawing attention to the dimension of orientation has a rather limited effect on performance. (The discussion here deals only with left-right discrimination since training studies have been directed primarily towards this discrimination.) Training studies can be divided roughly into two kinds: in one, procedures draw attention to the relevant dimension through instructions, demonstrations and feedback, and in the other, procedures focus on the child's encoding of orientation information. In the first group, drawing attention to orientation is associated with a significant increase in correct responses, but not a substantial increase (Cronin, 1967; Koenigsberg, 1973; Mandler & Day, 1975; Vogel, in press, Expt. 2). All the methods used to demonstrate the relevant cue appear to be equally effective in improving performance (Koenigsberg, 1973), as would be expected if attention played a role. The second kind of study provides specific training with the part of the figure that must be processed to make a correct judgment, and it is this kind of training that often results in a dramatic improvement in left-right discrimination (Caldwell & Hall, 1969; Hendrickson & Muehl, 1962; Jeffrey, 1958; Jeffrey, 1966; Vogel, in press). However, these latter studies do much more than draw attention to orientation, as Jeffrey (1958) pointed out: "It should be reiterated that the button pressing response apparently did more than simply call attention to the appropriate part of the stimulus inasmuch as the importance of the direction that the arms were pointing was demonstrated to S several times during the test trials" (p. 273). Although some part of the poor performance on left-right problems may be ascribed to lack of attention to orientation, the greater part of the difficulty lies elsewhere, probably in the initial coding of the orientation information (as will be discussed later).

A new focus developing out of the general rubric of attention refers to a difficulty in memory. Some years ago, Over and Over (1967) pointed out that one aspect of the difficulty in solving a left-right discrimination was in remembering to which particular side a picture was turned. A similar point has been made in more sophisticated ways recently by Vogel (1977). and by Mandler and her colleagues (Mandler & Day, 1975; Stein & Mandler, 1974). A memory difficulty could operate in a number of different ways. Does the child attend too poorly (or inappropriately) to get the relevant information? Is the child unable to code certain kinds of orientation information? Does the information fade rapidly after being encoded? Vogel and Mandler and her colleagues have independently concluded that focusing attention on the appropriate dimension plays a relatively small role in improving memory. Vogel (1977) has proposed that young children have difficulty with both the initial coding and the long-term retention of left-right information; Mandler and Day's discussion (1975) have focused on long-term retention rather than initial coding. Over and Over (1967) have concluded that the ability to retain left-right information was a necessary, but *not* a sufficient, condition for solving problems requiring recognition of the side to which an oblique line was turned. Although these studies have drawn different conclusions with respect to the role of memory in left-right tasks, there is general agreement that any memory deficit observed is not due primarily to inattention to the relevant information.

Before presenting an alternative theoretical view, I want to discuss a distinction between two different kinds of "perception" of orientation. In one kind, the specific orientation of a figure is identified—a figure is encoded as upright, upside down, turned sideways to the left, and so on. In the other kind, a figure is seen as oriented in the same way or a different way from another figure, or from itself on another occasion. These relative judgments can be made on the basis of a variety of cues— for example, judging one figure to be parallel to another (Bryant, 1974) or judging analogous parts (such as the tops) to be in the same location (Barroso & Braine, 1974). Similarly, Stein and Mandler's (1974) finding that the orientation of a diagonal was recognized more frequently when it appeared with other figures than alone suggests that the same-different judgment was made on the basis of the spatial relations among local contours; for example, the space between the top of the diagonal and the adjacent figure may have increased when the orientation of the diagonal changed. At an even more primitive level, a child may see two figures as looking different—a this-way-turned-dog and a that-way-turned-dog, but the perception may be a relatively unitary one in which orientation is not separable as an attribute that can be identified and encoded. It has often been implicitly assumed that the same-different judgment based on relational cues is a "purer" measure of the perception of orientation than identification of the orientation of a single figure. I would argue that the judgments are different, and that relative judgments represent a strategy for making judgments when the child does not yet have the capacity to identify the orientation (or the identification task is very difficult).

The need to distinguish between relative judgments and identification arises primarily in comparing the results obtained for up-down discriminations with those obtained for left-right discriminations (mirror-image obliques being considered as a special case of left-right discrimination). I would argue (for reasons which will become clearer in the next section), that judgments of the orientation of upright and upside-down figures, or of vertical and horizontal lines, are made on the basis of identification, whereas judgments of the orientation of left-right figures are made on a relative basis by young children. This view is helpful in understanding young children's responses to differently oriented lines under different conditions; a study by Over and Over (1967) is a case in point. Orientation perception was evaluated 1) with a detection method, in which one of two comparison items was selected as being oriented in the same way as a simultaneously presented standard, and 2) with a discrimination learning method, in which the child learned which of two items was designated as the correct one. With the detection method, discrimination of both mirror-image obliques and the vertical-horizontal lines was very good, whereas with the discrimination learning method, only the discrimination of the vertical-horizontal lines was at a high level. In the case of the detection method, both absolute and relative judgments of orientation can yield correct responses. For the vertical or horizontal standard, the orientation is identified, and the correct comparison item is selected; for the oblique standard, a relative judgment is made—the standard is judged to be parallel to one of the comparison items—and the correct choice is made. In the discrimination learning condition (with two stimuli) only the absolute judgment yields a correct response. The horizontal and vertical lines are identified, and coded in memory as vertical and horizontal; then the child need only learn which of the two categories is correct. However, relative judgments of the two obliques yield different codes with different spatial arrangements (e.g., as the side of the stimulus cards is changed to balance position), and multiple codings for a single orientation would make learning very difficult.* From this point of view, the same judgments or

---

* Support for this position appears in a study by Celia Fisher, "Children's discrimination of line orientation with simultaneous and successive presentation," reported at the meetings of the Eastern Psychological Association in 1978 at Washington, D.C. Dr. Fisher found that young children could recognize with ease the orientation of an oblique line presented successively when the line appeared in the same location on the card for each trial, but had difficulty in recognizing the orientation of the line when the line was presented in two locations on the card.

processes underlie performance under both detection and learning conditions (contrary to the usual interpretation of these data), whereas different prcesses underlie performance with the vertical-horizontal pair and the oblique pair.

The distinction between orientation judgments that are relative and those that are absolute (i.e., identifications) also helps clarify the effects of alignment of stimuli on performance. Starting with the early work of Sekuler and Rosenblith (1964), a number of studies (Huttenlocher, 1967a, 1967b; Cairns & Steward, 1970) have reported that up-down discriminations are made more readily when the stimuli are side-by-side and left-right discriminations are made more readily when stimuli are one above the other. That is, children tend to make mirror-image errors (mirror-image being defined here as 180° reversals around the axis separating the two figures). However, Barroso and I found (1974) that mirror-image confusion is not the basis for such errors because the same pattern of errors appears when the standard and matching figures consisted of different shapes which could not possibly form mirror-images of each other. Similarly, Bryant (1973) concluded that the difficulty in discriminating left and right oblique lines was independent of whether the lines were exact mirror-images of each other or not. The effects of alignment can be interpreted as due to a strategy of placing analogous parts close to each other, e.g., tops near tops; that is, a relative judgment of orientation is made and not an identification of the orientation of either of the figures.* When the data on alignment effects were first reported, they appeared to challenge the view that left-right identification was more difficult than up-down identification; however, it now seems clear that some testing conditions elicit relative judgments in young children, which may have little relevance to the processes underlying identification of orientation.

STAGES IN THE PROCESSING OF ORIENTATION INFORMATION

Thus far I have argued that an attentional theory of the development of orientation judgments is inadequate, and have pointed to the need to distinguish between identification judgments and judgments of relative orientation. Now I want to present an alternative interpretation of how the ability to identify orientation may develop. In order to give an

---

* This statement must be qualified somewhat. A fine-grained analysis of the Barroso and Braine data (1974) suggested the existence of a bias to place the matching card in the upright orientation. Such a response bias clearly involves an identification, and not simply a relative judgment, of the upright orientation of the single figure on the response card.

understandable account of this view, it is necessary to spend some time considering the possible basis for an identification of orientation that is not the usual framework judgment. Ordinarily, we assume that the identification of orientation involves describing the location of a particular feature—the top—with respect to the spatial framework; a picture of a person is upright when the head is at the top of the page, and so on. However, there is a body of data on judgments of the orientation of *non-representational* shapes that does not fit this assumption.

Some years ago, I found that preschool children gave highly consistent judgments of the upright and non-upright orientations of various geometric shapes (Ghent, 1961). Although most of the shapes were unfamiliar, the young children appeared to judge these geometric shapes as readily as the orientation of familiar, realistic shapes. These results have been replicated in the U.S. (Moeller & Goodnow, 1969; Pick, Klein & Pick, 1966), in Iran (Antonovsky & Ghent, 1964) and in Zambia (Serpell, 1971). As I have suggested elsewhere (Braine, 1978), analogous judgments may appear in adults. Arnheim (1954) reported that college students judge the upright orientation of non-representational art with significant consistency, and experimental studies using geometric shapes of various sorts have found that adults show significant consistency in their judgments of the upright orientation of many geometric shapes (Howard & Templeton, 1966, pp. 295-301). None of these judgments fit the usual definition of the upright being the familiar orientation of the shape, or the orientation in which the top of the shape is at the top of the spatial framework.

Some progress has been made in understanding the basis for the young child's judgments of the orientation of geometric figures (Ghent, 1961). Although the notion of stability is often invoked to explain the judgment, the data do not support this view, since the parts judged (by adults) to be heavier or more stable appeared as often at the top of the figure as at the bottom. Another interpretation sometimes offered is that the shape resembles a realistic object in the orientation called upright, but this view is also contradicted by the data. A substantial amount of evidence indicates that the children's judgments are determined by two characteristics—the presence of a focal* or salient feature

---

* A focal feature can be defined in a principled (nonintuitive and noncircular) way for very simple stimuli as the one differentiating feature in an otherwise homogeneous figure or card. Stimuli designed on the basis of this a priori definition of focal were indeed judged to be upright when the focal feature appeared at the top (Ghent, 1961, Figure 2). By extension, the focal feature for complex figures can be defined functionally—behaviorally—as whatever kind of feature the young child prefers at the top. Further discussion of this issue can be found in Braine (1972, pp. 183-184).

at the top of the shape, and a vertical orientation of the main lines (or long axis) of the shape (Braine, 1972; Ghent, 1961). I proposed that these characteristics determine the uprightness judgment in the following manner (Ghent, 1961). Let us assume, as Hebb proposed some years ago (1949), that young children process the features of a shape in a serial order at some point before identification occurs. Now assume also that this serial ordering does not proceed randomly from one feature to another, but begins with the focal feature and continues in a downwards direction. When a geometric shape is oriented with the focal feature at the top, the orientation of the shape is congruent with the processing mechanism just described, and the child calls the figure upright. That is, the child's judgment of the upright orientation of unfamiliar figures is a judgment of whether the figure is oriented so as to fit with the perceiving mechanism or to conflict with it.* Essentially, when young children look at geometric shapes (at least for many shapes), they see right-looking or wrong-looking shapes.

This proposal can be extended, in principle, to realistic shapes. Since realistic shapes do not have a single focal feature, let us assume that serial processing starts at the top (with respect to retinal cues) and continues in a downwards direction. For realistic figures that have a usual orientation on a page, the parts of the figure are then processed in a particular order, and in the same order on different occasions. A picture is judged as looking "right" or "familiar" when the features are processed in the familiar order. (For indirect evidence supporting these assumptions, see Ghent, 1960 and Braine & Knox, 1975.) An alternative but complementary way of looking at the link between recognition processes and the "looking right" judgment is to focus directly on constructs in memory. Earlier work suggested that representations of mono-oriented figures (i.e., figures with a single typical orientation) are coded in memory in the upright orientation (Braine, 1973). A mismatch between the input and the representation would provide the basis for perceiving the input as looking "wrong" or "unfamiliar"; comparison between the input and the representation would involve a sampling of parts tagged with the same spatial location (presumably as a consequence of the top-downwards order in which the features are processed).

The line of thought developed here proposes that the very young

---

* This interpretation implies that recognition of a form should be facilitated by presentation of the form in the upright orientation under conditions of brief exposure. Recognition of tachistoscopically presented geometric shapes was found to be better in young, preschool children for phenomenally upright forms than for upside-down forms (Ghent & Bernstein, 1961; Braine, 1972).

child makes a judgment of orientation which characterizes a shape as upright or non-upright, turned the "right" way, or turned the "wrong" way. I suggest that this primitive dichotomy constitutes the first stage, in a series of at least three stages, at which orientation information is processed. At this stage a child can distinguish only whether a shape is upright or not; the child cannot distinguish among non-uprights. That is, a child would not be able to discriminate between a figure turned sideways and one turned upside down, or between one figure turned to the left and another turned to the right (although this latter difficulty would not be a specific left-right difficulty). Previous work in this area has always presented the child with a discrimination between upright and upside-down pictures, and when young children made the distinction, it was assumed that the child identified one of the choices as upside down. However, this assumption has never been tested, and some evidence will be presented later to show that it is probably wrong— the young child may have been merely identifying one figure as non-upright. The observations cited earlier on orientation discrimination in infants and toddlers (Church, 1970; Fagan, 1972; Hunton, 1955; Mc-Gurk, 1970, 1972a; Watson, 1966) could be subsumed under the view that the children were identifying the shape as upright or non-upright.

Since uprightness can be identified at the first level, subsequent development occurs through a differentiation of the non-upright category (see Figure 1). At the second level, non-upright figures can be identified as upside down and sideways; this identification can also be made on a

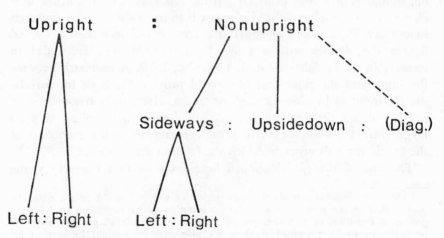

FIGURE 1. Levels of processing of orientation information. From Braine, 1978.

relatively primitive basis. Since the apparent vertical is a salient feature in the young child's response to orientation (Ghent, 1961), upside down is identified as a non-upright that looks vertical, i.e., in which the line joining the top and bottom features of the shape is parallel to the apparent vertical. Similarly, sideways is identified as a non-upright which is perpendicular to the apparent vertical. It is at this stage that the child has a specific difficulty in identifying left-turned from right-turned, in contrast to the first-stage difficulty in distinguishing among non-uprights. One of the untouched problems is the identification of diagonality, and there are two possibilities as to how diagonality is treated at this stage. One possibility is that diagonal figures are identified as non-uprights that are neither upside down nor sideways; another possibility is that diagonals are identified as crooked instances of the vertical.*

At the third level of processing, the leftness and rightness of shapes becomes identifiable: uprights are differentiated into left-turned and right-turned, and shapes tilted 90° or 45° are also differentiated into left-turned and right-turned. Identification of the attribute of turned to the left or turned to the right requires reference to a framework provided either by the child's body or by an external frame of reference. From this point of view, the left-right identification is based on a different mechanism than identifications of upright, upside down and sideways. because the former identification requires the child to code the orientation of the figure with respect to a framework whereas the latter identifications do not require reference to a framework. Although the ability to abstract the attribute of "left-turnedness" or "right-turnedness" appears at the third stage or level, the child at the second developmental level is able to make relative judgments of the sideways orientation of figures (as discussed earlier).

There is a certain face validity to the second and third stages proposed, whether or not the underlying processes are correctly described. We know that identification of turned-to-the-left or to-the-right is a late development; we also know that there is a long period when a young child is perfectly capable of distinguishing upright from upside down and each of these from sideways. The immediate empirical question is whether the first stage or processing level exists, and this issue is ad-

---

* Some findings of Rudel and Teuber (1963) offer support for the latter position. Preschool children found it more difficult to discriminate at 45° oblique line from a vertical line than from a horizontal line. This result would be expected if preschool children saw the oblique line as a crooked vertical, a line belonging in the same category as the vertical line.

dressed in the set of studies to be reported in the remaining part of this paper. Since the first stage is one in which a figure is perceived as looking "right" or looking "wrong," it should be easy to distinguish any upright figure from any non-upright figure, but difficult to distinguish among non-upright figures, such as upside down and sideways. This prediction was examined in three studies with young children.

TRAINING AND GENERALIZATION TASK IN TODDLERS

The first study posed two questions: Can the toddler discriminate upright from non-upright pictures such as upside-down pictures, and if so, can the child continue to pick upside-down pictures when they are paired with other non-upright pictures? The child was initially trained to discriminate between upright and non-upright pictures, with the non-upright pictures always being rewarded. If criterion was reached on the training, the child was tested on a generalization task in which the stimuli consisted of pairs of non-upright pictures (upside down and sideways) to see whether the child could continue to pick the *specific* non-upright that had been rewarded in the original training. Two groups of children were tested by different experimenters using different apparatus, but the results were very similar in the two groups and will be reported together.

Subjects

The children came from well-educated families, recruited on a word-of-mouth basis, and were tested in their homes. The first group comprised three girls and two boys between 22 and 28 months at the beginning of testing; the training problem for all these children was a discrimination between upside down and upright. The second group consisted of three girls and one boy between 24 and 27 months. The training task for two children was a discrimination between sideways and upright and, for the other two children, a discrimination between upside down and upright.

Apparatus

Two different forms of a two-choice apparatus were used. The first consisted of a panel almost perpendicular to the child's line of sight containing two square windows, 10 cm. on a side and separated by 15 cm., which housed the stimuli. The child would push one of the windows, and if the correct choice were made, the window would open and a buzzer would sound. (Other rewards were used, small trinkets or a favored food, when the buzzer appeared to be ineffective.) If the incorrect choice were made, the window remained closed, and the buzzer did not sound. At the end of a trial, curtains were drawn across the windows and new stimuli were inserted; opening of the curtains signalled a new trial.

The other apparatus consisted of a tabletop with a moveable tray, on which two boxes were placed, each 13 cm. on a side and 9 cm. high, separated from each other by 13 cm. The stimuli were placed on the front face of each box, and the reward (trinket or favored food) was placed in the shallow trough underneath each box; the child displaced the box to get the reward. (The apparatus resembled the Wisconsin General Test Apparatus.) The opening and closing of a curtain at the front of the tabletop signalled the beginning and end of each trial.

The stimuli consisted of outline drawings of realistic objects (dog, cat, car, girl, boy, man, flowers, clown, table, chair, sailboat, horse, cow, tricycle, cup, plant, truck, house). The child's ability to identify the pictures was checked (by the mother) before the task was begun, and any pictures that the child could not identify were omitted for that particular child.

Procedure

Training began with trials in which a single non-upright picture, usually the car, was presented in one of the two choice positions in a random order. When the child had followed the single, non-upright picture to a criterion of 8 out of 10 correct trials, the non-upright picture was paired with a blank card to criterion, and then with a different item in the upright orientation until criterion was reached. At this point, the non-upright picture was paired with an identical picture in the upright orientation; although the child had only to continue to respond positively to the same non-upright item, performance was disrupted by the presentation of two identical items, differing only in orientation. If the child did not solve this first problem in a few days, the experimenter tried to teach the child directly what the correct answer was. (For example, the picture of the upright car would be shown outside the apparatus, turned slowly to the non-upright position, and the experimenter would say that the car turned like this makes the window buzz, and that this car—upright—does not.) If the child reached criterion on

the non-upright vs. the upright car, a new pair of pictures was introduced, one non-upright and one upright, until the child reached criterion again. Then new pairs were introduced on each trial, and testing
continued until the child reached criterion.

After the response to the non-upright member of any pair was established, the child's ability to distinguish among non-uprights (upside
down from sideways) was tested. As in the previous trials, a different
pair of pictures was presented on each trial, but now one picture was
upside down and one was sideways (half to the left and half to the
right). The first two trials of each day consisted of non-upright vs.
upright pairs as used in training; then the upside-down vs. sideways
pairs were introduced, and the two different problems were intermingled
randomly. The child continued to be rewarded for picking the specific
non-upright orientation that had been rewarded during training (either
upside down or sideways), with the non-rewarded figure being the only
aspect of the problem that changed. The number of trials run each day
varied considerably, and averaged about 12.

Results and Discussion

During training, neither the problem presented, nor the apparatus
used, appeared to influence performance (in this small group of children). Of the 5 children trained on the upside-down/upright problem
with the window apparatus, three children reached criterion. Of the two
children trained on the upside-down/upright problem with the modified
WGTA, one child reached criterion; of the two trained on the sideways/
upright problem with the modified WGTA, one reached criterion. That
is, about half the toddlers in this narrowly selected group reached criterion on initial training, regardless of sex, problem or method. With the
exception of one child (who learned in a few sessions), 8 to 12 training
sessions were required before criterion was reached. The result of primary
interest here is the performance of the 5 children who reached criterion,
and were given the generalization task. Each child showed more difficulty in discriminating between two non-upright orientations than between one non-upright and one upright (Figure 2); the performance of
each child will be considered in turn.

Child M was performing at 87% correct before the introduction of
the upside-down/sideways problem. On the first day in which both the
sideways and the upright problems were presented, the upside-down
member of the pair was picked 100% of the time when paired with an

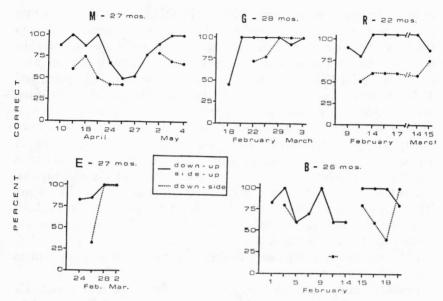

FIGURE 2. Percentage of correct responses by 2-year-old children in the generalization phase of the orientation discrimination task. The solid line indicates responses to upside-down/upright pairs, and the dotted line to upside-down/sideways pairs, for children M, G, R, and E. For child B, the solid line indicates responses to sideways/upright pairs, and the dotted line to sideways/upside-down pairs.

upright member, but the upside-down member was picked only 60% of the time when paired with a sideways member. For the first three sessions, the upside-down/upright pairs were performed with 87-100% accuracy, whereas the upside-down/sideways pairs were performed with 50-75% accuracy. Throughout the testing, M spontaneously said, "Both upside down" to almost every pair of upside-down vs. sideways stimuli; she never said that to pairs of upside-down vs. upright stimuli. M's behavior then deteriorated, and she did not want to continue the task. The upside-down/sideways problem was stopped at that point, and only the upside-down/upright problem was presented until performance improved. After the upside-down/sideways problem was reintroduced, performance was again inferior to that on the upside-down/upright problem. For the days on which both problems were given, 68 of the 77 trials on the upside-down/upright problem were correct, whereas only 34 of 57 trials were correct on the upside-down/sideways problem (Chi-square $= 13.97$, $p < .01$).

Several days after stopping the problem just described, another type of generalization test was done with M. In this case, we asked whether M (trained to pick the upside-down stimulus), would select a sideways stimulus when presented with a choice between a stimulus turned sideways and one turned upright. The same pairs of realistic figures were presented again; 15 trials consisted of upside-down vs. upright pairs, and 15 trials consisted of sideways vs. upright pairs, the two problems being intermingled in a random order. The 30 trials were presented on two separate days, and all responses were rewarded. With the upside-down vs. upright pairs, M selected the upside-down figure in 13 of the 15 trials; with the sideways vs. upright pairs, she selected the sideways figure in 13 of the 15 trials. M did not hesitate on the sideways vs. upright pairs, nor did she give any sign that the problem had changed. The similarity in response to the upside-down and sideways stimuli, both quantitatively and qualitatively, is particularly striking because of the many earlier trials in which the sideways stimuli were never rewarded, yet M spontaneously responded to the sideways stimuli as equivalent to the upside-down ones.

Another child, G, showed very stable performance throughout. He performed at 100% accuracy for almost all the upside-down/upright pairs. However, on the first day in which a sideways stimulus was paired with an upside-down stimulus, he performed at 70% accuracy on the upside-down pairs. (On the first trial with an upside-down/sideways pair, G pushed both windows!) Although there was only a small difference in the proportion of correct responses for the two problems, the data suggest that there was some confusion between the upside-down and sideways stimuli on the first day, followed by very quick learning.

The youngest child, R, showed a very consistent difference between the two problems, with performance on the upside-down/upright problem being almost perfect at the same time as performance on the upside-down/sideways problem was at a chance level. The data shown in Figure 2 were obtained by holding the two stimuli in the experimenter's hands, asking R to point to the one that was upside down or wrong, and rewarding her with a bit of graham cracker for a correct response. This procedure was adopted because R did not reach criterion with the apparatus after much training—R often pushed the window without looking—yet her mother claimed that R could distinguish between upside-down and upright. (The break of almost a month between testing periods was due to two factors—one, efforts to increase the child's interest with new pictures and to teach her the upside-down/sideways problem outside the testing sessions, and two, the fact that the family went on a trip for two weeks.) For the session in which both problems were presented, 32 of 34 trials were correct for the upside-down/upright problem, and only 21 of 34 trials were correct for the upside-down/ sideways problem (Chi-square = 10.35, $p < .01$).

Child E, trained with the upside-down/upright problem on the modified Wisconsin General Test Apparatus (WGTA), was performing at more than 80% correct on the day before the generalization trials began. During the first day of generalization testing, E was 85% correct on the upside-down/upright trials, but only 34% correct on the upside-down/sideways trials. (On the very first trial with an upside-down /sideways pair, she remarked that there were two upside-down pictures this time.) By the next day of testing, E achieved perfect performance on both problems, although with prolonged hesitations on most of the upside-down/sideways pairs. As with child G, the difference in performance on the two problems did not approach statistical significance.

Child B was trained with the sideways/upright problem on the modified WGTA. On the first day of generalization testing, B chose correctly 100% of the sideways/upright pairs and 80% of the sideways/upside-down pairs. On the next testing session, B was restless and reluctant to continue; she chose correctly on 60% of the trials, regardless of type. In an effort to restore B's previous performance, only the sideways/ upright pairs were presented and performance was 70% correct; performance rose to 100% correct on the following testing session (with only the sideways/upright pairs). When both problems (totaling 10 trials) were presented at the next session, performance fell to 60% correct with the sideways/upright and 20% correct on the sideways/upside-down; B refused to do more than five trials on the next test session. On a subsequent day (February 15 of Figure 2), I found that B could be tested by holding the stimulus cards in my hands, asking her to pick the sideways picture and rewarding her for correct responses. During four days of testing, B was correct on 95% of the trials with the sideways/upright pairs, and on 70% of the trials with the sideways/ upside-down pairs (although with perfect performance on the last test day). Combining the data for these four sessions with the other three sessions on which both kinds of stimuli were presented yields 35 trials for each problem, in which 86% of the sideways/upright trials were correct and 63% of the sideways/upside-down trials were correct (Chi-square = 4.79, $p < .05$). This estimate of the difference in performance on the two types of problems is conservative because it excludes those days when only the sideways/upright problem was presented and when B's performance was almost perfect. It is clear that the sideways/

upside-down problem was difficult (and distressing) to B, although she did seem to have solved it eventually.*

The data obtained from the five children who were tested on the generalization task are consistent with the view that toddlers initially identify upside-down and sideways pictures as non-upright, although a distinction between the two orientations can be achieved by at least some toddlers. The failure of almost half the toddlers to master the training task is a result requiring further investigation since there is evidence that much younger children can make discriminative responses to specific instances of upright and non-upright items (Church, 1970; Fagan, 1972; McGurk, 1970, 1972a).

The next task was to assess whether there is evidence for a difficulty in distinguishing among non-uprights in somewhat older subjects. To ask this question, one group of 3-year-old children was presented with the problem of distinguishing upside-down from upright, and another group was required to distinguish upside-down from sideways. For all children, the upside-down stimulus was the rewarded one, and the question was whether learning to select the upside-down stimulus was more difficult in the context of sideways pictures than in the context of upright pictures.

Subjects

The 12 boys and 12 girls came from a daycare center and a morning nursery school, both in the same area of downtown New York. The mean age of the 12 children receiving the upside-down/upright problem was 3:6 years (ranging from 3:4 years to 3:9 years), with half the children coming from each school. The 12 children receiving the upside-down/sideways problem had a mean age of 3:7 years (ranging from 3:3 years to 3:10 years); again, half the children came from each school.

Procedure

The stimulus cards were the same as those used with the toddlers, and the apparatus was the variant of the WGTA already described. On a day before the testing began, each child had a preliminary experi-

---

* B's difficulty in differentiating between sideways and upside down was particularly convincing because of the extra efforts made to facilitate the discrimination. First, B's mother gave her informal training on the problem (with my encouragement), using real objects to demonstrate the difference between the orientations. Second, the trials conducted outside the apparatus were prefaced with the instruction to pick the picture that was turned sideways, providing a consistent reminder of the relevant cue.

ence with the apparatus, and identified the stimulus cards (presented in the upright orientation).

The experimenter told the child that they were going to play a game in which a trinket was going to be hidden under one of the pictures, and the child was to try to find the trinket each time. Throughout the testing, the child was told to look carefully at the pictures, because that was the only way to tell where the prize was hidden. The problem was presented in two sessions of 32 trials each, one week apart. During session 1, the first 16 trials were distributed as follows:

1-4: an upside-down picture was presented alone, with correction trials following errors;

5-8: the same upside-down picture was paired with a blank card;

9-12: the same upside-down picture was paired with either an identical picture in the upright orientation (upside-down/upright group), or in the sideways orientation (upside-down/sideways group);

13-16: a different pair of identical pictures, differing only in orientation, as in trials 9-12.

On trials 17-32, new pairs of figures were introduced on each trial. For session 2, different pairs of pictures were presented on each trial. The side of the rewarded, upside-down stimulus was determined by a Gellerman series and was the same for all children, but the order of the items used was randomized for each child.

Results and Discussion

During the first eight trials (essentially shaping trials in which the same stimuli were presented to all children), both groups performed at a high level (Figure 3). When the problem became one of distinguishing between two orientations of the same figure, the two groups performed very differently. The children presented with the upside-down/upright discrimination learned the problem quickly, whereas most of the children given the upside-down/sideways problem never solved the problem at all (Figure 3). Two children in the upside-down/sideways group refused to continue after trial 48, accusing the experimenter of always changing the one that was right. Considering 11 correct responses on the last 12 trials as the criterion for solving the problem, 11 of the 12 children reached criterion on the upside-down/upright problem, whereas only 2 of the 12 children reached criterion with the upside-down/sideways problem. On the upside-down/upright problem, most of the children reached this criterion during the first session, and continued to

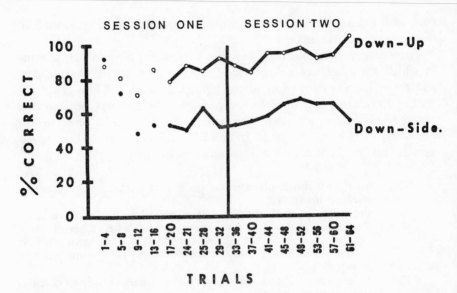

FIGURE 3. Percentage of correct responses to different problems by children of 3 years. From Braine, 1978.

perform at criterion level during the second session. There were no sex differences in performance.

The ease of solving the upside-down/upright problem indicates that this distinction matched the child's spontaneous categorization of the stimuli, in contrast to the upside-down/sideways distinction, which was a difficult categorization to train. An analogous study is in progress on the learning to select sideways stimuli in the context of either upright or upside-down stimuli; as predicted, the sideways/upright problem appears to be much easier to solve than the sideways/upside-down problem. The discrimination learning data from the children of 2 and 3 years strongly support the view that the first identification of orientation is of upright and non-upright shapes.

MATCHING TASK

Another way of getting information on the child's perception of orientation is to ask the child to match orientations (although, as pointed out earlier, this method may not always elicit identifications of orientation). There are two aspects of such data that can be examined—the number of errors made for each standard (upright, upside-down, etc.), and the *kind* of errors made for the different standards, which would provide a rough index of the equivalences existing for the child. Some years ago, I investigated the child's ability to match the orientation of standards presented upright, upside down, turned 90° left, and turned 90° right. At the time, I analyzed the results in terms of the number of errors made for the vertical dimension (the upright and the upside-down standards) and the errors made for the horizontal dimension (the left and right standards), which was the traditional way of treating such data. However, if the major orientation categories used by the young child are upright and non-upright, a different analysis suggests itself. The vertical errors should be separated into errors made when the standard was upright and errors made when the standard was upside-down, with the expectation that the upside-down standard would be matched to other non-uprights (figures turned to the right or the left) more often than the upright standard would be matched to such figures.

Subjects

The children were tested at a child care center in a low-income housing project in New York. Data were analyzed on 12 boys and 12 girls, with a mean age of 4:1 years and a range of 3:1 to 4:5 years.

Procedure

The stimulus was a V-shaped figure which was judged to be upright by young children when oriented with the angle at the top (Ghent, 1961). The "V" was presented in any one of four orientations; the child responded by selecting an item from a multiple-choice of four items, one in each of the four possible orientations. Each of the four orientations was presented three times, and two different multiple-choice arrays were presented. Two fixed, random orders of presentation were used. For the first condition (recall), the standard figure was presented for 1-2 seconds, removed, and then the multiple-choice was made available. The series was then repeated under a direct matching condition in which the child held the standard, and placed it directly on top of the matching figure in the multiple-choice. Throughout both conditions, the experimenter and the child sat side by side, and the experimenter presented the standards and the set of multiple-choices to the child one at a time. The three trials with the phenomenally upright standard and the three trials with the upside-down standard were selected for the present analysis. (The number of available trials was small because the task was not set up for this kind of analysis.) These six trials were drawn from the recall condition for 15 children, and from the matching condition for 9 children, depending on which condition yielded more errors, but gave performance that was above chance.

Results and Discussion

The question asked of the data was whether the upside-down and upright standards elicited different kinds of errors; specifically, whether more 90° errors were made in response to the upside-down standard. As can be seen in Figure 4, approximately the same number of 180° errors were made to both standards, but more 90° errors were made when the standard was upside down than when it was upright $(t = 3.41, p < .01)$. These confusions suggest that the young child categorized the upside-down standards as non-upright, and then selected a non-upright from the multiple-choice, sometimes matching the long axis of the standard (correct response) and sometimes not (90° error).

However, there was some evidence that all non-uprights were not equivalent. After doing the analyses described above, errors made with the left and right standards were analyzed in a similar way, with the

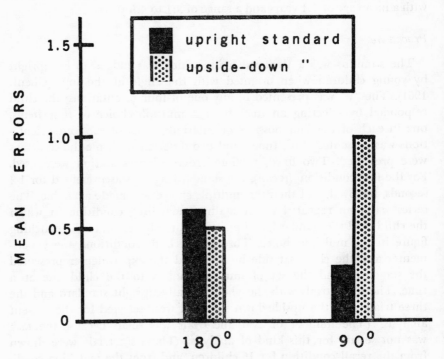

FIGURE 4. Analysis of errors made to different standards in a matching task.

prediction that errors to these standards should include more upside-down items than upright items. There was a slight difference in the predicted direction, but the left and right-standards were more likely to be confused with each other than with either the upright or the upside-down figures. Although these data might be specific to the figure used (a special effect of the points of the "V"), it is more likely that the data reflect an asymmetry in the order in which the members of the non-upright category are differentiated.* It is not surprising that some differentiation of the non-upright may have occurred in this group with a mean age of 4:1 years; new work with a matching task is in progress to investigate further the equivalences existing among non-uprights in children between 3:0 and 4:5 years.

Concluding Discussion

The results of these studies with children from 2 to 4 years support the view that shapes are identified as upright or non-upright at an early stage in development. As described in the first part of this paper, subsequent development involves the differentiation of the non-upright category in at least two steps. The second stage permits a distinction to be made between upside down and sideways (although the matching task suggests that this development may proceed asymmetrically), and the third stage permits shapes to be identified as turned to the left or turned to the right. Between the second and the third stage, the child presumably makes a variety of relative judgments (as discussed in the first part of this paper), by comparing some features of a figure with some features of another figure or with some feature in the environment (e.g., the edge of a card). These stages can be construed both as a sequence of developmental periods, and as different levels at which orientation information is processed at all ages. That is, I am suggesting that adults proceed through stages or levels in making orientation judgments, and that the hierarchy of levels replicates the sequence of developmental stages. The difference between children and adults is that,

---

* An asymmetrical differentiation could proceed in the following way. The first test applied to a non-upright standard is whether the line joining the top and bottom features of the figure is horizontal (parallel to the ground). If the answer is "yes," the standard is encoded as non-upright with a horizontal tag, and the choices conform to that description. If the answer is "no," the upside-down standard is encoded as non-upright without any additional tag, and the choices would be of any non-upright. The next developmental step would involve applying the test of whether the line joining the top and bottom features of the figure is vertical, and at this point, upside-down and sideways standards would be equally identifiable.

since the levels develop with age, only a limited number of levels is available to the young child.

Some recent studies of reaction time in adults are consistent with the view that adults process orientation information at several levels. In one set of studies (Braine & Relyea, unpublished), the question asked of adults was similar to that asked of children in the preceding studies; that is, does it take longer to identify the specific orientation of a non-upright figure in the context of other non-upright items than in the context of upright items? As predicted from the previous findings with children, adults took significantly longer to identify upside-down items presented in a block of trials containing both upside-down and sideways items than in a block of trials containing upside-down and upright items. Analogously, adults took longer to identify sideways items presented in a block of trials with upside-down items than in a block with upright items. Clearly adults processed orientation information from upside-down (or sideways) figures at a lower level, or more quickly, in the context of upright figures (level 1 of the proposed theory) than in the context of other non-upright figures (level 2). Another group of reaction-time studies in adults investigated discrimination of mirror-image stimuli, usually left-right pairs (Sekuler & Houlihan, 1968; Staller & Sekuler, 1976; Wolff, 1971). In general, left-right judgments required more time when the shapes were places to form "mirror-images"* of each other than when the placements did not form "mirror-images," a result which is similar to the findings on errors made by young children. However, the ingenious analysis of Staller and Sekuler (1976) indicated that "mirror-image" discriminations were not inherently difficult for either adults or children, but that "mirror-image" pairs tended to be perceived as turned the same way (inwards or outwards), and that additional processing was required to judge them as turned in different ways (towards different sides). The results of the two groups of reaction-time studies imply that adults' orientation judgments, although almost always correct, require different amounts of cognitive activity under different conditions, and further, that these different levels of processing appear to parallel developmental progress.

The view that orientation information may be processed at different levels in the adult provides a basis for understanding some anomalous

---

* "Mirror-image" is placed in quotation marks to indicate that high error rates occur with certain stimulus placements (in children) even when the stimuli do not form mirror-images of each other (Barroso & Braine, 1974; Bryant, 1973). The term is used to indicate the placements that yield mirror-images (with respect to the axis separating the two figures) when the stimuli are identical shapes.

orientation judgments made by adults. In discussing the uprightness judgments of geometric shapes made by young children (in the earlier part of this paper), I pointed out that adults also give consistent judgments of the uprightness of a wide range of nonrepresentational patterns, ranging from abstract art to randomly generated shapes. Such judgments are difficult to understand if one assumes that adults use a single basis for making orientation judgments, one that describes the location of the top feature (of the shape) with respect to the spatial framework. However, if orientation judgments are made at different levels by adults, judgment of an abstract shape can be seen as the "looks right" judgment, based on coding processes, as proposed for young children. As discussed elsewhere (Braine & Knox, 1975), Kohler (1940, pp. 32-33) also pointed out that adults may make an orientation judgment in which a figure is described as "looking familiar" (as when one looks at an upside-down face with one's head between one's legs).

Perhaps the most provocative implication of the line of thought developed here is the light it throws on the problem raised in the introduction—the orientation errors made in the reproduction of shapes. There is a relatively large literature showing that a pattern may be reproduced with the shape relatively correct, but not the orientation; such errors have been reported for normal young children (Eldred, 1973; Fabian, 1945), non-literate adults (Shapiro, 1952) and brain-injured adults and children (Bender, 1952; Royer & Holland, 1975). In general, rotational errors have been interpreted as errors of space perception, or as evidence for an unresponsiveness to space, but these observations can be interpreted in another way. Assume that some of the geometric shapes to be copied are presented in a phenomenally non-upright orientation rather than a neutral orientation. Both children and adults would perceive the shape as non-upright (level 1), and, under some circumstances, reproduce the shape in the apparent upright. This interpretation predicts first, that rotations would not be random (as implied by the error hypothesis), but to positions that are phenomenally upright, and second, that rotations should disappear when shapes presented for copying are in the upright orientation. The available data provide support for both predictions.

In recent years, a number of studies have pointed out that rotations are not random. Schack and I investigated the rotations produced by schizophrenic and handicapped children on the Bender-Gestalt, and (for the few figures which could be said to have an apparent upright) found that almost all of the rotations were to the predicted upright (Braine, 1973). In an analysis of the rotations made by brain-injured adults,

Shapiro (e.g., 1952) concluded that rotations were to positions in which the main lines of the figures were vertical, and the figures were bilaterally symmetrical about the vertical axis. Similarly, Fabian (1945) described the rotations made by normal young children as systematic shifts to the vertical. Finally, cross-cultural work by Deregowski (1972) and by Serpell (1971) indicates that rotations are not random; Deregowski proposed that rotated figures are characterized by vertical symmetry and stability. However, vertical symmetry is an inadequate description of many rotations (Braine, 1973); a more accurate description is that rotations are shifts to positions in which the figures are phenomenally upright.

There is very little material on the question of whether rotations disappear when the standard shapes are presented in the apparent upright. The only comprehensive study is an investigation of normal children of 4 and 5 years in which Eldred (1973) found that there were virtually no rotations in the copying of phenomenally upright geometric standards, in contrast to the considerable number of rotations appearing in the copies of upside-down standards. Eldred's study clearly reveals the inadequacy of the hypothesis that rotations are to vertical symmetry, because both the upright and the upside-down standards were presented with the long axis vertical and with symmetry about the vertical axis, yet rotations were elicited by the upside-down standards. In a dissertation in progress, Pamela Perkins is finding that rotations made by children with learning disabilities also disappear when the figures are presented for copying in the phenomenally upright orientation. Data are needed from adult groups who tend to make rotations (such as brain-injured or illiterate people) to see if their errors disappear when upright standards are presented.

Although Shapiro (1952) found that the rotations made by illiterate adults were similar to those made by brain-injured adults, the line of thought developed here suggests that the reasons for reproducing a shape in the apparent upright may be different in the two groups. The illiterate adults may only need some exposure to the task and feedback concerning the expected behavior in order to copy the form in the orientation presented, whereas the brain-injured person may be unable to process the information at a higher level.

At this point, we have come full circle, having started with the observation that both adults and children with brain-injury rotate shapes, and proceeding through an analysis of the normal development of orientation perception, we end with a new way of looking at the data from pathology. The point of view developed here suggests that neither children nor patients are adequately described as making orientation *errors* on various tasks. Rather, most errors are seen as based on particular kinds of orientation judgments, judgments which derive from different levels in the processing of orientation information. Since the levels correspond to stages in the development of orientation perception, the proposals provide a theoretical basis for understanding the development of orientation perception and some of the similarities observed between children and adults.

REFERENCES

ANTONOVSKY, H. F. and GHENT, L. Cross-cultural consistency of children's preferences for the orientation of figures. *American Journal of Psychology,* 1964, 77, 295-297.

ARNHEIM, R. *Art and Visual Perception.* Los Angeles: University of California Press, 1954.

BARROSO, F. and BRAINE, L. GHENT. "Mirror-image" errors without mirror-image stimuli. *Journal of Experimental Child Psychology,* 1974, 18, 213-225.

BENDER, L. *Child Psychiatric Techniques.* Springfield: Thomas, 1952.

BRAINE, L. GHENT. A developmental analysis of the effect of stimulus orientation on recognition. *American Journal of Psychology,* 1972, 85, 157-187.

BRAINE, L. GHENT. Perceiving and copying the orientation of geometric shapes. *Journal of Research and Development in Education,* 1973, 6, 44-55.

BRAINE, L. GHENT. A new slant on orientation perception. *American Psychologist,* 1978, 33, 10-20.

BRAINE, L. GHENT and KNOX, C. Children's orientation judgments: Retinally or environmentally determined? *Perception and Psychophysics,* 1975, 17, 473-479.

BROOKS, R. M. and GOLDSTEIN, A. G. Recognition by children of inverted photographs of faces. *Child Development,* 1963, 34, 1033-1040.

BRYANT, P. E. Discrimination of mirror-images by young children. *Journal of Comparative and Physiological Psychology,* 1973, 82, 415-425.

BRYANT, P. E. *Perception and Understanding in Young Children.* New York: Basic Books, 1974.

CAIRNS, N. U. and STEWARD, M. S. Young children's orientation of letters as a function of axis of symmetry and stimulus alignment. *Child Development,* 1970, 41, 993-1002.

CALDWELL, E. C. and HALL, V. C. The influence of concept training on letter discrimination. *Child Development,* 1969, 40, 63-72.

CHURCH, J. Techniques for the differential study of cognition in early childhood. In: J. Hellmuth (Ed.), *Cognitive Studies,* Vol. 1. New York: Brunner/Mazel, 1970.

CRONIN, V. Mirror-image reversal discrimination in kindergarten and first-grade children. *Journal of Experimental Child Psychology,* 1967, 5, 577-585.

DEREGOWSKI, J. B. Reproduction of orientation of Kohs-type figures: A cross-cultural study. *British Journal of Psychology,* 1972, 63, 283-296.

ELDRED, C. A. Judgments of right-side-up and figure rotation by young children. *Child Development,* 1973, 44, 395-399.

FABIAN, A. A. Vertical rotation in visual-motor performance—its relationship to reading reversals. *Journal of Educational Psychology,* 1945, 36, 129-154.

FAGAN, J. Infant's recognition memory for faces. *Journal of Experimental Child Psychology,* 1972, 14, 453-476.

GHENT, L. Recognition by children of realistic figures presented in various orientations. *Canadian Journal of Psychology,* 1960, 14, 249-256.

GHENT, L. Form and its orientation: A child's-eye view. *American Journal of Psychology*, 1961, 74, 177-190.

GHENT, L. and BERNSTEIN, L. Influence of the orientation of geometric forms on their recognition by children. *Perceptual and Motor Skills*, 1961, 12, 95-101.

GIBSON, E. J., GIBSON, J. J., PICK, A. D., and OSSER, H. A developmental study of the discrimination of letter-like forms. *Journal of Comparative and Physiological Psychology*, 1962, 55, 897-906.

HEBB, D. O. *The Organization of Behavior.* New York: Wiley, 1949.

HENDRICKSON, L. H. and MUEHL, S. The effect of attention and motor response training on learning to discriminate b and d in kindergarten children. *Journal of Educational Psychology*, 1962, 53, 236-241.

HOWARD, I. P. and TEMPLETON, W. B. *Human Spatial Orientation.* New York: Wiley & Sons, 1966.

HUNTON, V. D. The recognition of inverted pictures by children. *Journal of Genetic Psychology*, 1955, 86, 281-288.

HUTTENLOCHER, J. Discrimination of figure orientation: Effects of relative position. *Journal of Comparative and Physiological Psychology*, 1967a, 63, 359-361.

HUTTENLOCHER, J. Children's ability to order and orient objects. *Child Development*, 1967b, 38, 1169-1176.

JEFFREY, W. E. Variables in early discrimination learning: Motor responses in the training of a left-right discrimination. *Child Development*, 1958, 28, 268-275.

JEFFREY, W. E. Discrimination of oblique lines by children. *Journal of Comparative and Physiological Psychology*, 1966, 62, 154-156.

KOENIGSBERG, R. S. An evaluation of visual versus sensorimotor methods of improving orientation discrimination of letter reversals of preschool children. *Child Development*, 1973, 44, 764-769.

KOHLER, W. *Dynamics in Psychology.* New York: Liveright, 1940.

MANDLER, J. M. and DAY, J. Memory for orientation of forms as a function of their meaningfulness and complexity. *Journal of Experimental Child Psychology*, 1975, 20, 430-443.

McGURK, H. The role of object orientation in infant perception. *Journal of Experimental Child Psychology*, 1970, 9, 363-373.

McGURK, H. Infant discrimination of orientation. *Journal of Experimental Child Psychology*, 1972a, 14, 151-164.

McGURK, H. The salience of orientation in young children's perception of form. *Child Development*, 1972b, 43, 1047-1052.

MOELLER, C. E. and GOODNOW, J. J. Orientations called "Right-side UP": Effects of stimulus alignment. *Psychonomic Science*, 1969, 16, 213-215.

OLSON, D. R. *Cognitive Development: The Child's Acquisition of Diagonality.* New York: Academic Press, 1970.

OVER, R. and OVER, J. Detection and recognition of mirror-image obliques by young children. *Journal of Comparative and Physiological Psychology*, 1967, 64, 467-470.

PIAGET, J. and INHELDER, B. *The Child's Conception of Space.* London: Routledge & Kegan Paul, 1956.

PICK, H. L., JR., KLEIN, R. E., and PICK, A. D. Visual and tactual identification of form orientation. *Journal of Experimental Child Psychology*, 1966, 4, 391-397.

PUFALL, P. B. and SHAW, R. E. Analysis of the development of children's spatial reference systems. *Cognitive Psychology*, 1973, 5, 151-175.

ROYER, F. L. and HOLLAND, T. R. Rotational transformation of visual figures as a clinical phenomenon. *Psychological Bulletin*, 1975, 82, 843-868.

RUDEL, R. G. and TEUBER, H. L. Discrimination of direction of line in children. *Journal of Comparative and Physiological Psychology*, 1963, 56, 892-898.

SEKULER, R. and HOULIHAN, K. Discrimination of mirror-images: Choice time analysis of human adult performance. *Quarterly Journal of Experimental Psychology*, 1968, 20, 204-207.

SEKULER, R. W. and ROSENBLITH, J. F. Discrimination of direction of line and the effect of stimulus alignment. *Psychonomic Science*, 1964, 1, 143-144.

SERPELL, R. Preference for specific orientation of abstract shapes among Zambian children. *Journal of Cross-Cultural Psychology*, 1971, 2, 225-239.

SHAPIRO, M. B. Experimental studies of a perceptual anomaly. II. Confirmatory and explanatory experiments. *Journal of Mental Science*, 1952, 97, 605-617.

STALLER, J. and SEKULER, R. Mirror-image confusion in adults and children. *American Journal of Psychology*, 1976, 89, 253-268.

STEIN, N. L. and MANDLER, J. M. Children's recognition of geometric figures. *Child Development*, 1974, 45, 604-615.

VOGEL, J. M. The development of recognition memory for the left-right orientation of pictures. *Child Development*, 1977, 48, 1532-1543.

WATSON, J. S. Perception of object orientation in infants. *Merrill-Palmer Quarterly of Behavior and Development*, 1966, 12, 73-94.

WOHLWILL, J. F. Developmental studies of perception. *Psychological Bulletin*, 1960, 57, 249-288.

WOHLWILL, J. F. and WIENER, M. Discrimination of form orientation in young children. *Child Development*, 1964, 35, 1113-1125.

WOLFF, P. Mirror-image confusability in adults. *Journal of Experimental Psychology*, 1971, 91, 268-272.

5

Perceptual Asymmetries and Reading Proficiency

DIRK J. BAKKER

Traditionally, there has been much interest in the mechanisms subserving motor and perceptual asymmetries. These asymmetries appear to be closely related to hemispheric asymmetry of function (Mountcastle, 1962; Dimond & Beaumont, 1974). Kimura (1961) demonstrated that subjects with left or right hemispheric control of speech show right and left preference for spoken digits, respectively. Thus, the hemisphere which primarily mediates speech is a major determinant of contralateral ear advantage for verbal stimuli. Moreover, it may be that an increment in ear advantage reflects an increment in hemispheric asymmetry of function.

Cerebral lateralization is often considered prerequisite for the normal development of motor and cognitive functions (Orton, 1966; Satz & Sparrow, 1970). Hence, research workers, including Birch, have been interested in the relations between lateral asymmetry and a variety of language functions. Good evidence for functional lateralization in early childhood exists (e.g., Turkewitz, Moreau, & Birch, 1968; Turkewitz, Moreau, Davis, & Birch, 1969). In addition, Belmont and Birch (1963) mapped the development of hand, eye and foot preference in normal children, and later investigated relationships between lateral preferences and reading proficiency (Belmont & Birch, 1965).

Acknowledgments. I would like to thank Dr. Piet Reitsma who was willing to share his insights on visual asymmetries with me, and Dr. Mini den Hartog who critically read the manuscript. Part of the present author's research described in this chapter was supported by a grant from the Netherlands Organization for the Advancement of Pure Research (Z.W.O.).

This chapter deals only with laterality in perception. The aim is to review recent knowledge about the development of auditory and visual asymmetry in relation to reading proficiency.

Perceptual asymmetry may manifest itself subsequent to stimulation of the right and left sensory surfaces. Information presented to the right side may be perceived, retained and recalled better or worse than similar information presented to the left side. Apparently, which side is most proficient depends on the nature of the information. For example, it is generally accepted that verbal stimuli presented to the right side are more proficiently processed than verbal stimuli presented to the left side. The reverse holds for nonverbal stimuli. For example, digits spoken to the right ear are usually better recalled than digits spoken to the left ear (Kimura, 1967). But melodies played to the left ear are better recognized than melodies played to the right ear (Kimura, 1967). Similarly, digits perceived in the right visual half-field are generally better recalled than digits successively perceived in the left field (White, 1969). On the other hand, pictures of faces are best recognized if presented in the left visual half-field (Rizzolatti, Umiltà & Berlucchi, 1971).

Clearly, the terms verbal and nonverbal are global concepts and it is possible that the reported right-left differences in processing verbal and nonverbal inputs are based upon "inadvertent and uncontrolled differences at a simpler level" (Karp & Birch, 1969, p. 480). These authors, for example, found that, in measuring reaction times to spoken words, there was a right ear advantage for "jump" but not for "run." The consonants of these words differ both in number and in distinctive features: "jump" has a final stop consonant whereas "run" has no stops at all. Moreover, right ear advantage can be demonstrated more easily for consonants than for vowels (Shankweiler & Studdert-Kennedy, 1967; Studdert-Kennedy & Shankweiler, 1970), for stop consonants and fricatives than for nasals (Blumstein, 1974) and for pairs of consonants differing in two features (e.g., voice and place) than for pairs differing in only one feature (Shankweiler & Studdert-Kennedy, 1967; Morais & Darwin, 1974). Spellacy (1969) demonstrated left ear advantage for melodies but not for timbre, frequency patterns and temporal patterns. But the evidence is not consistent for temporal patterns, and Bakker (1967, 1968), unlike Spellacy, found left ear advantage in the recall of nonverbal temporal patterns. Finally, Doehring (1972) found the left ear to be more accurate in the discrimination of intensity variations in tonal sequences but not in frequency variations. It can be concluded from all of this that the nature and degree of perceptual asymmetry depend upon the various components of the sounds one listens to. Moreover, the reported research has clearly demonstrated that listening and visual half-field techniques are effective means for investigating the problem of asymmetry.

AUDITORY ASYMMETRY AND READING PROFICIENCY

It is reasonable to predict a relation between ear asymmetry and reading proficiency since both reading and processing of auditorially presented verbal stimuli are considered to be controlled by the language hemisphere. If reading retardation is caused by a lag in the cerebral lateralization of language one would expect deficient reading to be associated with atypical asymmetries (Satz & Sparrow, 1970; Satz & Van Nostrand, 1973). To test just such a hypothesis Sparrow and Satz (1970) presented 9- to 12-year-old normal and reading-retarded children pairs of digits simultaneously, one digit to the right ear and one to the left (i.e., dichotic stimulation). The reading-retarded children showed left ear advantage more frequently than the normals. This was confirmed in subsequent investigations (Satz & Van Nostrand, 1973; Satz, Rardin & Ross, 1971). Similar atypical ear advantage in older retarded readers has been reported by Bakker (1969), Zurif and Carson (1970), Witelson and Rabinovitch (1972) and more recently by Leong (1976) and Thomson (1976). All these findings support Satz and Sparrow's original hypothesis predicting less right ear advantage in older retarded than in older normal readers. Basic to the hypothesis is their theory that hemispheric specialization for language, though established around puberty in normal readers, is still incomplete in retarded readers. Moreover, at younger ages language will be more bilaterally represented in both normal and retarded readers. As a consequence, according to the hypothesis, language laterality tests will not differentiate between normal and retarded groups at younger ages. It would follow that patterns of ear asymmetry in young normal and retarded readers will not differ. Indeed, the results of investigations by Satz and his colleagues (Satz & Van Nostrand, 1973; Satz, Rardin & Ross, 1971) support these expectations.

However, one may question whether the failure of ear asymmetry to distinguish normal from retarded readers at early stages is due to the symmetrical representation of language in the brains of such children. If language functions are, in fact, bilaterally controlled at the beginning of the school period and unilaterally at the end of the school period, one might expect ear asymmetry to increase with age as a reflection of the developing lateralization during that period. The results of a few studies support this expectation (Bryden, 1973; Satz, Bakker, Teunissen, Goebel & Van der Vlugt, 1975). Satz et al., in presenting digit pairs to normal

5- to 11-year-old children, found that right ear advantage increased with age. Bryden presented normal 6- to 14-year-old children consonant-vowel syllables, and, like Satz et al., found that ear asymmetry increased with age.

However, most studies suggest an early onset of auditory asymmetry followed by a leveling off. Kimura (1963) and Knox and Kimura (1970) administered dichotic digit tasks to normal children 4 to 8 years old. The youngest subjects showed right ear advantage whereas the older subjects did not. Geffner and Hochberg (1971) and Geffner and Dorman (1976) demonstrated right ear superiority for verbal inputs in 4-year-olds, Nagafuchi (1970) and Ingram (1975) reported the same in 3-year-olds. The previously described expected increase in the magnitude of ear asymmetry with age did not occur in these studies. Similar results were obtained by Berlin, Hughes, Lowe-Bell and Berlin (1973). They presented consonant-vowel nonsense syllables to 5- to 13-year-old children and demonstrated right ear advantage across ages.

Van Duyne and Bakker (1976) recently reported ear asymmetry in the study of semantic coding strategies. Word strings of four different taxonomic categories and interpolated digit series were presented to the right and left ear successively (i.e., monaural stimulation). Word and digit recall was analyzed in relation to age, sex and ear receiving input. Girls showed stronger right ear advantage than boys. However, no age by ear interactions were demonstrated.

The preliminary results of a recent investigation that we carried out in collaboration with H. Van der Vlugt at the University of Leyden are pertinent to the problem of the onset and development of auditory asymmetry. Two hundred and fifty children consisting of 25 boys and 25 girls from the kindergarten, first, second, third and fifth grades participated in the project. The primary aim of the study was to establish the reliability of ear asymmetry measures at different levels of task complexity, and the subjects were therefore tested twice with two pairs of digits, then three pairs, and then four pairs. A sex effect in the development of ear asymmetry seems probable; the magnitude of the between-ear differences on all tests and retests increases up to grade 2 in girls and up to grade 3 in boys, and decreases at higher grades. The results (see Figure 1) suggest a non-linear relationship between age and asymmetry. This finding is in agreement with studies cited earlier which reported a leveling off or decrease in magnitude following the onset of asymmetry.

It will be recalled that these findings contrast with those of Satz et al. (1975) who found ear asymmetry increased with age. Porter and Berlin (1975), in discussing this disagreement in results, suggested that inter-

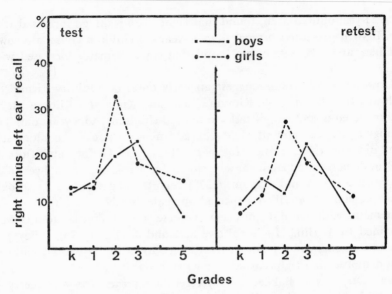

FIGURE 1: Mean right minus left ear differences for test and retest, by grade and sex, across complexity.

pretations regarding the development of auditory asymmetry will depend upon the processes that are tapped by the listening tasks. If reading-retarded children do, in fact, lag in the hemispheric specialization of function (Satz & Sparrow, 1970), one would certainly expect listening tasks which tap early lateralized aspects of language to be appropriate in differentiating between the ear asymmetries of young normal and young retarded readers. Thus, the failure of Satz et al. (Satz & Van Nostrand, 1973; Satz, Rardin & Ross, 1971) to show atypical between-ear differences in young dyslexics may simply indicate that their listening tasks were inadequate for the purpose of demonstrating early language lateralization.

However, a quite different explanation may be given. It seems reasonable to expect that the asymmetry-reading relationship depends not only on the processes tapped by the listening task but also on the nature of the learning-to-read process as well. The nature of both spoken and written language may change markedly during development. Belmont (1974) recently listed the numerous perceptual operations involved in early reading. In discussing the differences between early and fluent reading, Smith (1971) states that the novice reader crosses the bridge between surface structure and meaning from the side of the surface structure and the fluent reader from the meaning side. Whereas the beginning reader "must deduce meaning from surface structure" the fluent reader is "merely sampling the visual information to confirm his expectations" (Smith, 1971, p. 221). In view of these important qualitative differences between early and fluent reading it seems most unlikely that the same cerebral processes subserve both kinds of reading.

The cardinal question at this point is: What kind of relationship between ear asymmetry and reading ability can be expected in early stages of the learning-to-read process? Satz's model (Satz & Sparrow, 1970) predicts no relation at all because language is thought to be represented bilaterally in the brain at this stage of development. However, as has been stated, this theory is at variance with recent evidence suggesting early lateralization of language functions. In attempting to clarify the issue one should consider that a child entering the elementary school has had a great deal of experience with the processing of both language and visual form percepts. He is then required to "learn a complicated, arbitrarily organized system of visual signs and symbols which must become intimately associated with a previously learned auditory-vocal language system according to a rigidly prescribed and sometimes contradictory set of rules" (Belmont, 1974, p. 535).

Experimental work reviewed by Masland (1970) strongly suggests that such associations are much easier to make within one hemisphere than between the two hemispheres. Therefore, if the child had visual-form and auditory-language perception primarily controlled in the same hemisphere, this would be an advantage, especially in early stages of the learning-to-read process. Thus, young children whose language ability is mediated in the right hemisphere may be proficient readers since, as argued by Masland (1970), visual-spatial perception must be concentrated in the right hemisphere as well. However, in advanced reading, since syntactic and semantic operations instead of perceptual skills are required, and since these linguistic operations are probably mediated in the left hemisphere, then it is logical to expect proficient reading at older ages to be associated only with left hemispheric control of language.

The present theory, which predicts different laterality-reading relationships at different stages of the learning-to-read process, is substantially supported by the results of a series of investigations in our laboratory. Initial experiments with 7- to 13-year-old normal and reading-retarded children showed that above average reading proficiency was associated with large ear asymmetries in the older subjects and smaller ear asymmetries in the younger subjects (Bakker, Smink & Reitsma, 1973; Bakker, 1973). This suggests that advanced reading flourishes in the presence of a strong lateralization of receptive language, and that early reading is accompanied by a more moderate lateralization of that function. However, no inferences were made regarding the relation between *side* of lateral preference and reading proficiency since ear asymmetry was analyzed only in terms of *absolute* between-ear differences.

This limitation was overcome in subsequent investigations (Bakker, Teunissen, & Bosch, 1976) in which digit pairs were presented dichotically to normal third grade boys and girls. In addition, the subjects were administered a standard word naming test and a masked word naming test with partially sifted out letters. The sifting out was done to increase perceptual complexity which, in turn, may have forced an increased dependency upon the right hemisphere. Ear asymmetry was expressed in terms of the proportion of total information processed by the left ear. Regression analyses disclosed linear relations between ear asymmetry and reading proficiency in girls and non-linear relations in boys (Figure 2).

The results suggest that proficient reading in third grade girls is associated with left hemispheric language control, whereas in boys it is asso-

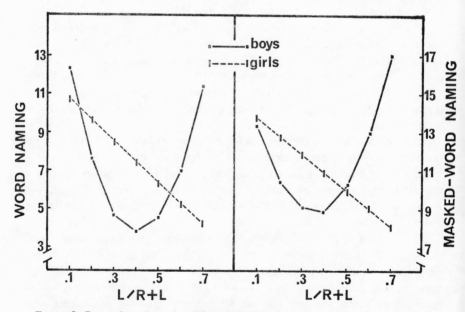

FIGURE 2: Regression of word naming (WNT) and masked-word naming (M-WNT) on ear asymmetry in normal third grade boys and girls (WNT boys: $Y = 18.523 -.729X + 008X^2$; WNT girls: $Y = 11.702 -.107X$; M-WNT boys: $Y = 17.845 -.501X +.006X^2$; M-WNT girls: $Y = 14.407 -.088X$). From Bakker et al., 1976.

ciated with either left or right hemispheric control. The girls show the laterality-reading pattern to be expected at advanced stages of the learning-to-read process; the boys may be in an intermediate stage already passed by the girls. Such an explanation for the sex effect implies that lower grade girls and higher grade boys will show asymmetry-reading patterns similar to those of the present third grade boys and girls respectively. This was later supported by the outcome of an investigation with second, third-fourth, and fifth-sixth grade boys and girls (Bakker, Teunissen, & Bosch, 1976). The second grade girls and the fifth-sixth grade boys showed ear asymmetry-reading proficiency relationships similar to those of the third grade boys and girls of the previous experiment.

The preliminary results of a recent investigation at Northern Illinois University (Van Duyne & Bakker, 1976) provide evidence of developmental changes in ear asymmetry-reading patterns. First, second and third grade children were presented word strings and digit series monaurally, in addition to a standard reading test. Asymmetric digit recall was analyzed in relation to reading proficiency in the second and third graders. Multiple correlation and partial regression coefficients were calculated with right and left ear recall serving as independent variables

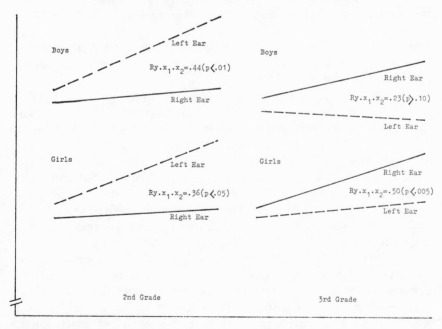

FIGURE 3: Regression of reading proficiency on right and left ear recall in normal second and third grade boys and girls.

and reading proficiency as the dependent variable. Figure 3 presents the multiple R's and partial regression slopes. In the second grade it is left ear performance which contributes most to the digit recall-reading relationship, whereas right ear performance contributes most to that relationship in third graders.

This shift may reflect the relative contribution of each hemisphere to reading proficiency at different stages of the learning-to-read process. In summary, the experimental evidence suggests that early reading is less dependent than advanced reading on left hemisphere functioning.

The shift in cortical mechanisms primarily subserving reading at early and advanced stages of the learning-to-read process may be related to the relative importance of perceptual and semantic analysis in these two stages. During a transitional stage proficient reading may be associated with either right or left hemispheric representation of language. Equally good reading proficiency may result when either the right or the left hemisphere is primarily involved but will be associated with quite different reading strategies. Children showing right hemispheric representation of language seem to be more sensitive to the perceptual features of the text. They explore the visual word configurations carefully, read slowly and make few errors. Children showing left hemispheric representation of language, like fluent readers, tend to read at relatively fast rates. They risk making many errors because they are still in a stage of the learning-to-read process that requires close attention to the perceptual features of the text.

These hypotheses were tested by Bakker, Teunissen and Bosch (1976), who split up a reading performance task in terms of speed, accuracy and proficiency by measuring the number of words read, the number of errors made and the difference between these measures. Second, fourth and sixth grade children were selected on the basis of their significant right or left ear advantage. These groups were then matched on reading proficiency. Measures of speed and accuracy were standardized by grade, across ear advantage groups and summed per subject. The summed speed and accuracy scores of children showing right ear advantage differed from children showing left ear advantage both across grades and in the second grade. Analysis of this finding indicated that right ear advantage was associated with fast and/or inaccurate reading, and left ear advantage was associated with slow and/or accurate reading.

Given that right and left ear advantage reflect left and right hemispheric control of language respectively, the reviewed investigations warrant the following conclusions:

1) Reading in older school age children flourishes when language is represented only in the left hemisphere, whereas in younger children either right or left hemispheric representation of language is equally effective.

2) The exclusive and unilateral control of proficient reading (i.e., right *or* left hemispheric representation of language) is effective in girls earlier than in boys.

3) Left and right representations of language are associated with different reading strategies, especially at younger school ages. Initial reading is psycholinguistically one thing; advanced reading another. This distinction seems to parallel a neuropsychological one: A left hemispheric representation of language subserves advanced reading; a right hemispheric representation subserves initial reading. Thus, functional maturity of the right hemisphere may be of importance to the early stages of the learning-to-read process. This conclusion is corollary to and extends the model of Satz and Sparrow (1970), who stress the importance of left hemispheric maturity to all modes of reading.

VISUAL ASYMMETRY AND READING PROFICIENCY

The use of listening techniques is based mainly on evidence that an auditory stimulus produces greatest activity in the decussating auditory pathways, and hence the contralateral cerebral hemisphere. It is known that in the visual system the fibers from the nasal half of the retina decussate at the optic chiasma and join the temporal fibers from the other eye prior to projection to the visual area in the striate cortex of the contralateral hemisphere. The effect of presenting stimuli to corresponding visual hemifields is, in fact, a selective stimulus presentation to either of the cerebral hemispheres. This selective presentation allows determination of relative superiority of the left and right cerebral hemispheres for the processing of alphabetic and non-alphabetic stimuli.

It is clear that the most appropriate approach to the laterality-reading relation is to study the way reading itself is lateralized. The efficiency of the reading of tachistoscopically presented words in the left or right visual fields is considered an indication of the proficiency of, respectively, the right and left hemisphere in dealing with reading material. Word recognition, while relying heavily on language-related processing, requires detailed visual-spatial analysis as well, especially in the early stages of the learning-to-read process, as has been argued in the preceding section. Thus, word recognition may be more proficient in the left or right visual field depending on whether perceptual or higher linguistic analyses are more prominent during the processing of the words.

Research on the *development* of visual asymmetries is rather scanty.

An early study by Forgays (1953) investigated the neural effects of acquired reading habits and directional scanning. He presented English words simultaneously to the right and left visual fields of children in grades 2 through 10 and the first 3 years of college. He found right field superiority at grades 8 and above only. Forgays concluded that 7 years of reading experience resulted in relatively greater retinal sensitivity to right field words. McKeever and Huling (1970) attempted to study the effects of acquired visual habits vs. cerebral dominance with a tachisto-scopic word recognition task in two groups of children in the seventh grade. Half the subjects had normal reading skills whereas the other half read at third grade level, presumably with poorly acquired reading habits. Both groups showed superior right field word recognition. According to the investigators this finding favors a cerebral dominance rather than a reading habit explanation of visual asymmetry.

Interest in the development of visual asymmetry is presently growing. Miller and Turner (1973) found right field superiority for the recognition of briefly presented words in fourth grade and older normal children. Reitsma (1975) presented three-letter words to either the right or left visual field of second, fourth and sixth grade boys and girls. In order to control for fixation, one-third of the words were presented centrally. The exposure times were determined beforehand for each child individually and set at such a level that 60-70% of all words presented could be recognized by all children. Reitsma found a significant grade by visual field interaction indicating right field superiority at grades 4 and 6 but not at grade 2. These findings confirmed those of Miller and Turner. Reitsma argued that the absence of a visual field difference in second graders may be due to the importance of visual-spatial analysis in word recognition at early stages of the learning-to-read process. Since visual-spatial processes are probably controlled by the right hemisphere they would tend to suppress right field (i.e., left hemispheric) superiority in visual word recognition. This explanation, while in accordance with our theory predicting different laterality-reading relations at younger and older school ages, does not account for an additional finding of Reitsma (1975) and Miller and Turner (1973) who demonstrated that right minus left field differences correlate positively with performance on standard reading tests. This finding may be related to the presence of a speed factor in their reading test. Children who show strong right field advantage also show left hemispheric specialization for written language. As argued before, children who show left hemispheric language control may prefer fast-reading strategies which, in turn, would explain the relation found between right field superiority and reading proficiency as measured by a speed-reading test.

The results of studies on the onset and development of visual asymmetry are otherwise not uniform. Olson (1973) flashed three- and four-letter words in the visual hemifields of second through sixth grade children. Right field superiority was found in all grade levels but no grade by field interaction was reported. Reitsma (1975), in an investigation with first, second and third grade children, required the identification of unilaterally presented numerals. An analysis of variance revealed better right than left field identification across grades. The between-field differences tended to decrease with age. The discrepant results of Reitsma's later and earlier investigations are best understood in terms of the different stimulus features that characterized the two studies: The earlier study utilized words; the later study utilized numerals.

A few studies are addressed to exploring atypical between-field differences in reading-retarded children. Marcel and Rajan (1975) presented five-letter words to 7- to 9-year-olds and found greater right field superiority in good readers than in poor readers. The authors attributed their results to the "differential extent of specialization for linguistic function in the left cerebral hemisphere in good and poor readers" (p. 495). The findings of Marcel and Rajan confirmed those of an earlier investigation (Marcel, Katz, & Smith, 1974) in which 8-year-old good readers, especially the girls, showed greater right field superiority in the identification of five-letter words than poor readers of the same age.

On the other hand, the results and conclusions of a study by Yeni-Komshian, Isenberg and Goldberg (1975) are diametrically opposed to those of Marcel et al. (1975). Yeni-Komshian et al. compared the between-field differences in the identification of numerals of normal-reading fifth to seventh grade children with those of age mates with a reading lag of three years. They found greater between-field differences in the poor readers than in the good readers. The group-by-field intraction was largely due to depressed left field performance in the poor readers. The authors considered that the depressed left field performance indicated a right hemisphere deficit in reading disability, perhaps related to "the abstracting of physical characteristics of words or transmission of this abstraction to the left hemisphere" (p. 92). A similar view was recently expressed by Witelson (1976) who on the basis of an extensive study of right-left differences in the tactual identification of letters and nonsense shapes concluded that the right hemisphere in dyslexics may be insufficiently specialized for spatial processing.

It is clear that at present no firm conclusions can be drawn as to whether retarded readers show atypical visual asymmetries or not. McKeever and Huling (1970) found no differences in this respect between normal and reading-retarded children, whereas Marcel et al. (1974; 1975) found right field superiority in normals and Yeni-Komshian et al. (1975) found right field superiority in reading-retarded children. These contradictory results are not surprising since the investigators: 1) utilized different age and reading levels, 2) used different types of stimulus material (numerals, words), 3) flashed at different locations in either field, and 4) required different types of response (identification, matching). Similar procedural differences hinder a comparison of studies dealing with the onset and development of visual asymmetry. However, the studies on word identification by Reitsma (1975) and Miller et al. (1973) *are* comparable in terms of sample characteristics (normal, second, fourth and sixth grade children), stimulus materials (words), stimulus presentation (unilateral) and response requirements (naming). In both studies, onset of right field superiority was found at grade four. The implication of these two studies, that at lower grades both cerebral hemispheres are equally proficient in the processing of written language, strengthens the inference expressed in the section on auditory asymemtry, namely, that proficient early reading is associated with either right or left hemispheric representation of spoken language.

PERCEPTUAL ASYMMETRIES: PROBLEMS AND PERSPECTIVES

Does the theory defended in this chapter have implications for the etiology of specific reading disability (dyslexia)? The suggested conclusion based on the investigations described is that proficient reading at advanced stages of the learning-to-read process is associated with left hemispheric representation of language only, and that proficient early reading may go with either left or right hemispheric language representation. Either fluency or accuracy may characterize early reading, depending on whether language is primarily mediated in the left or right hemisphere. The accurate but slow reading strategy, while appropriate at early stages of the learning-to-read process, may be unfavorable at later stages.

Girls seem to pass through the asymmetry-reading stages faster than boys, and the risk of getting stuck in early reading strategies associated with right hemisphere activity may be greater for boys than for girls. Such a stagnation could result in the reading retardation that is found more frequently in boys than in girls. In addition, it seems probable that right hemispheric representation of language will be more frequently observed in older dyslexics than in older normal readers. The results of studies comparing such reading groups tend to support this hypothesis (e.g., Sparrow & Satz, 1970).

Another implication of the theory is that young dyslexics would be hard to distinguish from young normals on the basis of their reading level alone as the reading level of dyslexics will be comparatively low once they are supposed to have exchanged their slow right hemispheric reading strategy for the faster left hemispheric one. This prediction, however, is refuted by the facts: Dyslexics *are* recognized from the onset of reading instruction. Finally, if dyslexics stick to strategies generated by the right hemisphere, one would expect them to be characterized primarily by slow reading. This expectation, too, is refuted by the facts: Dyslexics do read slowly but they make many errors as well. It is felt, therefore, that the theory of the development of language asymmetry-reading patterns in normal readers fails to account for some facts observed in early dyslexia. The problems encountered by young reading-disturbed children may be related to atypical lateralization of those non-linguistic functions crucial to early reading (Witelson, 1976). These children may be handicapped by having linguistic and non-linguistic functions lateralized in opposite hemispheres. The establishment of relationships between the visual patterns of letters and the meaning of these letters would then require interhemispheric associations. Since associations between hemispheres are more difficult to make than associations within hemispheres one would expect young school children showing opposed lateralization of visual-spatial and language functions to make more errors in reading than age-mates having these functions primarily controlled by the same hemisphere (Masland, 1970).

More detailed analysis is needed to unravel the complex relations between perceptual asymmetry and reading proficiency. Perceptual asymmetry should not be considered merely in terms of verbal vs. nonverbal and auditory vs. visual. Investigations of the perception of auditorially presented consonants showed ear asymmetry to vary with the nature and number of distinctive features involved (Blumstein, 1974). Therefore, it would be desirable to split up the visual-verbal stimuli used in half-field studies in an analogous manner. The way children read should be analyzed in more detail as well. It would be fruitful, for example, to gather information about the relation between perceptual asymmetry and types of errors made in reading and spelling.

The search for relationships between hemispheric asymmetry of function and reading proficiency through the investigation of perceptual asymmetry presupposes that perceptual asymmetry is, in fact, a reflection of hemispheric asymmetry. There is some evidence for the validity of this assumption. Kimura (1961), for example, found right ear advantage in subjects with verified left hemispheric control of language and left ear advantage in cases of right hemispheric language control.

Satz (1975, 1976), however, recently objected to the inference that right hemispheric representation of language is reliably predictable from left ear advantage for speech stimuli. Using Bayes' theorem on conditional probabilities, he concluded that the likelihood of having speech represented in the right hemisphere given left ear advantage is extremely low. His analysis was based on estimates that: 1) 95% of neurologically impaired patients have speech primarily represented in the left hemisphere and 5% in the right hemisphere (Milner, Branch, & Rasmussen, 1964); 2) 70% of normal right-handed adults show right ear advantage in dichotic listening; and 3) 60% of patients with verified right hemispheric speech representation show left ear advantage (Kimura, 1961).

Satz's conclusions are weakened by the fact that these percentages are, themselves, contestable. First, the figures given by Milner et al. refer to cerebral representation of language *production,* whereas inferences based on ear advantage refer to cerebral representation of language *reception.* Second, some studies (Bryden, 1975; Shankweiler & Studdert-Kennedy, 1975) report right ear advantage rates as high as 85%. Such figures are in close correspondence with the findings of Molfese, Freeman and Palermo (1975) indicating greater left than right hemisphere activity to speech stimuli in 80% of their normal cases. Third, Kimura (1967) reports that 10 of her 11 cases, i.e., 91%, having right hemispheric representation of speech showed left ear advantage. Moreover, the fact that antecedent probabilities are derived from examinations of both normal subjects and patients further obscures Satz's analyses and conclusions.

Hemispheric specialization of function is not the sole determinant of perceptual asymmetry; the reading and writing direction of a language is another. For example, Orbach (1952) found left field superiority in the recognition of Hebrew words by subjects who had learned Hebrew as their first language. English words, on the other hand, were better recognized in the right visual field. This finding exemplifies the effect of reading direction on visual asymmetry since Hebrew is read from right to left and English from left to right. However, in a subsequent study (Orbach, 1967), right-handed, native Hebrew readers showed right field superiority in the recognition of both Hebrew and English words. Orbach concluded that both cerebral asymmetry of function and reading habits must influence the differential recognition of words in the right and left visual fields.

Bertelson (1972) recently investigated the effects of reading habits on auditory asymmetry. He presented Hebrew and French spoken sentences with an extraneous signal to bilingual Israelis. The task was to locate the temporal position of the signal. Poorer performance resulted when the French sentences were presented to the right ear and the signal to the left, and when the Hebrew sentences were presented to the left ear and the signal to the right. Thus, direction of reading seems to influence both visual and auditory asymmetry, and this, in turn, would explain the relation between perceptual asymmetry and reading proficiency at older school ages. At younger school ages reading habits would still be too weak to account for such a relationship. Turner and Miller (1975) investigated the differential effect of hemispheric specialization and reading habits on visual asymmetry in children and adults. However, since both hemispheric specialization of the brain and directional scanning in reading may increase with age, clear-cut conclusions as to the specific influence of either factor are precluded. Moreover, it is possible that specific reading habits and perceptual asymmetry are subserved by the same cerebral mechanisms. In that case the relations between directional habits and ear advantage or visual field superiority would confound the more basic association between hemispheric specialization and perceptual asymmetry.

There are quite a few things to settle.

REFERENCES

BAKKER, D. J. Left-right differences in auditory perception of verbal and non-verbal material by children. *Quarterly Journal of Experimental Psychology,* 1967, 19, 334-336.

BAKKER, D. J. Ear-asymmetry with monaural stimulation. *Psychonomic Science,* 1968, 12, 62.

BAKKER, D. J. Ear-asymmetry with monaural stimulation: Task influences. *Cortex,* 1969, 5, 36-42.

BAKKER, D. J. Hemispheric specialization and stages in the learning to read process. *Bulletin of the Orton Society,* 1973, 23, 15-27.

BAKKER, D. J., SMINK, T., and REITSMA, P. Ear dominance and reading ability. *Cortex,* 1973, 9, 301-312.

BAKKER, D. J., TEUNISSEN, J., and BOSCH, J. Development of laterality-reading patterns. In R. M. Knights and D. J. Bakker (Eds.), *The Neuropsychology of Learning Disorders.* Baltimore: University Park Press, 1976, pp. 207-220.

BELMONT, I. Requirements of the early reading task. *Perceptual and Motor Skills,* 1974, 38, 527-537.

BELMONT, L. and BIRCH, H. G. Lateral dominance and right-left awareness in normal children. *Child Development,* 1963, 34, 257-270.

BELMONT, L. and BIRCH, H. G. Lateral dominance, lateral awareness, and reading disability. *Child Development,* 1965, 36, 57-71.

BERLIN, C. I., HUGHES, L. F., LOWE-BELL, S. S., and BERLIN, H. L. Dichotic right ear advantage in children 5 to 13. *Cortex,* 1973, 9, 394-402.

BERTELSON, P. Listening from left to right versus right to left. *Perception*, 1972, 1, 161-165.

BLUMSTEIN, S. E. The use of theoretical implications of the dichotic technique for investigating distinctive features. *Brain and Language*, 1974, 1, 337-350.

BRYDEN, M. P. Dichotic listening and the development of linguistic processes. Paper presented at the International Neuropsychological Society, New Orleans, LA, 1973.

BRYDEN, M. P. Speech lateralization in families: A preliminary study using dichotic listening. *Brain and Language*, 1975, 2, 201-211.

DIMOND, S. J. and BEAUMONT, J. G. (Eds.). *Hemisphere Function in the Human Brain*. London: Elek Science, 1974.

DOEHRING, D. G. Ear asymmetry in the discrimination of monaural tonal sequences. *Canadian Journal of Psychology*, 1972, 26, 106-110.

FORGAYS, D. G. The development of differential word recognition. *Journal of Experimental Psychology*, 1953, 45, 165-168.

GEFFNER, D. S. and DORMAN, M. F. Hemispheric specialization for speech perception in four-year-old children from low and middle socio-economic classes. *Cortex*, 1976, 12, 71-73.

GEFFNER, D. S. and HOCHBERG, I. Ear laterality performance of children from low and middle socio-economic levels on a verbal dichotic listening task. *Cortex*, 1971, 7, 193-203.

INGRAM, D. Cerebral speech lateralization in young children. *Neuropsychologia*, 1975, 13, 103-105.

KARP, E. and BIRCH, H. G. Hemispheric differences in reaction time to verbal and non-verbal stimuli. *Perceptual and Motor Skills*, 1969, 29, 475-480.

KIMURA, D. Cerebral dominance and the perception of verbal stimuli. *Canadian Journal of Psychology*, 1961, 15, 166-171.

KIMURA, D. Speech lateralization in young children as determined by an auditory test. *Journal of Comparative and Physiological Psychology*, 1963, 56, 899-902.

KIMURA, D. Functional asymmetry of the brain in dichotic listening. *Cortex*, 1967, 3, 163-178.

KNOX, C. and KIMURA, D. Cerebral processing of non-verbal sounds in boys and girls. *Neuropsychologia*, 1970, 8, 227-237.

LEONG, C. K. Lateralization in severely disabled readers in relation to functional cerebral development and syntheses of information. In R. M. Knights and D. J. Bakker (Eds.), *The Neuropsychology of Learning Disorders*. Baltimore: University Park Press, 1976, pp. 221-231.

MARCEL, T., KATZ, L., and SMITH, M. Laterality and reading proficiency. *Neuropsychologia*, 1974, 12, 131-139.

MARCEL, T. and RAJAN, P. Lateral specialization for recognition of words and faces in good and poor readers. *Neuropsychologia*, 1975, 13, 489-497.

MASLAND, R. L. Implications for therapy. In F. A. Young and D. B. Lindsley (Eds.), *Early Experience and Visual Information Processing in Perceptual and Reading Disorders*. Washington: National Academy of Sciences, 1970, pp. 457-464.

McKEEVER, W. F. and HULING, M. D. Lateral dominance in tachistoscopic word recognition of children at two levels of ability. *Quarterly Journal of Experimental Psychology*, 1970, 22, 600-604.

MILLER, L. K. and TURNER, S. Development of hemifield differences in word recognition. *Journal of Educational Psychology*, 1973, 65, 172-176.

MILNER, B., BRANCH, C., and RASMUSSEN, T. Observations on cerebral dominance. In A. V. S. De Reuck and M. O'Connor (Eds.), *Disorders of Language*. London: Churchill Ltd., 1964, pp. 200-214.

MOLFESE, D. L., FREEMAN, R. B., and PALERMO, D. S. The ontogeny of brain lateralization for speech and non-speech stimuli. *Brain and Language*, 1975, 2, 356-368.

MORAIS, J. and DARWIN, C. J. Ear differences for same-different reaction times to monaurally presented speech. *Brain and Language*, 1974, 1, 383-390.

MOUNTCASTLE, V. B. (Ed.). *Interhemispheric Relations and Cerebral Dominance*. Baltimore: The Johns Hopkins Press, 1962.

NAGAFUCHI, M. Development of dichotic and monaural hearing abilities in young children. *Acta Otolaryngologica*, 1970, 69, 409-415.

OLSON, M. E. Laterality differences in tachistoscopic word recognition in normal and delayed readers in elementary school. *Neuropsychologia*, 1973, 11, 343-350.

ORBACH, J. Retinal locus as a factor in the recognition of visually perceived words. *American Journal of Psychology*, 1952, 65, 555-562.

ORBACH, J. Differential recognition of Hebrew and English words in right and left visual fields as a function of cerebral dominance and reading habits. *Neuropsychologia*, 1967, 5, 127-134.

ORTON, S. T. *Word-Blindness in School Children and Other Papers on Strephosymbolia*. Compiled by J. L. Orton. Pomfret, Conn.: The Orton Society, Inc., 1966.

PORTER, R. J. and BERLIN, C. I. On interpreting developmental changes in the dichotic right-ear advantage. *Brain and Language*, 1975, 2, 186-200.

REITSMA, P. Visual asymmetry in children. Paper presented at the International Conference on "Lateralization of Brain Functions." Leiden, The Netherlands, 1975.

RIZZOLATTI, G., UMILTA, C., and BERLUCCHI, G. Opposite superiorities of the right and left cerebral hemispheres in discriminative reaction time to physiognomical and alphabetical material. *Brain*, 1971, 94, 431-442.

SATZ, P. Cerebral dominance and learning disabilities: Review. Paper presented at the International Conference on "The Neuropsychology of Learning Disorders." Korsør, Denmark, 1975.

SATZ, P. Cerebral dominance and reading disability: An old problem revisited. In R. M. Knights and D. J. Bakker (Eds.), *The Neuropsychology of Learning Disorders*. Baltimore: University Park Press, 1976, pp. 273-294.

SATZ, P., BAKKER, D. J., TEUNISSEN, J., GOEBEL, R., and VAN DER VLUGT, H. Developmental parameters of the ear asymmetry: A multivariate approach. *Brain and Language*, 1975, 2, 171-185.

SATZ, P., RARDIN, D., and ROSS, J. An evaluation of a theory of specific developmental dyslexia. *Child Development*, 1971, 42, 2009-2021.

SATZ, P. and SPARROW, S. Specific developmental dyslexia: A theoretical formulation. In D. J. Bakker and P. Satz (Eds.), *Specific Reading Disability: Advances in Theory and Method*. Rotterdam: Rotterdam University Press, 1970, 17-39.

SATZ, P. and VAN NOSTRAND, G. K. Developmental dyslexia: An evaluation of a theory. In P. Satz and J. Ross (Eds.), *The Disabled Learner: Early Detection and Intervention*. Rotterdam: Rotterdam University Press, 1973, pp. 121-148.

SHANKWEILER, D. and STUDDERT-KENNEDY, M. Identification of consonants and vowels presented to the left and right ears. *Quarterly Journal of Experimental Psychology*, 1967, 19, 59-63.

SHANKWEILER, D. and STUDDERT-KENNEDY, M. A continuum of lateralization for speech perception? *Brain and Language*, 1975, 2, 212-225.

SMITH, F. *Understanding Reading: A Psycholinguistic Analysis of Reading and Learning to Read*. New York: Holt, Rinehart and Winston, 1971.

SPARROW, S. and SATZ, P. Dyslexia, laterality and neuropsychological development. In D. J. Bakker and P. Satz (Eds.), *Specific Reading Disability: Advances in Theory and Method*. Rotterdam: Rotterdam University Press, 1970, 41-60.

SPELLACY, F. Lateral preferences in the identification of patterned stimuli. *The Journal of the Acoustical Society of America*, 1969, 47, 574-578.

STUDDERT-KENNEDY, M. and SHANKWEILER, D. Hemispheric specialization for speech perception. *The Journal of the Acoustical Society of America*, 1970, 48, 579-594.

THOMSON, M. E. A comparison of laterality effects in dyslexics and controls using verbal dichotic listening tasks. *Neuropsychologia*, 1976, 14, 243-246.

TURKEWITZ, G., MOREAU, T. and BIRCH, H. G. Relations between birth condition and neuro-behavioral organization in the neonate. *Pediatric Research*, 1968, 2, 243-249.

TURKEWITZ, G., MOREAU, T., DAVIS, L., and BIRCH, H. G. Factors affecting lateral differentiation in human newborn. *Journal of Experimental Child Psychology*, 1969, 8, 483-493.

TURNER, S. and MILLER, L. K. Some boundary conditions for laterality effects in children. *Developmental Psychology*, 1975, 11, 342-352.

VAN DUYNE, H. J. and BAKKER, D. J. The development of ear-asymmetry related to coding processes in memory in children. Paper presented at the Fourth Annual Meeting of the International Neuropsychological Society, Toronto, 1976.

WHITE, M. J. Laterality differences in perception: A review. *Psychological Bulletin*, 1969, 72, 387-405.

WITELSON, S. F. Abnormal right hemisphere specialization in developmental dyslexia. In R. M. Knights and D. J. Bakker (Eds.), *The Neuropsychology of Learning Disorders*. Baltimore: University Park Press, 1976, pp. 233-255.

WITELSON, S. F. and RABINOVITCH, M. S. Hemispheric speech lateralization in children with auditory-linguistic deficits. *Cortex*, 1972, 8, 412-426.

YENI-KOMSHIAN, G. H., ISENBERG, D., and GOLDBERG, H. Cerebral dominance and reading disability: Left visual field deficit in poor readers. *Neuropsychologia*, 1975, 13, 83-94.

ZURIF, E. B. and CARSON, G. Dyslexia in relation to cerebral dominance and temporal analysis. *Neuropsychologia*, 1970, 8, 351-361.

6

Temporal Changes in Information Processing After Cerebral Damage

IRA BELMONT

The study of altered neuropsychological processes underlying perceptual and perceptual-motor changes in individuals who have sustained brain damage is important for two reasons. First, elucidation of the deficient or altered neural processes can lead to more rational therapeutics for improving perceptual and perceptual-motor functioning, and second, the deficient processes may be related to more complex cognitive changes such as reduced ability to learn, remember and make adequate judgments.

The present chapter reviews a series of studies which we believe revealed one such altered neural process, an increase in the time required by the damaged nervous system to process information. The postulated lesion-induced inertia might help to explain certain modifications in perception, awareness, and action which, in part, underlie the deficient behavior of the affected individuals. It should also permit a more rational consideration of how to construct a more effective environment for them.

RESEARCH FINDINGS ON INERTIA

Our program of research used a variety of strategies and techniques which were applied to the examination of patients who had unilateral cerebral damage. We studied older left hemiplegic stroke patients (right cerebral damage) who were past the acute stage of the cerebral vascular accident (CVA) and resident in a large municipal chronic disease hospital. They were compared to socially similar and age-matched residents of the same hospital who had a variety of musculoskeletal disabilities (e.g., leg amputation, hip fracture) who showed no evidence of central nervous system damage and whose sensory and motor functioning were normal for age.

In one approach we examined the effect of antecedent stimulation upon the response to subsequent stimulation. For this we used the auditory time error technique first developed in psychophysics. The technique required that the patient judge whether the second of two successively presented identical tones was heard as louder or softer than the first when the time interval between the tones was varied. The auditory time error method makes it possible to study the time course of the effect of a prior stimulus upon the individual's responsiveness to a later stimulus. It is well-known that, in normals, as the time interval between the tones is increased, response shifts from judgments that the second tone is "softer" to judgments that it is "louder." In our studies (Birch, Belmont & Karp, 1964a, 1965a), we found that the pattern of response appeared to be the same for both the normal and brain-damaged individuals, but that the brain-injured patients required a very much longer time to evolve the response pattern. While the responses of normal persons indicated that mild inhibition (one-second interval) and then enhancement (three-second interval) had occurred, the brain-injured individuals exhibited strong inhibition of the subsequent tone in both circumstances. However, as the interstimulus interval was increased, the inhibition decreased regularly so that when nine seconds intervened between tones enhancement occurred similar to that shown by normals when there was a three-second interstimulus interval. This suggested that, while basic mechanisms of inhibition and arousal may be similar in both groups, when cerebral damage exists it takes longer to process stimuli and to recover to baseline levels.

It follows that if brain injury results in a delay in neural processing and the patients had unilateral damage, then the inertia may be associated with the damaged hemisphere. This inference was tested in studies using simple reaction time. We found that the brain-damaged patients not only showed a general slowing in reaction time (this has been consistently found by others), but they responded more slowly to stimula-

The work described here was done in collaboration with Dr. Herbert G. Birch and Dr. Eric Karp when we were part of the Program for Normal and Aberrant Behavioral Development of the Kennedy Center of the Albert Einstein College of Medicine, Yeshiva University. The concepts outlined and approaches taken to the work were our joint product. Those who knew Herbert Birch, who was director of the program, and the scope and depth of his thinking will know that his contribution had special value and weight in whatever may prove to be lasting in the work.

tion of the affected (left) side than to stimulation of the unaffected (right) side. In contrast, the non-brain-damaged individuals showed no such lateral differences in reaction time. Our reaction time experiments demonstrated that the lateralized increase in latency shown by the hemiplegic patients was not the result of simple sensory or motor changes frequently exhibited by stroke patients. To account for sensory changes, inputs to the two sides were equated for effective intensity by stimulating each side at its 100% threshold value (minimal intensity level to which a response is made on all threshold-determining trials). In addition, a vocal response, which is a non-lateralized common response indicator, was used to control for the possible effects of the unilateral motor deficit *per se*. Using these control conditions permitted the conclusion that the lateralized differences in reaction time reflected greater inertia in processing information by the affected than by the intact hemisphere. We found this on somesthetic stimulation (Karp, Belmont & Birch, 1971) and on auditory stimulation (Belmont, Handler & Karp, 1972). A similar effect was found by Benton and Joynt (1959) for the visual system. These studies suggest that the inertia is not limited to one or another sense system, but, rather, is characteristic of all afferent systems of the damaged hemisphere.

If the intact hemisphere processes information in advance of the affected one, then a number of behavioral inferences follow. One of these concerns the judgment of order of stimulation applied to the two sides. It was predicted that when two tones are successively presented, one to each ear, the brain-injured patients would judge order correctly when the right ear is stimulated first but would frequently err when the left ear is stimulated first. It was reasoned that a correct response is overdetermined when the right ear is stimulated first. Input is both provided earlier to and processed faster by the left intact hemisphere,* in contrast to the later stimulation and slower processing of the right (damaged) hemisphere. In this condition objective circumstances and subjective experience will coincide. However, when the order of stimulation is reversed, it was argued that the affected, right hemisphere would process the first applied stimulus sufficiently slowly so that the later applied but more rapidly processed input to the intact left hemisphere would be experienced as having been applied first. To test this prediction (Belmont & Handler, 1971), tones were provided at 20 db above the 100% threshold level for each ear and at interstimulus intervals ranging from 20 to 80 msec. We found that most of the brain-damaged

---

* Behavioral and electrophysiological evidence indicates that inputs to a particular ear are mediated predominantly by the opposite hemisphere.

patients followed the prediction of differential accuracy, while normal individuals judged order accurately no matter which ear was stimulated first. The results were consistent with the hypothesis that the damaged hemisphere processes information more slowly than does the intact one.

Another strategy we utilized argued that if delayed neural processing underlies certain behavioral deficiencies of brain-damaged individuals, then improvement in behavior should be made possible by creating external conditions to match the internal lateral imbalance in processing speed. Such matching should result in the brain-damaged patients behaving adequately and like normals. We successfully applied this strategy using a well-known test for indicating cerebral damage, the double simultaneous stimulation (face-hand) test (Bender, 1952). Patients with unilateral cerebral damage are frequently unresponsive (show "extinction") to a stimulus applied to the affected side when it is simultaneously presented with one applied to the intact side. This is so despite adequate responsiveness to the same stimulus when applied alone to the affected side.

In a first study of this phenomenon (Birch, Belmont & Karp, 1964b), we had argued that the response of the brain-damaged patients to single stimulation of the affected side but the failure to respond to the same stimulus on bilateral simultaneous stimulation represents a problem of modified awareness. By subjectively equating bilateral stimulation for intensity, we showed that extinction was not the result of threshold differences between the sides and that the modified awareness exhibited in response to double simultaneous stimulation probably reflected a direct alteration in the physiological functioning of the central nervous system. In a second study (Birch, Belmont & Karp, 1967), we specifically tested the notion that the extinction was caused by delay in processing time occurring in the damaged hemisphere. For this test we applied double bilateral stimulation, not simultaneously but successively, with the affected side stimulated first in order to compensate externally for the slower internal processing. Under these conditions the hemiplegic patients did not exhibit extinction but, rather, responded to both stimuli as did normals.* Table 1 contains the accuracy scores achieved by individual patients under simultaneous and successive stimulation conditions. In those few instances where extinction occurred, it was now equally divided between the right and left sides.

In order to explain the occurrence of extinction, however, another process in addition to inertia must be invoked. We argued that simul-

---

* Successivity *per se* was not the basis for successful response since reversal of order of stimulation (intact side stimulated before affected side) produced typical extinction.

TABLE 1*

Accuracy of Response Made by Patients to Simultaneous and to
Successive Stimulation When the Affected Side
Was Stimulated First

| | Number of Accurate Responses When Stimuli Were: | |
Patient	Simultaneously Presented	Successively Presented
1	0	7
2	0	7
3	1	7
4	1	7
5	1	7
6	1	7
7	1	6
8	1	5
9	2	7
10	3	5
11	3	5
12	4	7
13	4	7
14	4	5
15	5	7
16	6	7
17	6	7
18	6	7
19	6	7

* Reproduced from Birch, Belmont and Karp, 1967, with permission from Oxford University Press.

taneous stimulation at the periphery does not lead to simultaneous central nervous system processing but, rather, to successive arousals with the intact hemisphere being the first one to be effectively organized. This, we suggested, is accompanied by suppression (extinction) of the more slowly developing excitation in the damaged hemisphere by the more rapidly organized input to the intact hemisphere. A model of the mechanism for extinction is presented in Figure IA. This view of suppression was based on evidence which showed that successive stimulation results in the relative or complete inhibition of later aroused regions in the central nervous system and that it occurs in normal as well as in brain-damaged individuals (e.g., Crawford, 1947; Battersby, Wagman, Karp & Bender, 1960; Boynton, 1961; Schmid, 1961; Raab, 1963). Thus, in our experiment, prior stimulation of the affected side permitted the development of effective levels of organization in the damaged hemisphere before onset of interference from the input to the intact hemisphere. This led to the

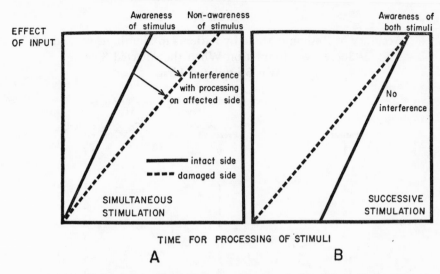

FIGURE 1A. Model for extinction of awareness to double bilateral simultaneous stimulation in patients with unilateral cerebral damage. FIGURE 1B. Model for overcoming extinction of awareness to double bilateral successive stimulation.
(Adapted from Birch, Belmont and Karp, 1967)

awareness of both stimuli. A model for overcoming extinction is presented in Figure 1B. It suggests that, for these patients, what was externally successive was internally simultaneous.

PROCESSES OF AROUSAL AND INHIBITION MAY BE THE SAME IN NORMAL AND BRAIN-DAMAGED

The results of our studies consistently suggested that certain processes of arousal and inhibition are the same for both normal and brain-damaged persons, but that differences in neural timing alter the way in which these processes are manifested and reach awareness. Extinction was shown to occur in normals—for example, when simultaneous bilateral stimuli were applied but the two stimuli were of different intensities (Bird, 1964). In this situation the less intense stimulus was suppressed and the individual was unaware of it. Yet awareness of the same stimulus did occur when it was applied singly. We have argued (Birch, Belmont & Karp, 1967) that this normal alteration in awareness occurs on the basis of differences in speed of processing, whereby the less intense stimulus is organized more slowly and is suppressed (masked) by the more intense, more rapidly processed one. That stimuli of higher intensity result in faster rising excitations and are processed at a more rapid rate is suggested by a number of studies (e.g., David, Guttman & Bergeijk, 1958; Rosner, 1961) and has been referred to by Rosner as the intensity-latency law. It is reflected in other behavioral findings also as, for example, in the increase in speed of reaction time elicited by increasing stimulus intensity (Teichner, 1954) and in electrophysiologic findings in which the latency of neuroelectric response is decreased as the intensity of the stimulus is increased (e.g., Cobb & Dawson, 1960; Vaughan & Hull, 1965). In fact, the size and the duration of the stimulus, as well as its intensity, affect the speed of arousal in the nervous system. It has been known for some time that increasing the area stimulated or the duration of stimulation has the same behavioral effect as increasing the intensity of a stimulus, and that size, duration and intensity have interchangeable effects so that increasing one and appropriately decreasing another produces a constant behavioral effect (Graham & Margaria, 1935; Graham & Kemp, 1938; Osgood, 1953). It may well be that much of the modified awareness reported as masking, perceptual blanking, raised thresholds, etc. is based on differential neural processing time and the resultant suppression of given stimuli of an array depend upon the interplay of the size, duration, intensity and interstimulus interval of the stimulus elements.

The issue of differences in neural processing time may also be important for the study of normal behavioral development over the life span. The baseline evidence we obtained from normal, aged controls suggests that this is so. For example, their response to the auditory time error technique indicated that neural effects of successive stimulation are similar to those of young normal adults when stimuli are close in time but that, different from young adults, they cease to show effects when stimuli are increasingly separated in time (Birch, Belmont & Karp, 1964a, 1965a). Thus, with aging, a time-related narrowing of stimulus interaction occurred. Also, on double simultaneous stimulation, the older normal individuals differed from young adults in that they required longer periods of experience with the two stimuli before they successfully responded to both of them (Belmont, Birch & Karp, 1968). Interestingly, the same pattern of response is also characteristic of pre-teenagers (Bender, Fink & Green, 1951), while children younger than 6 or 7 years of age consistently show extinction of one of the two stimuli (Fink & Bender, 1952). Thus, a developmental gradient is evident ranging from extinction at very young ages, to delayed full response to multiple stimulation by older children, to immediate full response by younger adults, to delayed full response by older adults, to consistent extinction by older brain-damaged adults. The study of changes in the speed of neural processing and its relation to facilitation and suppression effects of multiple stimulation may prove to be a promising area for examining neural mechanisms of developmental change.

CONCLUSIONS

Our studies, then, suggest that certain of the processes of inhibition and arousal are the same in both normal and brain-injured people but that these processes are radically affected by the inertia which we believe is operating on the affected side of patients with unilateral cerebral damage. This creates a condition whereby the intact hemisphere processes sensory inputs in advance of the affected one. When incoming information is bilateral and within a given sense modality, the damaged hemisphere shows increased and prolonged inhibition.* Moreover, the more organized and active processes in the intact hemisphere interfere with the functioning of the more slowly integrating hemisphere. Such slowed processing and interference may, in part, underlie certain deficiencies in perception and awareness, and in the organization and coordination of action (Belmont, Karp & Birch, 1971) frequently seen in cerebrally damaged individuals.

If our findings do, in fact, reflect a unilateral delay in information processing, then it clearly has implications for more complex cognitive functioning in brain-damaged persons. The changes in awareness indicate that what is effective stimulation for normals is frequently ineffective for the brain-damaged. Comprehension of the environment, both external and internal, would be altered particularly on the affected side as is seen, for example, in the unilateral astereognosis shown by the patients (Birch, Belmont & Karp, 1964b). It has implications for what is an effective learning situation for them. Major modifications in methods of rehabilitation management and training must be designed to match changes in information processing (Belmont, 1957, 1966; Belmont, Benjamin, Ambrose & Restuccia, 1969).

It has even been suggested (Efron, 1963) that altered temporal processing may underlie aphasia, that it is not language *per se* that is controlled by the left hemisphere but, rather, that sequencing and temporal order functions are mediated by that hemisphere and that symptoms of disordered language derive from disordered temporal processing. Memory, judgment, and reasoning too would be affected either indirectly through

---

* The effect of brain damage on intersensory in contrast to intrasensory processing appears to be different (Birch, Belmont & Karp, 1965b).

faulty perceiving and action, or directly through altered reticulo-cortical relations or reduced cortical tone, as postulated, for example, by Luria (1973). While the locus, size, and nature of brain damage produce specific kinds of defects which underlie deficiencies in behavior, the examination of the role of altered rates of processing in these disorders should be a productive endeavor.

REFERENCES

BATTERSBY, W. S., WAGMAN, I. S., KARP, E., and BENDER, M. B. Neural limitations of visual excitability: Alterations produced by cerebral lesions. *A.M.A. Arch. Neurol.*, 1960, 3, 24-42.

BELMONT, I. Psychoneurologic problems of the hemiplegic patient in rehabilitation. *N.Y. State Jour. Med.*, 1957, 57, 1383-1385.

BELMONT, I. The relation of afferent changes to motor performance in the rehabilitation of cerebrally damaged patients. *Bull. N.Y. Acad. Med.*, 1966, 42, 918-922.

BELMONT, I., BENJAMIN, H., AMBROSE, J., and RESTUCCIA, R. D. Effect of cerebral damage on motivation in rehabilitation. *Arch. Phys. Med. Rehab.*, 1969, 50, 507-512.

BELMONT, I., BIRCH, H. G., and KARP, E. The sequence of errors made to double simultaneous stimulation in older persons. *Cortex*, 1968, 4, 280-287.

BELMONT, I. and HANDLER, A. Delayed information processing and judgment of temporal order following cerebral damage. *Jour. Nerv. Ment. Dis.*, 1971, 152, 353-361.

BELMONT, I., HANDLER, A., and KARP, E. Delayed sensory motor processing following cerebral damage. II. A multisensory defect. *Jour. Nerv. Ment. Dis.*, 1972, 155, 345-349.

BELMONT, I., KARP, E., and BIRCH, H. G. Hemispheric incoordination in hemiplegia. *Brain*, 1971, 94, 337-348.

BENDER, M. B. *Disorders in Perception*. Charles C Thomas, Springfield, Ill., 1952.

BENDER, M. B., FINK, M., and GREEN, M. Patterns in perception on simultaneous tests of face and hand. *Arch. Neurol. Psychiat.*, 1951, 66, 355-362.

BENTON, A. L. and JOYNT, R. J. Reaction time in unilateral cerebral disease. *Confin. Neurol.*, 1959, 19, 247-256.

BIRCH, H. G., BELMONT, I., and KARP, E. Excitation-inhibition balance in brain-damaged patients. *Jour. Nerv. Ment. Dis.*, 1964a, 139, 537-544.

BIRCH, H. G., BELMONT, I., and KARP, E. The relation of single stimulus threshhold to extinction in double simultaneous stimulation. *Cortex*, 1964b, 1, 19-39.

BIRCH, H. G., BELMONT, I., and KARP, E. The prolongation of inhibition in brain-damaged patients. *Cortex*, 1965a, 1, 397-409.

BIRCH, H. G., BELMONT, I., and KARP, E. The disordering of intersensory and intra-sensory integration by brain damage. *Jour. Nerv. Ment. Dis.*, 1965b, 141, 410-418.

BIRCH, H. G., BELMONT, I., and KARP, E. Delayed information processing and extinction following cerebral damage. *Brain*, 1967, 90, 113-130.

BIRD, J. W. Parameters of double tactile stimulation. *Cortex*, 1964, 1, 257-268.

BOYNTON, R. M. Some temporal factors in vision. In: W. A. Rosenblith (Ed.), *Sensory Communication*. New York: Wiley, 1961.

COBB, W. A. and DAWSON, G. D. The latency and form in man of the occipital potentials evoked by bright flashes. *J. Physiol.*, 1960, 152, 108-121.

CRAWFORD, B. H. Visual adaptation in relation to brief conditioning stimuli. *Proc. Roy. Soc. London*, 1947, Series B, 134, 283-302.

DAVID, E. E., GUTTMAN, N., and VAN BERGEIJK, W. A. On the mechanism of binaural fusion. *J. Acoust. Soc. Am.*, 1958, 30, 801-802.

EFRON, R. Temporal perception, aphasia and déjà vu. *Brain*, 1963, 86, 403-424.

FINK, M. and BENDER, M. B. Perception of simultaneous tactile stimuli in normal children. *Neurology*, 1952, 3, 27-34.

GRAHAM, C. H. and KEMP, E. H. Brightness discrimination as a function of the duration of the increment in intensity. *J. Gen. Psychol.*, 1938, 21, 635-650.

GRAHAM, C. H. and MARGARIA, R. Area and the intensity-time relation in the peripheral retina. *Amer. J. Physiol.*, 1935, 113, 299-305.

KARP, E., BELMONT, I., and BIRCH, H. G. Delayed sensory-motor processing following cerebral damage. *Cortex*, 1971, 7, 419-425.

LURIA, A. R. *The Working Brain. An Introduction to Neuropsychology*. New York: Basic Books, 1973.

OSGOOD, C. E. *Method and Theory in Experimental Psychology*. New York: Oxford University Press, 1953.

RAAB, D. Backward masking. *Psychol. Bull.*, 1963, 60, 118-129.

ROSNER, B. S. Neural factors limiting cutaneous spatiotemporal discriminations. In: W. A. Rosenblith (Ed.), *Sensory Communications*. New York: Wiley, 1961.

SCHMID, E. Temporal aspects of cutaneous interaction with two-point electrical stimulation. *J. Exp. Psychol.*, 1961, 61, 400-409.

TEICHNER, W. H. Recent studies of simple reaction time. *Psychol. Bull.*, 1954, 51, 128-149.

VAUGHAN, H. G. and HULL, R. C. Functional relation between stimulus intensity and photically evoked cerebral responses in man. *Nature*, 1965, 206, 720-722.

Section II
INTELLECTUAL PROCESSES

7

Race and Intelligence

Current controversies over the extent to which genetic factors are responsible for racial differences in intelligence raise all the major problems surrounding intelligence and its measurement, race and its definition, and relations between biological structure and psychological function. The genetic issue has been debated throughout the whole of the century and remains unresolved. It is the contention of this paper that in the form in which it is usually posed it is unresolvable, and that the controversy owes its continuing interest to political rather than scientific concerns. In short, as Birch and Gussow (1970) put it, the genetic inferiority theory, which many have found insupportable, can more properly be described as unsupportable.

THE GENETICAL CASE

By far the most cogent statement of the case that the causes of race differences in IQ are largely genetic in origin is that presented by Jensen (e.g. 1969, 1973, 1975) in a number of papers and books. Jensen starts with a well-attested empirical finding which has been replicated in a large number of studies, especially in the United States. When black and white children of the same age are given IQ tests, the blacks on average do very much worse than the whites. Figure 1 shows the distribution of IQs obtained in one study carried out in five southern states of the U.S.A. The mean IQ of black children was only 80.7 as compared with a mean of 101.8 for whites; and the distribution of scores was more peaked—the SD was only just over 12 points for blacks as compared with 16 for whites.

FIGURE I

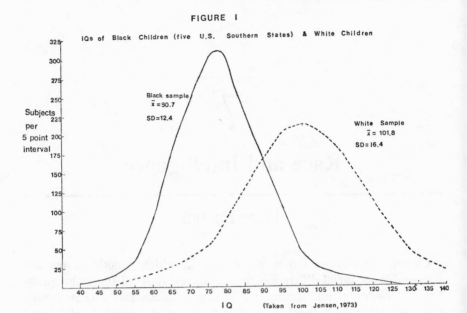

IQs of Black Children (five U.S. Southern States) & White Children

Black sample
x̄ = 90.7
SD = 12.4

White Sample
x̄ = 101.8
SD = 16.4

Subjects per 5 point interval

IQ   (Taken from Jensen, 1973)

The black children in this sample were more disadvantaged by poverty, ignorance, poor health and poor schooling than the average American black; and the general view is that when representative samples of U.S. blacks and whites are tested they differ on average in IQ by about 15 points—one standard deviation.

People have disputed the significance of this large difference, saying that it is simply an artefact of the tests or that it has no functional significance. There is some truth in this; nonetheless it is a mistake to dismiss all the findings that point to a deficiency in the ability of blacks, as compared with whites, to solve the puzzles that make up IQ tests. Their relative lack of success in them is, after all, not a bad indicator of their relative lack of success educationally. If we take the tests at face value, the findings would suggest that whereas 50% of whites have IQs of 100 or more, only 16% of blacks do. And whereas 16% of whites have IQs of over 115, only 2½% of blacks do. These differences are uncomfortably large and their significance as indicators is reflected in the dif-

This chapter is based on a paper given to the International Congress on Transcultural Psychiatry held at the University of Bradford, England, July 1976.

I am indebted to Ian Plewis, Jill Hodges and Barbara Tizard for comments on this paper.

ferences in the proportions of blacks and whites who do well in school and in, for example, the professions.

Until fairly recently, most pyschologists have followed Klineberg (1935) in accounting for IQ differences in environmental terms: American blacks grew up in a culture of poverty; disproportionate numbers were born to the most ignorant and depressed sections of the population; they suffered *intense* racial discrimination; they went to the worst schools; opportunities for intellectual and academic advancement were largely blocked. All of these things were true, and many of them are still true. What Jensen, Eysenck (1971) and others have tried to prove is that even making allowance—or some allowance—for these inequalities, large differences in performance still remain. The reason, they say, is that the potential to develop a high IQ is largely genetically determined; in contemporary America, and elsewhere in industrial society, most of the variation in IQ is determined by hereditary, not environmental, factors. In technical terms, Jensen and others say that about 80% of IQ variance is genetic in origin.

If this is so, then, it is argued, the amount that can be done through environmental change to shift the mean IQ or to improve educational attainments so that they reach satisfactory standards is fairly limited. Hence the claim that attempts to raise the intellectual and academic competencies of disadvantaged children through widescale programs of preschool education—such as the American Project Head Start—are bound to fail because they are attempting the impossible. Disadvantaged children don't benefit much from such measures, it is said, because they are *genetically* incapable, by and large, of doing so. Their IQs and academic performance remain low because that is all they are capable of, whatever the circumstances of their upbringing.

This is a profoundly pessimistic doctrine. In effect it implies that the majority of blacks are inherently backward in intelligence and that in consequence they will only really benefit educationally from some form of "special" education. For inasmuch as educability depends upon intelligence (as it surely does, to an extent) and inasmuch as blacks by and large are deficient in intelligence, they will not profit from the methods and curriculum appropriate for the (mostly white) children of normal ability, but will make progress only if taught by methods which rely on rote learning and a highly simplified curriculum. A few exceptional blacks will of course do all right but the majority won't.

Jensen and others think that intelligence is not subject to environmental manipulation except in a limited way. If, for example, only 20% of the IQ variance is environmental, it can be shown that it would

FIGURE   2

HYPOTHESISED   MECHANISM   TO   EXPLAIN
'PROGRESSIVE   ACHIEVEMENT   GAP'

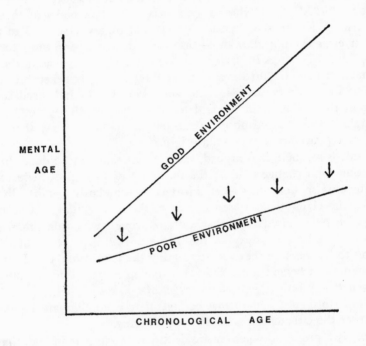

(Arrows   represent   adverse   circumstances,
disease etc)

require an improvement of 2.24 standard deviations in the environmental conditions of blacks that are relevant to the development of intelligence to raise their mean IQ to that of whites*—or to put it another way Jensen says that if *all* the observed differences between whites and blacks are due to environmental factors (and assuming that environmental effects are normally distributed and that variances are equal), then it follows that only just over 1% of whites have an environment which is

---

* See Appendix.

as poor as that of the average black (Jensen, 1973; Tizard, 1975). Jensen regards this conclusion as so implausible that he rejects the hypothesis that mean differences in IQ between blacks and whites can be accounted for solely in environmental terms.

Jensen advances a number of other arguments to support his case for the genetic determination of race differences in IQ. For example, he says, environmentalists claim that, because harsh conditions continue to operate on disadvantaged groups throughout their childhood, there is a *progressive achievement gap* between groups, as children grow older: IQ and other attainments differ increasingly with age. Figure 2 shows how mean attainment scores would look if that were so.

However, when children of different ages are tested on the same

FIGURE 3

MEAN T SCORES ON RAVEN

PROGRESSIVE MATRICES

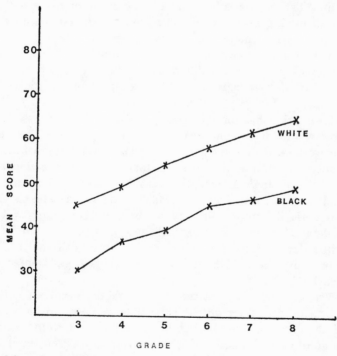

Adapted from Jensen, 1973.

intelligence test, this is not by and large what we find. Figure 3 presents one set of results reported by Jensen. It can be seen that the curves with age run virtually parallel—they don't diverge as would be the case if the environment deficit exerted a cumulative effect.

Other supporting lines of evidence in favor of the genetic hypothesis may be mentioned. One that is when blacks and whites are tested on tasks that have no very obvious relation to intelligence, the blacks do quite well on those that require only rote learning, but quite badly on those that involve more cognitive complexity. This is supposed to show that it is covert, genetic factors that are responsible for the differences in performance on tasks that demand intelligence for their completion.

Another line of argument is that other disadvantaged groups don't do as badly on IQ tests as do blacks. American Indians, for example, live in very poor environmental conditions, but tend to score higher on IQ tests than do American blacks—whose conditions of life seem a good deal better on the whole than those of Indians or Mexican-Americans. Similarly, "hybrids"—that is, children with a mixture of black and white ancestry—are said to do better on IQ tests than "pure" blacks.

All this adds up to a substantial case in favor of the genetic determination of intelligence. It is, however, one which rests entirely on the validity of applying inferences about heritability *within* groups to explain differences *between* groups. The assumption is that if you can estimate the extent to which differences *within* any group or subgroup are genetically determined you can arrive at "probabilistic estimates" about the cause of differences *between* groups.

This assumption has for the most part been accepted even by those psychologists who have contested Jensen's other claims. They have in consequence tended to argue about the proportion of the within-groups IQ variance attributable to genetic factors and by implication the proportion of the residual variance which *is* subject to environmental manipulation. Jensen says only 20%, others 50% and so on. The varying estimates are derived from correlational analyses of twin studies and similar kinship data. The shaky basis for these has been pointed out by Kamin (1974) in a devastating critique (which has been answered in part, but only in part, by Fulker, 1975) and by many others (e.g., Bronfenbrenner, 1972; Jencks, 1972).

However, my main point is that this whole debate about heritability has no bearing whatsover on the issue it is supposed to be explaining. Even if the within-groups heritability was 100%, it would still throw no light at all on the reason why groups living in different environments differed in biometric or social characteristics.

This no doubt will seem an extreme, not to say extravagant, statement to those who have followed the heated controversy about the genetics of intelligence. How can we decide between the two diametrically opposed points of view?

APPLICATION OF HERITABILITY THEORY TO STATURE

An obvious way to test the validity of the heritability model is to apply it to another set of data to see whether the deductions drawn from it make sense. Fortunately it is easy to do this. We can apply Jensen's theory that the higher the within-groups heritability of a biometric attribute, the less likely it is that between-groups differences can be accounted for in environmental terms, to an attribute which can be much more reliably measured than IQ, and whose meaning is much less ambiguous than intelligence, namely stature. By looking at the *heights* of children growing up in different circumstances, we can test the cogency and validity of heritability models. For stature is a highly heritable characteristic: Tall parents tend to have tall children, and marked differences in stature—e.g. between men and women, or Watusi and Pygmies—are considered, and no doubt rightly considered, to be almost entirely due to differences in genetic make-up. Jensen (1973) himself has made this point and used Watusi/Pygmy data to illustrate it.

The within-groups heritability of stature is very high—it is estimated that over 90% and perhaps as much as 95% of the subpopulation variation in stature is genetically determined. Does it therefore follow that if we examine the distribution of heights of different subpopulations living in, say, the United States or Britain, we can, by using our knowledge of this very high within-groups heritability, arrive at any sort of conclusion as to whether any differences found between groups are likely to be environmental rather than genetic in origin? The answer is no, not at all.

To illustrate this, I have brought together data bearing on the heights of three generations of London schoolboys, one measured in 1909, a second in 1938 and a third in 1959. Table 1 presents the data (Tizard, 1975).

The data are drawn from special surveys, carried out by school doctors, of very large and representative samples of the school population of London. The children measured in 1938 and 1959, if not the sons and grandsons of those measured in 1909, are drawn from much the same gene pool. The social class distribution of the families is quite similar and, indeed, many must have attended the same schools and lived in the very same houses.

TABLE 1

Mean Heights in Centimeters of London Schoolboys in
1909, 1938 and 1959

Age	1909 mean	SD	1938 mean	1959 mean	SD
7.5	114.2	6.04	120.5	123.1	5.69
8.5	119.7	6.12	125.8	129.0	6.07
9.5	124.7	6.23	130.9	134.2	6.51
10.5	129.0	6.56	135.8	139.1	6.48
11.5	133.4	6.69	140.4	144.9	7.20
12.5	137.6	7.33	144.8	149.5	7.65
7.5-12.5	126.4	6.51	133.0	136.6	6.63

Pooled variance 43.17, S.D. 6.57. From Tizard, 1975.

Children in all three samples grew on average about 5 cm a year between the ages of 7 and 12, and the generation gap remained almost constant during the six-year period of growth. The difference in the mean stature of children growing up in 1909 and 1959 is, in fact, enormous: It amounts to 10.2 centimeters (4 inches), or a full two years of growth. So 7-year-olds growing up in 1959 were as tall as 9-year-olds in 1909, and 10-year-olds in 1959 as tall as 12-year-olds 50 years earlier. The difference in mean height at each age and over the whole range of 1.55 standard deviations, one and a half times as great as the difference in the IQ of whites and blacks.

If we apply Jensen's model to the London height data (assuming the heritability to be 95%) we arrive at the conclusion that to account for the difference between the 1909 and 1959 samples the environment must have differed by nearly 7 standard deviations units—nearly 5 if the heritability is only 0.90.* Following Jensen's reasoning, a difference of this magnitude is virtually impossible to account for in environmental terms. But this is a preposterous conclusion: It leads us therefore either to reject the hypothesis that the two populations are genetically similar (which would be an equally preposterous thing to do, or to reject the theory upon which the whole case is built. And this, as Feldman and Lewontin (1975) Moran (1974) and other population geneticists have argued, is precisely what we should do.

It should be noted that all the other arguments that Jensen advances to support his genetic hypothesis are similarly demolished when they

---

* See Appendix.

are applied to height data. There is no evidence of cumulative deficit—
but that proves nothing at all. Nor would measurements of other physical
attributes—calf circumference, weight, subscapular skinfold and so on)
provide any evidence whatsoever either to help predict, or explain the
reason for, the long-term increase in the growth of children which has
been going on for more than a century and of which the London data
presented in Table 1 are but a small sample. Interestingly, if all we
knew in the present instance was the measurements of the three "subpopulations," we might be led to infer that the data strongly supported
a genetic explanation of differences between the 1909 and 1959 samples,
the "hybrid" 1938 sample falling neatly in between according to prediction. So a secular, environmentally determined change would be mis-
interpreted as providing evidence of genetic differences.

Similarly, social class differences in height cannot be explained in
genetic terms, since they show the same secular trends and time lag.
And even racial or ethnic differences (with a few exceptions) in the
growth of children have been shown to depend almost entirely on differences in nutrition rather than between-groups differences in genetic
make-up (Habicht et al., 1974). In short, we cannot, using Jensen's
model, make any valid inference at all as to the extent to which genetic
factors are responsible for subpopulation differences in stature, among
groups growing up in changing, and therefore differing, environments. If
we used the model to predict change, or to estimate the limits of growth,
we would be hopelessly wrong—because the theory doesn't fit: it's a false
theory based on false and inadequate premises. If there really are genetic
differences between individuals and subpopulations in biomtric attributes
—as there surely are (in color for example)—we won't learn anything
about them this way. A quite different strategy of research is required.

Secular Trends in IQ

Because IQs are measured as deviation scores from sample means, and
because intelligence test items are changed from time to time as their
cultural familiarity changes, little attention has been paid to the possibility that secular changes may also have occurred in measured intelligence. The matter is difficult to study but would repay inquiry. We
know, for example, that several studies carried out over a period of
10-15 years by British investigators (Scottish Council for Research in
Education, 1949; Cattell, 1950; Giles-Bernadelli, 1950) to test the prediction, based on a genetic hypothesis, that the "national intelligence"
must be decreasing, uniformly reported modest rises in IQ. These were
not anticipated, and the authors attributed them (probably rightly,

though post hoc) to test sophistication. However, more marked effects have been reported by Jencks (1972):

> During World War II, for example, many elementary schools in Holland were closed. The IQ scores of children entering at least one secondary school after the end of the war appear to have dropped about 7 points as a result. Also, the schools in Prince Edward County were closed by the local board of education during the early 1960s, in order to avoid integration. When schools were reopened, black children who had not attended school for several years scored substantially lower than most black children of their age. So too, the New York City schools were closed for several months in the fall of 1968 as a result of a strike, and the city reported a drop in test scores the following spring.

Similarly, *gains* are reported by Tuddenham (1948) for American men tested by the U.S. Army in World War I and World War II. Tuddenham estimates that the rise in IQ was 0.7 to 0.8 SD (11-12 IQ points), though Jencks, who corrects the scores for restriction in range, thinks the true gain to be only 0.57 SD (about 9 IQ points). Likewise, studies of children matched for IQ at 11, but staying on at secondary school for varying periods after compulsory school age, have shown, both in England (Vernon, 1957) and in Sweden (Husen, 1951), differences in IQ of up to 12 points at the time of induction for military service.

All of these differences are explicable within a genetical framework; but their implications for between-groups comparisons have not really been faced because underlying all such comparisons is the belief that different subpopulations live in conditions which are roughly comparable in their nurturance of the factors that determine IQ. It was to expose the falsity of this belief that Birch devoted so much of his professional life (notably in Birch and Gussow, 1970).

RACE AND IQ: THE COLLABORATIVE PRENATAL PROJECT (CPP)

A recent publication bearing on social and biological factors related to IQ at age 4 gives a graphic illustration of the systematic bias affecting the development of the poor in the United States, and calls into question the basic assumption about homogeneity of environment which underlies all heritability analysis. Broman et al. (1975) have presented tables and a commentary describing data on 169 prenatal and developmental characteristics of 12,210 white children and 14,550 black children born in 12 university-based maternity units and followed up for 4 years when they were tested on a short form of the 1960 Revision of the Stanford Binet Scale.

TABLE 2

Percentage of Population by S E I

	0-9	10-19	20-29	30-39	40-49	50-59	60-69	70-79	80-89	90-95
US whites (%)	0.9	3.3	6.1	10.3	14.0	17.8	17.3	14.5	9.8	6.1
(cum. %)	0.9	4.2	10.3	20.6	34.6	52.4	69.7	84.2	94.0	100.0
CPP whites (%)	—	1.4	7.5	18.2	21.0	19.6	14.0	10.7	4.7	2.8
(cum. %)	—	1.4	8.9	27.1	48.1	67.7	81.7	92.4	97.1	100.0
US blacks (%)	10.2	15.8	19.1	19.1	15.8	8.8	5.1	3.7	1.9	0.5
(cum. %)	10.2	26.0	45.1	64.2	80.0	88.8	93.9	97.6	99.5	100.0
CPP blacks (%)	—	7.5	23.0	30.0	21.1	11.3	5.2	1.4	0.5	—
(cum. %)	—	7.5	30.5	60.5	81.6	92.9	98.1	99.5	100.0	100.0

Compiled from Figures 3.2 and 3.3 in Broman et al. (1975)

By far the most interesting parts of an otherwise pedestrian book are the tables showing socioeconomic status, measured on a socioeconomic index (SEI), and race differences. These are presented but scarcely commented on or analyzed in the text. However, the difference between the white and black population and between the CPP index cases and their racial groups throughout the U.S. can be seen very clearly from Table 2 which has been calculated from the information presented in figures 3.2 and 3.3 of the Broman monograph. Throughout the U.S. there are six times as many blacks as whites in the lowest two deciles of the SEI categories (and the proportion of blacks in the lowest decile, namely 10.2%, is eleven times as great as the proportion of whites, 0.9%). In the highest SEI category there are six times as many whites as blacks (and in 90+ percentile there are 12 times as many; 6.1% whites, 0.5% blacks). And the CPP groups are by no means representative of the populations from which they are drawn, having much smaller proportions in both the lowest and highest SEI categories.

In the other tables presented in the monograph, SEI is divided into only three categories: category I consists of the lowest 25% of the combined CPP aggregate, category II the middle 50% and category III the highest 25%. This broad grouping reduces the apparent differences. Even so, from Broman et al.'s table 4.1 (which incidentally, contains a misprint—5579 should be 5779 in category II for the white population) it can be calculated that 10.6% of whites are in the lowest 25% in socioeconomic status, 48.5% in the middle 50% category ,and 40.9% in the highest category; the corresponding figures for blacks are 32.5%, 57.1%, and 10.4%. And "equating" for social class still leaves a very substantial bias in favor of whites.

The same point is illustrated even more clearly in the two-way tables, as in Table 3 which analyzes birthweight in grams by SEI for whites and blacks. It is based on a re-analysis of table 9.4 in Broman et al. (1975).

In the white and black groups as a whole (bottom rows) the proportions of birth of under 2000 grams are 1.3% for whites but 2.7% for blacks; and for births under 2,500 grams they are $1.3 + 4.8 = 6.1\%$ for whites and $2.7 + 9.4 = 12.1\%$ for blacks. The differences are not simply due to the much larger numbers of blacks in the lower socioeconomic groupings, but are shown consistently across the SEI categories presented in the table. The same pattern emerges in regard to mother's education. Further analysis of Broman's table 5.1 (not reproduced here) shows that 12.4% of white mothers had less than 8 years of education as compared with 19.3% of black; 18.2% of whites had 13 or more years of educa-

TABLE 3

Birthweights of Whites and Blacks: %s by S E I

| | Birthweight (grams) | | | | | | |
	≤ 2000	2001-2500	2501-3000	3001-3500	3501-4000	4001 +	Total %
SEI I (lowest 25%)							
Whites	1.8	6.0	23.5	37.8	23.6	7.3	100
Blacks	2.8	10.0	31.1	39.1	14.2	2.7	100
SEI II (middle 50%)							
Whites	1.5	5.3	20.1	40.4	25.2	7.5	100
Blacks	2.7	9.3	29.5	40.0	15.6	3.0	100
SEI III (highest 25%)							
Whites	0.8	3.9	19.0	40.8	27.8	7.7	100
Blacks	2.7	9.4	29.8	40.0	15.2	2.9	100
All SEI							
Whites	1.3	4.8	20.0	40.3	26.1	7.6	100
Blacks	2.7	9.4	29.8	40.0	15.2	2.9	100

Reanalyzed from Table 9.4 in Broman et al. (1975)

tion as compared with 5% of blacks. And of those with 8 or fewer years of education, 30% of the whites were in the lowest SEI category as compared to 61% of the blacks; and 10% of whites were in the highest educational category (13 or more years of education) but only 2% of blacks were in that category. For those with 13 or more years of education there were only 9 out of 1261 (0.7%) white mothers in SEI category I and 87% in category III: but 8% of the black mothers with tertiary education were in SEI category I and only 40% in category III.

Analyzed in this way, the data provide a stark illustration of what Light and Smith (1969) described as the "malicious social allocation" of blacks, on a non-random basis, to the worst environments. A further analysis of the data would be of profound importance for the current IQ debate.

IMPLICATIONS FOR POPULATION GENETICS

What could we infer from the fact that the proportion of blacks who are disadvantaged socially and economically is very much higher than the proportion of whites? Broman et al. report that "the distribution of 30 of the 31 race-related variables would be expected to favor the subsequent development of white children. For example, white mothers had higher socioeconomic index scores, more education, higher scores on the nonverbal SRA intelligence test, were more often married, were of lower parity, made more prenatal visits, and had higher hemoglobin readings during pregnancy. The white children were larger at birth, 4 months, 8 months and I year. The Negroes had a significant advantage on only 1 of the 31 variables; they were slightly taller at age 4," (though shorter at birth, and at 4, 8 and 12 months). There is a need to explore in a more sophisticated way the effects of these adverse circumstances, recognizing that within each socioeconomic category the blacks are still gravely disadvantaged in that they tend to be at the lower end of the distribution within categories. An associated point is that for most of the variables there is an excess of black cases among those whose biomedical or sociocultural environment is adverse enough to be considered a *clinical* hazard. Broman et al. computer-tested the slope of the regression lines for linearity: Few departures were reported. But as Snedecor and Cochran (1967) point out, this is not a very satisfactory procedure for dealing with statistically small but biologically potentially important discrepancies from linearity, and a sensitive investigator would have looked carefully at the tail ends of the distributions and analyzed relationships among clinically related attributes (Tizard & Plewis, 1977).

Finally, the data would permit a more adequate exploration of the limits of an environmental explanation of the observed differences in IQ between whites and blacks. Jensen (1975) dismisses an environmental explanation of the differences between Negroes and whites on the grounds that the populations would have to differ by "some three or four standard deviations" in the environmental factors that influence IQ if the usually reported 15 to 20 points IQ difference is to be explained entirely in environmental terms. In the present instance the IQ differences ranged from about 8 points in the lowest socioeconomic level to 13 points in the highest level, that is, from 1-2 standard deviation times the value of "environmental effect." Both estimates assume, incidentally, that the within-groups heritability is 80% in both the black and white subpopulations—a highly questionable assumption in any case and virtually meaningless in an American context in view of the enormous within-groups variability in environmental conditions. (In other words the arguments that Feldman and Lewontin (1975) and others (e.g., Moran, 1974; Deaken, 1976; Tizard, 1975, 1976) have raised as to whether heritability estimates throw any light at all on between-groups differences apply with only slightly less force to estimates of within-groups heritability when the "groups" are as heterogeneous as these.)

The real point here, however, is that in order to question the cogency of Jensen's analysis one does not have to "hypothesize" the existence of "as yet unidentified and unmeasured factors, which produce IQ differences *between* racial groups, but do not appreciably contribute to IQ variance *within* groups." (Jensen, 1975). The many differences are there for all to see, and it is not the case that no one has clearly specified the nature of these factors so they have to be simply labeled as "factor X," an ad hoc entry "invoked to explain the IQ gap still left when known measurable environmental differences are taken into account." If the present set of data do one thing, it is to show that on virtually all of the variables relevant to IQ which were measured, blacks are seriously disadvantaged as compared with whites. The cumulative result of this multitude of adverse factors is to depress mean IQ and reduce variance so that fewer variables are associated with IQ among blacks; the patterns of association differ, and the magnitude of the relationships is smaller.

Because their standpoint is one of benign psychological apartheid, Broman et al. do not discuss these race differences or look in any detail at differences in the index cases attending the different centers. They do remark, however, that within the 8 samples from biracial research centers, where the average white-Negro difference in socioeconomic index score was only 3 points, the average IQ difference was only 5 points. Furthermore, by putting together data given in Broman et al.'s monograph on p. 24 and a casual remark made on p. 286, one discovers that in one center, in which the mean SEI for blacks was only 30.1, the mean IQ was only 87; but in two others centers, in which the blacks' mean SEI score was respectively 62.8 and 60.8, their mean IQ was 102. Whether, if at all, the black families in the two well functioning "samples" differed from the average white family in other characteristics on which in general blacks are shown to be disadvantaged, one cannot say, since no relevant data to answer this question are presented. But if one is interested in black-white differences, it is here that one might start one's inquiries.

ECOLOGICAL STUDIES OF RACE DIFFERENCES

Once we stop trying to use dubious correlational data to explain differences in means, and start to examine the actual conditions that affect the development of children, we get on to much more interesting ground —still, unfortunately, largely unexplored because most effort so far has gone into entirely futile debates about heritability. Already, however, there are many other leads to follow. They arise mainly out of recent work. This, in contrast to many of the earlier studies which reported merely IQs and gave only sketchy accounts of the circumstances of the people tested, has paid particular attention to the specific characteristics of different environmental settings which influence development. Three recent investigations illustrate the manner in which this type of inquiry throws light on the mechanisms that influence cognitive development.

Yule et al. (1975), in a large ecological study in an inner London borough, tested all 9-year-old children on a group test of nonverbal intelligence. The mean IQ of white children was 92 and that of colored (Caribbean) children 82. However, some of these children of West Indian parents were born outside the UK—they had scores of only 76—16 points below that of whites. But others were born in the U.K., and they had scores of 85—only 7 points below that of whites, though they still suffered from substantial environmental disadvantages. The 9-point difference gives an indication of the extent of adaptation. It is also relevant that the IQs of other immigrant groups showed similar differences. Greek Cypriot children born in the U.K. had a mean IQ of 91, but those born in Cyprus a mean of only 81. A small group of Turkish children born in the U.K. had a mean of 85. All these children are culturally disadvantaged as compared with indigenous children—but they have nothing in common racially.

In another study, carried out in the Thomas Coram Research Unit, B. A. Akhurst tested all available children aged 9-11 years and 13-15 years in a representative sample of Children's Homes serving London. The test used was the short form of the WISC. There were 127 white children and 55 black. At ages 7-9 the mean IQ of the whites was 107 and that of blacks 101; but the differences between them were not significant. However of those aged 13-15, the means for whites and blacks were 92 and 93—almost identical, with both showing a significant drop in IQ with age. Of course, the interpretation of the findings is not entirely straightforward; but the implication is that a common environment leads to a lessening of between-groups differences, and that some conditions of deprivation do lead to cumulative deficits.

A third and much more detailed series of studies has been carried out by Barbara Tizard and colleagues in the Thomas Coram Research Unit (Tizard and Rees, 1976; Tizard and Hodges, 1978; Hodges and Tizard, 1977). All the subjects were children growing up in residential nurseries from birth until the age of two. After their second birthday some of the children were adopted, some restored to their families, and some transferred to other institutions. There is no evidence that selective factors relating to biosocial attributes of the children played a significant part in their subsequent adoptive placement, restoration to their natural parents, or transfer to another children's home.

At the age of two a group of similar children in residential nurseries, which included some but not all of the present sample, were on average slightly backward: Their mean IQ was 94. Those who remained in the nurseries until the age of four however showed a rise in IQ: The mean at 4½ was 101 for white children and 105 for black children. The blacks, in fact, scored higher, but the difference was not significant, no doubt because the environment was the same for both groups. The social environment was also, as was shown by observational studies, much richer for 3- and 4-year-old children than for children under 2: The IQ rise of 10 points, between ages 2 and 4, is no doubt attributable to this enrichment.

Some of the children were adopted after the age of 2, mostly into middle-class homes. At age 4½ these children had IQs that were very much higher than those who had not been adopted: The mean was 116 points, in fact. Again there was no significant difference in the mean IQ of blacks and whites, though the blacks did as a matter of fact again do somewhat better than the white adoptees.

Nearly all the children tested at 4½ were again tested at the age of 8½, this time on the WISC. The results (Hodges and Tizard, 1977) were as follows (see Table 4). The early adopted children retained their high IQs: The mean was 116 at age 4, 115 at age 8. The mean IQ of a group of 5 children adopted *after* the age of 4 fell slightly from 105 to 101 points—14 points lower than that of the children adopted at a younger age. The 9 children restored to their natural parents before the age of 4 also showed no significant change in IQ; the mean at 8 was the same as that of the children adopted *after* the age of 4. However, the fourth group, who moved out of the nurseries to their own families or stayed in institutional care, decreased in IQ, by an average of 7 points, by the time they were 8.

This study was not designed to investigate race differences in intelligence, and, as the authors point out, the cell sizes in the different race/ placement categories were "too small for statistical analysis of the findings to be appropriate." However, there was "a consistent trend for the black children, wherever placed, to have higher IQs than the white children." Clearly no unambiguous interpretation can be given to this finding—but the 8-year test results do at least indicate that there was no differential falling off in the IQs of blacks as compared with whites between the ages of 4 and 8. The data thus answer a query raised when

TABLE 4

IQ Changes: 4-8½ Years

(children who spent their first two years in institutions)

GROUP	N	WPPSI IQ at 4	WISC IQ at 8½
Adopted before 4 years	20	116	115
Adopted between 4 & 8 years	5	105	101
Restored to parents before 4 years	9	98	103
Restored after 4 or remained in care	11	103	97

Data from B. Tizard and J. Hodges, 1978. See also B. Tizard and J. Rees, 1976.

the original 4-year-old data were published—critics doubted whether anything much could be made of group differences in the IQs of children as young as 4.

The answer seems to be that transfer out of a less stimulating environment—in this case a good institution—into an intellectually more stimulating private home before the age of 4 is highly beneficial to the development of a child's IQ. The IQ rise of perhaps 20 points, from a mean around 94 at age 2 to 116 at age 4, holds up unchanged to age 8. But children adopted after the age of 4 show no comparable rise, nor do children restored to a less stimulating environment before the age of 4. These findings are in line with those obtained in longitudinal studies of children of different social class or racial backgrounds growing up in their own homes. (See Smilansky et al., 1976 for a review and an excellent study of Israeli infants from two ethnic groups.) They are also in conformity with the findings of Dennis (1973) regarding the effect of adoption on orphanage children in the Lebanon—though, as Clarke and Clarke (1976) point out, the evidence does not necessarily imply that the first 2 to 4 years are "critical" for the development of IQ.

Clearly there is a great deal more to be done to tease out the factors that are responsible for the development of a good intelligence. We do, however, have some ideas of where to look. (Clark & Clarke, 1976, have explored many of the issues in their editorial comments on a stimulating set of papers which discuss the "myth and evidence" surrounding the topic of early experience.) By concentrating our attention on race differences, and carrying out further large-scale psychometric surveys and elaborate statistical analyses based on crude and misleading concepts of heritability, we will simply get nowhere. What we need instead are detailed but objective studies of processes that affect the child, and experimental studies to test our findings in action. Until this is done, sterile debates about the importance of so-called race are likely to continue. Their only outcome, in my view, will be to distract psychologists and educators from the study of meaningful and important problems, and fan racial prejudice.

SUMMARY

There is a current controversy about relations between "race," which in practice means ethnic group defined by color, and IQ. It is well established that American blacks score on average about 15 points below whites in IQ. Some think genetic factors are primarily responsible for their poor showing. The debate centers on three issues: the meaning that can be ascribed to IQ scores; the estimation of within-group "heritability"; and the proportion of between-groups differences in mean IQ that can be attributed to genetic factors using coefficients derived from within-groups estimates of heritability.

It is argued here that even if we take IQ scores at face value and assume within-groups heritability to be 80%, we can draw no conclusions whatsover about the cause of any biometric differences between groups growing up in different environments. Furthermore, there is evidence that when environmental conditions are the same there are no differences in the mean IQs of black and white children.

Recent studies are summarized. They suggest that large and characteristic mean differences in the environment of children growing up in different circumstances, especially in their early years, account for the observed mean differences in test performance, and that race is not a factor influencing it. Advances in knowledge are most likely to come from further detailed study, preferably experimental, of the manner in which large numbers of experiential factors influence the development of competencies.

APPENDIX

JENSEN'S HERITABILITY MODEL APPLIED TO IQ AND STATURE

Consider first a single (white) group or subpopulation. The SD (standard deviation) of IQs is 15 points and the variance the square of the standard deviation, 225 (15^2). Jensen claims that the heritability coefficient of intelligence *within* a group is 0.80. This means that 80% of the variance of 225 points is due to genetic factors, which leaves 20% to be accounted for by non-genetic or environmental factors. From this we can calculate that the environmental component of IQ variance is $0.20 \times 225 = 45$ and that the standard deviation is 6.71 IQ points (the square root of 45). If we now find two genetically identical individuals (e.g. monozygotic twins) whose IQ scores differ by say 10 points, we can say that they differ by $10/6.71 = 1.49$ standard deviations in the effects of all non-genetic factors influencing IQ.

Now apply the same analysis to *between-groups* differences. The mean IQ of whites is 100 and of blacks 85, so the mean difference is 15 points. The standard deviation of the environmental components is, as before, 6.71 IQ points. So for *all* the observed differences of 15 points to be due to environmental factors, blacks and whites would have to differ by $15/6.71 = 2.24$ standard deviations in the effects of environment on differences in intelligence. Jensen considers that the figure is implausibly high; he therefore rejects the hypothesis that differences in IQ between blacks and whites can be accounted for solely in environmental terms.

What happens if we apply Jensen's analysis to the London height data?

Standard deviations in height are not given for the 1938 sample but those for the 1909 and 1959 samples agree closely, and for statistical purposes, the pooled variance (43.17) and SD (6.57) can be used without distorting the analysis. Similarly, the mean heights of each sample, over all 6 age groups, give an accurate picture of what is happening at each age and can likewise be used as data from which to analyze the trends over time. The within-group heritability may be assumed to be 0.95. Hence the total range of environmental components only accounts for 5% of the observed variance (or 10% if we follow Jensen's worked example using Watusi and Pygmy data). The mean observed variance for the entire age group 7-12 is $6.57^2 = 43.17$ cm. The environmental variance is $43.17 \times 0.05 = 2.17$ c.m. and the standard deviation of the environmental effects, 1.47 cm. The mean observed difference is 10.2 cm. This is $10.2/1.47 = 6.94$ times the "environmental effects" expressed in standard deviation units (4.90 SD units if as much as 10% of the variance is environmental).

Clearly, if Jensen believes it difficult to account for a standard deviation value of 2.24 for the IQ data by an environmental hypothesis, it is very much more difficult to account for a standard deviation value of 6.94, or even 4.90, for the height changes in environmental terms. And even if the heritability coefficient for height in children is less than 0.90, it is nonetheless almost certainly greater than the heritability coefficient of IQ, and the phenotypic difference in height between 1909 and 1959

(10.2 cm.), expressed in SD units is 1.55 times as great (10.2/6.57 = 1.55) as the corresponding difference of one SD in IQ between blacks and whites.

REFERENCES

BIRCH, H. G. and GUSSOW, J. D. *Disadvantaged Children: Health, Nutrition and School Failure.* New York: Harcourt, Brace & World and Grune & Stratton, 1970.

BROMAN, S. H., NICHOLS, P. L. and KENNEDY, W. A. *Preschool IQ: Prenatal and Early Developmental Correlates.* Hillsdale, New Jersey: Lawrence Erlbaum Associates, 1975.

BRONFENBRENNER, U. *Influences on Human Development.* Hinsdale, Ill.: Dryden Press, 1972.

CATTELL, R. B. The fate of national intelligence: test of a thirteen-year prediction. *Eugen. Rev.,* 1950, 42, 136-148.

CLARKE, A. M. and CLARKE, A. D. B. *Early Experience: Myth and Reality.* London: Open Books, 1976.

DEAKIN, M. On Urbach's analysis of the IQ debate. *Brit. J. Philosophy of Science,* 1976.

DENNIS, W. *Children of the Creche.* New York: Appleton-Century Crofts, 1973.

EYSENCK, H. J. *Race, Intelligence and Education.* London: Temple Smith, 1971. (American edition titled: *The IQ Argument.* Freeport, New York: Library Press, 1971).

FELDMAN, M. W. and LEWONTIN, R. C. The heritability hang-up. *Science,* 1975, 190, No. 4220, 1163-1168.

FULKER, D. W. Book Review of L. J. Kamin. *The Science and Politics of IQ. Am. J. Psychology,* 1975, Vol. 88, No. 3.

GILES-BERNADELLI, B. M. The decline of intelligence in New Zealand. *Population Studies,* 1950, 4, 200-208.

HABICHT, J-P., MARTORELL, R., YARBROUGH, C., MALINA, R. M., and KLEIN, R. E. Height and weight standards for preschool children. *The Lancet,* 1974, 1, 7858, 611-614.

HODGES, J. and TIZARD, B. The effects of adoption, restoration to the natural mother, and continued institutionalization on the cognitive development of eight year old children. To be published, 1977.

HUSEN, T. The influence of schooling upon IQ. *Theoria,* 1951, 17, 61-88.

JENCKS, C. *Inequality: A Reassessment of the Effect of Family and Schooling in America.* New York: Basic Books, 1972.

JENSEN, A. R. How much can we boost IQ and scholastic achievement? *Harvard Educational Review,* 1969, 39, 48.

JENSEN, A. R. *Educability and Group Differences.* London: Methuen, 1973.

JENSEN, A. R. Race and mental ability. In: S. J. Ebling (Ed.), *Racial Variation in Man.* Symposium of the Institute of Biology No. 22. London: Institute of Biology, 1975.

KAMIN, L. J. *The Science and Politics of IQ.* Potomac, Maryland: Lawrence Erlbaum Associates, 1974.

KENNEDY, W. A., VAN DE REIT, V., and WHITE, J. C. A normative sample of intelligence and achievement of Negro elementary school children in the Southeastern United States. *Monographs of the Society for Research on Human Development,* 1963, 28, No. 6.

KLINEBERG, O. *Negro Intelligence and Selective Migration.* New York: Columbia University Press, 1935.

LIGHT, R. J. and SMITH, P. V. Social allocation models of intelligence: A methodological inquiry. *Harvard Educational Review,* 1969, 39, 484-510.

MORAN, P. A. P. The estimation of psychological genetic differences between classes and races. *Brit. J. Psychiatry,* 1974, 124, 228-292.

SCOTTISH, COUNCIL FOR RESEARCH IN EDUCATION. *The Trend of Scottish Intelligence.* London: University of London Press, 1949.

SMILANSKY, S., SHEPHATIA, L., and FRENKEL, E. *Mental Development of Infants from Two Ethnic Groups: Findings from the Jerusalem Study of Growth and Development.* Jerusalem: Ruth Bressler Center for Research in Education. Research Report No. 195, 1976.

SNEDECOR, G. W. and COCHRAN, W. G. *Statistical Methods.* Ames, Iowa: Iowa State University Press, 1967.

TIZARD, B. and HODGES, J. The effect of early institutional rearing on the behavior problems and affectional relationships of 8 year old children, 1978. (To be published.)

TIZARD, B. and REES, J. A comparison of the effects of adoption, restoration to the natural mother, and continued institutionalization on the cognitive development of four-year-old children. In: A. M. Clarke and A. D. B. Clarke (Eds), *Early Experience, Myth and Reality.* London: Open Books, 1976, pp. 135-152.

TIZARD, J. Race and IQ: The limits of probability. *New Behaviour,* 6, April, 1975.

TIZARD, J. Progress and degeneration in the 'IQ debate': Comments on Urbach. *Brit. J. Phil. Sci.,* 1976, 27, 251-274.

TIZARD, J. and PLEWIS, I. Critical notice of Broman, S. H., Nichols, P. L. and Kennedy, W. *Preschool IQ: Prenatal and Early Developmental Correlates.* Hillsdale, N. J.: Lawrence Erlbaum Associates, 1975.

TUDDENHAM, R. D. Soldier intelligence in World Wars I and II. *Amer. Psychologist,* 1948, 3, 54-56.

VERNON, P. E. Intelligence and intellectual stimulation during adolescence. *Indian Psychol. Bull.,* 1957, 2, 1-6.

YULE, W., BERGER, M., RUTTER, M., and YULE, B. Children of West Indian immigrants: II. Intellectual performance and reading attainment. *J. Child Psychol. Psychiat.,* 1975, 1-17.

8

Heterogeneity in Children with Neurological Impairment

MORTON BORTNER

INTRODUCTION

There are two good reasons to study the relationship between neurological status and cognitive function in children. First, such investigations form the empirical foundation for a science of brain-behavior relationships. Second, children with neurological impairment often suffer cognitive deficits and as a consequence require special attention from the educational community. It is most unlikely that each neurologically impaired child is unique both in the nature of his physical signs and in their cognitive concomitants. It is far more likely that there are constellations of physical and cognitive signs based on location and pathological nature of the lesion. Without a relationship between biology and cognition, we are reduced to a trial-and-error approach to the education of these children. However, if we can connect educational procedures and their outcome to specific impairments, then we can evaluate and identify what is effective and what is not. The data to be presented, therefore, are directed at clarifying the heterogeneous nature of the neurological signs found in so-called minimally brain-damaged children, the heterogeneous nature of their cognitive consequences, and finally, the relationships between these two sets of events.

The research reported is based on work that was supported in part by the U.S. Office of Education Grant OEG-0-8-071272-3317 (032), and the Joseph P. Kennedy, Jr. Foundation.

Thanks to Dr. I. Leon Smith for his constructive criticism of an earlier version of this chapter.

187

It is probably fair to say that we still do not have any very clear ideas about how to educate minimally brain-damaged children. There was an obvious implication in the work of the 1950s and the 1960s that these children required something special (never specified), something different from what normal children got. This was certainly not hard to justify since it was clear that they had been unable to profit from instruction in normal classes and were increasingly receiving special attention precisely because of their failure to learn from standard approaches in standard settings.

Attempts to arrive at rational instructional strategies have, to date, emphasized either language development or perceptual and perceptual-motor skills, since these represent two major areas of deficit and therefore two differing viewpoints as to origin of educational handicaps. (See Frostig, 1964 for the perceptual viewpoint and Kirk, 1968 for the language viewpoint.) Proponents of each perspective, incidentally, have been criticized for the inadequate connection between their programs and the theories upon which they were allegedly based. There is doubt, therefore, that either of these viewpoints has ever been empirically tested in any relevant and systematic fashion (Bortner, 1971). Moreover, to complicate the issue still further, there is good evidence to suggest that a perceptual handicap may not even be as primary as it has been made out to be in the hierarchy of difficulties shown by neurologically impaired children. For example, Boll (1972) has reported that tests of conceptual ability show more serious impairment in these children than visual, auditory or tactual perception, and concluded that a term such as "conceptually handicapped" might be more useful in describing them than the ubiquitous term "perceptually handicapped."

It is ironic, therefore, in the light of the disagreement which exists about the nature and extent of cognitive and perceptual deficit in these children, that the stereotype persists that they are, from a psychological viewpoint, a homogeneous group. Such a stereotype is certainly perpetuated by such terms as "organic impairment" and "minimal brain damage." It will be the purpose of the ensuing discussion to demonstrate the necessity of viewing these children as constituting a heterogeneous aggregation, and to present some psychometric and neurological data which provide limited support for the assertion that they are indeed anything but a homogeneous group. It follows from such a view that describing neurologically impaired children as primarily language impaired or primarily perceptually impaired or primarily anything else is misleading since it implies that we are dealing with an essentially uniform group and a single entity. This simplistic tendency to view children's learning problems as stemming from some single mechanism or disability has certainly delayed the development of individualized instructional strategies.

The category of "brain damage" is seen in the present paper as non-specific and functionally meaningless. The tenacity and persistence of such labeling are difficult to understand in light of the progress made in the mapping of the brain in human clinical neuropsychology. Reitan's (1973) work with adults has made it eminently clear that it is naive to conceive of "brain damage" as an entity. In an attempt to document the nature of meaningful brain-behavior relationships, he and his colleagues have studied the effects of brain damage and have defined lesions that are diffuse, focal, localized in the left or the right hemisphere, acute or chronic, and in such neuropathological terms as traumatic, vascular or neoplastic. Smith made essentially the same point long ago (1962) and again more recently (1975). Bortner and Birch (1968) said the same thing with special reference to children. More recently, in the field of liaison psychiatry, Lipowski (1975) challenged the reductionistic character of the so-called organic brain syndrome which implied a "non-existent homogeneity of psychiatric aspects of cerebral disease," and called attention to the variety of impairments seen in patients with cerebral dysfunction.

Empirical findings make it clear that verbal function is associated with the left cerebral hemisphere. Patients with left cerebral damage usually have difficulties in receptive and/or expressive language (Berent, Cohen & Silverman, 1975). Patients with right cerebral damage show perceptual inadequacy in any combination of the visual, auditory or tactual modalities (Parsons, 1970). More generally, there is much evidence that the type and location of the lesion are associated with specific behavioral deficits (Yates, 1966). Moreover, such deficits do not merely permit the psychologist to confirm a diagnosis that is already known but rather they permit the identification of neurological disorders even when neurological procedures themselves have proven equivocal (Fisklov & Goldstein, 1974).

Perhaps, because most (although not all) of this work has been reported for adults and has not yet been corroborated for children, the label "brain damage" lives on. It is true that some evidence suggests that general deficit rather than specific deficits characterizes the behavior of children with known brain lesions (Ernhart, Graham, Eichman, Marshall & Thurston, 1963; Reed, Reitan & Klove, 1965), although, as stated earlier, some areas of function seem to be more affected than others (Boll, 1972). Thus, the problem of the relationship, in children, between various forms of cognitive behavior on the one hand and type and location of lesion on the other remains open. Despite such lack of closure on brain-behavior relationships in children, it is clear enough by now from the work with adults that the term "brain damage" is, at best, a gross category which subsumes a variety of neurological entities and, at worst, an obscurantist label.

SOME RECENT HISTORY

Because of its implications for the future history of children, with central nervous system (CNS) impairment, it is instructive to digress for a moment and point to the issue of homogeneity-heterogeneity among mentally retarded children. For these children, the short history of attempts to demonstrate the value of special classes (and of presumed homogeneity) ended in failure. In retrospect, the finding of "no difference" in the educational achievement of retarded children in regular and special classes was probably inevitable, in part, not because the special classes failed to provide sufficiently pertinent special instruction, but because the assumption that children benefit when classes are more uniform was never validated. It was logical to expect that such uniformity, if it could be achieved, would make both pedagogical and management issues easier for the teacher and thereby lead to increased improvement in the children. Unfortunately, such homogeneity does not appear to have ever been achieved, and, in fact, it was recently suggested (Smith, 1974) that special classes "reproduce rather than reduce" the individual differences found in regular classes (albeit, at lower cognitive levels).

Despite such findings, educators have continued their work as if classes composed of retarded children were by definition more homogeneous than groups of age-comparable children of normal intellect. On the other hand, the individualized teaching that is commonly found in special classes reflects the teachers' recognition that many individuals with the same general level of intelligence may be different from each other. Such individualized teaching is indirect evidence, at the level of practice, that such children are a heterogeneous aggregation.

In reaction to the failure of special classes, Dunn (1968) and others proposed the abolition of the practice of grouping children on the basis of labels, and proposed instead the mainstreaming of poor learners. These proposals and their inherent admission of the earlier failure of special classes notwithstanding is more like walking away from the problem, the abolition of labels is not a solution to mislabeling. Mainstreaming, which needs no apology for its social value, is essentially irrelevant to the need for pertinent teaching based on knowledge of the child's intellectual and educational strengths and weaknesses. In retrospect and in summary, despite changes in the social grouping of these children, there is little now that is newer, or educationally more pertinent, in their classroom instruction than before. They have simply moved from a context of lower level cognitive heterogeneity (special classes) to a context of higher level cognitive heterogeneity (mainstream). There is as yet no demonstration of educational gain.

Recent developments in the education of "brain-damaged" children suggest that, unless a major conceptual shift occurs, a similar fate of relabeling, regrouping, and mainstreaming without appreciable changes in teaching strategy, awaits them. In the 1950s and early 1960s, using such terms as "brain-injured" or "minimal brain damage," parents seeking something special in the education of their children brought pressure to bear upon boards of education, who responded with "special classes for the brain-injured." From the mid 1960s to the present, educators became more "nationalistic" and terms using the word "brain" gave way to more behaviorally and educationally oriented labels such as "learning-disabled." Classes for the brain-injured were now called classes for the learning-disabled. It didn't matter. In neither case were instructional tactics designed that could meet the variety of cognitive-educational needs that such children have. Now that the pendulum is swinging under the banner of mainstreaming, learning-disabled, née brain-injured, children are gradually being integrated into normal classes. As was the case with mentally retarded children, such mainstreaming may have some (far from clear) impact on their social development, but there is little to suggest that their cognitive-educational skills will be improved in the slightest.

What does the brief history of recent attempts to reconstitute and/or dissolve special classes teach us? It tells us, at the very least, what we have *not* learned from such actions, namely, we have not learned anything about instructional strategies. Energy might be better spent identifying those cognitive and learning characteristics that operationally define different clinical entities. Children with these entities may or may not have different educational needs. Let's find out!

How are we to define these entities? Interestingly, schools have no trouble making similar decisions. They define children with minimal brain damage, e.g. by using such information as presence of neurological signs of abnormality, IQ level, reading disability-learning disability, and level of social maturity. Such considerations are in part, of course, administrative, and stem from the practical need (financial in origin) to have state-approved categories within which to place children in order that the school may be reimbursed for their education. These ways of characterizing children are certainly meaningful, but how educationally pertinent are they? They are clearly part of a political-economic process, and somewhat less clearly related to pedagogy. Yes, it is true that characteristics such as reading grade level and social maturity are certainly related to matters of instruction, but they equally certainly do not lead in any direct way to classroom strategies, and of course, the fact of neurological impairment, in itself, suggests absolutely nothing to the teacher.

MENTAL ABILITY PATTERNS

Investigations into the cognitive functioning of children with known cerebral lesions often report generalized rather than specific deficits, i.e., these children evidence depressed scores in all ability areas when compared with normal children. But, it is not clear why this should be so. Indeed, the large number of neurological disorders makes it seem plausible to expect differential cognitive deficit roughly in accordance with differential neurological status. Such differential cognitive deficit might be manifested, if it existed at all, in different degrees of defect in various subtests of the WISC. Thus pattern analysis in neurologically impaired children represents an attempt to deal with the questions of differential cognitive defect as it relates to neurological status.

From the view of education, pattern analysis reveals the nature of the child's uneven abilities. For example, strength in language and weakness in perceptual skills will result in inconsistent classroom performance which interferes with smooth classroom practices. Since it is reasonable to assume that different neurological lesions will result in differential alteration of cognitive function, one may speculate that meaningful patterns exist among these children. It is constructive to view such patterns as potential bases for instructional approaches. After all, if each child is uniquely different in his cognitive deficits, then educational prescriptions can never transcend trial and error.

It is sometimes reported that in children with neurological impairment of Verbal-Performance discrepancies. What does it matter? While superior judgment that neurologically impaired children "can say but they can't do." Most of these reports were based on relatively small samples, raising the inevitable questions of the representativeness of the study samples and the generalizability of the reported findings. But, far more importantly, one must ask how important it is at all for the teacher to learn of Verbal-Performance discrepancies. What does it matter? While superior functioning in one or the other area may have some implications for whether to stress academic or vocational subject matter, the fact is that the Verbal-Performance message conveys very little of practical value with respect to instructional procedures.

In an effort to document the nature of the heterogeneity of these children, and to deal with the methodological difficulties referred to above, Bortner (1976) studied 210 neurologically impaired children in a school setting which educated approximately one-half of all the neurologically impaired children who had been identified in a large New York county. If not actually representative of CNS impaired school children, this large sample certainly came close to being so, and was defined with respect to such variables as age, sex, race, socioeconomic status, and most fundamentally, nature and number of CNS signs. The Verbal-Performance discrepancy was examined not because of its educational significance but because of its potential value in discriminating discrete groups. Many children were superior in Verbal scores, but, then, many were superior in Performance scores. What might this mean? Since the investigator assumed that these children were a heterogeneous aggregation, then, of course, there was no reason to expect that either Verbal or Performance scores would be consistently superior, or that any other *single* pattern would emerge. The attempt was made merely to establish the fact of cognitive heterogeneity and something about its nature among such children.

What is the potential value of such an effort? Some workers have suggested that mental ability profiles may be useful in developing educational provisions for these children. For example, Guilford (1959) has suggested that if mental ability patterns can be identified they can be ameliorated. Indeed, it has even been suggested that highly specific instructional strategies can be designed on the basis of these profiles (Meeker, 1969). Similar views have been expressed by others (Belmont, Birch & Belmont, 1967; Gallagher, 1960; Sabatino & Hayden, 1970). Despite such high hopes, very little empirical data describing patterns of mental abilities of neurologically impaired children are available (Belmont, Birch & Belmont, 1967; Benton, 1964).

Are Guilford and Meeker justified in their claims that identification leads to amelioration? No! according to Mann (1971). He says that interest in mental ability patterns is based on the twin assumptions that certain abilities (e.g., perception) underlie and are basic to academic achievement, and secondly, that these abilities are susceptible to training. He doubts that either assumption is true. Somewhat more optimistically, Bortner (1971) suggested that knowledge of these patterns may permit restructuring of instruction which, in turn, will maximize the child's strengths.

The restructuring of instruction to facilitate learning, contains, admittedly, more hope than is presently justified by the state of research findings. There is already a considerable body of research, (e.g., Berliner & Cahen, 1973; Cronbach & Snow, 1969) dealing with aptitude-treatment interactions, i.e., the effect of different types of instruction on learners with different abilities. The results are essentially negative. One can accept the findings, however, without necessarily being deterred by them. The fact is, of course, that knowledge of mental ability patterns has not yet led directly to more successful teaching strategies.

In addition, Bortner suggested that such knowledge of abilities may also permit the hierarchical reordering of instructional objectives to coincide with the child's emerging competencies and thereby provide a rational basis for the modification of educational objectives. This simply suggests that when a child's cognitive-developmental level is identified and when that child is out of phase with age-grade expectancies, then the teacher will need to modify her goals in accordance with the reality of the child's aptitudes. One functional description of his aptitudes and his developmental level is the so-called mental ability pattern, and it is certainly pertinent to suggest that this objective criterion be included among the bases for instructional decision.

THE IMPLICIT MODEL

Obtaining knowledge of patterns of abilities is a way of addressing oneself to a model which suggests that learners should be taught (not necessarily placed) according to empirically derived cognitive categories. The model suggests that knowledge of such categories will have *some* meaningful application in the construction of rational strategies of instruction. If such information is not helpful, what are the alternatives? Shall we continue to base instructional strategies on the intuitions of experienced teachers who have found that their method "works"? Shall we continue to base educational decisions on the manifestly unsatisfactory educational utility of such labels as "brain-damaged" and "learning-disabled"? There does not seem to be much choice in the matter; the search for mental ability patterns will probably proceed as one necessary (if insufficient) step in the identification of those processes and mechanisms which underlie academic learning. Ultimately, empirically based teaching strategies will need to deal with such underlying learning mechanisms.

One might argue that there is no more magic in an empirically derived cognitive category than in an administrative assignment; that, indeed, groups defined as empirically different may not be important to differentiate from an educational point of view. But, we are not arguing for a classroom assignment. We are not arguing that cognitive categories, once identified, should be the basis for classroom grouping. Instead, it is being suggested that such cognitive categories be one basis for instructional strategies no matter what classroom they are in.

It might be argued that the search for "underlying learning mechanisms" is a chimera, since, once identified, any mechanism can be subjected to interminable analysis, that "mechanism" is subject to infinite regression. No doubt, "mechanisms" may be interminably regressed, but that is not to say that at any given level of explanation they are not functionally useful. After all, no one ever viewed the bacterium as an ultimate mechanism, which was not to deny the utility of its discovery.

With this background of hope, during the course of a descriptive study of neurologically impaired children by the present investigator (Bortner, 1976), it became feasible to explore a variety of methods which describe the nature of these children's heterogeneity and lay a foundation for defining subgroups. The methods ranged from those that were frankly crude through those employing moderate levels of statistical sophistication. All except one failed. Even the "successful" method defied unequivocal interpretation. One thing seems clear: We are merely at the beginning.

STUDY SAMPLE

The subjects of the presently reported longitudinal study were 210 children who had been administratively designated as brain-damaged and assigned to a special school and special class placement. They ranged in age from six through twelve years. There were three times as many boys as girls in the sample. This sex distribution is in line with that in other studies (Birch, 1964; Rutter, Graham & Yule, 1970). The children were followed for a period of four years.

Thirty children were selected on a random basis from the existing total pool at each age level in the chosen age range. Slightly less than the original 210 children were followed in the second, third, and fourth years of the study because of moves, transfers and illnesses. Even so, there was remarkable stability in the school population, and the second, third, and fourth years of the study contained N's, respectively, of 203, 193, and 177. The high quality of this special school undoubtedly influ-

enced parents to remain in the school district and prevented greater
out-migration.

The school from which the children of this study were drawn served
an entire suburban county of 56 school districts and approximately 350,-
000 pupils. The social class and ethnic characteristics of children attending this special school have been described in detail in a previous report
(Bortner & Birch, 1970). In brief, the pupils were predominantly white,
from upper working-class and middle-class backgrounds, and with a
scattered representation of other social and ethnic groups. There was a
marked underrepresentation of children from significantly deprived
social and economic backgrounds.

Placement in this school was based on criteria that were uniform
throughout the year in which the study sample was admitted. The
county's educational policy was to admit those children with learning
disabilities and/or behavioral problems for whom a physician had at-
tested to the presence of neurological impairment. To be sure, such
medical evidence was not uniform and relied variously on history, the
clinical neurological examination, and/or electroencephalography. However, while data were not uniform, there was positive evidence in the
school records from at least one of these three sources. Hence, some
children came with a history of seizures, others with pathological reflex
status, others with positive EEG, and still others with some combination
of these or other signs. All children, therefore, presumably came to the
school with some evidence of neurological impairment plus a history of
difficulty in school achievement.

Tests and Procedures

All children were given a clinical neurological examination and a
WISC. The WISC was re-administered in each of three subsequent
years. It is obvious that no single test can hope to capture the complexity of brain-behavior relationships. The WISC was chosen because
it is an omnibus test and contains samples of a variety of cognitive
abilities, including the ubiquitous Verbal-Performance dichotomy. As
such, it provides information on language, visual-perceptual adequacy,
perceptual-motor integration and other skills known to be affected by
brain damage.

In the present series of studies, both cross-sectional and longitudinal
methods of analysis were used. Previous research has concentrated, for
the most part, on levels of performance at a fixed point in time. Of
course, such cross-sectional reports cannot deal with the question of

whether a given subject has improved or declined in his performance, and yet it is entirely possible that certain forms of impairment in interaction with growth and development may result in one level of function at time A and a quite different level of function at time B. Longitudinal analysis is the only method that can deal effectively with this issue.

Two sets of data were analyzed which included cognitive and neurological information. In an effort to determine the heterogeneous nature of the cognitive deficit, the WISC data were analyzed in three different ways.

1) There is the question of the depiction of an intellectual profile for a given age group. The method used here is a variation of a procedure previously described by Belmont and Birch (1966). The method is graphic. A zero abscissa is established by using the mean of all the scaled scores of a given age group, above and below which are plotted the group mean of the scaled scores for each subtest. Hence, all subjects aged six are summed for each subtest individually, and the mean of all subtests combined is then obtained. Thus, if the mean scaled score for all subtests combined for age six years is eight, this value becomes the zero abscissa. If the mean scaled score for Information is six, this would be plotted as a two-point negative deviation below the zero abscissa of eight. The plotting of such deviation values around the mean of all subtest scores for a given age group provides a visual depiction of the magnitude of individual subtest variations, or in effect, an intellectual profile. The presence of different profiles as a function of age would provide one kind of support for the hypothesis of heterogeneity of cognitive abilities among neurologically impaired children.

2) The second method described is based on R factor analyses. Consecutive factor analyses of the WISC for "brain-damaged" children have not previously been reported. The reported factors for the standardization sample include a general, a Verbal, and a Performance factor. While it was not anticipated that this study sample would depart in any important way from this frequent finding, one could ask whether the structure of intellectual functioning in so-called brain-damaged children undergoes differentiation with increasing age, or indeed, whether age exerts any influence on obtained factors. Again, differences in factor structure at different ages would argue for heterogeneity of cognitive ability patterns among such children.

3) The third method reported is based on Q factor analyses. Such procedures have not frequently been reported for intelligence tests results. This analysis is based upon age groupings, and in this sense, like

the previous two methods, uses development, *per se*, as a vehicle for investigating the issue of heterogeneity. This method was found to be useful in permitting subgroups not otherwise recognized to be identified, and thus provided the strongest support for the hypothesis of heterogeneity in neurologically impaired children.

In an effort to determine the heterogeneous nature of the neurological impairment, both hard and soft signs of CNS abnormality were recorded. The relationship between these signs and intellectual impairment was then studied.

COGNITIVE STATUS

Method 1—A Graphic View of Patterns
of Intellectual Functioning

Does the organization or patterning of abilities in neurologically impaired children remain the same or does it change in meaningful ways over the crucial span of the school years? This question may be addressed by comparing the graphic subtest profiles of the WISC that characterize successive years in a given age range.

For a given age level each subtest mean was plotted in terms of its deviation above or below the mean value of the 12 subtests which served as the abscissa. This procedure resulted in four sets of deviation scores, one for each of four successive years in the progress of a given initial age group. For example, in Figure 1 the mean scaled score for all 12 subtests for six-year-olds in the first year of the study was 5.38; this served as the abscissa for six-year-old children in the first year of the study. The mean scaled score for Information was 5.47. The difference between these two figures (+.09 or .1) is the required deviation value and was plotted one-tenth of a scaled value point *above* the abscissa for six-year-old children in the first year of the study. The mean scaled value for all 12 subtests for the six-year-olds in the second year of the study (they are now seven years old) was 5.44; this served as the abscissa for six-year-old children in the second year of the study. The mean scaled score for Information was 5.36. The difference between these two figures (—.08 or —.1) is the required deviation value and was plotted one-tenth of a scaled value point *below* the abscissa for six-year-old children in the second year of the study. The same procedure was followed for six-year-olds in the third and fourth years of the study. Problems of interpretation resulting from differences in level of ability among the four groups were overcome since each member of a set of four scores was plotted around its own mean. The resulting graph is therefore presumed to depict relative rather than absolute subtest strength and weakness.

What kind of results would attest to the existence of heterogeneity among these children? Heterogeneity is, itself, a slippery concept and has several meanings, but, in general, is concerned with the existence of discrete subgroups (what Cattell calls subpopulations in a nonhomogeneous population). The process of deciding whether a subject belongs to any given subgroup is probably related to the process of defining "types." Cattell's (1944) discussion of the different concepts that underlie this term makes it clear that we need to distinguish which kind of typing we are engaged in. What is being addressed here is the possibility that the same neurological lesion results in differential cognitive deficit depending on the age of the subject, thus defining cognitive subpopulations. If this proposition is correct, then discrete psychometric patterns should emerge. There are two kinds of findings that are relevant: 1) For graphs of different groups of children at successive age levels (not shown here), individual subtest variation in opposite directions (above or below the abscissa) may differ according to age in the initial year of the study. Hence, children who entered the study at age seven may differ from those who entered the study at age six in the pattern of their subtest variations over the four-year time span, and cross-sectional data could show that neurological impairment manifests itself in differential cognitive patterns associated with age. 2) Within any given age group individual subtest variation in opposite directions would suggest that as a given age group grows older its cognitive profile of relative strengths and weaknesses changes. Thus, longitudinal data could also show that neurological impairment manifests itself in differential cognitive patterns associated with age.

Figure 1 shows the pattern of subtest variation for six-year-olds in the first year of the study compared with themselves in the second, third, and fourth year of the study at ages seven, eight and nine respectively. Inspection of Figure 1 shows that on five of the 12 subtests (Information, Comprehension, Digit Span, Picture Arrangement and Coding) children aged six in the initial year of the study varied in opposite directions at different times during the four years of the study. For Information and Comprehension the trend was mildly regressive, with the children doing relatively more poorly as they grew older; for Coding the trend was toward relative improvement with increasing age. Such directionalities in subtest strength and weakness suggested that differences in cognitive patterning are associated with age.

When similar graphs were constructed for children who were age 7, 8, 9, 10, 11 or 12 years in the first year of the study it was found that subtest variation in opposite directions occurred persistently with changes

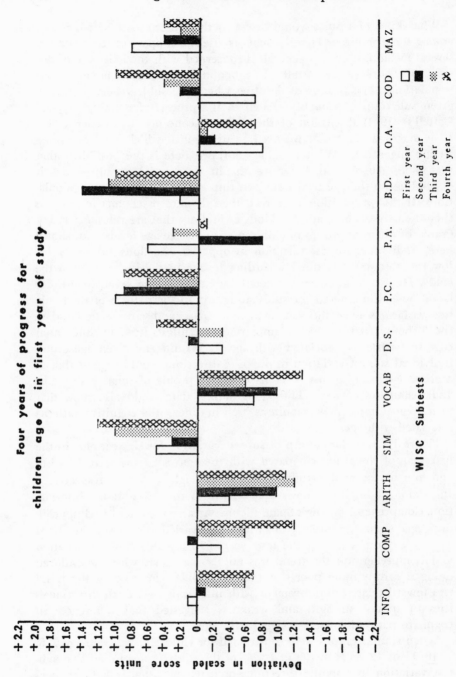

Figure 1. Four years of progress for children age 6 in first year of study.

in age for certain subtests. Such consistent variation in association with age constituted support (both cross-sectionally and longitudinally based) that cognitive patterning in children with neurological impairment changes with age. Thus, the age-cognitive pattern interaction implied that one could not view these children as a homogeneous group.

This procedure had been reported earlier in an attempt to compare emotionally disturbed and brain-damaged children (Bortner & Birch, 1970) and was of some value in presenting in pictorial fashion cognitive similarities and differences. However, the technique left much to be desired since the scaled score deviations were hardly better than arbitrary in size, and being pictorial were not accessible to standard statistical treatment, thus leaving the question hanging as to what constituted a statistically significant or psychologically meaningful deviation. Moreover, in retrospect, it became clear that one or two subtests could inflate the abscissa (mean of the mean of all subtests), thus casting the whole procedure into doubt. Hence, not much was done with this method and it was essentially abandoned, even though it does provide a crude and approximate picture of the organization of abilities and can easily be adapted to a variety of cognitive measures. The weakness of the procedure prevented confident acceptance of the finding of heterogeneity. It was necessary to find a procedure with more power.

Method 2—Factor Analyses of the WISC for Four Consecutive Years: R Analyses of Test Variables*

Factor analysis was another method used to determine the presence of subtest patterns of the WISC. What kinds of findings would lend support to the idea of heterogeneity of cognitive functioning among CNS impaired children? Again, using the fact of development, *per se,* as a vehicle for studying the issue, an age-specific analysis might reveal systematic, age-related differences in factor structure. Differences could occur in both the nature and the number of factors. Only those differences pertaining to number of factors will be discussed here. Inevitably, the discussion of number of factors and their association with age becomes intertwined with the issue of the differentiation of intelligence, with older children expected to show more factors than younger children.

The factor analyses reported here were based on the intercorrelations of 11 subtests (Mazes were excluded) using the principal component method of extraction with the highest coefficients in each column serving as communality estimates. This method was used in conjunction with

---

* Thanks to Dr. I. Leon Smith for his considerable help with the R analysis.

TABLE 1

Factor Loadings on WISC Subtests for Brain Damaged Children Age 6-12 Years in First Year of Study Followed for Four Year Period

WISC Subtest	Year 1 Age Span 6-12 N = 210			Year 2 Age Span 7-13 N = 203			Year 3 Age Span 8-14 N = 193			Year 4 Age Span 9-15 N = 177		
	A	B	h^2	A	B	h^2	A	B	h^2	A	B	h^2
1. Info.	−76	03	63	88	13	65	75	00	56	81	01	67
2. Comp.	−51	20	44	52	−17	41	62	08	46	67	05	49
3. Arith.	−45	38	57	49	−39	63	45	34	52	42	37	51
4. Sim.	−78	−08	54	70	00	50	81	−07	59	78	01	63
5. Vocab.	−85	−04	69	77	00	60	86	−08	66	89	−08	70
6. D.S.	−42	26	40	41	−29	40	45	19	35	25	33	28
7. P.C.	−22	56	54	18	−57	49	23	49	44	13	60	47
8. P.A.	−08	67	54	35	−52	62	40	44	58	35	50	60
9. B.D.	06	79	56	−06	−85	66	−08	85	64	−15	93	71
10. O.A.	10	88	67	−11	−88	67	−07	88	70	−04	84	67
11. Cod.	−18	51	42	11	−59	45	22	51	45	26	43	40

From Bortner, 1976.

TABLE 2

Factor Loadings on WISC Subtests for Brain Damaged Children Age 6-9 Years in First Year of Study Followed for Four Year Period

WISC Subtest	Year 1 Age Span 6-9 N = 120			Year 2 Age Span 7-10 N = 114			Year 3 Age Span 8-11 N = 107			Year 4 Age Span 9-12 N = 98		
	A	B	h²	A	B	h²	A	B	h²	A	B	h²
1. Info.	70	14	64	84	00	71	—62	26	63	—84	06	78
2. Comp.	50	23	47	63	11	50	—74	06	59	—73	01	53
3. Arith.	33	52	62	32	59	69	—32	59	67	—42	49	68
4. Sim.	76	—05	53	58	11	43	—78	—03	58	—78	03	63
5. Vocab.	84	—03	67	86	—07	66	—86	—06	68	—84	—02	68
6. D.S.	26	46	44	25	50	48	—34	39	42	—20	41	31
7. P.C.	26	56	58	17	56	47	—25	50	42	—09	60	44
8. P.A.	—05	80	59	16	67	62	—19	65	61	—28	60	65
9. B.D.	—06	80	58	—09	85	64	19	92	67	18	96	74
10. O.A.	—08	87	66	—14	89	65	06	79	57	06	81	60
11. Cod.	15	56	45	02	68	48	—10	64	49	—24	42	36

From Bortner, 1976.

TABLE 3

Factor Loadings on WISC Subtests for Brain Damaged Children Age 10-12 Years in First Year of Study Followed for Four Year Period

WISC Subtest	Year 1 Age Span 10-12 N = 90				Year 2 Age Span 11-13 N = 89				Year 3 Age Span 12-14 N = 86				Year 4 Age Span 13-15 N = 79			
	A	B	C	h²	A	B	C	h²	A	B	C	h²	A	B	C	h²
1. Info.	46	—06	47	59	62	—21	—32	57	65	16	16	46	69	02	03	52
2. Comp.	79	17	—20	—7	00	18	—65	55	56	—20	—02	46	60	12	06	50
3. Arith.	06	26	64	68	68	29	00	69	05	—09	72	64	11	—03	83	76
4. Sim.	60	00	18	49	51	—02	—39	57	68	—05	12	61	70	01	16	64
5. Vocab.	71	00	23	72	10	01	—84	81	94	00	—08	81	95	—08	—02	81
6. D.S.	00	07	72	58	68	14	10	49	06	01	68	51	08	06	54	39
7. P.C.	27	54	02	53	—10	58	—40	62	27	—61	—15	55	25	75	—21	68
8. P.A.	28	48	09	51	22	37	—40	62	53	—25	09	57	41	38	08	55
9. B.D.	—13	72	14	53	18	78	08	70	—02	—71	17	60	—18	76	29	71
10. O.A.	00	91	—12	75	—07	82	—09	70	—04	—94	04	86	00	88	01	78
11. Cod.	10	49	10	37	24	49	—05	43	11	—40	33	47	24	39	17	44

From Bortner, 1976.

the equimax method of rotation which yields an oblique solution (Harman, 1960).

The results of the factor analyses are presented in Tables 1-4. The symbols assigned to the factors are consistent with those reported by Cohen (1959) where "A" refers to a verbal factor, "B" a performance factor, and "C" an attention, distractibility, or memory factor. The verbal factor (A) and the performance factor (B) emerged with equal clarity in the first year of the study and in each succeeding year for the group as a whole (Table 1). Thus, these identified patterns showed stability over a four-year period. Moreover, since the C factor did not emerge, one could infer that cognitive functioning is less differentiated in CNS impaired children than in normal children. While this may be true for the group as a whole, it is nevertheless misleading as the age-specific analyses below indicate.

Tables 2-3 report the results when the group was divided into a younger age group (6-9 years in year one of the study) and an older age group (10-12 years in year one of the study). A difference in number of factors emerges. The younger age group shows only two of the three major factors previously reported by Cohen (1959), a Verbal and a Performance factor. However, the older age group manifests the third factor, the "C" factor of attention, distractibility, or memory that had earlier been reported by Cohen for the standardization group. This factor changes in its composition over the four-year period studied, but most frequently (three out of the four years) contains the expected Arithmetic and Digit Span.

We should recall that both Arithmetic and Digit Span appeared in the performance factor in the younger children (Table 2). One might interpret its emergence as the separate C factor in the older children (Table 3) as a confirmation of the differentiation hypothesis of intelligence, where it is posited that intelligence is relatively global initially and differentiates with increasing age. However, a closer look at these tables militates against such an easy interpretation, and will be elaborated below.

Until now we have discussed only the cross-sectional data. Do the longitudinal data support the inferences based on the cross-sectional data? In order to answer this, it is necessary to compare the longitudinally defined older group (children age 6-9 years in first year of study who became 9-12 years in fourth year of study) with the cross-sectionally defined older group (children age 10-12 years in first year of study). Children who started out at ages 6-9 years in the first year of the study were followed for four years until they became 9-12 years.

Within Table 2 are the longitudinal data. These data show no tendency for a given group of younger children to differentiate in the number of factors they manifest as they grow older. Quite the contrary—the stability of the two factors shown by the younger children and their resistance to differentiation are indicated by the proportion of the total variance accounted for by these two factors. Table 4 shows these proportions, where it can be seen that factor A never varies during the four years beyond the limited range of 53.1% of the variance (in year three) to 54.4% (in year four). Factor B shows the same stability and varies within the same narrow range of 10.3% of the variance (in year one) and 12.2% (in year three). Hence, the differentiation hypothesis is supported only if one refers to the cross-sectional data, i.e., if one compares *different* groups of younger and older children.

In summary, when the total group was split into two age ranges (younger group 6-9 years, older group 10-12 years), the results obtained

TABLE 4

Proportion of Variance Accounted for by Each Factor

	Younger Children (6-9 Years in First Year) (2 factors)		Older Children (10-12 Years in First Year) (3 factors)	
	Factor	% Variance	Factor	% Variance
Year 1	A	54.4	A	48.2
	B	10.3	B	11.9
			C	9.3
Year 2	A	53.5	A	49.1
	B	11.7	B	12.9
			C	9.9
Year 3	A	53.1	A	49.1
	B	12.2	B	11.7
			C	9.5
Year 4	A	53.9	A	49.8
	B	11.2	B	11.9
			C	9.9

Adapted from Bortner, 1976.

and the inferences to be made depended upon the method of analysis. Thus, if we relied on cross-sectional data and compared the results of Table 2 with Table 3, we found that the younger children showed two factors and the older children showed three factors. The differentiation hypothesis of intelligence appeared to be confirmed. But, when we looked at the longitudinal data in Table 2, we found that the younger children were reliably defined over a four-year time span by two factors of intelligence. As they grew older in this four-year time span, they remained defined by the same two factors and there was no evidence of further intellectual differentiation. The group initially defined as the older group (10-12 years, see Table 3) was equally reliably defined for the same time span, not by two but by three factors of intelligence. As they grew older they remained defined by the same three factors. It could, therefore, be inferred from the longitudinal data that discrete subgroups of CNS impaired children exist with different cognitive factor structures—some with two, others with three factors. If one considers the cross-sectional data in conjunction with the longitudinal data, one might conclude that intelligence differentiates from two into three factors for some children with CNS impairment and remains at two factors for others. (Of course, it is possible that the process of admitting these children into the school varied in some unkown way from younger to older children, administrative exigencies being what they are. If that were the case, the composition of the cross-sectionally defined older children could have differed in systematic ways from the younger children. Such differences in composition might then have been reflected in the factor differences reported here. However, no such differences in admission procedures were evident).

What light do these findings shed on the possible existence of discrete subgroups of neurologically impaired children? It will be recalled that the cross-sectional data revealed that the younger children proceeded from two factors to three factors as they grew older. The longitudinal data failed to confirm this. Had the longitudinal data confirmed this finding, we might conclude that *all* neurologically impaired children start out with two factors and differentiate to three factors. The absence of such confirmation suggests the possibility that the cross-sectionally defined younger and older groups were uniquely different from each other in some meaningful way (behaviorally? neurologically?) in the first place, and that the obtained difference in factor structure was the psychological representation of this fact. Hence, the idea of cognitively discrete subgroups was again suggested. It was not as clear as it might be, and R factor analysis based on age-splits is probably an insufficient method for the clarification of this issue.

*Method 3—Factor Analysis of the WISC: Q Analyses of Person Variables**

A Q-group analysis was done on the WISC data as part of the continuing strategy designed to characterize meaningful subgroups of children according to patterns of cognitive performance. However, since Q analysis is not a frequently reported procedure (see Cattell, 1950) it is discussed here in detail.

The question asked is whether the children we are studying represent a homogeneous or heterogeneous group with respect to their cognitive performance. If they represent a homogeneous entity, then we are justified in describing their performance on cognitive tasks in terms of a single set of average scores based on the behavior of the group as a whole. If, on the other hand, they are not homogeneous but represent, instead, several groups with different patterns of cognitive behavior, then the use of average scores based on the total group's performance will be misleading. In an attempt to discover whether the cognitive performance of these subjects can best be described in terms of a single group whose members all perform in a similar way or, instead, whether it can be described in terms of several different, uniquely performing subgroups, Q-group analyses were made of the subject's WISC scores for two consecutive years.

The technique

The typical use of correlation coefficients enables us to measure the degree to which two sets of scores rank a group of individuals in the same way. Just as we can group together variables, e.g., tests, through factor analysis, we can also group persons together. In an R factor analysis, variables are grouped together which have a high relationship to each other and a low relationship to other variables. Thus, clusters of variables result which are maximally independent of (unrelated to) each other. Similarly, subjects can be grouped together in such a way that they form maximally independent groups. The subjects forming a given group would perform in a similar fashion and the performance which characterizes one group would bear only a minimal relationship to the performance which characterizes another.

When dealing with only a few subjects, we can group the subjects together on the basis of inspection. When larger numbers of subjects are involved, however, a Q-group analysis, or factor analysis based on

---

* Thanks to Robert L. Cooper for his considerable help with the Q analysis.

subject correlations, must be used if we are to obtain the most accurate clustering of subjects.

The procedure

For purposes of data analysis, the children were divided into two age groups: a "younger" group, who were aged 6-9 during the first year of testing, and an "older" group, who were aged 10-12 during the first year of testing. For each of these groups, two Q analyses were performed: one on the first year WISC subtest scaled scores and one on the second year scores. Thus, four Q analyses of WISC scaled scores were performed: 1) year one scores of ages 6-9 ($N = 120$); 2) year two scores of ages 7-10 ($N = 109$; not reported here); 3) year one scores of ages 10-12 ($N = 90$); 4) year two scores of ages 11-13 ($N = 89$; not reported here).

The coefficients which were factor analyzed were not product-moment coefficients but cross-products. (A cross-product is the sum of the products of one subject's score on each test multiplied by another subject's score on each test.) Thus, where A_1, A_2, ... A_{12} represent subject A's scores on tests 1, 2, ... 12, and where B_1, B_2, ... B_{12} represent B's scores on tests 1, 2, ... 12, the cross-product for AB would be $A_1 \times B_1$ plus $A_2 \times B_2$ plus . . . . $A_{12} \times B_{12}$. The rationale for using cross-products instead of product-moment coefficients can be summarized as follows. If product-moment coefficients are employed, the children who define a type, i.e., have the highest loadings on the factor, can display grossly discrepant means and standard deviations, thus making it difficult to characterize the cluster as a whole. When cross-products are used, on the other hand, it is necessary that children who define a cluster be alike both in mean and standard deviation. Hence, cross-products were the coefficients which were factored.

For each analysis, three centroids were extracted, but only the second and third centroid were rotated. The first centroid was omitted from the rotation in order to obtain clusters in which total IQ did not prove to be the defining feature. If all three centroids had been rotated, high IQ children would have defined each cluster because their cross-products were the largest ones. Since the first centroid essentially ordered the children in terms of their total IQ score, and since the second and third centroids were by definition minimally related to the first, by rotating only the second and third centroids, clusters could be obtained in which the total IQ was not the defining feature. The resulting clusters would still, however, be defined by children whose means and standard deviations were alike.

Results of Q analysis

For each age group, two clusters of children or Q groups were obtained. Each Q group in turn consisted of two subgroups, each of which was the mirror image of the other. Thus, for each age group, four subgroups were obtained.

Just as an R factor (a cluster of scores) is defined or characterized by its highest loading *items*, a Q group (a cluster of subjects) is defined or characterized by its highest loading *subjects*. In order to facilitate interpretation of the Q analyses, the scores of the six children with the highest positive loadings and the scores of the six children with the highest negative loadings were examined for each Q group. If the cluster of children who constitute a Q group can be viewed as varying along some trait or dimension, then the six children with the highest positive loadings can be considered as archetypes of one pole of the dimension and the six children with the highest negative loadings can be considered as archetypes of the other pole. Thus, for each Q group, two subgroups of archetypal subjects were identified, one with positive loadings and one with negative loadings.

For each archetypal subgroup, the mean and standard deviation of the scaled scores obtained on each subtest was calculated as well as the mean and standard deviation based on all 12 subtests. It was possible to identify for each archetypal subgroup those subtests on which it was relatively strong and those subtests on which it was relatively weak. The criterion of "strength" and "weakness" which was employed was an arbitrary one—namely, a difference of at least one scaled score point from the archetypal subgroup's overall mean score. This criterion was chosen because the standard deviation of each subtest's scaled scores is three, and hence one scaled score point represents one-third of a standard deviation. A difference from the mean of one-third of a standard deviation seemed large enough to provide a reasonably reliable rough index of strength or weakness. Thus, for example, for the Q analysis performed on the 6-9-year-olds' scores, the positive archetypes of Q group I subgroup A had an average scaled score of 7.3. The subtests on which these children performed relatively well, therefore, were those on which they obtained scores equal to or higher than 8.3, whereas the subtests on which they performed relatively poorly were those on which they obtained scores equal to or lower than 6.3. The tests on which they performed well relative to their overall average are summarized for the archetypal subjects in Table 5. Mean subtest configurations for archetypal subgroups are shown in Figures 2 and 3. Note that whereas subgroup 1A (positive archetypes) obtained relatively better scores on the Performance subtests, subgroup 1B (negative archetypes) obtained its better scores on the Verbal subtests.

Both archetypal subgroups had about the same average Full Scale IQ (79 and 72) but each displayed a marked discrepancy between their Verbal and Performance IQ scores. Archetypal subgroup 1A's average Verbal IQ was 30 points *lower* than its average Performance IQ, and archetypal subgroup 1B's average Verbal IQ was 16 points *higher* than its average Performance IQ. This 6-9-year-old Q group appears to be defined, therefore, in terms of a general Verbal-Performance discrep-

TABLE 5

Profile of Mean WISC Subtest Performance of Q Subgroups—Archetypal
Younger and Older Subjects

	Age 6-9 Yr 1		Age 6-9 Yr 1		Age 10-12 Yr 1		Age 10-12 Yr 1	
	QIA	QIB	QIIA	QIIB	QIA	QIB	QIIA	QIIB
Inform.	L				H		H	L
Comp.	L		L		H	L	L	
Arith.			L	L			H	L
Simil.	L	H	H		H	L		H
Vocab.	L		L		H	L		
D.S.		L	H	L			H	L
P.C.			H				L	
P.A.	H	L	H					H
B.D.	H	L		H	L	H	L	
O.A.	H	L	L		L	H	L	H
Coding	H	L	H	L	L	H		
Mazes	H	L			L	H	L	
VQ	67	83	78	67	87	69	88	79
PQ	97	67	78	72	61	86	66	91
FSQ	79	72	76	67	72	80	75	83

Note: H = subtest mean ≥ one scaled score point *above* mean of all subtests for subgroup.
    L = subtest mean ≥ one scaled score point *below* mean of all subtests for subgroup.

Adapted from Bortner, 1976.

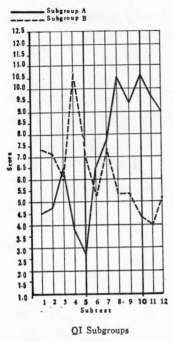

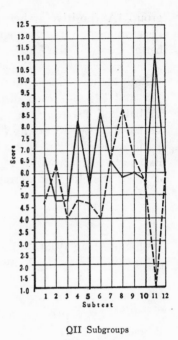

QI Subgroups   QII Subgroups

FIGURE 2. Mean WISC subtest scores of younger archetypal children. Adapted from Bortner, 1976.

ancy. Each of its archetypal subgroups displayed a discrepancy, but each subgroup's discrepancy was the mirror image of the other. Although this Q group can be defined in terms of a general Verbal-Performance discrepancy, it can also be defined more specifically in terms of the six subtests on which the two subgroups performed in opposite directions. In a similar fashion, each Q group obtained in each analysis can be defined by identifying those subtests on which the archetypal positive and negative subgroups performed in opposite directions.

While characteristics arrived at in this manner seem clear when only the archetypal subjects are considered, it might be argued that such characteristics would not hold for the Q group as a whole—for all the subjects entering it. In order to check whether the characterizations determined by the archetypal subjects would also apply when subjects with lower or marginal loadings were included, the procedure followed with the highest loading subjects was also followed with 1) all subjects having loadings equal to or greater than .0200 (which excluded about one-third of the subjects entering each group) and 2) all subjects enter-

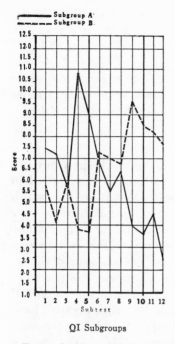

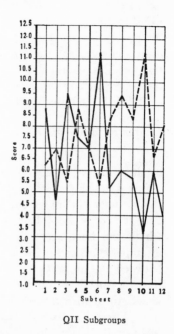

QI Subgroups   QII Subgroups

FIGURE 3. Mean WISC subtest scores of older archetypal children. Adapted from Bortner, 1976.

ing the Q group. Substantially the same results were obtained. That is to say, the same relative strengths and weaknesses were observed on most of the same tests for each Q subgroup whether based on the highest loading subjects, or on the subjects with loadings equal to or higher than .0200, or on all subjects.

An examination of sets of profiles for two consecutive years (not shown here; see Bortner, 1976) for the archetypal younger children and for the archetypal older children indicated that, with the exception of the younger children's second Q group, their patterns were maintained in broad outline from one year to the next.

The correlations between Q group loadings in year one with those in year two for the younger and for the older children were calculated. For the older children, the correlation between the loadings on Q group I in years one and two, and for Q group II in years one and two were substantial $(r = .67$ and .76 respectively). The younger children, however, displayed a substantial correlation only between loadings on Q group I in years one and two $(r = .66)$. Although the correlation between year one and year two loadings on Q group II was statistically significant $(p < .01)$, it was at a much lower order of magnitude $(r = .37)$. Thus, the second Q group was not very stable for the younger children, either in terms of the children who entered it or in terms of the subtest profiles characterizing it. However, Q group I for the younger children and both Q groups for the older children were stable in terms of the children entering them as well as in terms of the subtest profiles.

Characterization of children

We can now characterize the younger and the older children in terms of the subtest profiles. Based on the archetypal profiles summarized in Table 5 and Figures 2 and 3, we can characterize the groups into which the younger and older children are divided as follows: For the younger children, only the QI group maintained a stable subtest configuration, which can be characterized in terms of a general Verbal-Performance discrepancy, there being a difference of at least one standard deviation between PQ and VQ for the Q subgroups. Children with positive loadings in this Q group tended to have higher Performance than Verbal scale scores, with the reverse being true for children with negative loadings. There are six subtests on which subgroups IA and IB performed in opposite ways: Similarities, Picture Arrangement, Block Design, Object Assembly, Coding and Mazes. On each of these tests, if one archetypal subgroup performed relatively well, the other performed poorly. Following standard clinical interpretation, QIA for the younger children may be seen as strong in interpersonal and perceptual skills and weak in abstract verbal ability. QIB demonstrates the reverse of these tendencies.

For the older children, the QI group was characterized by differences in Comprehension, Similarities, Vocabulary, Object Assembly, Coding and Mazes. Positive QI loadings were associated with high scores in Comprehension, Similarities and Vocabulary, and low scores in Object Assembly, Coding and Mazes. Negative QI loadings showed the reverse pattern. QIA for the older children may be seen as strong in abstract verbal ability and social judgment and weak in perceptual skills. QIB is characterized by the reverse pattern.

The older children's QIIA group can be characterized in terms of relatively higher scores on Information, Arithmetic and Digit Span, and poor Performance scores. QIIA, therefore, describes strength in attention and memory in the context of good Verbal and poor Performance skills. QIIB describes the reverse of this pattern.

In summary, only QI was stable in the younger children; QII was stable in both the younger and the older children.

1) QIA (younger) defines children with good social judgment and perceptual skills, but who are weak in abstract verbal ability. QIB shows the reverse pattern.

2) QIA (older) defines children with good social judgment and abstract verbal ability, but who are weak in perceptual skills. QIB shows the reverse pattern.

3) QIIA (older) defines children with good verbal skills and good attention and memory, but who are weak in perceptual skills. QIIB shows the reverse pattern.

Whereas Table 5 and Figures 2 and 3 summarize Q group profiles for the archetypal subjects, later tables (Bortner, 1976) describe each Q group for *all* the children whose highest loadings were found on that group. The characteristics identified for archetypal subjects held up fairly well for all the subjects entering each Q group.

So, what does it all mean? And, was it worth all the trouble? The answer lies in comparing the Q group profiles of Figures 2 and 3 with the profile obtained for all-children-combined in the younger group (ages 6-9) and the profile for all-children-combined in the older group (ages 10-12). The later profiles based on mean subtest scores in the first year of testing are shown in Figure 4. It can be seen that these profiles are relatively flat. For the younger children ($N = 120$), not one of the subtest averages differed from the overall mean score (6.0) by as much as one scaled score point. For the older children ($N = 90$) only two subtests were at least one scaled score point above or below the overall mean

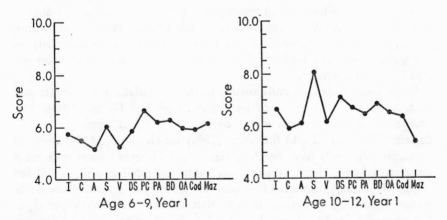

FIGURE 4. Mean WISC subtest performance, All subjects combined, Year 1. From Bortner, 1976.

(6.5). These were Similarities, which was 1.5 points above the mean, and Mazes, which was 1.0 points below the mean.

If one had only the information which is presented in Figure 4, one could have concluded that these children could be characterized as subnormal, and that their performance was uniformly and unrelievedly poor across all or almost all subtests. It is now clear that such a characterization would have been grossly misleading since it would not reflect the marked differences that have been found to exist in uniquely performing subgroups. The use of Q analyses has revealed the existence of markedly different clusters of children whose different patterns of cognitive performance are obscured by more simplistic analyses.

NEUROLOGICAL STATUS

The examination of clinical neurological status was independent of the examination of intellectual competence. The psychologist and the physician were unaware of each other's test results. Each child was given a clinical neurological examination during school hours in a specially designated area. To control for the influence of examiner bias, 36 age-matched children who attended a nearby regular school were brought in and interspersed among the subjects. The examiner did not know whether a given child came from the regular school or the special school.

The neurological evaluation was limited to clinical examination and included the study of cranial nerve intactness, reflex organization, the presence of pathological reflexes, muscle strength and tone, balance and gait, motor coordination and sensory organization. In addition, information was obtained about responses to double simultaneous tactual stimulation, presence or absence of adventitious motor overflow, ability to engage in imitative motor activity and clinical assessment of speech and language functions.

Responses to double simultaneous tactual stimulation were evaluated according to criteria described by Bender, Fink and Green (1951). The evaluation of adventitious motor overflow was based upon procedures described by Prechtl and Stemmer (1966) which required the children to stand still with feet together, head upright, eyes closed and arms outstretched with the fingers of both hands extended and separated for a period of one minute. The examiner noted choreiform movements occurring during this time in any part of the body, with principal focus upon face, limbs and hands. The ability to engage in imitative voluntary movements was evaluated by requesting the child to copy the movements of the examiner's fingers as they were selectively opposed to the thumb of each hand. Speech and language functions were evaluated by listening to the child's spontaneous speech and to his replies to a variety of standard questions.

On the basis of the neurological examination, two kinds of abnormalities were identified. The first were hard signs of cerebral dysfunction which are routinely relied upon in diagnosis and whose presence constitute a neurological syndrome. These are believed to have localizing value and include abnormalities in reflex, cranial nerve and motor organization; lateralized dysfunctions; and the presence of pathological reflexes.

The second kind of abnormality consisted of soft signs of cerebral dysfunction (Wikler, Dixon & Parker, 1970). These included speech and language disturbance (excluding dysarthria and aphasia), inadequacies in gait, balance and coordination, adventitious motor overflow, imitative fine motor movements, extinction to double simultaneous tactual stimulation and inadequacies in graphesthetic and stereognostic responses, muscle tone and position sense.

In the first of two reports (Hertzig, Bortner & Birch, 1969), both the number and nature of hard signs were quite variable. The classical neurological syndromes found included residual quadriplegia, diplegia, right and left hemiplegia and monoplegia, and athetosis, with 29% of the group $(N = 90)$ having such hard signs of central nervous system abnormality. Residual hemiplegia was the most frequent finding. In all cases the motor component was mild and the most striking findings were weakness and abnormal reflexes.

When soft signs were considered, 90% of the children had one or more such findings, if we included those children who also had hard signs. If hard sign children were excluded, two-thirds of the children had soft signs. More importantly, the variability in terms of number of signs was great, with roughly 7% having two signs, 13% with three, 19% with four, 12% with five, 5% with six, 9% with seven, 9% with eight, 4% with nine, 5% with ten, and 2% with 11 soft signs.

The most frequent soft signs were inadequate balance (66%), incoordination (58%), and disturbance of speech and language (54%). Disturbance in position sense was the least frequently seen (2%). Intermediate in frequency of occurrence were choreiform movements and disturbances in muscle tone, gait, imitative movements, graphesthesia and stereognosis, with percentages of children showing such disturbances ranging from a high of 44% to a low of 24%. Thus, children were quite heterogeneous in their neurological manifestations, with variety in number and nature of both hard signs and soft signs of abnormal cerebral function.

This neurological heterogeneity was sustained in the findings of the second study (Bortner, Hertzig & Birch, 1972) which encompassed a larger study sample ($N = 198$). Attempts to relate neurological abnormality with different age levels failed to disclose any meaningful associations.

The attempt to relate neurological findings with IQ levels was successful. The neurological findings made it possible to classify the children into three groups: 1) hard signs, 2) two or more soft signs, and 3) one or no soft signs. These three groups were then compared with respect to level of Verbal IQ, Performance IQ and Full Scale IQ. The children with hard signs and the children with two or more soft signs were essentially similar to each other in level of intellectual functioning, but were significantly duller than the children with one or no soft signs. The finding that children with two or more soft signs had lower IQs than children with one or no soft signs made it seem likely that the number of soft signs might be systematically related to level of IQ. This hypothesis was sustained and the larger the number of soft signs the lower the IQ that was obtained. This finding held true for Verbal, Performance and Full-Scale IQ. Although some preliminary analyses failed to determine whether any particular soft sign or constellation of signs played a special role in depressing the IQ, this question remains essentially open.

SUMMARY

Graphic studies, through R factor analyses, through Q factor analyses represented progressively refined indices which showed that neurologically impaired children can be defined in terms of distinct cognitive patterns. Moreover, hard signs and soft signs of neurological abnormality were found to be quite variable in their number and nature. It seems fair to conclude that these children are heterogeneous from the point of view of both neurological and intellectual patterning. It was found that the number of neurological signs was related to level of intelligence; the greater the number of soft signs, the lower the level of intellectual functioning. Although not confirmed, it is a good bet that particular constellations of soft signs are related to the degree of cognitive deficit. The most difficult task remains—that of formulating educational recommendations on the basis of observed brain-behavior relationships.

REFERENCES

BELMONT, LILLIAN and BIRCH, H. G. The intellectual profile of retarded readers. *Perceptual and Motor Skills*, 1966, Monograph Supplement 6-V22.

BELMONT, I., BIRCH,, H. G. and BELMONT, L. The organization of intelligence test performance in educable mentally subnormal children. *American Journal of Mental Deficiency*, 1967, 71, 969-976.

BENDER, M., FINK, M., and GREEN, M.: Patterns in perception on simultaneous tests of face and hand. *Archives of Neurology and Psychiatry*, 1951, 66, 355-362.

BENTON, A. L. Psychological evaluation and differential diagnosis. In: H. A. Stevens and R. Heber (Eds.), *Mental Retardation: A Review of Research*. Chicago: University of Chicago Press, 1964.

BERENT, S., COHEN, B. D., and SILVERMAN, A. J. Changes in verbal and nonverbal learning following single left or right unilateral electroconvulsive treatment. *Biological Psychiatry*, 1975, 10, 95-100.

BERLINER, D. C. and CAHEN, L. S. Trait-treatment interaction and learning. In: F. N. Kerlinger (Ed.), *Review of Research in Education*, Vol. 1. Itasca, Ill.: F. E. Peacock, 1973.

BIRCH, H. G. (Ed.). *Brain Damage in Children*. Baltimore, Md.: Williams & Wilkins, 1964.

BOLL, T. J. Conceptual vs. perceptual vs. motor deficits in brain-damaged children. *Journal of Clinical Psychology*, 1972, 28, 157-159.

BORTNER, M. Phrenology, localization, and learning disabilities. *Journal of Special Education*, 1971, 5, 23-29.

BORTNER, M. *Cognitive Development in Children with Brain Damage*. Final Report No. OEG-8-0-071272-3317. Office of Education, Department of Health, Education & Welfare. New York: Yeshiva University, 1976.

BORTNER, M. and BIRCH, H. G. Brain damage: An educational category? In: M. Bortner (Ed.), *Evaluation and Education of Children with Brain Damage*. Springfield, Ill.: Thomas, 1968.

BORTNER, M. and BIRCH, H. G. Patterns of intellectual ability in emotionally disturbed and brain-injured children. *The Journal of Special Education*, 1970, 3 (4), 351-369.

BORTNER, M., HERTZIG, M. E., and BIRCH, H. G. Neurological signs and intelligence in brain-damaged children. *Journal of Special Education*, 1972, 6, 325-333.

CATTELL, R. B. Psychological measurement: Normative, ipsative, interactive. *Psychological Review*, 1944, 51, 292-303.

CATTELL, R. B. *Personality: A Systematic Theoretical and Factual Study*. New York: McGraw-Hill, 1950.

COHEN, J. The factorial structure of the WISC at ages 7-6, 10-6 and 13-6. *Journal of Consulting Psychology*, 1959, 23, 285-299.

CRONBACH, L. J. and SNOW, R. E. *Individual Differences in Learning Ability as a Function of Instructional Variables*. Final Report, Contract No. OEC-4-6-061269-1217, U.S. Office of Education. School of Education, Stanford University, 1969.

DUNN, L. M. Special education for the mildly retarded: Is much of it justifiable? *Exceptional Children*, 1968, 35, 5-22.

ERNHART, C. G., GRAHAM, F. K., EICHMAN, P. L., MARSHALL, J. M., and THURSTON, D. Brain injury in the preschool child: Some developmental considerations: II. Comparison of brain injured and normal children. *Psychological Monographs*, 1963, 77, 17-33 (Whole No. 573).

FISKLOV, S. and GOLDSTEIN, S. Diagnostic validity of the Halstead-Reitan neuropsychological battery. *Journal of Consulting and Clinical Psychology*, 1974, 42, 382-388.

FROSTIG, MARIANNE and HORNE, D. *The Frostig Program for the Development of Visual Perception*, pictures by Bea Mandell. Chicago: Follett, 1964.

220 Cognitive Growth and Development

GALLAGHER, J. J. The Tutoring of Brain-Injured Mentally Retarded Children. Springfield, Ill.: Thomas, 1960.

GUILFORD, J. P. Three faces of intellect. American Psychologist, 1959, 14, 469-479.

HARMAN, H. A. Modern Factor Analysis. Chicago: University of Chicago Press, 1960.

HERTZIG, M. E., BORTNER, M., and BIRCH, H. G. Neurologic findings in children educationally designated as "brain damaged." American Journal of Orthopsychiatry, 1969, 39, 437-446.

KIRK, S. A., McCARTHY, J. J., and KIRK, W. D. Illinois Test of Psycholinguistic Abilities (rev. ed.). Urbana, Ill.: University of Illinois Press, 1968.

LIPOWSKI, Z. J. Organic brain syndromes: Overview and Classification. In: D. F. Benson and D. Blumer (Eds.), Psychiatric Aspects of Neurological Disease. New York: Greene, 1975.

MANN, L. Psychometric phrenology and the new faculty psychology: The case against ability assessment and training. Journal of Special Education, 1971, 5, 3-14.

MEEKER, M. N. The Structure of Intellect: Its Interpretation and Uses. Columbus, Ohio: Merrill, 1969.

PARSONS, O. A. Clinical neuropsychology. In: C. Speilburger (Ed.), Current Topics in Clinical and Community Psychology, Vol. 2. New York: Academic Press, 1970.

PRECHTL, H. and STEMMER, C. The choreiform syndrome in children. Developmental Medicine and Child Neurology, 1966, 8, 149-159.

REED, H. B. C., REITAN, R. M., and KLOVE, H. The influence of cerebral lesions on psychological test performances of older children. Journal of Consulting Psychology, 1965, 29, 247-251.

REITAN, R. M. Psychological testing of neurological patients. In: J. R. Youmans (Ed.), Neurosurgery: A Comprehensive Reference Guide to the Diagnosis and Management of Neurosurgical Problems. Philadelphia: Saunders, 1973.

REITAN, R. M. and DAVISON, L. A. Clinical Neuropsychology: Current Status and Application. New York: Winston/Wiley, 1974.

RUTTER, M., GRAHAM, P., and YULE, W. A Neuropsychiatric Study in Childhood. London: Heinemann, 1970.

SABATINO, D. A. and HAYDEN, D. L. Information processing behaviors related to learning disabilities and educable mental retardation. Exceptional Children, 1970, 36, 21-29.

SMITH, A. Ambiguities in concepts and studies of "brain damage" and "organicity." Journal of Nervous and Mental Disease, 1962, 135: 311-326.

SMITH, A. Neuropsychological testing in neurological disorders. In: W. J. Friedlander (Ed.), Advances in Neurology, Vol. 7. New York: Raven Press, 1975.

SMITH, I. L. Statistical realities of special-class distributions. American Journal of Mental Deficiency, 1974, 78 (6), 740-747.

WIKLER, A., DIXON, J., and PARKER, J. B. Brain function in problem children and controls: Psychometric, neurological and electroencephalographic comparisons. American Journal of Psychiatry, 1970, 127, 634-645.

YATES, A. J. Psychological deficit. Annual Review of Psychology, 1966, 17, 111-144.

9

Birth Order and Family Size Associations with Mental and Physical Development

LILLIAN BELMONT

BACKGROUND

At the time we began our studies of birth order and family size there were two generalizations possible concerning the variables of interest. Associations between family size and intelligence and other variables seemed well established, whereas associations with birth order were not.

Family size was found to be negatively related to intellectual level (Anastasi, 1956; Terhune, 1974; Wray, 1971). The children of large families tend to make poorer showings on intelligence and achievement tests, even when social class is controlled (Akesson, 1967; Douglas, 1964; Nisbet & Entwistle, 1967; Rutter et al., 1970; Scottish Council for Research in Education, 1953; Vernon, 1951). Thus, for example, in the well-known Scottish mental survey, average intelligence test score decreased as family size became larger. The association of test score with family size is less pronounced in the upper social classes (Anastasi, 1959; Douglas, 1964; Nisbet & Entwistle, 1967). Children from large families tend to be overrepresented among those with mild mental retardation (Birch et al., 1970), and, among groups of mentally retarded, those from larger families have lower IQs (Anastasi, 1959). At the outset of our research, then, we expected to find inverse associations with family size.

I thank the Department of Defense of the Netherlands for permission to use the data from the military pre-induction screening examination. This report was supported in part by N.I.H. grant #HD-06808.

221

We were less certain about whether we would find birth order effects. Birth order has been studied in relation to personality differences and affiliative behavior (e.g., Burke, 1956; Koch, 1955; Sampson & Hancock, 1967; Schachter, 1959; Schooler, 1961; Warren, 1966); findings have been inconclusive. Another area of interest has been the association of birth order with intelligence, achievement and eminence (Altus, 1965, 1966; Bradley, 1968; Sampson, 1965; Schachter, 1963). What is clear is that there is an association between birth order and eminence (outstanding intellectual achievement); firstborn are overrepresented among eminent men of science.

The overrepresentation of firstborn among the eminent could represent increased opportunity for academic exposure, greater or different motivation and drive or, of course, higher intelligence. Schachter (1963) suggested that the potentiality for outstanding achievement among firstborn derives from their overrepresentation in college and graduate school. Schachter concluded that firstborn are more capable as far as school work is concerned but are not necessarily brighter than lastborn.

A number of birth order studies were based on small samples or selected populations (e.g., Schoonover, 1959; Altus, 1966). However, the Scottish Mental Survey of 1947 (Scottish Council for Research in Education, 1949) was a study of a population of over 70,000 11-year-old children; it could not be called either select or small. In the Scottish study firstborn were not at particular advantage, nor were lastborn at particular disadvantage; this held for boys and girls.

On the other hand, in a British longitudinal study of children born in 1946, there was a generally consistent firstborn advantage on achievement tests and school success for boys from 2- and 3-child families (Douglas et al., 1968). The pattern for girls was both different and less compelling. In a study of American high school students, birth order associations, favoring firstborn and earlier born, were found for both boys and girls (Breland, 1974).

Schooler's review with the provocative title "Birth order effects? Not here, not now!" appeared in 1972. In it Schooler argued that changing fertility patterns over time (see Hare & Price, 1969; Price & Hare, 1969) could lead to an apparent excess of firstborn or lastborn in groups studied and that, therefore, most findings of higher rates of psychiatric conditions, for example, among given birth orders were more parsimoniously explained by the prevalence of given birth orders in the general population when the subjects were born, rather than by birth order effects.

With the publication of the results of 2 large-scale studies (Belmont &

Marolla, 1973; Breland, 1974) and the elaboration of the confluence model (Zajonc & Markus, 1975), there has been another resurgence of interest in birth order research. In 1977 the *Journal of Individual Psychology* devoted an entire issue to birth order research; among its articles the issue contains three reviews (Belmont, 1977; Breland, 1977; Falbo, 1977) and a bibliography (Forer, 1977).

In what follows, we present the details (method, findings) of our various studies of birth order and family size among a population of 19-year-old men from the Netherlands. Finally, we discuss the implications of the results.

METHOD

Data Source

Our studies used the records of the military preinduction examinations of some 400,000 19-year-old young men who were born in the Netherlands between January 1, 1944 and December 31, 1947. The data were made available on magnetic tape. On the tape, young men are identified by their military registration numbers (made up of date of birth plus 3 additional digits). All records were therefore anonymous.

The data were originally made available to our Research Unit by the Ministry of Defense of the Netherlands for the study of the effects on mental and physical development of the Dutch famine of 1944/45 (Stein et al., 1975). Stein and her colleagues found that intrauterine exposure to the famine produced no measurable adverse effects on survivors at military induction age (19 years). It was thus possible to use the data for the study of other issues, including birth order and family size associations.*

In the Netherlands the young men are required to appear for their pre-induction screening examination *before* a decision is reached on whether they will be required to serve in the armed forces. This procedure assures that information was available on virtually the total population of young men.

For the birth cohorts considered, total losses were under 10% (Stein et al., 1975) and included loss due to death, migration, and exemptions. Young men could claim exemption from military service if 2 (1947 birth cohort) or 3 (1944-1946 birth cohorts) older brothers had served in the Dutch armed forces; this represented a loss of 2% for the entire population but more for later birth orders (in larger families).*

---

* The data set has proved to be an invaluable source for a whole series of studies (e.g. Mittelman, et al., 1978; Ravelli, et al., 1976; Stein, et al., 1976a, b).

Screening Procedure

The screening procedure for military service can be divided into three parts:

1) Each young man completed a form which included questions concerning the size (number of children) of his family of origin, his birth order in that family, the number of older brothers, the level of education he had attained and his father's occupation.

2) Each young man took a battery of 5 tests: the Raven Progressive Matrices (Dutch modification with 40 items); a test of mechanical comprehension (Bennett); two achievement tests (language/grammar and arithmetic/mathematics); and a test of clerical aptitude. Raw scores on each test were converted by the military to a 6-point rating, with 1 representing the best and 6 the poorest performance. A total score was also available; the ratings on the 5 tests were summed and converted to a rating from 1 to 6 (see Belmont, Wittes & Stein, 1977, for a fuller description.)

3) Each young man was given a health examination and height and weight were recorded. The results of the examination were noted on a health rating scale with fitness ratings in 7 areas (general health, upper extremities, lower extremities, hearing, vision, intelligence and psychological stability). Ratings of "unfit" were assigned a diagnosis using the codes of the 1948 International Classification of Diseases (World Health Organization, 1948). Psychiatric diagnoses required review by a psychiatrist.

We had information on birth order, family size, father's occupation, subject's education, scores on psychometric measures, height, weight, ratings of health status and diagnoses. These data were collected by the military authorities for other than research purposes. Therefore, we do not have systematic information on other variables which might also be of interest to research workers. Thus, for example, we do not have systematic information on such family characteristics as paternal age or IQ, spacing interval between siblings, the birth order of older brothers and sisters or spacing and sex of younger siblings. Further, we have no information on women.

Through the cooperation of the Department of Defense and the civil authorities in Amsterdam we were able to obtain information on parental age and spacing interval for a subset of young men from 2-child

---

* In our initial paper, we reported on all young men for whom we had a test score and information on birth order and family size. In subsequent studies we excluded family sizes in which we estimated the loss in later birth orders might be large.

families who were from Amsterdam. Records were made anonymous; by linking military registration numbers we were able to identify 535 brother pairs for a study of spacing effects.

Methodologic Issues

We have reasoned that since all young men were 19 years old, family size was complete. Incomplete families (which very likely would result if young children were studied) might distort findings by family size.

In some birth order studies the wide ranges in age encompass many different birth cohorts with differing birth rates and infant mortality. Our studies have overcome this problem since the young men were all born within a 4-year period and were all the same age when the data were collected.

It is possible that birth order effects are an artifact of family size or that family size effects are reflections of social class membership or both. Therefore, in our studies we were careful to control for social class.

In order to sort out birth order from family size effects, data were cross-classified, resulting in a triangular array. Birth order gradients were examined within specific family sizes and family size gradients within specific birth orders.

Precautions must be taken in analyses because birth order and family size are statistically confounded with each other. Each variable contains information about the other: Family size sets the upper limit of possible birth positions (a family size of 5 cannot contain sixth- and seventh-born members); birth order sets the lower limit of family size (a fifthborn cannot be a member of a family size smaller than 5). Given equal cell sizes, the correlation between birth order and family size is exactly 0.5 (Wittes & Belmont, submitted for publication). We have overcome this problem by using hierarchical (nested) models of analysis of variance.

FINDINGS

We studied the associations of birth order and family size with a number of different outcome measures, tapping mental and physical development in adulthood and childhood, using standardized measures and clinical assessment.

Mental Development

Intelligence and Achievement. Our first study (Belmont & Marolla, 1973) reported on birth order and family size effects on a nonverbal test of intelligence (Raven Progressive Matrices) for the total population of

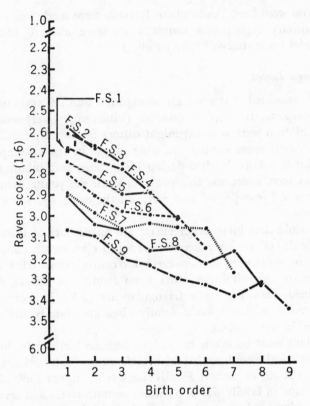

FIGURE 1. Mean Raven score (1-6) by birth order within family size (F.S.) across the population (N = 386,114) From Belmont & Marolla (1973). Copyright 1973 by the American Association for the Advancement of Science.

19-year-old young men born between 1944 and 1947 (N = 386, 114). Our focus was on the progression of mean test scores by birth order within given family sizes and the gradients by family size within given birth orders. These data are displayed in Figure 1. At given family sizes, first-born had a better score on the average than secondborn, who in turn had a better score on the average than thirdborn and so on. The finding of a downward gradient as birth order increased was very consistent.*

---

* We inspected the distributions of the scores from 1 (best) to 6 (worst) for each birth order within family size. There was a larger proportion of "high" (1) scorers and a smaller proportion of "low" (6) scorers among firstborn than among secondborn. At each succeeding birth order, there were slight but regular declines in the proportion of high scorers and slight increases in low scorers.

In general, the same trend was apparent when family size was examined within the context of birth order: The average performance of a given birth order was better in small families than in larger families (this did not hold for one-child families).

These gradients were examined within social class groupings as well. (Social class was based on father's occupation; an 11-point occupational scale was collapsed into three groups: manual, non-manual and farm). As expected, we found social class differences in level of ability; our focus, however, was on birth order and family size associations within social class. Family size effects were not always present but birth order position continued to have an association with intellectual competence in all three social classes. The "atypical" performance of only children was present in all three social classes.

We also analyzed patterns on the full battery of 5 psychometric measures (Belmont, Wittes & Stein, 1977). Our study population consisted of (a) young men born between 1944 and 1946 who were (b) members of 1- to 6-child families, (c) in the manual and non-manual social class for whom (d) there were scores on all five tests. We excluded all those born in 1947, sons of farmers, and young men from families containing 7 or more children.

Findings were consistent across the five tests. In Table 1 we present the mean total ability scores (a rating from 1 to 6 based on the individual test ratings, equally weighted) for each birth order/family size cell; the total ability scores reflect the findings on the 5 separate tests: (i) At all birth order/family size positions the mean scores in the non-manual social class were better than those in the manual social class. (ii) The birth order pattern was similar in the two social classes; there was a consistent birth order gradient in 2- to 4-child families. For larger size families the birth order gradient was less consistent but firstborn had better mean scores than laterborn. (iii) Family size gradients for given birth order positions were dissimilar in the two social classes. In the manual social class, with one exception, there was a consistent family size gradient for all birth order positions. In the non-manual social class, family size gradients within birth order positions were present only for third and fourthborn. Inconsistencies were due to the relatively poor average score of only children (F.S.1.) and to the overall superiority of 3-child families (rather than 2-child families). However, the scores of all birth orders in the larger families were poorer than were those in smaller families.

We assessed the relative influence of birth order and family size in the two social classes by analyses of variance using hierarchical (nested)

TABLE 1

Mean Total (T) Scores by Birth Order and Family Size for the Manual Social Class (N = 110,645) and for the Non-Manual Social Class (N = 88,853)

MANUAL

Family Size		Birth Order 1	2	3	4	5	6
1	M	3.009					
	SD	1.326					
	N	6484					
2	M	2.947	3.088				
	SD	1.317	1.328				
	N	11280	11106				
3	M	3.031	3.136	3.220			
	SD	1.345	1.338	1.362			
	N	8889	9501	7878			
4	M	3.105	3.244	3.274	3.330		
	SD	1.375	1.358	1.361	1.370		
	N	6115	6476	6317	4710		
5	M	3.205	3.349	3.423	3.361	3.454	
	SD	1.388	1.382	1.373	1.348	1.400	
	N	3808	4016	4313	3329	2679	
6	M	3.296	3.442	3.508	3.507	3.494	3.593
	SD	1.406	1.394	1.362	1.372	1.383	1.422
	N	2377	2626	2721	2455	1915	1650

NON-MANUAL

Family Size		Birth Order 1	2	3	4	5	6
1	M	2.315					
	SD	1.130					
	N	5505					
2	M	2.166	2.339				
	SD	1.101	1.163				
	N	10990	9824				
3	M	2.164	2.278	2.363			
	SD	1.127	1.139	1.191			
	N	7939	8613	6664			
4	M	2.177	2.337	2.400	2.403		
	SD	1.141	1.177	1.194	1.196		
	N	4894	5369	4921	3265		
5	M	2.216	2.361	2.463	2.444	2.581	
	SD	1.184	1.222	1.244	1.222	1.307	
	N	2700	3064	3069	2249	1603	
6	M	2.299	2.361	2.512	2.515	2.438	2.656
	SD	1.196	1.201	1.275	1.245	1.192	1.385
	N	1530	1605	1726	1459	1028	836

Footnote: The standard errors of the mean are small, due in part to the large N.

models (see Belmont, Wittes & Stein, 1977). Family size effects were stronger than birth order effects in the manual social class, whereas in the non-manual social class birth order effects were considerably stronger than family size effects.

School Performance. The previous two studies used psychometric measures and refer to functioning in adulthood. We were also able to study birth order and family size associations in relation to school performance, which represented an experience begun in childhood. Schachter (1963) had shown that firstborn are overrepresented at college and graduate school. We wondered whether there were birth order and family size associations with school failure (Belmont, Stein & Wittes, 1976).

Level of education attained by age 19 had been ordered into a 7-point educational scale to reflect the Dutch educational system (de Bruijn, 1950). The first two categories—1) attendance at special school for the mildly retarded and 2) failure to graduate from lower school (first 6 years of school)—were combined into an index of school failure. (In the Netherlands during the period concerned, 8 years of schooling was compulsory. Those designated as "failed lower school" were the children who probably repeated several grades before reaching school-leaving age and thus never successfully completed lower school).

For school failure, which refers to an experience of childhood, it was less reasonable to assume that family size was completed than in other of our studies, where measures refer to adulthood. Those designated as firstborn or lastborn at 19 years would have had that designation during childhood. However, those who at 19 were neither first- nor lastborn could in fact have been lastborn at some time during schooling. We avoided this ambiguity by combining into one category, middleborn, all those who during childhood could have been in potentially variable birth order positions.

The study population consisted of young men, born in 1944-1946, from 1- through 6-child families in the manual and non-manual classes.

In general, school failure rates increased as family size increased (Table 2). The rate of school failure was significantly related to birth order position; for each family size and in both social classes, lastborn were at greater risk of school failure than firstborn. (The rates for only children were 42.4 and 13.9 for the manual and non-manual groups respectively.)

This study is of interest because it shows a similar pattern to that found with adult measures and thus suggests the persistence of the associations through a long period in the course of development. The over-

Table 2

School Failure Rates per 1000 within Family Size for First-, Middle- and Lastborn Children by Social Class

Manual social class (n = 112,437)

Birth Order — School Failure Rates

Family size	First	Middle	Last	Family size rate
2	37·7	—	45·5	41·6
3	47·1	53·9	61·1	53·8
4	54·8	64·5	77·3	64·6
5	64·0	74·0	82·6	73·2
6	75·4	90·8	110·4	90·5

χ^2 Values

Family size	Over-all χ^2	df	P	Linear Trend χ^2	df	P	Last vs. Others χ^2	df	P
2*	8·55	1	<·025	8·55	1	<·025	8·55	1	<·025
3	16·37	2	<·001	16·36	1	<·001	12·06	1	<·001
4	22·65	2	<·001	22·42	1	<·001	16·11	1	<·001
5	8·49	2	<·025	8·46	1	<·01	4·20	1	<·05
6	14·95	2	<·001	14·80	1	<·001	9·33	1	<·005
Total	71·01	9	≪·001	70·59	5	≪·001	50·24	5	≪·001

Non-manual social class (n = 89,401)

Birth Order — School Failure Rates

Family size	First	Middle	Last	Family size rate
2	11·0	—	15·5	13·1
3	11·9	11·7	14·6	12·6
4	14·2	17·6	21·6	17·4
5	18·4	21·0	40·7	23·0
6	23·9	24·5	43·8	26·4

χ^2 Values

Over-all χ^2	df	P	Linear Trend χ^2	df	P	Last vs. Others χ^2	df	P
7·85	1	<·01	7·85	1	<·01	7·85	1	<·01
3·09	2	N.S.	1·97	1	N.S.	3·07	1	<·10
6·23	2	<·05	6·20	1	<·025	4·04	1	<·05
26·90	2	≪·001	17·89	1	<·001	26·28	1	≪·001
11·16	2	<·001	5·69	1	<·025	11·15	1	<·001
55·23	9	≪·001	39·60	5	≪·001	52·39	5	≪·001

* For two-child families, both models (linear trend and 'last vs others') will necessarily account for all the χ^2.

representation of lastborn at the low end of achievement complements that of the firstborn at the upper end (entry to college). They do not support Schachter's hypothesis that the firstborn's advantage is one of opportunity to attend college.

Physical Development

We studied two aspects of physical development: the height of the young men and the prevalence of obesity among them.

Height. In our study of height (Belmont, Stein & Susser, 1975) we were interested in contrasting the consistency of birth order and family size associations with height on the one hand and with intelligence test score (Raven Progressive Matrices) on the other (Figure 2). (The data presented in Figure 2 refer to all men born in 1944-46 who were members of 1- through 6-child families.)

Figure 2 repeats the birth order and family size associations with Raven score (described above); it also shows the average height by birth order within given family sizes. The birth order associations with height are different from those with test score. Thus, family size was associated with height but birth order was *not*. Except for 1-child families, young men from smaller families were, on the average, taller than those from larger families. The family size findings for height and intelligence were similar to those for 11-year-old Scottish children (Scottish Council for Research in Education, 1953). Family size associations with height were present in both the manual and non-manual classes.

Obesity. We examined birth order and family size associations with obesity in this population of young men (Ravelli & Belmont, in press). Studies of obesity in children have reported (i) that the prevalence of obesity declines with increasing family size, (ii) that in small families lastborn tend to have higher rates of obesity than firstborn, and (iii) most particularly, that only children tend to be obese more often than those with siblings (Bruch, 1940; Bruch and Touraine, 1940; Hillman, 1963; Crisp et al., 1970; Whitelaw, 1971; Wilkinson et al., 1977).

Obesity was defined by a relative weight index, that is by a measure of weight 20% or more above the ideal weight for a given height (Ravelli, 1976). The study included all young men born between 1944 and 1947 from 1- through 5-child families.

The overall prevalence of obesity was higher in the manual social class than in the non-manual social class (Table 3). In both social classes obesity rates declined with increasing family size, leveling off at family size 4 and 5. The rate differences by family size were highly significant.

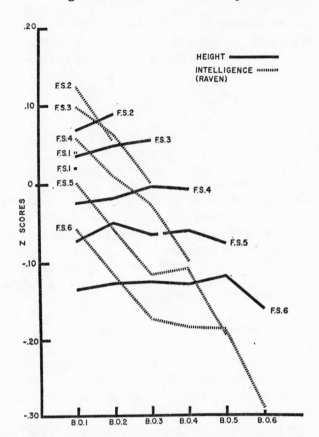

FIGURE 2. Height and intelligence (Raven) by birth order within family size (F.S.) across the population (N = 234,837). Height (cm.) and test score (1-6) were converted to a common scale (z-scores).

The family size difference in obesity rates was more regular in the manual group, whereas in the non-manual group differences were better explained by the high rate for one-child families. There was no clear birth order pattern discernible; rates for firstborn tended to be lower than those for lastborn, but these differences were small, and generally not statistically significant. What is most prominent is that young men from 1-child families (only children) had by far the highest obesity rate of all family sizes and birth orders. Indeed the rates of only children in the 2 social classes were very similar; regardless of social class membership, only children were at high risk for obesity. Our findings for obesity in adults are similar to those reported for children.

TABLE 3

Obesity Rates (Percent) by Family Size and Birth Order for the Manual Social Class (N = 136,811) and for the Non-Manual Social Class (N = 132,590)

MANUAL

Family Size	Birth Order 1	2	3	4	5	Total
1	3.33					3.33
2	2.43	2.57				2.50
3	1.96	1.85	2.15			1.98
4	1.51	1.61	1.79	2.12		1.73
5	1.69	1.45	1.52	2.01	2.18	1.73

Overall rate 2.09

NON-MANUAL

Family Size	Birth Order 1	2	3	4	5	Total
1	3.13					3.13
2	1.69	1.86				1.77
3	1.32	1.35	1.45			1.37
4	1.32	1.06	1.33	1.41		1.27
5	1.36	1.17	0.95	1.45	1.47	1.25

Overall rate 1.54

Special Study: The Only Child

We reviewed all the characteristics of only children and studied their psychiatric status (Belmont, Wittes & Stein, 1976). As a group, only children were at some disadvantage on indices of mental and physical development.

Only children can be described accurately in terms of family size: They are unambiguously members of the smallest sized family. Their birth order is less clear: They can be viewed as firstborn or lastborn (or even without rank) and they have usually been grouped with firstborn.

We contrasted only children with firstborn or lastborn from 2-, 3- and 4-child families. (We studied young men born between 1944-1947 in the manual and non-manual social classes.) On measures of intellectual competence and school performance, only children were at a disadvantage when contrasted with firstborn but at an advantage when contrasted with lastborn. They did not fit any firstborn pattern but they fit a family size gradient for lastborn. (For example, they had better scores than lastborn from 2-child families who in turn had better scores than lastborn from 3-child families who in turn had better scores than lastborn from 4-child families. Similarly they had higher rates of university attendance than lastborn from 2-, 3- and 4-child families.)

In earlier studies (e.g., Douglas, 1964; Douglas et al., 1968; Scottish Council for Research in Education, 1949; Vernon, 1951) only children had achieved the highest score. However, in addition to our findings, Breland (1974) also found that only children were atypical.

With regard to the frequency of psychological disorder among only children, there is little evidence comparable to that available for intelligence to suggest regular associations with family size and birth order. As children, only children have been reported to have more problems (e.g., Shrader & Leventhal, 1968) and also fewer problems (e.g., Levy, 1931; Tuckman & Regan, 1967). As adults, only children have been reported to be overrepresented among neurotics (Gregory, 1958; Norton, 1952; Riess & Safer, 1973; Taintor, 1970; Vogel & Lauterbach, 1963). As indicated in the opening review, the associations found between birth rank and psychiatric conditions have been brought into question by a series of recent papers (Hare & Price, 1969; Schooler, 1972).

At the outset it was apparent that the study population had relatively low rates of psychiatric disorder; the highest overall rate was under 5%, lower than others have reported (Dohrenwend & Dohrenwend, 1967).

In our study of the only child, psychiatric disorder was assessed with two measures: 1) an unfit rating on the "psychological stability" item of the health rating scale (see above) and 2) psychiatric diagnoses. All diagnoses were classified to conform to the terminology of the 1968 *Diagnostic and Statistical Manual* (*DSM-II*) (American Psychiatric Association, 1968). We studied the two diagnoses with greatest frequency, Neurosis and Personality Disorder.

In both social classes only children had the highest rates on indices of psychological disorder: They had the highest rate of "unfit" (on psychological stability) and the highest rate of Neurosis. Also, in the non-manual social class only children had the highest rate of Personality Disorder.

We were less certain of characterizing only children as firstborn or lastborn on measures of psychological disorder. (Firstborn tended to have lower rates than lastborn.) Only children "looked like" lastborn at times (Figure 3) but appeared to be uniquely at risk for a diagnosis of Neurosis (Figure 4).

What was apparent was that there was a family size association with psychiatric disorder (all psychiatric diagnoses combined) in both social classes (Table 4); these rates were not compelling. Only children had a significantly higher rate of overall psychiatric disorder than firstborn from 2-, 3- and 4-child families.

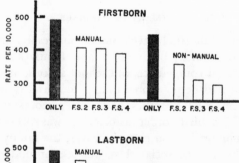

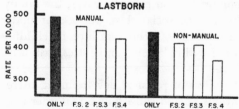

FIGURE 3. Rate for "unfit" on psychological stability item of health rating scale for only children, firstborn and lastborn from 2-, 3-, and 4-child families in the manual and non-manual social classes. From Belmont, Wittes & Stein (1976).

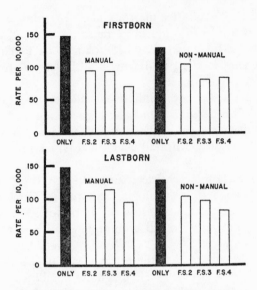

FIGURE 4. Rate for Neurosis for only children, firstborn and lastborn from 2-, 3-, and 4-child families in the manual and non-manual social classes. From Belmont, Wittes & Stein (1976).

SUMMARY OF FINDINGS

With regard to intellectual development our results have shown that, except for 1-child families, birth order and family size were inversely related to intellectual competence and school success. Within given family sizes, firstborn had better scores than laterborn. Within given birth orders, those from small families had better scores than those from larger families. The birth order association was present in both the manual and non-manual social class; however, the famliy size association was regular in the manual social class, but less pronounced in the non-manual social class. Rates of school failure in childhood increased as family size increased; within given family sizes, lastborn had the highest risk of school failure.

In contrast, on indices of physical development, there were consistent family size associations but no consistent birth order associations. Except for 1-child families, family size was inversely related to height; those from small families were taller than those from large families. Family size was inversely related to obesity: Those in small families, and particularly in 1-child families, had the higher rates of obesity and large families had the lower rates.

TABLE 4

Overall Rate of Psychiatric Disorder per 10,000
Population by Family Size for the Manual
Social Class (N = 107,723) and for the
Non-Manual Social Class (N = 95,335)

Famliy Size	MANUAL	NON-MANUAL
1	471.1	441.4
2	422.8	385.8
3	419.5	358.7
4	412.9	332.9

A gradient similar to the one found with obesity characterized psychiatric condition; rates of psychiatric disorder tended to be higher in small families. Although firstborn had lower rates than lastborn, these results were not compelling. As for only children, they tended to be at some disadvantage on indices of intellectual and physical development. They were uniquely at risk for obesity and, perhaps, psychiatric disorder. They occupied an intermediate position on indices of mental development in that they did not have the advantages of firstborn from small families but had advantages relative to lastborn.

IMPLICATIONS OF FINDINGS

Implications for Family Planning

Our results have shown a persistence of family size associations with indices of mental and physical development. Small family size was an asset for mental development and for stature: Members of small families had better achievement and intelligence test scores on the average than members of larger families; they had lower rates of school failure than those from larger families; and, indeed, they were taller than those from larger families. Small family size was a liability for the prevalence of obesity and of psychiatric disorder: The rates were higher in small families than in larger families.

Only in a general way did the 1-child family share the benefits of small family size: Their average test scores were better and their school failure rates were lower than were those from larger families. But they never equaled firstborn from small families. Where small family size was a disadvantage (rates of obesity and of psychiatric disorder), only children showed the most disadvantage.

On a population level, these results are pertinent to decisions involved in family planning (Terhune, 1974). Whatever the processes might be which underlie these findings, they suggest that there are both advantages and disadvantages to small family size. However, with the increased emphasis today in some societies on small family size (probably including increase in the proportion of only children), studies of more current generations could determine whether a changed view of what is normative for family size results in changes in the at-risk characteristics of only children.

On a population level, our findings have relevance. They are less useful for individual prediction. The findings refer to *groups* of young men defined by family size/birth order characteristics. We highlighted the consistency of effects within measures and persistence of effects between measures. These effects, though consistent, are small (Belmont & Marolla, 1973; Belmont, Wittes & Stein, in press), accounting for a small proportion of individual variance. Despite the small size of the effects, their consistency suggests that they are real and the search for explanations should prove to be productive.

Implications for Theory Building and Testing

There have been a number of views advanced to account for family size and birth order effects (see Belmont & Marolla, 1973; Breland, 1977). Recently, one hypothesis has gained prominence; Zajonc and Markus (1975) proposed a process to explain family size and birth order associations in their confluence model which was originally developed on the basis of the findings contained in Figure 1 (above) and later extended to other findings as well (Zajonc, 1976). Briefly, the confluence model postulates an "intellectual environment" for each family at a particular point in time. This intellectual environment is a function of the absolute intellectual level of its members (parents and children combined) at a given time; the intellectual environment changes with the growth, recruitment and departure of members. When the first child is born, the intellectual environment of the two parents $(30 + 30/2)$ is reduced to $30 + 30 + 0/3$. (At birth, the child's contribution is considered to be zero.)

If one postulates that after a time the first child contributes "4" to the intellectual environment, with the birth of the second child the intellectual environment is reduced from the one-child environment of $30 + 30 + 4/3$ to the average of 30, 30, 4, and 0. The actual numbers assigned are of no import as long as the child's contribution does not exceed that of the parents. Zajonc and Markus argue that with increasing family size the intellectual environment for the entire family becomes more impoverished. Therefore, large family size must necessarily lead to lower scores of all members of the large family.*

In the model, differences in birth order effects are postulated to be associated with differences in spacing interval between siblings. With short intervals, the intellectual environment is more impoverished (see formula for intellectual environment above); this process is ameliorated or reversed with longer intervals between siblings. Clearly, spacing is critical to tests of the confluence model.

The confluence model was recently tested by Grotevant and his co-workers on a sample of 101 middle-to-upper-middle-class families with both biological and adopted children (Grotevant, Scarr & Weinberg, 1977). Then concluded that the confluence model is "a very poor fit to the data on individual differences in IQ." Only 2% of the variance is accounted for when individual scores are entered into the equation. (Indeed, 2% may be an overestimate caused by the statistical confounding of birth order and family size). The study also reported on the effects of birth order, family size and spacing for the 251 children in the sample. Spacing and family size were found not to be significant but birth order was significantly related to children's IQ differences.

A major strut of the Zajonc model is the effect of spacing in explaining the birth order effect. We were able to study this question (Belmont, Stein & Zybert, in press) in a subsample of men from 2-child families for whom we had been able to obtain information on spacing. We had two series: one composed of unrelated individuals—firstborn and lastborn for whom we knew the date of birth of the sibling, the other composed of firstborn and secondborn men who were brothers (228 pairs in the manual social class and 307 pairs in the non-manual class). Spacing between siblings ranged from 11 months to more than 12 years. Despite the wide range of spacing intervals, we did not find any association between test score and spacing in either social class. There was a significant negative association between maternal age and spacing (women who were older when they had their first child had closer spacing); controlling for maternal age did not change the spacing results.

---

* In order to explain the poorer performance of only children another factor is introduced. The explanation offered is that mastery is gained by having someone to teach, and the only child, like the lastborn, cannot gain this added proficiency because he has no younger siblings to teach. (An implicit assumption of the theory is that parental mental age is immutable; parents gain no benefit from teaching nor lose by living in an impoverished environment.)

The confluence theory is an intriguing one and probably it will continue to generate research interest. The model was developed using findings for *groups* identified by birth order and family size characteristics. Implicit in the confluence model is that adjacent birth orders in the population series represent siblings; as formulated, the theory is an *individual* family hypothesis. However, our studies, as well as all other large-scale studies, are cross-sectional; they are age-specific and therefore do not refer to siblings. In our series, the largest majority of these young men, especially in larger sized families, would *not* be brothers. (In any case, in our series there can be no information concerning sisters.) Similar restrictions hold for other large data sets. (Breland, 1974, could identify twins in his series.)

Birth order effects among lastborn in larger families may be related in part to cohort effects (Susser, 1973); for example, in our series the oldest (firstborn) siblings of later and lastborn of larger families would have grown up in a pre-World War II environment, perhaps including the economic hard times of the 1930s. So, too, the mothers of these lastborn necessarily would have begun their families in earlier times and might have had less education than women who started their families at a later point in time. Breland (1974) was able to examine the effect of maternal age and education in his series and found that birth order effects persisted after such factors were controlled.

Theories must also take into account the puzzling social class differences in the relative influence of family size and birth order (our studies), as well as possible cross-cultural differences (Davis et al., 1977). Indeed, birth order associations may shift with changing times with different cultures (compare Scottish study findings with our findings); it is questionable whether such shifts are satisfactorily explained by changing birth rates alone (see Hare & Price, 1969). In our sample of brothers, the birth order effect, though small, persisted.

However, it is unlikely that any one "cause" can explain individual differences in complex mental and physical development. In our data, for example, the two social classes differed in ability level. It might actually be more parsimonious to assume that individual differences in ability are the result of multiple causes (of which family size and birth order are but two) which exert their influence at different periods and in different ways in the course of development.

REFERENCES

AKESSON, H. O. A study of fertility and mental deficiency. *Acta Genetica*, 1967, 17, 234-252.

ALTUS, W. D. Birth order and scholastic aptitude. *Journal of Consulting Psychology*, 1965, 29, 202-205.

ALTUS, W. D. Birth order and its sequelae. *Science*, 1966, 151, 44-49.

American Psychiatric Association. *Diagnostic and Statistical Manual of Mental Disorders—DSM-II*. Washington, D.C., 1968.

ANASTASI, A. Intelligence and family size. *Psychological Bulletin*, 1956, 53, 187-209.

ANASTASI, A. Differentiating effect of intelligence and social status. *Eugenics Quarterly*, 1959, 6, 84-91.

BELMONT, L. Birth order, intellectual competence, and psychiatric status. *Journal of Individual Psychology*, 1977, 33, 97-104.

BELMONT, L. and MAROLLA, F. A. Birth order, family size, and intelligence. *Science*, 1973, 182, 1096-1101.

BELMONT, L., STEIN, Z., and SUSSER, M. Comparison of associations of height with intelligence test score. *Nature*, 1975, 255, 54-56.

BELMONT, L., STEIN, Z., and WITTES, J. Birth order, family size and school failure. *Developmental Medicine and Child Neurology*, 1976, 18, 421-430.

BELMONT, L., STEIN, Z., and ZYBERT, P. Child spacing and birth order: Effects on intellectual ability in two-child families. *Science* (in press).

BELMONT, L., WITTES, J., and STEIN, Z. The only child syndrome: Myth or reality. Paper presented at the Meeting of the Society for Life History Research in Psychopathology, October 1976.

BELMONT, L., WITTES, J., and STEIN, Z. Relation of birth order, family size and social class to psychological functions. *Perceptual and Motor Skills*, 1977, 45, 1107-1116.

BIRCH, H. G., RICHARDSON, S. A., BAIRD, D., HOROBIN, G., and ILLSLEY, R. *Mental Subnormality in the Community—A Clinical and Epidemiologic Study*. Baltimore: Williams & Wilkins, 1970.

BRADLEY, R. W. Birth order and school-related behavior: A heuristic review. *Psychological Bulletin*, 1968, 70, 45-51.

BRELAND, H. M. Birth order, family configuration, and verbal achievement. *Child Development*, 1974, 45, 1011-1019.

BRELAND, H. M. Family configuration and intellectual development. *Journal of Individual Psychology*, 1977, 33, 86-96.

BRUCH, H. Obesity in childhood. *American Journal of Diseases of Childhood*, 1940, 59, 739-781.

BRUCH, H. and TOURAINE, G. Obesity in childhood: V. The family frame of obese children. *Psychosomatic Medicine*, 1940, 2, 141-206.

BURKE, M. O. A search for systematic personality differentiae of the only child in young adulthood. *Journal of Genetic Psychology*, 1956, 89, 71-84.

CRISP, A. H., DOUGLAS, J. W. B., ROSS, J. M., and STONEHILL, E. Some developmental aspects of disorders of weight. *Journal of Psychosomatic Research*, 1970, 14, 313-320.

DAVIS, D. J., CAHAN, S., and BASHI, J. Birth order and intellectual development: The confluence model in the light of cross-cultural evidence. *Science*, 1977, 196, 1470-1472.

DE BRUIJN, J. The Netherlands. In: *The Year Book of Education*. London: University of London Institute of Education, 1950.

DOHRENWEND, B. S. and DOHRENWEND, B. P. Field studies of social factors in relation to three types of psychological disorder. *Journal of Abnormal Psychology*, 1967, 72, 369-378.

DOUGLAS, J. W. B. *The Home and the School*. London: MacGibbon & Kee, 1964.

DOUGLAS, J. W. B., ROSS, J. M., and SIMPSON, H. R. *All Our Future—A Longitudinal Study of Secondary Education*. London: Peter Davies, 1968.

FALBO, T. The only child: A review. *Journal of Individual Psychology*, 1977, 33, 47-61.

FORER, L. Bibliography of birth order literature in the '70's. *Journal of Individual Psychology*, 1977, 33, 122-141.

GREGORY, I. An analysis of familial data on psychiatric patients: Parental age, family size, birth order, and ordinal position. *British Journal of Preventive and Social Medicine*, 1958, 12, 42-59.

GROTEVANT, H. D., SCARR, S., and WEINBERG, R. A. Intellectual development in family constellations with adopted and natural children: A test of the Zajonc and Markus model. *Child Development*, 1977, 48, 1699-1703.

HARE, E. H. and PRICE, J. S. Birth order and family size: Bias caused by changes in birth rate. *British Journal of Psychiatry*, 1969, 115, 647-657.

HILLMAN, R. W. Infant feeding patterns and oral habits of overweight and underweight children. *American Journal of Clinical Nutrition*, 1963, 13, 326-330.

KOCH, H. L. Some personality correlates of sex, sibling position, and sex of sibling among five- and six-year-old children. *Genetic Psychology Monographs*, 1955, 52, 3-50.

LEVY, J. A. A quantitative study of behavior problems in relation to family constellation. *American Journal of Psychiatry*, 1931, 10, 637-654.

MITTELMAN, M., STEIN, Z., SUSSER, M., and BELMONT, L. Psychiatric fitness and cognitive function: A causal connection? Paper presented at the Annual International Symposium of the Kittay Scientific Foundation, 'Cognitive Defects in the Development of Mental Illness,' April 1977. New York: Brunner/Mazel, 1978.

NISBET, J. D. and ENTWISTLE, N. J. Intelligence and famiy size, 1949-1965. *British Journal of Educational Psychology*, 1967, 37, 188-193.

NORTON, A. Incidence of neurosis related to maternal age and birth order. *British Journal of Social Medicine*, 1952, 6, 253-258.

PRICE, J. S. and HARE, E. H. Birth order studies: Some sources of bias. *British Journal of Psychiatry*, 1969, 115, 633-646.

RAVELLI, G. P. Patterns of obesity and thinness prevalence in a national population of nineteen-year-old men. Unpublished doctoral dissertation, The Faculty of Medicine, Columbia University, 1976.

RAVELLI, G. P. and BELMONT, L.: Obesity in nineteen-year-old men: Family size and birth order associations. *American Journal of Epidemiology* (in press).

RAVELLI, G. P., STEIN, Z. A., and SUSSER, M. W. Obesity in young men after famine exposure in utero and early infancy. *New England Journal of Medicine*, 1976, 295, 349-353.

RIESS, B. F. and SAFER, J. Birth order and related variables in a large outpatient population. *The Journal of Psychology*, 1973, 85, 61-68.

RUTTER, M., TIZARD, J., and WHITMORE, K. (Eds.). *Health, Education and Behavior*. London: Longman Group Limited, 1970.

SAMPSON, E. E. The study of ordinal position: Antecedents and outcomes. In: B. A. Maher (Ed.), *Progress in Experimental Personality Research*. New York: Academic Press, 1965.

SAMPSON, E. E. and HANCOCK, F. T. An examination of the relationship between ordinal position, personality and conformity: An extension, replication, and partial verification. *Journal of Personality and Social Psychology*, 1967, 5, 398-407.

SCHACHTER, S. *The Psychology of Affiliation*. Stanford, California: Stanford University Press, 1959.

SCHACHTER, S. Birth order, eminence and higher education. *American Sociological Review*, 1963, 28, 453-456.

SCHOOLER, C. Birth order and schizophrenia. *Archives of General Psychiatry*, 1961, 4, 91-97.

SCHOOLER, C. Birth order effects: Not here, not now! *Psychological Bulletin*, 1972, 78, 161-175.

SCHOONOVER, S. M. The relationship of intelligence and achievement to birth order, sex of sibling, and age interval. *Journal of Educational Psychology*, 1959, 50, 143-146.

Scottish Council for Research in Education. *The Trend of Scottish Intelligence.* London: University of London Press, 1949.

Scottish Council for Research in Education. *Social Implications of the 1947 Scottish Mental Survey.* London: University of London Press, 1953.

SHRADER, W. K. and LEVENTHAL, T. Birth order of children and parental report of problems. *Child Development,* 1968, 39, 1165-1175.

STEIN, Z., SUSSER, M., and SAENGER, G. Mental retardation in a national population of young men in the Netherlands. I. Prevalence of severe mental retardation. *American Journal of Epidemiology,* 1976a, 103, 477-485.

STEIN, Z., SUSSER, M., and SAENGER, G. Mental retardation in a national population of young men in the Netherlands. II. Prevalence of mild mental retardation. *American Journal of Epidemiology,* 1976b, 104, 159-169.

STEIN, Z., SUSSER, M., SAENGER, G., and MAROLLA, F. *Famine and Human Development: The Dutch Hunger Winter of 1944, 1945.* New York: Oxford University Press, 1975.

SUSSER, M. *Causal Thinking in the Health Sciences—Concepts and Strategies in Epidemiology.* New York: Oxford University Press, 1973.

TAINTOR, Z. Birth order and psychiatric problems in boot camp. *American Journal of Psychiatry,* 1970, 126, 1604-1610.

TERHUNE, K. W. *A Review of the Actual and Expected Consequences of Family Size.* Calspan Report No. DP-5333-G-1. Washington, D.C.: Public Health Service, 1974.

TUCKMAN, J. and REGAN, R. A. Ordinal position and behavior problems in children. *Journal of Health and Social Behavior,* 1967, 8, 32-45.

VERNON, P. E. Recent investigations of intelligence and its measurement. *Eugenics Review,* 1951, 43, 125-137.

VOGEL, W. and LAUTERBACH, C. G. Sibling patterns and social adjustment among normal and psychiatrically disturbed soldiers. *Journal of Consulting Psychology,* 1963, 27, 236-242.

WARREN, J. R. Birth order and social behavior. *Psychological Bulletin,* 1966, 65, 38-49.

WHITELAW, A. G. Association of social class and sibling number with skinfold thickness in London schoolboys. *Human Biology,* 1971, 43, 414-420.

WILKINSON, P. W., PEARLSON, J., PARKIN, J. M., PHILIPS, P. R., and SYKES, P. Obesity in childhood: A community study in Newcastle upon Tyne. *Lancet,* 1977, 1, 350-352.

WITTES, J. and BELMONT, L. A comparison of models for the analysis of data from birth order—family size arrays. Submitted for publication.

World Health Organization. *Manual of the International Statistical Classification of Diseases, Injuries, and Causes of Death* (6th revision), Geneva, 1948.

WRAY, J. D. Population pressure on families: Family size and child spacing. In: R. Ravelle (Ed.), *Rapid Population Growth: Consequences and Policy Implications,* Vol. 2. Baltimore: Johns Hopkins Press, 1971.

ZAJONC, R. B. Family configuration and intelligence. *Science,* 1976, 192, 227-236.

ZAJONC, R. B. and MARKUS, G. B. Birth order and intellectual development. *Psychological Review,* 1975, 82, 74-88.

10

Some Effects of the Dutch Hunger Winter of 1944-1945

Zena Stein *and* Mervyn Susser

The relation of early nutrition and mental development was a central concern of Herbert Birch at the time we knew him, and his stimulating research in this field did much to kindle our own interest in this topic (Birch, 1972).

Poor mental performance, social deprivation, and nutritional deprivation are commonly found in the same strata of society. Over the last decade it has been realized that poor nutrition, in particular early malnutrition, could be a major factor in the social distribution of depressed mental competence. No one will dispute the importance of mental competence, for societies as well as individuals, in coping with the modern world. If poor nutrition is a cause of poor mental competence, the social implications are immense.

Malnutrition is preventable, yet widespread. The vast extent of general calorie-protein malnutrition in the Third World came to be better understood after World War II, although Cicely Williams first described kwashiorkor in 1933. In the mid-1960s, a U.S. congressional committee gave shocked recognition to the existence of widespread hunger even in the affluent U.S.

The broad hypothesis generated by these circumstances and related scientific work is that early malnutrition retards brain growth and that the brain's organic deficit in turn leads to behavioral and mental deficits. The likely population-wide manifestations of the effects of malnutrition on mental performance would be depressed IQs and the so-called cultural-familial syndrome of mild mental retardation, both of which are

244

concentrated among the poor and deprived. Brain damage with severe mental retardation is an unlikely outcome; the severe forms of retardation do not display the same dramatic social gradient as the mild form without brain damage.

The hypothesis has been refined by the notion of the "critical period" —when the brain grows most actively and supposedly is most vulnerable to insult and irreversible damage. This growth involves hyperplasia and hypertrophy at different phases for different cell types. Although in human beings hyperplasia of neurons seems mainly to occur in utero during the second trimester of pregnancy, maximum velocity of brain growth begins in the last trimester and continues after birth. Both neuronal hypertrophy and glial hyperplasia are thought to contribute to rapid growth during these months. The hypertrophy of neurons, with arborization into dendrites and synapses, probably continues into the second year of life.

When we designed our studies in this field, rapid growth was thought to occur, in the human infant, mainly in the latter part of pregnancy and in early prenatal life (Dobbing, 1964). More recent studies show the phase of rapid growth extending from the second and third trimesters of gestation through the second year of life (Dobbing & Sands, 1973.

A number of experiments in rats, dogs, and pigs supports the critical-period hypothesis, although interpretations of such animal studies must allow for the fact that species differ in the phase at which maximum brain growth takes place. In pigs, for instance, the peak growth rate is prenatal, while in rats it is postnatal. Winick and his colleagues showed that nutritional deprivation at the time of maximum brain growth reduced the estimated number of rat brain cells, and the number remained deficient thereafter (Winick & Noble, 1966). Myelin deposition also has been found to be restricted and to remain deficient in malnourished dogs and pigs.

The World War II famine studies by A. N. Antonov in Leningrad and Clement Smith in Holland showed that human maternal starvation caused fetal growth retardation and consequently reduced birthweight. Since many studies, although not all, have found that low birthweight is associated with retarded subsequent development, it was a short step to the assumption that causal pathway exists from maternal malnutrition, through reduced birthweight, to retarded mental and motor development with an outcome in poor mental performance and short stature.

The famine in the Netherlands took place between October and May 1944-45. We realized that the documented effect of the famine in re-

ducing birthweight might have great significance for an understanding
of the relation between mental competence and nutrition. By following
the offspring of affected pregnancies through the postwar years of relative plenty we could define human populations that had suffered demon-
strable nutritional deprivation at specified times in intrauterine life, and
only at such times. Such pathologies or handicaps that had resulted
would be observed in survivors or, in some cases, noted in early deaths.
Our initial concern was to test the effect of malnutrition during the so-
called "critical period" of brain development in the latter part of
pregnancy.

In the course of the research our interest broadened to include a
range of effects of prenatal starvation. In this chapter, we summarize
the effects of the famine on fertility, on the immediate outcome of pregnancy, on infant mortality, on mental performance and on mental
retardation, and on health state and obesity in 19-year-old men who survived. The methods and the full array of findings can be found in the

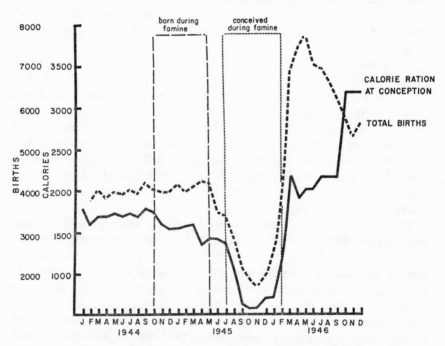

FIGURE 1. Number of births in famine cities, June 1944 to December 1946, and
estimated caloric rations at the time of conception of those births. From Stein et al.,
1975.

sources given at the end of the chapter (Stein et al., 1975; Ravelli et al., 1976).

FERTILITY

Associated with severe famine, there was a marked reduction in the number of conceptions resulting in births (see Figure 1). This reduction did not take place unless the nutritional deprivation exceeded a threshold of severity. Thus in those parts of the country which did not experience the full impact of famine, there was no variation in births with levels of food rations, nor was there variation in the famine-exposed areas until the available food had reached a very low level. Infertility, we concluded, is associated with starvation but not with milder forms of undernutrition.

We attributed the reduction of births to social and biological factors, but particularly to the cessation of ovulation in women. Although we could not exclude an increase in spontaneous abortions as a cause, the data suggested that it was unlikely to have been an important factor. The steep rise in successful conceptions that followed immediately after restoration of the diet gave evidence that physiological as well as social recovery was swift.

The fall in number of births was evident in all sections of the exposed population but it was most marked in low income occupational groups. We inferred that in spite of rationing and soup kitchens, nutritional deprivation hit the poorer families the hardest. This unequal impact was sufficient to change the social class composition of birth cohorts and had repercussions on our findings among survivors, a problem to which we shall return.

THE OUTCOME OF PREGNANCY

A starting point of our inquiry, we have noted, was Clement Smith's careful documentation of a reduction in mean birthweight in hospitals of Rotterdam and The Hague, associated with exposure of pregnant women to famine in the latter part of pregnancy (Smith, 1947; Bergner & Susser, 1970). Our findings (see Figure 2) are in accord with the earlier reports. Food deprivation in the third trimester affected birthweight. The effect was not linear but, as with fertility, became apparent only when the famine was most severe. Besides birthweight, placental weight, infant length, and head circumference at birth were reduced under the same conditions, namely only with third trimester deprivation and only when the famine was most severe. Gestation, however, was only slightly reduced in duration.

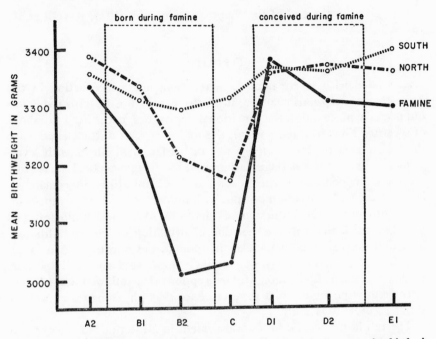

FIGURE 2. Birthweight by time and place (mean birthweight in grams for births in maternity hospitals for seven cohorts; famine, Northern control, and Southern control areas compared for the period August 1944 to March 1946 inclusive). From Stein et al., 1975.

In one hospital, mothers were weighed as a routine on the tenth day after delivery. We found that maternal post-partum weight, unlike birthweight, related closely to changes in diet in a linear fashion. We inferred from this and other analyses that above a certain level of nutritional deprivation the mother is able to buffer her fetus against an inadequate diet, but eventually a point is reached when she cannot do so. At that point the nutrition of the fetus is adversely affected and intrauterine growth retardation becomes evident.

MORTALITY

Infant mortality rates (see Figures 3 and 4) in the Netherlands were extraordinarily high in the year 1945, compared to earlier and subsequent rates in that country. To establish that even part of the mortality could be attributed to intrauterine famine exposure proved difficult, because unusual mortality occurred also in the parts of the country not

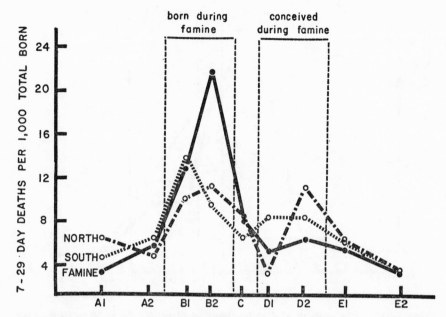

FIGURE 3. Deaths at 7 to 29 days by time and place (deaths at 7 to 29 days per 1000 total births: famine, Northern control, and Southern control areas by cohort for births January 1944 to December 1946). From Stein et al., 1975.

exposed to famine. Moreover, effects related to the postnatal period had to be distinguished from effects related to the prenatal period. We succeeded in showing to our satisfaction that there were substantial prenatal effects on infant mortality, and that famine exposure contributed a distinctive part of these.

The outstanding effect of prenatal exposure to famine was seen in infants aged between one week and three months of life who experienced intrauterine famine exposure and growth retardation in the latter part of pregnancy. The reason for their greater vulnerability was not obvious, the causes on death certificates being various, e.g., respiratory and intestinal infections, "atrophy," sclerema. Nor did it appear that premature delivery in itself was an important cause. We speculated that possibly maternal starvation in late pregnancy adversely affects immune competence in the young infant (Chandra, 1972).

Among those infants *conceived* at the height of the famine, but who were not exposed to maternal starvation during the middle and third trimesters, effects although less in magnitude, were of some theoretical

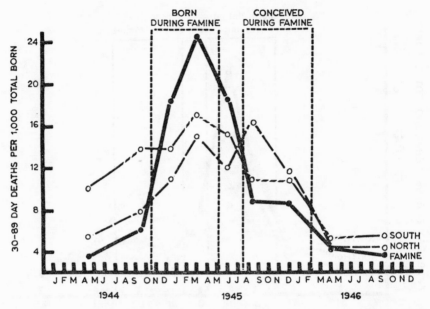

FIGURE 4. Deaths at 30 to 89 days by time and place (deaths at 30 to 89 days per 1,000 total births: famine, Northern Control, and Southern Control areas by cohort for births, January 1944 to December 1946). (Taken from Stein, Z., Susser, M., Saenger, G., and Marolla, F., 1975. *Famine and Human Development: The Dutch Hunger Winter of 1944-1945.* Oxford University Press, New York, p. 158.)

interest. These birth cohorts experienced an increase particularly in stillbirths and neonatal (first-week) deaths. In addition, there was an excess of very low birthweight infants and of premature deliveries (although the mean birthweight of these infants as a group was not reduced). Among the male survivors of these cohorts studied as young adults at military induction, the rate of congenital defects in the central nervous system was doubled (among 6,687 men 4 cases of spina bifida and hydrocephalus were expected and 8 were found). Deaths from meningitis, sometimes a complication of such malformations, were also raised in these cohorts.

At ages older than 3 months, and less than 20 years, there was no raised mortality, either overall or for specific causes, that could be attributed to prenatal famine exposure. Effects of prenatal famine exposure grave enough to threaten life did not express themselves beyond the first 3 months of life, although other unspecified prenatal effects in both famine and control areas probably did express themselves in later mortality.

THE OUTCOME IN YOUNG ADULT MALE SURVIVORS

From the coded results of the systematic examinations carried out on virtually the whole population of 19-year-old men for the purpose of military induction, it was possible to analyze a number of outcomes among those exposed to the famine and comparison groups. These outcomes included health status, anthropometric measures, and measures of mental performance.

Health Status

Only one clear association was found between prenatal exposure to famine and any of three different medical criteria. One medical criterion was the prevalence of health disorders recorded under the code of the International Classification of Diseases (World Health Organization, 1948) in the population at military induction. Twenty-six conditions had a frequency of more than 1 per 1,000, a rate which was taken to be a minimum for the purpose of examining trends among cohorts. In only one, congenital anomalies of the central nervous system, there was evidence of a raised prevalence related to first trimester exposure. An epidemic of congenital heart disease occurred across the country during the first half of 1944, but this was not related to the famine. Rising time trends for asthma, obesity, "immature personality," and psychoneurosis are also not famine-related.

A second medical criterion was the rating of health status of individuals in the population on 7 scales, each relating to a particular area of examination. A third medical criterion was the category of fitness for military service to which individuals were assigned. No distributions were famine-related by the second and third criteria.

Body Size

Height, weight, and various measures of body weight controlled for height provided the basis of our studies of prenatal famine effects on body size (see Figure 5). Although associations between food rations and body height were found, these were not related to prenatal famine exposure, but rather to a secular trend towards increasing height. The possibility that selective survival of infants removed those who would have grown into adults of small stature was not sustained by the relations between famine exposure, height, and mortality required by such an hypothesis. A secular trend was present also for weight controlled by height (Quetelet's index) especially in the manual working class.

With regard to the frequency of obesity at the extreme of the dis-

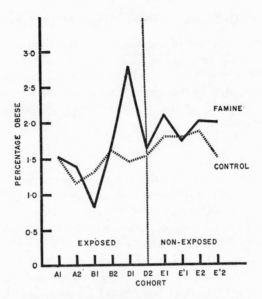

FIGURE 5. Obesity prevalence rates among birth cohorts in famine and control areas. From Ravelli et al., 1976 with permission from *The New England Journal of Medicine.*

tribution, however, we detected two contradictory prenatal famine effects.

We defined obesity as a value of weight for height equal to or greater than 120% of an international standard (Jelliffe, 1966) and related rates of obesity in young men to their estimated intrauterine exposure. In accord with a current hypothesis that early fat cell deposition influences later obesity (Knittle, 1971), and that such deposition takes place late in gestation and in the postnatal months, we found lower obesity rates in those exposed to famine in the last part of pregnancy and in the early postnatal period. Another hypothesis holds that nutritional deprivation in mid-pregnancy affects hypothalamic differentiation, which could, in turn, affect appetite regulation (Dorner & Staud, 1952). In accord with that hypothesis, we found a marked rise in the frequency of obesity among those exposed to famine through the first half of pregnancy.

Mental Performance and Mental Retardation

From the military induction examination we obtained scores on 5 psychometric tests—Raven Progressive Matrices, Language Comprehension, Arithmetic, Clerical Aptitude, Mechanical Comprehension—and a score

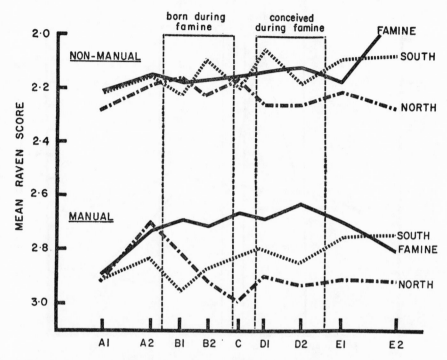

FIGURE 6. Raven scores by area and class (mean Raven scores by cohort in famine, Northern control, and Southern control areas, comparing manual and non-manual occupational classes). From Stein et al., 1975.

combining the results of all tests (see Figure 6). All tests were in agreement in failing to detect an effect of prenatal famine exposure. We found no evidence of persistent famine effects under unfavorable conditions associated with social class, religious affiliation, family size and birth order. The absence of such effects was not a function of the insensitivity of the measures. Thus the altered social class composition of the cohort exposed at the height of the famine, with its deficiency of lower class births, was reflected in better mental performance. This advantage disappeared when social class was controlled in the analysis.

One should perhaps note that those infants exposed in the latter part of pregnancy, who endured retarded fetal growth manifested in size at birth, and who survived the wave of early infant mortality, were conceived before the famine (which lasted only six months). The social class composition of this group was not affected by changes in the birth rate, and we would not expect it to have been. Among this group mental scores

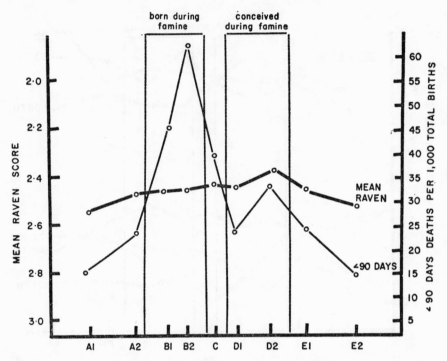

FIGURE 7. Raven scores and mortality by area (mean Raven scores and deaths occurring at ages less than 90 days, per 1000 total births by monthly cohort, famine cities). From Stein et al., 1975.

were neither higher nor lower, at 19 years, than expected from those born at other times and other places.

We explored the relation of measures of mental performance to famine-induced mortality in order to test the explanation that selective survival might have masked an association of previous famine exposure with mental competence (Figure 7). As with height, the prerequisite associations between famine exposure, mortality and mental performance were not found. Thus no distortion was apparent, and this alternative hypothesis can be dismissed.

Mental retardation data were obtained from two sources. The main source was the medical diagnosis assigned at the military induction examination. In addition, we obtained data from a survey of both women and men in about two-thirds of the residential institutions in the country. In neither data set could we detect a relation to famine exposure in the intrauterine period. Although potential cases could have been lost among the excess of infant deaths, the available evidence does not support this view. For one thing, the rate of severe mental retardation among the 19-year-old men, 3.8 per 1,000 irrespective of prenatal famine exposure, is virtually identical to the expected, based on other times and places (Stein et al., 1976a). Unusual selective loss of the severely retarded is an unlikely explanation of the absence of a detectable effect.

Similarly with mild mental retardation, for which we relied entirely on the military data, there were no discernible effects of intrauterine famine exposure. As with the other results for mental performance, the coherence of the epidemiological findings entrench our confidence in the sensitivity of the frequency measure: Variation with social class, degree of urbanization, family size, and birth rank was present in the anticipated direction. Moreover, the diagnosis could be assessed according to the standards of the military authorities, or according to our own assessment, based on scores on psychometric tests, or according to history of special school attendance (Stein et al., 1976b). Whichever the measure, we could find no excess with prenatal famine exposure.

In the path diagram we set out our inferred causal model (Figure 8).

In summary, we conclude as follows:

1) Below a threshold value of food rations, fertility in the population declined parallel with the availability of food. Infecundity, it is inferred, contributed to such infertility. There was an appreciable social class gradient in these effects, with the lowest classes affected most.

2) Above a threshold value of food rations a mother afforded the fetus protection from nutritional deprivation.

3) Below the nutritional threshold, the fetus was vulnerable to some extent in the first trimester of gestation to abnormal development of the central nervous system, premature birth and very low birthweight, and perinatal death. These effects depended on the interaction of nutritional deprivation with some other cooperating cause, possibly infection. The numbers affected were small.

4) Below the nutritional threshold, the fetus was most vulnerable in the third trimester of gestation in terms of intrauterine growth and early postnatal mortality. Of the fetal dimensions measured, weight was most sensitive to nutritional effects, and length and head size least sensitive. Slowed fetal growth was a mediating factor between prenatal nutritional deprivation and raised death rates in the first 3 months of life. The numbers affected were substantial.

5) Prenatal brain cell depletion in fetuses exposed to the famine during the third trimester probably occurred. If it occurred, this outcome

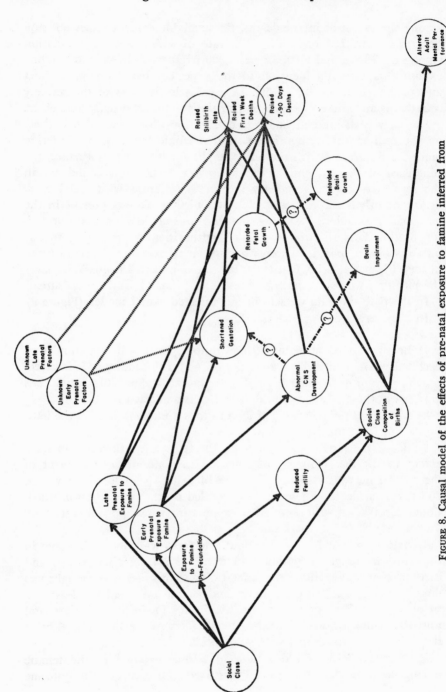

FIGURE 8. Causal model of the effects of pre-natal exposure to famine inferred from study of Dutch hunger winter 1944-1945. From Stein et al., 1975.

points to great resilience on the part of surviving fetuses, for the organic impairment did not become manifest in dysfunction.

6) Among adult survivors, we could find no evidence that prenatal nutrition impaired mental competence under some social conditions and not others. That is to say, if postnatal learning compensated for such adverse effects of prenatal nutrition as may have occurred, it did so equally well across all the social conditions that could be specified.

7) Famine exposure during the first half of pregnancy markedly raised the rate of obesity in young men, while later intrauterine and early postnatal exposure was associated with a moderate reduction of the rate of obesity.

8) Finally, we believe we must accept that poor prenatal nutrition cannot be considered a factor in the social distribution of mental competence among surviving adults in industrial societies. This is not to exclude it as a possible factor in combination with poor postnatal nutrition, especially in preindustrial societies.

REFERENCES

BERGNER, L. and SUSSER, M. W. Low birthweight and prenatal nutrition: An interpretative review. *Pediatrics*, 1970, 46, 946-966.

BIRCH, H. G. Malnutrition, learning and intelligence. *American Journal of Public Health*, 1972, 62, 773-784.

CHANDRA, R. K. Immune competence in undernutrition. *Journal of Pediatrics*, 1972, 81, 1194-1200.

DOBBING, J. The influence of early nutrition on the development and myelination of the brain. *Proceedings Royal Society* (Biology), 1964, 159, 503-509.

DOBBING, J. The later growth of the brain and its vulnerability. *Pediatrics*, 1974, 53, 2-6.

DOBBING, J. and SANDS, J. Quantitative growth and development of human brain. *Archives of Disease in Childhood*, 1973, 48, 757.

DORNER, G. and STAUD, J. Vergleichende morphologische untersuchungen der hypothalamusdifferenzierung bei ratte und memsch. *Endokrinologie*, 1972, 59, 152-155.

JELLIFFE, D. B. The assessment of the nutritional status of the community. *World Health Organization Monograph Series*, 1966, 53, 3-271.

KNITTLE, J. L. Childhood obesity. *Bulletin of New York Academy of Science*, 1971, 47, 579-589.

RAVELLI, G., STEIN, Z., and SUSSER, M. W. Obesity in young men after famine exposure in utero and early infancy. *New England Journal of Medicine*, 1976, 295, 349-353.

SMITH, C. A. Effects of wartime starvation in Holland on pregnancy and its products. *American Journal of Obstetrics and Gynecology*, 1947, 53, 599-608.

STEIN, Z., SUSSER, M., and SAEGER, G. Mental retardation in a natural population of young men in the Netherlands. I. Prevalence of severe mental retardation. *American Journal of Epidemiology*, 1976a, 103, 477-485.

STEIN, Z., SUSSER, M., and SAENGER, G. Mental retardation in a national population of young men in the Netherlands. I. Prevalence of severe mental retardation. *American Journal of Epidemiology*, 1976b, 104, 159-169.

STEIN, Z., SUSSER, M., SAENGER, G., and MAROLLA, F. *Famine and Human Development* (The Dutch Hungerwinter of 1944/45). New York: Oxford University Press, New York, 1975.

WINICK, M. and NOBLE, A. Cellular response in rats during malnutrition at various ages. *Journal of Nutrition*, 1966, 89, 300.

World Health Organization. Manual of the International Statistical Classification of Diseases, Injuries, and Causes of Death. Geneva, 1948.

Section III

COMPLEX PROCESSES AND COMPLEX BEHAVIORS

11

Temperament and the Dynamics of Development

ALEXANDER THOMAS *and* STELLA CHESS

A central consideration in Herbert Birch's research and thinking was that behavioral phenomena should always be considered within a developmental framework and analyzed in terms of a constantly evolving organism—environment interactional process. We ourselves were committed to this same approach when we started the New York Longitudinal Study in 1956. The primary goals of this study were the definition of temperamental characteristics in early childhood, the development of criteria for their categorization and scoring, the determination of the significance of temperament for psychological development, and the delineation of the vicissitudes of temperament in individual children over time. Birch joined this research effort several years after its inception and remained committed to it until his untimely tragic death. His contribution to our study of temperament was at all times imaginative and stimulating. In his typical style, he demanded conceptual and methodological rigor, sharpened our developmental and interactional approaches, and formulated one important generalization after another from masses of detailed behavioral data presented to him.

Birch always emphasized that no attitude of psychological functioning ever operated *sui generis,* in isolation from other aspects and characteristics. Whether one examines affect, cognition or overt behavior, there is always a constant dynamic interplay and interaction among all these factors. Specifically, as regards the prime focus of this volume and that of this chapter, temperament and cognition interact significantly throughout the developmental process. Behavioral style affects learning, thinking, problem-solving, etc. Cognitive characteristics shape the form and

261

quality of expression of individual temperamental characteristics. Specific examples of this temperament-cognition interplay are indicated, even when not highlighted, in this chapter.

CONCEPT OF TEMPERAMENT

The concept of temperament, the definition and criteria for categories and constellations of temperamental characteristics, scoring techniques, methods of quantitative and qualitative analyses, and the functional significance of temperament for normal and deviant behavioral development have been reported over the years in a large number of publications. Our latest volume, *Temperament and Development* (Thomas & Chess, 1977), as well as the rapidly increasing number of studies in this area by other investigators, details these reports. The present paper will summarize this material very briefly, and then discuss several pertinent issues related to the dynamics of development.

In the past, concepts and studies of psychological development focused in the main on the child's motivations (the *why* of behavior) and abilities (the *what* of behavior). The most influential theoretical system of the nature and dynamics of motivational factors came from the psychoanalytic movement. In recent years learning theorists have provided a different conceptual approach to this issue. The study of abilities and their functional significance has involved a number of psychometric approaches to the definition and measurement of intelligence, perception and sensory responses, as well as attempts to categorize and quantify more complex abilities, talents and cognitive patterns.

Important insights on both normal and deviant psychological development have been provided by these studies of the *why* and *what* of behavior. They have included increasing knowledge of the role of heredity, biochemical and neurophysiological factors, prenatal development, the birth process, parental practices and attitudes, intrafamilial dynamics, social and cultural forces, and the nature of the learning process.

By contrast, when we began our first longitudinal study in the 1950s, little systematic knowledge of the role of temperament or behavioral style (the *how* of behavior) existed, and very few investigators were interested in this issue. A number of observations on individual differences in behavioral style had been reported (see Thomas, Chess & Birch, 1968, for a bibliography of these reports) over the preceding decades, but they were too fragmentary and narrow in focus to provide a systematic and comprehensive understanding of temperament and its significance for psychological development and functioning.

Two serious limitations in theoretical and practical consideration of the developmental process are both cause and consequence of this failure to give importance to the study of temperament. First, behavioral patterns in any individual are analyzed primarily in terms of motivational forces or differences in intelligence and perception. The child with slow adaptation to any new situation becomes an anxious, insecure youngster with defensive withdrawal. The slowly moving, mildly expressive school child is labeled as having inferior intelligence. Temperamental characteristics that are inconvenient to the parent or teacher, or deviant from the average are interpreted by them—and the professional mental health worker as well—as the result of undesirable intrapsychic motivations in the child. The behavior is, in effect, made to fit a Procrustean bed of motivations.

The second cause and consequence of ignoring the significance of temperament involve the *tabula rasa* concept. In this environmentalist view, which dominated dynamic psychology and psychiatry from the beginning of this century until very recently, the newborn child and young infant has little patterned organization of individuality. Individuality in behavioral patterning and organization is then presumed to develop in response to the formative influences of the surrounding environment.

The increasing dominance of an exclusively environmentalist view of psychological development can be attributed in the main to two currents: 1) a rejection of the static, mechanistic beliefs of past centuries which conceived development as the mere unfolding and elaboration of fixed characteristics already present in the newborn infant, and 2) the progressive accumulation of research and clinical data indicating that the child's environment—his conditions of life, relationships with his parents and other family members, and the extrafamilial sociocultural setting—had a profound influence in shaping physical and psychological development. With regard to the second point, the psychoanalytic movement has been especially influential. Freudian theory does center around the concept of a fixed and predetermined evolution of a hypothetical instinctual drive for pleasure, the libido. Individual variations in the progressive movement of the young child from one libidinal stage to another, however, are conceptualized as primarily due to the influence of parental and sib relationships to the child. In essence, this represents an environmentalist view, which has been reinforced by the neo-Freudian cultural psychoanalytic group, with its emphasis on the importance of social and cultural as well as intrafamilial influences.

THE ENVIRONMENTALIST APPROACH

The environmentalist approach, in contrast to previous simplistic constitutionalist views, has contributed important information and insights on the role of intrafamilial and extrafamilial environmental influences to the cause of the developmental process. Numerous studies have delineated constellations of parental attitudes and practices, sib and other family relationships, social values, and cultural norms that significantly affect individual healthy and pathological behavioral evolution. However, as with the earlier constitutionalist view, recent studies made it increasingly evident that individuality in psychological development cannot be adequately explained on the basis of environmental factors alone (Thomas & Chess, 1977). Recent research on the infancy period has also documented dramatically the active participation of the infant, even in the newborn state, in the dynamic of child-environment interaction. The young baby's perceptual, behavioral and cognitive capacities are developed to an extent not imagined by students of development even 10 years ago (Kagan, 1971; Bower, 1974; Calder, 1976). The newborn infant not only responds actively to stimulation from the mother but initiates communication with vocalizations, facial expressions and body movements. Rutter (1975) summarizes this research:

> First, it is evident that, although limited in many ways, the young infant has a surprisingly sophisticated response to his environment and quite substantial learning skills. Second, these skills and capacities have a marked influence on the process of parent-child interaction. In many instances it is the baby who shows initiative and the parent who responds by following. Third, even in the early months of life there are striking temperamental differences between infants which influence both their response to the environment and also how other people react to them (p. 208).

In addition to the very dubious validity of the exclusively environmentalist view, such an approach has serious deleterious practical consequences. Parents of problem children are identified as the primary cause of the pathology, and frequently develop severe guilt feelings because of this assumption that they are solely responsible for their children's psychological difficulties (Chess, Thomas & Birch, 1965). These guilt feelings may result in anxiety, defensiveness, increased pressures on the children, and even hostility toward them for "exposing" the parents' inadequacy by their disturbed behavior. The consequences of these reactions by the parent can then be deleterious to the child, creating a self-fulfilling prophecy which deceptively appears to validate the assumption that the parents were the original sinners.

Furthermore, the environmentalist approach assumes that all children will tend to react similarly to the same developmental influences. This has resulted in a recurrent search for one set of rules for the parent and teacher which can be applied successfully to all children. The search for this "fool's gold" shuts the door on formulations and approaches which recognize that children have individual differences in their response to environmental demands and expectations—differences which negate the possibility of finding one set of rules applicable to all children.

THE NEW YORK LONGITUDINAL STUDY

It was with these considerations in mind that we launched our first longitudinal study in 1956. We started with 141 infants in the first few months of life and have followed their sequential behavioral development to identify specific categories of temperamental individuality, to formulate quantitative and qualitative methods of rating temperament, to trace the vicissitudes of temperament over time, and to determine its influence on both normal and deviant psychological development. Only 5 children have been lost to the study over time. The findings of this first study, the New York longitudinal study (NYLS) have been expanded by the data from several other longitudinal studies we have also conducted and from the work of other investigators. As indicated above, the methods and findings have been reported in a number of publications and are detailed in our latest volume (Thomas & Chess, 1977).

To summarize, we have found that the objective details of the behavior of all children in the routines of daily living and in new situations can be rated for 9 categories of temperament: activity level, rhythmicity of biological functions, ease of adaptability, approach/withdrawal reactions to new stimuli and new situations, sensory threshold, mood (preponderance of positive vs. negative mood), intensity of mood, distractibility, and persistence and attention span. Three functionally significant constellations of temperament have also been identified. The *Easy Child* is characterized by biological regularity, a preponderance of approach reactions to the new, positive mood of mild to moderate intensity, and easy adaptability. The *Difficult Child*, by contrast, has biological irregularity, a preponderance of withdrawal reactions to the new, many negative mood expressions of marked intensity and slow adaptability. The *Slow-To-Warm-Up Child*, like the Difficult Child, has withdrawal responses, negative mood, and slow adaptability, but, by contrast, has mild reactions and may or may not have irregularity of biological functions. As might be expected, individual children vary widely in the degree and sharpness with which they exhibit one or another of these constellations. Also, combinations of other categories may be functionally important in influencing the developmental process in specific children.

These 9 categories of temperament do not exhaust all the possibilities of behavioral style. Abrams and Neubauer (1975) have described a characteristic which they label Person- or Thing-Orientedness, defined as "individual variation in development characterized by an inclination in orientedness either toward the animate or toward the inanimate world. This variant becomes manifest at the second month of life. It casts its impressions on the surrounds, on the continuing developmental process, and on certain aspects of character formation." Graham and his associates (1973), in a British study of children 3-8 years of age, confirmed a number of our findings on temperament, and added an additional characteristic, which they labeled "fastidiousness." Hertzig et al. (1968) analyzed to the characteristics of the responses of 3-year-old children to task demands of a standard IQ test and defined a number of stylistic categories by an inductive analysis of the data. It can be expected that future investigators will identify additional characteristics of behavioral style, which reflect the *how,* rather than the *what* or *why* of behavior.

SIGNIFICANCE OF TEMPERAMENT

We have found that temperament plays a highly significant role in the child-environment interactional process at sequential age-stage levels of development. The child's temperament influences significantly the behavior and attitudes of peers, older children, parents and teachers. Conversely, the effect of these individuals' behavior and attitudes is markedly influenced by the child's temperament. Furthermore, temperament, motivations, cognitive attributes, and special abilities or handicaps enter into a mutually reciprocal interactional process in helping to shape the child's development at each age period. These findings have now been abundantly confirmed by a number of other investigators both in this country and abroad (Thomas & Chess, 1977).

These studies make it clear that a systematic analysis of the behavioral characteristics and their ontogenesis in any individual will necessarily be incomplete if temperament is ignored. Similarily, therapeutic and preventive programs for psychological disorders will be incomplete, and even misdirected, if the role of temperament is not identified. In addition, optimal structuring of the schoolroom routines and schedules requires attention to the individual child's temperament if maximum learning is to occur. Gordon (1973) puts it well: "The nature and quality of behavioral development and its expressions may be significantly influenced by affective response tendencies or temperament. It is quite likely that what surfaces as success or failure, achievement or developmental lag, adjustment or maladjustment in play, in school, in work, or in one's more personal life is a reflection of the extent to which certain affective response tendencies are accommodated, complemented, or frustrated by one's environmental encounters and existential conditions. Now, if this is true, those of us who would design and manage developmental and learning experiences certainly must give greater attention to the identification and understanding of temperamental traits and their implications for developmental and teaching/learning transactions" (p. 18).

GOODNESS OF FIT AND MASTERY

The finding that temperament plays a significant role in influencing the course of individual psychological development creates a temptation to make temperament the heart and body of a general theory. To do so would be to repeat a frequent approach in psychiatry which, over the years, has been beset by general theories of behavior based upon fragments rather than the totality of influencing mechanisms. A one-sided emphasis on temperament would merely repeat and perpetuate such a tendency and would be antithetical to our viewpoint, which insists that we recognize temperament as only one attribute of the organism. Temperament must at all times be considered in its internal relations with abilities and motives and in its external relations with environmental opportunities and stresses. In the elaboration of this approach we have found the evolutionary concept of "goodness of fit" (Henderson, 1913) to be very useful. This concept suggests that the adequacy of an organism's functioning is dependent upon the degree to which the properties of its environment are in accord with the organisms's own characteristics and style of behaving. Optimal developmental then derives from a *consonance* between an individual's temperament, abilities and motivational patterns and the expectations and demands of the environment. Dissonance between the capacities and characteristics of the individual and his environment, on the other hand, will lead to excessive stress and the danger of disorders in development.

Healthy psychological growth will result if the child achieves consistent mastery of successive environmental expectations and demands at successive age-periods. Such mastery is never an abstract process, but shaped by the social values and goals of the culture, which determine which behavioral outcome in the child-environmental interaction is desirable and productive, and which is undesirable and unproductive.

Furthermore, the possibility of mastery of any new expectation cannot be determined by the presence or absence of stress or discomfort as such. Stress can be considered to represent a demand upon the child (or adult) either for an alteration in a habitual pattern of functioning or for the mastery of a new activity or task that is difficult to achieve. If the demand, even if very difficult, stressful, and productive of discomfort, is consonant with the child's characteristics and capacities, then mastery and developmental progress are possible. If, however, the demand is dissonant with the child's behavioral style and abilities, excessive stress and discomfort will result, and mastery will not be possible. An unhealthy outcome will then occur unless the demand is appropriately modified or defined, or specific and selective assistance given to the child.

The concept of goodness of fit, therefore, should not be used as a homeostatic principle in the area of behavioral functioning, but as a homeodynamic one, which has as its end result developmental change and expanded competence rather than the maintenance of an equilibrium. This concept is central to the consideration of goodness of fit between a child's temperament and environmental expectations and demands. The degree to which an environmental expectation or new demand for mastery will be stressful and potentially excessively stressful will depend upon the temperamental characteristics of the individual child. Thus the stressful demands for the Difficult Child are typically those of socialization, namely the demands for alteration of spontaneous responses and patterns to conform to the rules of living of the family, the school, the peer group, etc. Once they do learn the rules and the situation is routinized, these children characteristically function easily, consistently and energetically. The Easy Child, by contrast, usually copes smoothly and easily with the demands of socialization, and is less vulnerable to the development of a behavior disorder than is the Difficult Child. However, the very ease of adaptability characteristic of the Easy Child may under certain circumstances be the basis for problem behavior disorder. Most typically, we have seen this occur when there is a severe dissonance between the expectations and demands of the intra- and extrafamilial environments. The child first adapts easily to the standards and behavioral expectations of the parent in the first few years of life. When he then moves actively into functional situations outside the home, such as in peer play groups and school, excessive stress and malfunctioning will develop if the extrafamilial standards and demands conflict sharply with the patterns learned in the home.

For the Slow-To-Warm-Up Child, a key issue is whether parents and teachers allow him to make an adaptation to the new at his own characteristically gradual tempo, or insist on an immediate positive involvement which is very difficult or impossible for such a child. By contrast, the very persistent child is most likely to experience stress not with the initial contact with a situation but during the course of ongoing activity after the first positive adaptation has been made. His quality of persistence leads him to resist interference or attempts to divert him from an activity in which he is absorbed. If the adult interference is arbitrary and forceable, tension and frustration tend to mount quickly in these children and may reach explosive proportions.

Type-specific stress and maladaptive child-environment patterns can be identified for other temperamental characteristics as well (Thomas, Chess & Birch, 1968). It is, of course, true, as with all generalizations of the dynamics of development, that individual children may show special and presumably atypical responses because of exceptional idiosyncratic factors which influence the child-environmental interactional process.

Goodness of fit is also significantly influenced for temperament by socioeconomic and cultural factors, as for other determinants of behavioral development. A child with hard-driving professional or business executive parents may be denigrated as "lazy" and "lacking will power" if he is temperamentally easily distractible and non-persistent (Thomas, Chess & Birch, 1968). In a socioeconomic group not dominated by such a "work ethic," such a child will find much easier acceptance and be permitted to function effectively within his own behavioral stylistic characteristics. A very high activity child will be excessively frustrated growing up in a small apartment in a congested urban area. Such a child is even more likely than others to be cooped up at home for fear that if he ran around in the streets he would be in special danger of accidents (Thomas et al., 1974). By contrast, a high activity child growing up in a middle-class suburban area can have adequate space to satisfy his motor activity needs without family conflict. Many other examples can be cited (Thomas et al., 1974) to emphasize the need for understanding a child's social and cultural background if one is to evaluate what constitutes excessive stress.

NATURE-NURTURE INTERACTION

The inadequacy of a simplistic environmentalist approach to the study of early individual differences in behavior, as discussed above, does not in any way imply a similarly simplistic genetic-constitutionalist view as the alternative. Modern biology has resolved the age-old debate of nature vs. nurture by the concept that the development of any living species is the product of the interaction between genetic-constitutional factors and environment. Whether it is an individual's height, weight, bone structure, cognitive and perceptual capacities, or temperament, the final phenotypic outcome is always the product of the constantly evolving interaction of nature and nurture. This issue is well-stated by Lehrman (1970), "the ontogenetic development of species-specific behavior patterns may often depend upon influences from the environment, which interact with processes internal to the organism at all stages of development, in such a way that it is misleading to label those behavior patterns that seem to depend upon ordinary learning, and those that do not, as 'learned' and 'innate,' with the implication that they have dichotomously different developmental origins" (p. 20). The studies of temperament thus far suggest an appreciable genetic role in the determination of temperamental individuality in the young infant. Prenatal or perinatal brain damage does not appear to influence temperament in any striking fashion. The data also indicate that parental attitudes and functioning, as shaped by the sex of the child or special concerns for a premature infant, at the very most have a modest etiological influence on temperament (Thomas & Chess, 1977).

CONSISTENCY OVER TIME

Once temperamental individuality is established in early infancy it cannot be considered immutable as development proceeds, any more than any other characteristic of the growing child. Environmental influence may very well accentuate, modify or even change temperamental traits over time. This has been strikingly evident as we have followed the behavioral development of the subjects in the New York longitudinal study from early infancy through adolescence. As documented in our latest volume with case vignettes (Thomas & Chess, 1977), 5 patterns of consistency of temperamental characteristics in individual children over time can be defined: 1) clear-cut consistency; 2) consistency in some aspects of temperament at one period and other aspects of temperament at other times; 3) distortion of the expression of temperament by other factors, such as psychodynamic patterns; 4) consistency in temperament but qualitative change in temperament-environment interaction; and 5) change in a conspicuous temperamental trait. Any individual child may show a combination of several of these 5 possibilities, i.e., consistency over time with one or several temperamental traits, distortion in another, change in several others, etc.

These findings that temperament may show strikingly different patterns of consistency over time are consistent with an interactionist concept of the dynamics of the developmental process. Temperament is a phenomenologic term in which the categorization of any individual is derived from the constellation of behaviors exhibited at any one age-period. These behaviors are the result of all the influences, past and present, which shape and modify these behaviors in a constantly evolving interactive process. Consistency of a temperamental trait or constellation in an individual over time, therefore, may require stability in these interactional forces, such as environmental influences, motivations and abilities. The same considerations also apply to other categories of behavior, such as motivations psychodynamic patterns, and intellectual functioning.

Continuity and predictability can thus not be assumed for any specific attribute or pattern of a child, whether it be temperament, intellectual functioning, motivational attributes or psychodynamic defenses. What is predictable is the process of organism-environment interaction. Consistency in development will come from continuity over time in the organism and significant features of the environment. Discontinuity will result from changes in one or the other which make for modification and change in development. This point of view is emphasized by Sameroff (1975) in a comprehensive review of the literature on early influences on development. "Despite the reasonableness of the notion that one should be able to make long-range predictions based on the initial characteristics of a child or his environment, the above review has found little evidence for the validity of such predictions. One view of the inadequacy of developmental predictions sees their source in the scientist's inability to locate the critical links in the causal chain leading from antecedents to consequence. A second view, propounded above, is that such linear sequences are non-existent and the development proceeds through a sequence of regular restructuring of the relations within and between the organism and his environment" (p. 286).

CONCLUSION

Our studies of the role of temperament in the dynamics of development have affirmed the basic principle of an interactionist approach—the necessity for the simultaneous scrutiny and analysis of the responses of the organism and of the objective circumstances in which these responses occur. To a constant stimulus a given response may vary from individual to individual in intensity, in direction, or in both. The determination of the effective environment—those features that are effective in influencing function—is dependent upon the characteristics of the organism. Viewed obversely, our knowledge of the characteristics of the organism defines its effective environment. This theme has been given a precise general statement by Schneirla and Rosenblatt (1961), and appropriately concludes this presentation:

Behavior is typified by reciprocal stimulative relationships . . . Behavioral development, because it centers on and depends upon reciprocal stimulative processes between female and young, is essentially social from the start. Mammalian behavioral development is best conceived as a unitary system of processes changing progressively under the influence of an intimate interrelationship of factors of maturation and experience—with maturation defined as the developmental contribution of tissue growth and differentiation and their secondary processes, and experience defined as the effects of stimulation and its organic traces on behavior" (p. 230).

REFERENCES

ABRAMS, S. and NEUBAUER, P. B. Object orientedness: The person or the thing. Presented at the meeting of the Psychoanalytic Association of New York, Jan. 1975.

BOWER, T. G. R. *Development in Infancy*. San Francisco: W. H. Freeman, 1974.

CALDER, N. *The Human Conspiracy*. London: British Broadcasting Corp., 1976, pp. 45-72.

CHESS, S., THOMAS, A., and BIRCH, H. G. *Your Child Is A Person*. New York: Viking Press, 1965.

GORDON, E. W. Affective response tendencies and self-understanding. *Proceedings of the 1973 Invitational Conference on Testing Problems—Measurement for Self-Understanding and Personal Development*. Educational Testing Service, Princeton, N.J., 1973, 14-20.

GRAHAM, P., RUTTER, M., and GEORGE, S. Temperamental characteristics as predictors of behavior disorders in children. *Amer. Jour. Orthopsychiatry*, 1973, 43, 328-339.

HENDERSON, L. J. *The Fitness of the Environment*. New York: MacMillan Co., 1913.

HERTZIG, M. E., BIRCH, H. G., THOMAS, A., and MENDEZ, O. A. Class and ethnic differences in the responsiveness of preschool children to cognitive demands. *Monographs of the Society for Research in Child Development*, 1968, 33, 1-69.

KAGAN, J. *Change and Continuity in Infancy*. New York: John Wiley, 1971.

LEHRMAN, D. S. Semantic and conceptual issues in the nature-nurture problem. In: Aronson, et al. (Eds.), *Development and Evolution of Behavior*. San Francisco: W. H. Freeman, 1970, p. 20.

RUTTER, M. A child's life. In: R. Lewin (Ed.), *Child Alive*. London: Temple Smith, 1975, p. 208.

SAMEROFF, A. Early influences on development: Fact or fancy. *Merrill-Palmer Quarterly*, 1975, 21, 267-294.

SCHNEIRLA, T. C. and ROSENBLATT, J. S. Behavioral organization and genesis of the social bond in insects and mammals. *Amer. Jour. Orthopsychiatry*, 1961, 31, 223-253.

THOMAS, A., CHESS, S., and BIRCH, H. G. *Temperament and Behavior Disorders in Children*. New York: New York University Press, 1968.

THOMAS, A., CHESS, S., SILLEN, J., and MENDEZ, O. Cross-cultural study of behavior in children with special vulnerabilities to stress. In: Ricks, Thomas, and Roff (Eds.), *Life History Research in Psychopathology*, Vol. 3. U. Minnesota Press, 1974, pp. 53-67.

THOMAS, A. and CHESS, S. *Temperament and Development*. New York: Brunner/Mazel, 1977.

12

Autism: Psychopathological Mechanisms and Therapeutic Approaches

MICHAEL RUTTER

INTRODUCTION

Herbert Birch was an extremely productive research worker whose investigations spanned an incredibly wide field in which his own writings repeatedly showed new ways of looking at old issues and provoked controversy by his constant questioning of the given "truths" of the day. The frequent references in the world literature to his many papers attest to his influence. However, such a measure greatly underestimates the extent of his impact on his colleagues and friends. Herbert Birch had a quite unusual talent for the quick and penetrating grasp of other people's ideas and problems and he was always ready to engage in vigorous and uninhibited discussion of these (this usually meant intellectual combat when he was talking!). As a result, any meeting with Birch usually resulted in an enforced rethinking of one's own work. This was not always comfortable but it was consistently stimulating and helpful.

This chapter outlines some findings and ideas from a program of research extending over some dozen years in which Herbert Birch took no part in planning or execution. However, it is a good example of work which nevertheless owes a lot to his thinking. The studies were started just after I had spent a most formative year (1961-62) working with Birch in New York and during subsequent years we often argued over the findings. He frequently spoke of his ideas on the importance of sensory integration in the process of intellectual development (Birch & Bitterman, 1949, 1951). He emphasized the role of cognitive factors in social and emotional development and suggested that impaired cognitive

273

processing was likely to have widespread disruptive effects. While in his published writings he never directly applied these ideas to the syndrome of autism, they were discussed in connection with "childhood schizophrenia"—a broader concept which included autism as well as other disorders. In this connection he wrote: "The possession of disordered response and input systems necessarily predisposes the child to abnormal patternings of organism-environment interaction. . . . The tasks for future research appear to include the need for a more refined definition of these disordered interactions, so that more effective procedures for modifying the impact on growth and development by means of parent counseling, special education, drug management and environmental re-ordering should be evolved" (Gittelman & Birch, 1967). The research program described in this chapter attempted to do just that for the syndrome of autism—an analysis of psychopathological mechanisms was used to develop therapeutic approaches which in turn had to be systematically evaluated.

DIAGNOSIS AND DEFINITION

The starting point of our research was the definition of the syndrome to be studied. Kanner (1943), in a paper which has rightly become a classic, sifted the heterogeneous population of psychotic, retarded, and disturbed children referred to his psychiatric clinic, and identified 11 whose disorder seemed to be distinctive and different from those shown by others. Various clinical features were noted but particular emphasis was laid on the children's inability to develop relationships with people, the delay in speech acquisition and non-communicative use of speech after it develops, repetitive behavior with distress at any change, good rote memory and normal physical appearance. In the years that followed, numerous other workers confirmed Kanner's observations (see Rutter, 1974), but controversy continued on the boundaries of the syndrome and on the criteria for its diagnosis. The very richness of Kanner's description intensified the problems. Which of the numerous features he described *had* to be present for autism to be diagnosed? Which behaviors were *specific* to autism and which were common to a broader range of disorders?

We tackled this problem by making a systematic comparison between the symptoms shown by children with infantile psychosis (or autism) and those shown by children with other forms of psychiatric disorder (Rutter, 1966; Rutter & Lockyer, 1967). The choice of the comparison group was crucial. First, it had to include children with a psychiatric condition (rather than normal children), since the differentiation proposed by Kanner was that between autism and other forms of mental disorder. Second, the groups had to be closely matched for age, sex and IQ—features known to be associated with differences in symptomatology (see e.g., Rutter, Tizard & Whitmore, 1970). This was essential in order to be sure that any differences found were specific to autism and not merely an artefact of age, sex, or IQ associations. Third, the form of data gathering had to be comparable in the two groups. Fourth, it was necessary that the anamnestic information be checked by direct observations of the children. Fifth, it was essential to include a long-term follow-up of both groups. This was needed in order to be sure that the differences reflected *enduring* characteristics and not merely transient features associated with clinic referral.

The results showed that there were only three symptoms that were both universal and specific—that is they were present in all (or nearly all) autistic children and they were significantly more frequent in the autistic group than the control group (Rutter, 1965a, 1966; Rutter, Greenfeld & Lockyer, 1967). The three symptoms were 1) a general failure to develop social relationships together with various specific abnormalities in interpersonal functioning; 2) language retardation with impaired comprehension, echolalia, and pronominal reversal; and 3) ritualistic or compulsive phenomena associated with repetitive stereotyped play patterns. Follow-up into adolescence and adult life (in which the children were personally seen) confirmed that these differences continued to differentiate the autistic group many years after clinic referral (Rutter, Greenfeld & Lockyer, 1967). These features, together with an onset before 30 months (as also emphasized by Kanner), were then taken as defining characteristics of the syndrome.

The initial study described the symptoms in relatively crude terms and it was necessary to add precision by more detailed clinical observation and experimental study. During the last decade this has been done by many different research groups as well as our own and it is now possible to outline the diagnostic criteria in more subtle and discriminating terms (see Rutter, 1978a).

VALIDITY OF THE SYNDROME

It will be appreciated that this initial study did no more than provide a working definition. Moreover, even this was based on various British psychiatrists' concept of infantile psychosis rather than directly on Kanner's own criteria. Comparison with Kanner's (1943) original description suggested that the two were closely similar so that this limitation probably mattered little. On the other hand, the crucial question of the *validity* of the syndrome remained to be determined. This was a matter for empirical study. In these circumstances validity meant that the behavioral designation of autism should carry implication about *other* features such as etiology, epidemiological characteristics, course of disorder or response to treatment (Rutter, 1965b).

Our first study provided evidence of the validity of the differentiation between autism and other forms of psychiatric disorder. The diagnosis of autism was associated with a distinctive pattern of scores on IQ tests, with persisting language delay and with poor employment prospects (Rutter et al., 1967; Lockyer & Rutter, 1969, 1970). In each of these respects the autistic children differed significantly from their matched controls. Autism also differed from the general run of emotional and conduct disorders in childhood in terms of the high frequency with which epileptic fits developed in adolescence (as well as in sex distribution, socioeconomic background and long-term outcome—Rutter, 1971).

There are three groups of disorders in which there might seem to be a particular overlap with autism: mental retardation (because autistic children often have low IQ scores), schizophrenia (because of the severe abnormalities of behavior and relationships in both conditions), and developmental disorders of receptive language (because all autistic children have abnormalities in language development). However, Hermelin and O'Connor (1970) in a series of well-planned experiments demonstrated a host of ways in which autistic children differed from matched groups of retarded children; Kolvin (1971) and his colleagues found many crucial differences between autism and schizophrenia; and our own studies (Bartak et al., 1975, 1977; Cox et al., 1975) have shown the many contrasts between autism and developmental language disorders.

The evidence is clear-cut in indicating that autism is a meaningful and valid diagnostic entity which differs not only from the broad run of common psychiatric conditions in early childhood, but also from schizophrenia and the other psychoses of later childhood (Rutter, 1972a).

Nevertheless, many questions remain. First, while it has been shown that the syndrome of autism has good validity, the question of whether our diagnostic criteria are the most appropriate has still to be examined. Second, it remains to be determined whether or not the syndrome represents a single unitary condition. Probably it does not. Certainly the behavioral syndrome can occur in association with quite different medical disorders, including congenital rubella (Chess et al., 1971), infantile spasms (Taft & Cohen, 1971), and a mixed bag of metabolic abnormalities of uncertain meaning (Coleman, 1976). Moreover, autistic children of normal nonverbal intelligence differ strikingly from mentally retarded autistic children, not only in their educational attainments and employment—as one might expect—but also in the frequency with which epileptic fits occur during adolescence (Bartak & Rutter, 1976).

These findings do not yet indicate whether or not there should be behavioral subgroupings within the overall syndrome of autism. On the other hand, they do emphasize that a behavioral diagnosis is not sufficient in itself. It is necessary also to specify the child's intellectual level and whether there is some associated medical condition. This is best done by means of separate designations on independent axes referring to clinical psychiatric syndrome, intellectual level and medical conditions, as in the World Health Organization multiaxial scheme (Rutter et al., 1969; Rutter, Shaffer & Shepherd, 1975).

PROGNOSIS

Information on the "natural history" of a disorder is always important in its implications for treatment, and often also it throws light on the nature of the condition in ways which provide leads for etiological research. Autism is no exception. Data on the course of development as autistic children pass through adolescence into adult life are provided by several long-term follow-up studies, including Kanner's cases (Eisenberg, 1956; Kanner, 1971; Kanner et al., 1972), Creak's cases (Creak, 1963a, b), Lotter's cases (Lotter, 1974a, 1974b, 1978), and children seen at the Maudsley Hospital (Rutter et al., 1967; Rutter, 1970).

The findings are in remarkably good agreement. Some two-thirds of autistic children remained severely handicapped but one-sixth obtained regular paid employment and another sixth made a fair social adjustment. About half remained without speech and many of those who gained speech continued to show a persisting language disability. Social relationships improved in many children and an appreciable minority showed some interest, friendliness and involvement with people. Even so, only rarely did the autistic individuals make close friends and none married. The best adjustment seemed to follow the development of self-awareness. Ritualistic and compulsive phenomena followed a more variable course but these tended to be most marked in middle childhood.

Our own follow-up study (Rutter et al., 1967; Rutter, 1970) also showed that about a quarter of autistic children developed epileptic fits during adolescence. In most cases there had been no suggestion up to that time of an organic component. Similar findings have come from other studies (Kanner, 1971; Creak, 1963b; Lotter, 1974b; Menolascino & Eaton, 1967). Seizures were most common in mentally retarded autistic children and there was the strong implication that their disorders had arisen as a result of organic brain dysfunction. This was less clear-cut with respect to autistic children of normal intelligence but even in this group some showed indications of brain pathology.

We found that only three measures obtained in early childhood were significantly related to social outcome in adolescence and adult life. These were the initial IQ, the degree of language impairment and the total symptom score (reflecting general severity of disorder). However, apart from language, no single symptom predicted outcome and, in particular, social abnormalities did not. Again, the results of other studies were in very good agreement (see Lotter, 1978). The findings strongly suggested the importance of a basic cognitive deficit in the development of autistic children—and possibly also in the genesis of the autistic syndrome itself. This was the next issue to investigate.

The only treatment measure related to outcome was the children's experience of schooling. Accordingly, we decided also to study further the effects of special educational treatment.

INTELLIGENCE

In his first description of infantile autism, Kanner (1943) drew attention to the children's often good rote memory, their serious facial expression and their lack of physical stigmata. He concluded that basically the children were of normal intelligence and that their often poor functioning on IQ tests were simply a secondary consequence of their social handicaps. We sought to test this hypothesis by further examination of the nature of intellectual performance in autistic children.

The first observation was that autistic children who were closely similar in their social and behavioral features varied widely in their intellectual performance, with IQ scores ranging from severely retarded to highly superior (Rutter & Lockyer, 1967). Clearly, autism was entirely compatible with high scores on at least some kinds of IQ tests.

The second approach was to determine if the IQ scores of autistic children had the same properties as those shown in other children. We found that they did. Thus, like others (Gittelman & Birch, 1967; Mittler et al., 1966; DeMyer et al., 1974), we observed considerable stability of IQ scores throughout middle childhood and adolescence (Lockyer & Rutter, 1969). Indeed, in this respect the findings were closely similar to those obtained for IQ stability in normal and retarded children without autism. Even more important, as in other children, IQ scores proved to be reasonable predictors of later educational attainments. This was so both in autistic children who received very little schooling (Lockyer & Rutter,

1969) and in those who received skilled special education (Bartak & Rutter, 1971; Rutter & Bartak ,1973).

The third strategy was to find out how intellectual performance varied with the children's psychiatric state. The long-term follow-up indicated that some autistic children made major social and behavioral improvements, but, in spite of this, their IQ level remained much the same (Lockyer & Rutter, 1969). Subsequent investigations of other groups of autistic children receiving intensive educational (Rutter & Bartak, 1973) or behavioral treatment (Hemsley et al., 1978; Rutter, 1978b) have confirmed this observation.

The fourth strategy involved a study of motivational factors in autistic children's intellectual performance. Cowan et al. (1965) had earlier produced evidence which indicated that hospitalized autistic children of low IQ exhibited negativism. Because some children obtained scores significantly *worse* than chance on a discrimination learning task, it was argued that they must have known the right answers in order to avoid them so systematically. The implication was that the children's low IQ scores might be attributable to motivational factors. However, in a replication of the Cowan study, we did *not* find this kind of negativism in any of a group of autistic children receiving special education (Clark & Rutter, 1977). It appeared that the negativism may have been a consequence of an institutional upbringing rather than of autism as such.

Of course, this study examined only one special aspect of the problem and it was necessary to go on to investigate others. Another approach was to determine how far the children's performance was explicable solely in terms of the difficulty level of the task they were given. For this purpose we used a board form of Raven's (1965) Progressive Matrices in which exactly the same mode of response was required for test items which varied greatly in the cognitive skills required (Clark & Rutter, 1978). The items were given in a series in which easy items were followed by more difficult items and then easier items and then more difficult items again and so on. It was found that whether the children made correct responses was strongly related to the difficulty level of the item rather than to the duration of testing or any other feature of the situation. Autistic children who made consistently wrong answers could be "made" to get correct answers by simply giving them an easier problem, even though the overall task and test situations remained identical. In short, as with other children, autistic children's scores on an IQ test were explicable in terms of cognitive factors without the need to involve motivation. Of course, that is not to say motivation is unimportant. Motivational factors will influence the performance of autistic children just as they do the performance of others. The question is whether motivational factors are sufficient to account for the low IQ scores of many autistic children. The available findings suggested that they are not. This is also borne out by Hingtgen and Churchill's (1969, 1971) demonstration that even when motivation had been greatly increased through the use of operant techniques, the cognitive skills of many autistic children were still considerably below normal.

The final evidence with respect to the significance of low IQ scores comes from the follow-up study again. This showed that the biological outcome also differed sharply according to IQ (Bartak & Rutter, 1976). Whereas a third of mentally retarded autistic children developed epileptic seizures (usually during adolescence), very few of those of normal intelligence did so. There is no plausible way that this could be explained in motivational terms. It was concluded that the IQ in autistic children functions in much the same way as in any other group of individuals. Autism and mental retardation frequently coexist and in these cases the retardation is just as "real" as in anyone else with a low IQ.

LANGUAGE

However, that is not to say that there is nothing unusual about autistic children's cognitive performance. Our first study (Rutter, 1966; Lockyer & Rutter, 1970) had shown that autistic children exhibited marked variability, with superior skills in some tasks and gross deficits in others. Characteristically the deficits involved language, sequencing and abstraction tasks. This, together with the almost universal language abnormalities in autistic children suggested the importance of investigating autistic language further.

The first question was whether there was a true inability or incapacity in the field of language, as distinct from an emotional or social block to the usage of language. There are three main pieces of evidence in this connection (Rutter, 1978c). First, it is well established from many studies (Shapiro, Roberts & Fish, 1970; Shapiro, Fish & Ginsberg, 1972; Cunningham & Dixon, 1961; Cunningham, 1968; Wolff & Chess, 1965; Tubbs, 1966), including our own (Rutter, 1965a, 1966), that it is *not* just that autistic children use little speech but rather that their language when it develops is abnormal in many respects. Echolalia and pronominal reversal are very frequent features, defects in the understanding of language are widespread and pecularities in the form of neologisms or metaphorical usage are common. This is quite different from the picture in elective mutism in which children fail to speak because of emotional disturbance or from that in which speech delay is due to a lack of adequate stimulation or appropriate experiences in early life (see Rutter, 1972b, 1977). It has been suggested that echolalic autistic children avoid the use of "I" as part of a psychic defense mechanism (Bettelheim, 1967). However, we found that the lack of use of "I" was simply a consequence of the fact that it is the last parts of sentences which are echoed and "I" rarely occurs at the end (Bartak & Rutter, 1974).

The second piece of evidence comes from autistic children's pattern of IQ scores (Lockyer & Rutter, 1970). We found that even on tests which did not involve any use of speech, autistic children performed badly when verbal or sequencing skills were required. This pattern was most marked in those with poor performance in spoken language. The implication is that the problem in autism is *not* lack of speech as such but rather a serious deficit in cognitive skill involving sequencing, abstraction and other language-related functions.

The third piece of evidence came from the experimental studies undertaken by Hermelin, O'Connor and their associates (Hermelin & O'Connor, 1970). They showed through a series of well-planned experiments that, unlike normal children, autistic children made relatively little use of *meaning* in their memory and thought processes.

All three sets of data indicated that autistic children's failure to use speech adequately is *not* a motivational problem. Rather, the speech and language problems involve an incapacity or lack of basic skills.

The next issue was to better define the nature of autistic children's language problems. We decided to tackle this by making a systematic comparison between the language and cognitive characteristics of autistic children and those of children with developmental receptive dysphasia— the condition which appeared most similar to autism in terms of the language disorder (Churchill, 1972; Pronovost et al., 1966; Rutter, 1966, 1968; Wing, 1969). Accordingly, we made a detailed investigation of all the boys we could find who showed a severe disorder of receptive language present from infancy (Bartak et al., 1975, 1977; Cantwell et al., 1978a; Boucher, 1976). In order to focus on specific language problems, we restricted the sample to boys of normal nonverbal intelligence. The group was then divided up on behavioral grounds into those with the syndrome of autism, those with an uncomplicated development language disorder, and a much smaller mixed group. The children's language and cognition was then assessed by means of parental reports, psychometric tests, and a detailed analysis of audiotape recordings made in the children's own home (Cantwell et al., 1977a).

The first finding was that there was a large group of children with a severe deficit in language comprehension who were not at all autistic.

Clearly, a severe impairment in spoken language did not constitute a sufficient basis for the development of autism.

Secondly, the crucial difference between the two groups did not lie in either articulation or grammatical competence. Articulation errors were actually more frequent in the dysphasic children (Boucher, 1976) and the groups did not differ on any of the measures of syntax or grammar.

On the other hand, the language deficit in the autistic children tended to be both more severe and more extensive. The deficit in spoken language comprehension was greater and more autistic children showed impairment in the use of gesture and of written language.

However, the biggest differences lay in the children's functional usage of language. Abnormalities of spoken language—including pronoun reversal, delayed echolalia, stereotyped utterances, metaphorical language and inappropriate remarks—were all much more frequent in autistic children. Moreover, the autistic children show less spontaneity in their use of spoken language, they talked less readily, they made less use of speech for social communication or "chat" and they showed less imaginative play. We concluded that, whereas autistic children suffered from a severe language impairment, they chiefly differed from most other children with language problems in terms of the fact that their language was *deviant* as well as *delayed*.

The next step was to examine cognitive performance in the two groups. They were closely matched on their overall level of nonverbal skills but they differed markedly both in their pattern of skills and in the much greater deficit of verbal skills in the autistic group. On the whole, the dysphasic group performed quite well on tasks not involving spoken language even when sequencing and abstraction were required. But this was not the case for autistic children. They showed marked deficits on most tasks which required anything other than visuo-spatial skills and short-term memory. It was clear that autism involved a quite widespread cognitive deficit which involved much more than difficulties in spoken language.

The next issue in the study concerned the relationship between this language abnormality with cognitive deficit and the social/behavioral problems of autistic children. A series of discriminant function analyses showed that there was little overlap between the autistic and dysphasic groups and that the functional language and the cognitive features differentiated the groups *as well* as did the social and behavioral measures. It appeared that autism was as much a cognitive and language disorder as it was a social and behavioral syndrome. Moreover, even *within* the autistic group the children who were most autistic in their functional language usage tended to be also the most autistic in their social and behavioral abnormalities. We concluded that a cognitive deficit associated with a variety of specific language abnormalities constituted a central feature of autism.

However, the precise nature of the relationship between the cognitive deficit and the social/behavioral abnormalities has still to be determined. Rather different methods of investigation are required to examine this matter. First, it is necessary to determine how far autistic children's social difficulties are *part of* the cognitive deficit. Thus, it could be that there are important impairments in the children's social perception—in their ability to recognize emotions in facial expressions, for example. Secondly, it is possible that at least some of the behavioral problems are *secondary* responses to cognitive deficits. In order to examine this possibility it is necessary to manipulate the children's environment experimentally. This constitutes the stage in our research program which has still to be completed. However, a few leads are available from other research. Churchill (1971) found that autistic children's social avoidance increased when they were given a task which led to failure but decreased when the task was followed by success. Similarly, Koegel and Covert (1972) showed that when children were taught improved cognitive skills, the amount of self-stimulation diminished. More recently, Carr et al. (1975) have demonstrated that autistic children are more likely to echo speech they do not understand. Thus, it appears worthwhile exploring further the possibility that some of autistic children's deviant behavior arises as a response to cognitive failure or a lack of understanding. However, it is equally important to identify the ways in which the social context and interpersonal interactions influence autistic children's behavior. Again, a few leads are available (Richer, 1978), but much more remains to be done.

FAMILY STUDIES

It was clear from early on in our studies that it was unlikely that most cases of autism were completely psychogenetically determined. The development of epileptic fits during adolescence, as well as other evidence, indicated the importance of organic factors in etiology. On the other hand, it remained quite possible that environmental influences might interact with biological handicaps to cause the behavioral syndrome. We set out to investigate this possibility. The findings in the literature were contradictory and inconclusive. However, most of the studies suffered from several crucial limitations (see Cantwell et al., 1978b). First, the children studied were diagnostically heterogeneous.

Second, several of the samples were unrepresentative with large numbers of families not willing to cooperate in the research. This could well seriously distort the findings (Cox et al., 1977). Third, the controls usually consisted of normal children—so failing to take into account the well demonstrated effect of the child's handicap on parent-child interaction. Fourth, in many cases the measures were both unreliable and open to bias.

We attempted to deal with these problems by comparing the families of autistic children with those of dysphasic children; by keeping noncooperation rates low; by using a wide variety of both standard tests and specially developed measures; and by taking steps to ensure that the instruments used were reliable and valid.

Initially, we examined the possibility that autism might follow severe stresses in the children's early years of life. However, we found no differences between autistic and dysphasic children in this respect (Cox et al., 1975). Next, we sought to test the suggestion that the parents of autistic children were deviant in terms of personality and psychiatric state. Systematic interview techniques (Brown & Rutter, 1966; Rutter & Brown, 1966) were used to measure parental warmth to the children. Measures were specially devised to assess parental demonstrativeness and responsiveness using data on verbal and physical expressions of sympathy, pleasure and enthusiasm in various specified situations. Sociability was judged from the frequency and range of contacts with other people, and the quality of friendships from their duration and the degree to which confidences were exchanged. Again, there were no differences between the groups on any of these measures or on standard questionnaire assessments of extraversion, neuroticism, or obsessionality (Cox et al., 1975; Cantwell et al., 1978c). Two different measures of thought disorder also showed no abnormalities in the parents (Lennox et al., 1977). However, there was a clinical impression (not reflected in test findings) that various marked oddities of personality, although present in only a minority of cases, were more frequent among the parents of autistic children (Cantwell et al., 1978c). Psychiatric illness was no more frequent among the parents of autistic children than among the parents of children with non-psychotic mental disorders (Rutter & Lockyer, 1967).

A wide range of measures was employed to study family activities and parent-child interaction. These included a detailed minute-by-minute description of the child's "standard day" (Douglas et al., 1968; Lawson & Ingleby, 1974); interview counts of the frequency of positive activities between parent and child (Brown & Rutter, 1966); the Ittleson Center family scales (Behrens et al., 1969); detailed time-sampled observations in the home (Hemsley et al., in preparation), and systematic analysis of audiotape recordings of the mother's communication with the child at home (Howlin et al., 1973a). Once more, no differences between the groups were found (Cantwell et al., 1977a, 1978c). Altogether the evidence gave no support to the notion that certain familial factors were necessary cause of autism (Cantwell et al., 1978b).

On the other hand, almost all studies (see Cantwell et al., 1978b), including our own (Rutter & Lockyer, 1967; Cox et al., 1975), have indicated that the parents of autistic children tend to be of a slightly higher IQ and social status than the general population. The explanation for this puzzling finding remains totally obscure. Also, however, it has been observed that some autistic children have a family history of language delay (Rutter et al., 1971). This raised the possibility of genetic factors in some cases.

BIOLOGICAL BASIS

Although a variety of medical conditions have been associated with autism in individual children, there is no consistent evidence that any particular biochemical abnormality, chromosomal anomaly, or structural pathology is causally related to more than the occasional case of autism (see Rutter, 1967; Guthrie & Wyatt, 1975; Darby, 1976; Ritvo et al., 1978; Coleman, 1976).

Perhaps the most promising lead is provided by the demonstration of dilatation of the anterior horn of the lateral ventricle in some cases of autism (Hauser et al., 1975; DeLong, 1978), but this finding still awaits replication. Biochemical studies suffer from the difficulties of controlling diet, from problems of neurochemical assessment, and from heterogeneous samples. This makes it difficult to reconcile contradictory findings. For example, Coleman and her colleagues (1976) found abnormal zinc levels in some autistic children, whereas Jackson and Garrod (1977), using a group of autistic children studied by us, did not. Boullin et al. (1971) found increased serotonin efflux, whereas Yuwiler et al. (1975) did not. Further research is required to determine the reasons for these disparities in findings.

Although, from the outset, Kanner (1943) wrote about an "inborn" defect, there has been little systematic genetic research into autism (see Rutter, 1967; Hanson & Gottesman, 1976; Folstein & Rutter, 1977a). Isolated reports of single pairs of twins with autism have been largely non-contributory because of both biased sampling and inadequate reporting. Nevertheless, despite the rarity of a family history of autism, there are two reasons for suspecting hereditary influences: the 2% rate of autism in sibs is 50 times that of the general population (Rutter, 1967) and a family history of speech delay is found in about a quarter of the families (Bartak et al., 1975). Accordingly, we undertook a detailed study of a systematically collected sample of 21 pairs of same-sexed twins, one or both of whom had autism as diagnosed by the criteria of Kanner (1943) and Rutter (1971). Apart from two pairs in which dermatoglyphics were used, zygosity was determined by blood grouping in all cases not markedly different in clinical appearance. Diagnoses were made from case summaries, numbered randomly to prevent sorting by pair and from which name, exact age and zygosity had been deleted.

Four of the 11 MZ pairs but none of the 10 DZ pairs were concordant for autism (Folstein & Rutter, 1977a, 1977b). This difference suggested a genetic component to autism. However, the concordance for a broader range of cognitive disorders (defined in terms of no phrase speech until 3 years, IQ 70 or below, severely abnormal articulation after 5 years, or scholastic difficulties requiring special schooling) was even more striking. Nine of the 11 MZ pairs (82%) were concordant for cognitive disorder, compared with only one of the 10 DZ pairs. These findings strengthened the suggestion of genetic determination and indicated that what is inherited is a form of cognitive abnormality which includes but is not restricted to autism.

In addition, however, brain injury associated with perinatal complications was found to be relevant to *dis*cordance. In 12 of the 17 pairs discordant for autism, the autistic member probably or possibly suffered a brain injury, whereas in none of the discordant pairs did this occur only in the non-autistic member. It appeared that brain injury, especially during the perinatal period, may operate on its own or in combination with a genetic predisposition to cause autism.

IMPLICATIONS FOR TREATMENT

These experimental, clinical and longitudinal studies of autism led us to the view that autistic children have a central defect in the cognitive processes associated with language, sequencing, symbolization and abstraction (Rutter, 1968, 1974; Rutter & Bartak, 1971). Circumstantial evidence suggested that this cognitive defect constituted the primary handicap and that at least some of the social and behavioral abnormalities arose as secondary consequences. We considered that the most fruitful road to therapy was to regard autism as an abnormality of development rather than as a unique mystical psychosis to which the ordinary principles of development did not apply (Rutter & Sussenwein, 1971).

With this premise, we sought to analyze the main ways in which the autistic child's development departed from normality, to determine the possible defects which led to this departure, to consider what was required for normal development, and finally to work out what was needed for a more normal development. We focused on the three chief handicaps typical of autism: 1) the failure of social development and, in particular, the failure to develop normal attachment behavior in early childhood, 2) the global failure of language development accompanied by certain abnormal linguistic characteristics; and 3) the tendency to develop rigid, stereotyped patterns and quasi-obsessive, compulsive or ritualistic behavior.

The autistic infant frequently appears unresponsive to social stimuli, not developing a social smile, not engaging in the normal amount of eye-to-eye gaze, not putting up his arms to be picked up, not responding to his parents' voices, not making normal differentiations between adults, not showing normal social or separation anxiety and, most of all, not forming strong personal bonds or attachments. Consideration of the available evidence on normal bond formation (Bowlby, 1969; Rutter, 1978d) suggested that intense, personal and reciprocal interaction was that most likely to foster attachment. Autistic children were handicapped in this in that they neither sought parental attention nor responded positively to it when it was given. We concluded that the most appropriate remedy was to *intrude* on the child in order to deliberately engage him in interaction which was meaningful and pleasurable (Rutter & Sussenwein, 1971). Autistic children had to be "taught" that reciprocal personal interactions could be both useful and fun. To do this effectively there would have to be careful observation to find out just what type of activity which could give rise to personal interaction was rewarding for each individual child. Attachment is also fostered by the provision of relief and comfort at times of distress and anxiety, and hence parents had to be helped to "read" the cues provided by their autistic child.

The evidence that autistic children were retarded in all aspects of language and not just delayed in speech also had implications for treatment. The children's receptive language defect meant that their "effective" environment would not be the same as that for ordinary children (Rutter & Sussenwein, 1971). If, because of his receptive defect, the autistic child only understands short sentences of simple vocabulary, people talking to him in long complex sentences may merely create confusion, causing the child to "shut off." The implication was to keep spoken communications simple enough to be within the child's grasp and to use gesture and demonstration as appropriate. However, it was also likely to be important not to use too many methods of communication at once in order not to tax the child's limited perceptual processing capacity.

Because the autistic child's defect lies first in pre-linguistic skills and in language comprehension rather than in the production of words, the first goal was to aid the development of these skills. Play and the encouragement of imitative behavior both had an important role in this connection. To aid the development of comprehension of spoken language, the adult needed to introduce talking into the play situation in a way which was linked with what the child or adult was doing.

Communication, rather than speech as such, was the objective and hence it seemed desirable to do all that could be done to encourage the child's communications in whatever form they appeared—speech, gesture, writing, demonstration or sign. Moreover, because autistic children were especially impaired in their *social* usage of speech, there should be a particular emphasis on the social components of communication. In short, the aim was to help the child not only gain greater language skills but also to use better whatever skills he had.

The most difficult question was *how* all this should be done. It appeared that contingent reinforcement probably played only a small part in normal children's development of language (Rutter & Martin, 1972). On the other hand, behavior modification (Yule & Berger, 1972; Yule, 1977) seemed to provide a means by which language might be encouraged in handicapped children whose receptive difficulties made it difficult for them to learn from the normal linguistic environment. Certainly this seemed worth further exploration.

The third task in the treatment of autistic children was to reduce and, where possible, eliminate the various deviant behaviors which so often developed. These could be usefully divided into two groups: 1) those that constituted rigid and stereotyped patterns, and 2) the less specific problem of tantrums, feeding difficulties, sleep disturbance, aggression and so forth.

The non-specific deviant behaviors did not appear fundamentally any different from those seen in any group of disturbed children. The treatment methods could be correspondingly similar except that the autistic child's impaired concept formation and symbolization would limit the use of psychotherapeutic techniques. This meant that behavioral approaches were likely to provide the most immediate means of intervention in the majority of cases. The best way to tackle each problem should be provided by a careful functional analysis of the long-lasting circumstances which played a part in determining behaviors (e.g., lack of communication skills giving rise to frustration, lack of parental attention leading to the use of tantrums to gain attention, etc.); of precipitants (e.g., the phobic stimuli which give rise to a fear or panic response); and of the contingencies or events following a behavior which serve to encourage it (see Rutter, 1975).

Stereotyped patterns of behavior constituted a somewhat different problem insofar as they seemed to comprise a more basic part of the autistic syndrome (Frith, 1971). Accordingly, it was likely to be difficult to entirely eliminate all such behavior. Rather, the aim should be to insure that the frequency was kept sufficiently low so that deviant behaviors did not interfere with normal activities and did not occur at times when they could constitute a social embarrassment. The principle of graded change appeared most appropriate. By gradually introducing minor changes and minor complexities, apparently useless rituals can be reduced or modified to form part of some more adaptive function. This principle was tried out and found to work in practice with autistic children (Marchant et al., 1974).

Not only do parents need skilled and experienced counseling to help them work out constructive and acceptable ways of coping with the difficulties presented by their autistic children, but also they need help in dealing with their feelings about having an unresponsive, disruptive, handicapped child. It is also crucial that parents are assisted in finding a balance between meeting the needs of the autistic child, meeting those of their other normal children and meeting their own needs as individual people and as marital partners. Some parents respond by severely reducing their social life (Tizard & Grad, 1961; Rutter, Graham & Yule, 1970) and this can lead to family tensions.

Lastly, there was the need for special schooling. The factors likely to foster more normal development in autistic children at home were likely also to apply at school. However, there was the added issue of how to aid learning in children whose behavior was often so disturbed as to make any teacher-directed task difficult, and whose learning was likely to be impeded by their considerable language and cognitive defects. Several quite different approaches were being advocated by various leading authorities and it seemed important to investigate directly the merits and demerits of contrasting educational regimes.

SPECIAL EDUCATION

In order to do this we selected three well-established units which took sizeable groups of autistic children and which differed markedly in both theoretical orientation and therapeutic practice (Bartak & Rutter, 1971,

1973; Rutter & Bartak, 1973). One unit (A) was primarily a psychotherapeutic unit with little emphasis on teaching; the second (B) provided a permissive classroom environment in which regressive techniques and an emphasis on relationships was combined with special educational methods; and the third (C) provided a structured and organized setting with a focus on the teaching of specific skills.

The design involved two main features. First, the characteristics of the three units were systematically assessed through the use of time- and event-sampled observations in the classroom, observations in the boarding setting (in the case of the two units with residential as well as day places), analysis of the time tables and interview with staff. Styles of staff-child interaction, qualities of staff's verbal and nonverbal behavior, and patterns of contingent responses to the children's behavior were assessed using measures of demonstrated reliability (Bartak & Rutter, 1975).

It was found that the three units differed markedly in actual practice as observed, as well as in their stated philosophy. The amount of formal teaching varied from 40 minutes per week at unit A, through 4 hours per week at B to 9 hours per week at C. Staff approval was most freely given at unit A but was given with most discrimination at C. In Unit A warmly expressed approval tended to follow whatever the child did whereas the staff at C differentiated their response according to whether the child's behavior was acceptable or disruptive. Observations also showed that instruction was frequently given by the staff at both units B and C whereas play occupied much of the time at A.

The follow-up findings showed that whether assessed in terms of educational attainment, on-task behavior in the classroom or cooperative play with others, the autistic children at C had made most progress and those at unit A the least. However, there were no differences between the units in terms of the children's behavior at home, and although the children at C tended to have made more progress in language than those at the other two units the differences fell short of significance. There was no tendency for the children in any of the units to improve in IQ and in all units there were large individual differences between the children in the progress made. Mentally retarded autistic children made the least progress and those with nonverbal IQ scores in the normal range made the most.

It was concluded that the children's progress depended to a significant extent on the type of unit they attended. Educational progress was greatest in unit C where there was the most structure and organization and the greatest emphasis on teaching. It appeared that autistic children responded best in a planned organized environment in which the teachers provide both a task orientation and specific teaching which is well adapted to both the child's level of development and his particular pattern of cognitive strengths and weaknesses. Given such a setting, many autistic children made real and worthwhile progress—with some later moving on to ordinary schools.

On the other hand, there were three important caveats to that general conclusion. First, the extent of progress was limited by the severity of the children's initial handicaps. Even with the best schooling, there was no tendency for IQs to rise and the mentally retarded autistic children remained quite seriously impaired in their social and scholastic functioning. Second, many of the children continued to have substantial difficulties in understanding what they learned—this was so at all three units. The nature of the autistic cognitive deficit means that teaching needs to be planned specifically to aid children's comprehension and appreciation of meaning. Third, there was very little generalization of the children's behavioral gains at school to the home environment. The implication is that greater efforts need to be made to integrate what is done at home and at school and also that treatment needs to be specifically designed to ensure that generalization occurs.

HOME-BASED TREATMENT

The last project in the research program to be described is our evaluation of a home-based treatment program in which the prime focus was helping parents by seeing them in their homes to aid them in utilizing behavioral techniques in a development context (Rutter, 1973). Previous research had shown the utility of behavioral methods but equally it had indicated that the benefits were only likely to endure and to generalize to the home if the parents were actively involved in treatment (Lovaas et al., 1973; Browning, 1971). Accordingly, we decided to carry out all treatment at home with the parents acting as the principal therapists for their children, and not just as aides. We sought both to foster the more normal development of language and social relationships and also to diminish deviant behaviors of all kinds. For this purpose we utilized a wide range of behavioral techniques including operant methods of reinforcement and withdrawal of attention (or "time-out"), desensitization, flooding, graded change and social intrusion (see Howlin et al., 1973b; Berger et al., 1974). Naturally, intervention in the home brought to the fore many personal, family and marital problems of the parents, and counseling and case-work techniques were freely combined with other treatment methods. Practical help with housing, babysitting and holidays was offered as appropriate; there was also close liaison with schools.

Several issues were crucial in evaluating the efficacy of this form of treatment (see Hemsley et al., 1978; Rutter et al., 1977). First, we had to determine, using each patient as his own control, whether the short-term changes in behavior were as marked as those obtained in the more controlled inpatient or laboratory setting. We found that they were. Second, we had to determine whether these changes were not only associated with treatment but also were greater than those which would have occurred without treatment. For this purpose we used a comparison of changes over a six-month period between the "experimental" treatment group and a matched group of autistic children attending other clinics or not receiving treatment. The results showed that the home-based treatment group had made significantly more progress in both language and cooperative, goal-directed play.

The third task was to determine whether the treatment had led to changes in *parental* behavior. This was crucial because our prime aim was to help autistic children by helping their parents learn better how to deal with them in ways that promoted normal development. In order to examine this issue we used the same matched control group and assessed changes in parental behavior over a six-month period. Parent-child interaction and communication were assessed using systematic time-sampled observations in the home. In addition, interview techniques were used to assess other aspects of parenting. Special emphasis was laid on the measurement of parental coping skills—that is their efficiency and sensitivity in developing ways of dealing with new problems as they arose. The results showed that our treatment methods had led to significantly improved parenting. The parents in the home-based treatment group showed more flexible and efficient coping strategies, were better able to assess their child's developmental level, were more actively involved with child, provided better feedback for him and more often spoke to the child in a way likely to foster language and communication.

The fourth issue was how far the treatment had led to *long-term* gains. For this purpose we used an individually matched control group of autistic children seen at the same clinic, who had received advice from us on the same general principles but who had attended only occasionally on an outpatient basis because they lived too far away for a home-based approach. The average length of time between first clinic attendance and follow-up was 33 months for the experimental group and 63 months for the controls. Statistical regression techniques were used to parcel out the effects of age. The findings showed that the home-based treatment group had made significantly greater improvement in all aspects of their behavior. They were more socially responsive, they showed fewer tantrums and less disruptive behavior, and there were fewer ritualistic behaviors, abnormal attachments and obsessional preoccupations. The home-based treatment group were also superior in their social usage of spoken language. However, there was only a slight (and non-significant) difference in any of the measures of language competence. The two groups did not differ in terms of IQ change: Both showed a negligible shift in mean score.

Although all children showed some improvements with treatment, the extent of change varied greatly from child to child. Some remained without any useful speech, whereas others had good conversational skills. Some presented very few behavioral problems, whereas others still required constant supervision in spite of treatment. The children who made least progress in language were more handicapped in this area from the outset. They made few spontaneous sounds, showed little comprehension of spoken language, were very limited in their play and showed little spontaneous imitation. In this group initial IQ did not predict outcome but the range was limited as the treatment group had been restricted by design to children with an IQ of at least 60.

We concluded that the home-based behavioral approach was a useful and effective method of treatment in terms of both short-term and long-term success. It led to greater improvement than that achieved by ordinary outpatient methods and was considerably cheaper (and probably more effective) than inpatient treatment. However, it was most effective in dealing with disruptive or maladaptive behavior. This suggests that these are not invariable concomitants of autism but rather arise as secondary responses to the basic cognitive handicap. Treatment was totally ineffective in raising IQ levels and made only a minor difference in the long-term to language competence (in spite of short-term gains). It appears, therefore, that language and cognitive impairments are more central and that, even with treatment, these deficits are likely to remain.

CONCLUSION

The research program is not yet complete and many questions remain unanswered. Even so, we have moved some way down the road towards a better understanding of the nature of the syndrome of autism and towards a better means of helping children with this chronically handicapping condition. As Birch foresaw, the research findings have clearly shown the extent to which a serious disorder of cognitive processing disrupts social and behavioral development. As he also argued, studies of cognitive and social mechanisms have had implications for treatment and studies of treatment have in turn cast new light on the nature of this unusual syndrome.

REFERENCES

BARTAK, L. and RUTTER, M. Educational treatment of autistic children. In: M. Rutter (Ed.), *Infantile Autism: Concepts, Characteristics and Treatment.* London: Churchill Livingstone, 1971, pp. 258-280.

BARTAK, L. and RUTTER, M. Special educational treatment of autistic children: A comparative study. I. Design of study and characteristics of units. *Journal of Child Psychology and Psychiatry,* 1973, 14, 161-179.

BARTAK, L. and RUTTER, M. The use of personal pronouns by autistic children. *Journal of Autism and Childhood Schizophrenia,* 1974, 4, 217-222.

BARTAK, L. and RUTTER, M. The measurement of staff-child interaction in three units for autistic children. In: R. V. G. Clark, I. Sinclair, and J. Tizard (Eds.), *Varieties of Residential Experience.* London: Routledge, 1975.

BARTAK, L. and RUTTER, M. Differences between mentally retarded and normally intelligent autistic children. *Journal of Autism and Childhood Schizophrenia,* 1976, 6, 109-120.

BARTAK, L., RUTTER, M., and COX, A. A comparative study of infantile autism and specific developmental receptive language disorder. I. The children. *British Journal of Psychiatry,* 1975, 126, 127-145.

BARTAK, L., RUTTER, M., and COX, A. A comparative study of infantile autism and specific developmental receptive language disorder. III. Discriminant function analysis. *Journal of Autism and Childhood Schizophrenia,* 1977, 383-396.

BEHRENS, M., MEYERS, D., GOLDFARB, W., GOLDFARB, N., and FIELDSTEEL, N. The Henry Ittleson Center family interaction scales. *Genetic Psychology Monographs,* 1969, 80, 203-295.

BERGER, M., HOWLIN, P. A., MARCHANT, R. L., HERSOV, L. A., RUTTER, M. L., and YULE, W. Instructing parents in the use of behavior modification techniques as part of a home-based approach to the treatment of autistic children. *Behavior Modification Newsletter,* 1974, Issue 5, 15-27.

BETTELHEIM, B. *The Empty Fortress: Infantile Autism and the Birth of the Self.* New York: Free Press, 1967.

BIRCH, H. G. and BITTERMAN, M. E. Reinforcement and learning: The process of sensory integration. *Psychological Review,* 1949, 56, 292-308.

BIRCH, H. G. and BITTERMAN, M. E. Sensory integration and cognitive theory. *Psychological Review,* 1951, 58, 355-361.

BOUCHER, J. Articulation in early childhood autism. *Journal of Autism and Childhood Schizophrenia,* 1976, 6, 297-302.

BOULLIN, D. J., COLEMAN, M., O'BRIEN, R. A., and RIMLAND, B. Laboratory predictions of infantile autism based on 5-hydroxytryptamine efflux from blood platelets and their correlation with the Rimland E-2 score. *Journal of Autism and Childhood Schizophrenia,* 1971, 1, 63-71.

BOWLBY, J. *Attachment and Loss, Vol. 1: Attachment.* London: Hogarth Press, 1969.

BROWN, G. W. and RUTTER, M. L. The measurement of family activities and relationships: A methodological study. *Human Relations,* 1966, 19, 241-263.

BROWNING, R. M. Treatment effects of a total behavior modification program with five autistic children. *Behaviour Research and Therapy*, 1971, 9, 319-327.

CANTWELL, D. P., BAKER, L., and RUTTER, M. A comparative study of infantile autism and specific developmental deceptive language disorders. IV. Analysis of syntax and language function. *Journal of Child Psychology and Psychiatry*, 1978a, in press.

CANTWELL, D. P., BAKER, L., and RUTTER, M. Family factors in autism. In: M. Rutter and E. Schopler (Eds.), *Autism: A Reappraisal of Concepts and Treatment*. New York: Plenum, 1978b.

CANTWELL, D. P., BAKER, L., and RUTTER, M. Families of autistic and dysphasic children. I. Family life and interaction patterns. *Archives of General Psychiatry*, 1978c, in press.

CANTWELL, D. P., BAKER, L., and RUTTER, M. Families of autistic and dysphasic children. II. Mothers' speech to the children. *Journal of Autism and Childhood Schizophrenia*, 1977a, 7, 313-328.

CANTWELL, D. P., HOWLIN, P., and RUTTER, M. The analysis of language level and language function: A methodological study. *British Journal of Disorders of Communication*, 1977b, 12, 119-135.

CARR, E. G., SCHREIBMAN, L., and LOVAAS, O. I. Control of echolalic speech in psychotic children. *Journal of Abnormal Child Psychology*, 1975, 3, 331-352.

CHESS, S., KORN, S. J., and FERNANDEZ, P. B. *Psychiatric Disorders of Children with Congenital Rubella.* New York: Brunner/Mazel, 1971.

CHURCHILL, D. W. Effects of success and failure in psychotic children. *Archives of General Psychiatry*, 1971, 25, 208-214.

CHURCHILL, D. W. The relation of infantile autism and early childhood schizophrenia to developmental language disorders of childhood. *Journal of Autism and Childhood Schizophrenia*, 1972, 2, 182-197.

CLARK, P. and RUTTER, M. Compliance and resistance in autistic children. *Journal of Autism and Childhood Schizophrenia*, 1977, 7, 33-48.

CLARK, P. and RUTTER, M. Task difficulty and task performance in autistic children, 1978. (Submitted for publication.)

COLEMAN, M. (Ed.). *The Autistic Syndromes.* New York: Elsevier, 1976.

COWAN, P. A., HODINOTT, B. A., and WRIGHT, B. A. Compliance and resistance in the conditioning of autistic children: An exploratory study. *Child Development*, 1965, 36, 913-923.

COX, A., RUTTER, M., NEWMAN, S., and BARTAK, L. A comparative study of infantile autism and specific developmental receptive language disorder. II. Parental characteristics. *British Journal of Psychiatry*, 1975, 126, 146-159.

COX, A., RUTTER, M., YULE, B., and QUINTON, D. Bias resulting from missing information: Some epidemiological findings. *British Journal of Preventive and Social Medicine*, 1977, 31, 131-136.

CREAK, M. Schizophrenia in early childhood. *Acta Paedopsychiatrica*, 1963a, 30, 42-47.

CREAK, M. Childhood psychosis: A review of 100 cases. *British Journal of Psychiatry*, 1963b, 109, 84-89.

CUNNINGHAM, M. A. A comparison of the language of psychotic and non-psychotic children who are mentally retarded. *Journal of Child Psychology and Psychiatry*, 1968, 9, 229-244.

CUNNINGHAM, M. A. and DIXON, C. A study of the language of an autistic child. *Journal of Child Psychology and Psychiatry*, 1961, 2, 193-202.

DARBY, J. K. Neuropathologic aspects of psychosis in children. *Journal of Autism and Childhood Schizophrenia*, 1976, 6, 339-352.

DELONG, R. A neuro-psychological interpretation of infantile autism. In: M. Rutter and E. Schopler (Eds.), *Autism: A Reappraisal of Concepts and Treatment*. New York: Plenum, 1978.

DEMYER, M. K., BARTON, S., ALPERN, G. D., KIMBERLIN, C., ALLEN, J., YANG, E., and

STEELE, R. The measured intelligence of autistic children. *Journal of Autism and Childhood Schizophrenia,* 1974, 4, 42-60.

DOUGLAS, J., LAWSON, A., COOPER, J., COOPER, E. Family interaction and the activities of young children. *Journal of Child Psychology and Psychiatry,* 1968, 19, 157-171.

EISENBERG, L. The autistic child in adolescence. *American Journal of Psychiatry,* 1956, 112, 607-612.

FOLSTEIN, S. and RUTTER, M. Infantile autism: A genetic study of 21 twin pairs. *Journal of Child Psychology and Psychiatry,* 1977a, 18, 297-321.

FOLSTEIN, S. and RUTTER, M. Genetic influences and infantile autism. *Nature,* 1977b, 265, 726-728.

FRITH, U. Spontaneous patterns produced by autistic, normal and subnormal children. In: M. Rutter (Ed.), *Infantile Autism: Concepts, Characteristics and Treatment.* London: Churchill Livingstone, 1971, pp. 113-131.

GITTELMAN, M. and BIRCH, H. G. Childhood schizophrenia: Intellect, neurologic status, perinatal risk, prognosis, and family pathology. *Archives of General Psychiatry,* 1967, 17, 16-25.

GUTHRIE, R. D. and WYATT, R. J. Biochemistry and schizophrenia. III. A review of childhood psychosis. *Schizophrenia Bulletin,* Issue No. 12, 18-32.

HANSON, D. R. and GOTTESMAN, I. I. The genetics, if any, of infantile autism and childhood schizophrenia. *Journal of Autism and Childhood Schizophrenia,* 1976, 6, 209-234.

HAUSER, S. L., DeLONG, G. R., and ROSMAN, N. P. Pneumographic findings in the infantile autism syndrome: A correlation with temporal lobe disease. *Brain,* 1975, 98, 667-688.

HEMSLEY, R., CANTWELL, D., HOWLIN, P., and RUTTER, M. The adult-child interaction schedule. In preparation.

HEMSLEY, R., HOWLIN, P., BERGER, M., HERSOV, L., HOLBROOK, D., RUTTER, M., and YULE, W. Treating autistic children in a family context. In: M. Rutter and E. Schopler (Eds.), *Autism: A Reappraisal of Concepts and Treatment.* New York: Plenum, 1978.

HERMELIN, B. O'CONNER, N. *Psychological Experiments with Autistic Children.* Oxford: Pergamon, 1970.

HINGTGEN, J. N. and CHURCHILL, D. W. Identification of perceptual limitations in mute autistic children. *Archives of General Psychiatry,* 1969, 21, 68-71.

HINGTGEN, J. N. and CHURCHILL, D. W. Differential effects of behavior modification in four mute autistic boys. In: D. W. Churchill, C. D. Alpern, and M. K. DeMyer (Eds.), *Infantile Autism.* Springfield, Illinois: Charles C Thomas, 1971.

HOWLIN, P., CANTWELL, D., MARCHANT, R., BERGER, M., and RUTTER, M. Analyzing mothers' speech to young autistic children: A methodological study. *Journal of Abnormal Child Psychology,* 1973a, 1, 317-339.

HOWLIN, P., MARCHANT, R., RUTTER, M., BERGER, M., HERSOV, L., and YULE, W. A home-based approach to the treatment of autistic children. *Journal of Autism and Childhood Schizophrenia,* 1973b, 3, 308-336.

JACKSON, M. J. and GARROD, P. J. Plasma zinc, copper and amino acid levels in the blood of autistic children. *Journal of Autism and Childhood Schizophrenia,* in press, 1977.

KANNER, L. Autistic disturbances of affective contact. *Nervous Child,* 1943, 2, 217-250.

KANNER, L. Follow-up study of eleven autistic children originally reported in 1943. *Journal of Autism and Childhood Schizophrenia,* 1971, 1, 119-145.

KANNER, L., RODRIGUEZ, A., and ASHENDEN, B. How far can autistic children go in matters of social adaptation? *Journal of Autism and Childhood Schizophrenia,* 1972, 2, 9-33.

KOEGEL, R. L. and COVERT, A. The relationship of self-stimulation to learning in autistic children. *Journal of Applied Behavior Analysis,* 1972, 5, 381-387.

KOLVIN, I. Psychoses in childhood—a comparative study. In: M. Rutter (Ed.), *Infantile*

Autism: Concepts, Characteristics and Treatment. London: Churchill Livingstone, pp. 7-26, 1971.

LAWSON, A. and INGLEBY, J. D. Daily routines of pre-school children: Effects of age, birth order, sex and social class, and developmental correlates. *Psychological Medicine,* 1974, 4, 339-415.

LENNOX, C., CALLIAS, M., and RUTTER, M. Cognitive characteristics of parents of autistic children. *Journal of Autism and Childhood Schizophrenia,* 1977, 7, 243-261.

LOCKYER, L. and RUTTER, M. A five to fifteen year follow-up study of infantile psychosis. III. Psychological aspects. *British Journal of Psychiatry,* 1969, 115, 865-882.

LOCKYER, L. and RUTTER, M. A five to fifteen year follow-up study of infantile psychosis. IV. Patterns of cognitive ability. *British Journal of Social and Clinical Psychology,* 1970, 9, 152-163.

LOTTER, V. Social adjustment and placement of autistic children in Middlesex: A follow-up study. *Journal of Autism and Childhood Schizophrenia,* 1974a, 4, 11-32.

LOTTER, V. Factors related to outcome in autistic children. *Journal of Autism and Childhood Schizophrenia,* 1974b, 4, 263-277.

LOTTER, V. Follow-up studies of autistic children. In: M. Rutter and E. Schopler (Eds.), *Autism: A Reappraisal of Concepts and Treatment.* New York: Plenum, 1978.

LOVAAS, O. I., KOEGEL, R., SIMMONS, J. Q., and LONG, J. S. Some generalizations and follow-up measures on autistic children in behavior therapy. *Journal of Applied Behavior Analysis,* 1973, 6, 131-166.

MARCHANT, R., HOWLIN, P., YULE, W., and RUTTER, M. Graded change in the treatment of the behavior of autistic children. *Journal of Child Psychology and Psychiatry,* 1974, 15, 221-227.

MENOLASCINO, F. J. and EATON, L. Psychoses of childhood: A five year follow-up study of experiences in a mental retardation clinic. *American Journal of Mental Deficiency,* 1967, 72, 370-380.

MITTLER, P., GILLIES, S., and JUKES, E. Prognosis in psychotic children. Report of follow-up study. *Journal of Mental Deficiency Research,* 1966, 10, 73-83.

PRONOVOST, W., WAKSTEIN, M. P., and WAKSTEIN, D. J. A longitudinal study of speech behavior and language comprehension of fourteen children diagnosed as atypical or autistic. *Exceptional Children,* 1966, 33, 19-26.

RAVEN, J. C. *Guide to Using the Coloured Progressive Matrices.* London: H. K. Lewis, 1965.

RICHER, J. The partial non-communication of culture to autistic children: An application of human ethology. In: M. Rutter and E. Schopler (Eds.), *Autism: A Reappraisal of Concepts and Treatment.* New York: Plenum, 1978.

RITVO, E., RABIN, K., YUWILER, A., FREEMAN, B., and GELLER, E. Biochemical and hematologic studies: A critical review. In: M. Rutter and E. Schopler (Eds.), *Autism: A Reappraisal of Concepts and Treatment.* New York: Plenum, 1978.

RUTTER, M. Speech disorders in a series of autistic children. In: A. W. Franklin (Ed.), *Children with Communication Problems.* London: Pitman Medical, 1965a.

RUTTER, M. Classification and categorization in child psychiatry. *Journal of Child Psychology and Psychiatry,* 1965b, 6, 71-83.

RUTTER, M. Behavioral and cognitive characteristics of a series of psychotic children. In: J. K. Wing (Ed.), *Early Childhood Autism: Clinical, Educational and Social Aspects.* Oxford: Pergamon, pp. 51-81, 1966.

RUTTER, M. Psychotic disorders in early childhood. In: A. J. Coppen and D. Walk (Eds.), *Recent Developments in Schizophrenia.* Ashford, Kent: Headley Brothers, pp. 133-158, 1967.

RUTTER, M. Concepts of autism: A review of research. *Journal of Child Psychology and Psychiatry,* 1968, 9, 1-25.

RUTTER, M. Autistic children: Infancy to adulthood. *Seminars in Psychiatry,* 1970, 2, 435-450.

RUTTER, M. The description and classification of infantile autism. In: D. W. Churchill, G. D. Alpern, and M. K. DeMyer (Eds.), *Infantile Autism.* Springfield, Illinois: Charles C Thomas, 1971.

RUTTER, M. Childhood schizophrenia reconsidered. *Journal of Autism and Childhood Schizophrenia,* 1972a, 2, 315-337.

RUTTER, M. Psychiatric causes of language retardation. In: M. Rutter and J. A. M. Martin (Eds.), *The Child with Delayed Speech.* Clinics in Developmental Medicine No. 43. London: Heinemann/SIMP, pp. 147-160, 1972b.

RUTTER, M. The assessment and treatment of pre-school autistic children. *Early Child Development and Care,* 1973, 3, 13-29.

RUTTER, M. The development of infantile autism. *Psychological Medicine,* 1974, 4, 147-163.

RUTTER, M. *Helping Troubled Children.* Harmondsworth: Penguin, 1975; New York: Plenum, 1976.

RUTTER, M. Speech delay. In: M. Rutter and L. Hersov (Eds.), *Child Psychiatry: Modern Approaches.* Oxford: Blackwell Scientific, pp. 688-716, 1977.

RUTTER, M. Diagnosis and definition of autism. In: M. Rutter and E. Schopler (Eds.), *Autism: A Reappraisal of Concepts and Treatment.* New York: Plenum, 1978a.

RUTTER, M. Developmental issues and prognosis. In: M. Rutter and E. Schopler (Eds.), *Autism: A Reappraisal of Concepts and Treatment.* New York: Plenum, 1978b.

RUTTER, M. Language disorder and infantile autism. In: M. Rutter and E. Schopler (Eds.), *Autism: A Reappraisal of Concepts and Treatment.* New York: Plenum, 1978c.

RUTTER, M. Early sources of security and competence. In: J. S. Bruner and A. Garton (Eds.), *Human Growth and Development.* London: Oxford University Press, 1978d.

RUTTER, M. and BARTAK, L. Causes of infantile autism: Some considerations from recent research. *Journal of Autism and Childhood Schizophrenia,* 1971, 1, 20-32.

RUTTER, M. and BARTAK, L. Special educational treatment of autistic children: A comparative study. II. Follow-up findings and implications for services. *Journal of Child Psychology and Psychiatry,* 1973, 14, 241-270.

RUTTER, M., BARTAK, L., and NEWMAN, S. Autism: A central disorder of cognition and language. In: M. Rutter (Ed.), *Infantile Autism: Concepts, Characteristics and Treatment.* London: Churchill Livingstone, pp. 148-171, 1971.

RUTTER, M. and BROWN, G. W. The reliability and validity of measures of family life and relationships in families containing a psychiatric patient. *Social Psychiatry,* 1966, 1, 38-53.

RUTTER, M., GRAHAM, P., and YULE, W. *A Neuropsychiatric Study in Childhood.* Clinics in Developmental Medicine Nos. 35/36. London: Heinemann/SIMP, 1970.

RUTTER, M., GREENFELD, D., and LOCKYER, L. A five to fifteen year follow-up study of infantile psychosis. II. Social and behavioral outcome. *British Journal of Psychiatry,* 1967, 113, 1183-1199.

RUTTER, M., LEBOVICI, S., EISENBERG, L., SNEZNEVSKIJ, A. V., SADOUN, R., BROOKE, E., and LIN, T.-Y. A tri-axial classification of mental disorders in childhood. *Journal of Child Psychology and Psychiatry,* 1969, 10, 41-61.

RUTTER, M. and LOCKYER, L. A five to fifteen year follow-up study of infantile psychosis. I. Description of sample. *British Journal of Psychiatry,* 1967, 113, 1169-1182.

RUTTER, M. and MARTIN, J. A. M. (Eds.). *The Child with Delayed Speech.* Clinics in Developmental Medicine No. 43. London: Heinemann/SIMP, 1972.

RUTTER, M., SHAFFER, D., and SHEPHERD, M. *A Multi-Axial Classification of Child Psychiatric Disorders.* Geneva: WHO, 1975.

RUTTER, M. and SUSSENWEIN, F. A developmental and behavioral approach to the treatment of pre-school autistic children. *Journal of Autism and Childhood Schizophrenia,* 1971, 1, 376-397.

RUTTER, M., TIZARD, J., and WHITMORE, K. (Eds.). *Education, Health and Behaviour.* London: Longmans, 1970.

RUTTER, M., YULE, W., BERGER, M., and HERSOV, L. The evaluation of a behavioural approach to the treatment of autistic children. Final report to the Department of Health and Social Security, London, 1977.

SHAPIRO, T., FISH, B., and GINSBERG, G. L. The speech of a schizophrenic child from two to six. *American Journal of Psychiatry,* 1972, 128, 92-98.

SHAPIRO, T., ROBERTS, A., and FISH, B. Imitation and echoing in schizophrenic children. *Journal of the American Academy of Child Psychiatry,* 1970, 9, 548-567.

TAFT, L. T. and COHEN, H. J. Hypsarrhythmia and infantile autism: A clinical report. *Journal of Autism and Childhood Schizophrenia,* 1971, 1, 327-336.

TIZARD, J. and GRAD, J. C. *The Mentally Handicapped and Their Families.* Institute of Psychiatry Maudsley Monographs No. 7. London: Oxford University Press, 1961.

TUBBS, U. K. Types of linguistic disability in psychotic children. *Journal of Mental Deficiency Research,* 1966, 10, 230-240.

WING, L. The handicaps of autistic children: A comparative study. *Journal of Child Psychology and Psychiatry,* 1969, 10, 1-40.

WOLFF, S. and CHESS, S. An analysis of the language of fourteen schizophrenic children. *Journal of Child Psychology and Psychiatry,* 1965, 6, 29-41.

YULE, W. Behavioral approaches .In: M. Rutter and L. Hersov (Eds.), *Child Psychiatry: Modern Approaches.* Oxford: Blackwell Scientific, pp. 923-948, 1977.

YULE, W. and BERGER, M. Behavior modification principles and speech delay. In: M. Rutter and J. A. M. Martin (Eds.), *The Child with Delayed Speech.* Clinics in Developmental Medicine No. 43. London: Heinemann/SIMP, p. 204-219, 1972.

YUWILER, A., RITVO, E., GELLER, E., GLOUSMAN, R., SCHEIDERMAN, G., and MATSUNO, D. Uptake and efflux of serotonin from platelets of autistic and non-autistic children. *Journal of Autism and Childhood Schizophrenia,* 1975, 5, 83-98.

13

The Role of Intention in Subjective and Objective Responsibility

MARTIN WHITEMAN

Over 40 years ago, Piaget (1962) put forth a distinction between objective and subjective responsibility. Since then there has been a sizable number of studies devoted to this problem. It is clear that Piaget hit upon a significant topic, located at the intersection of cognition and feeling. What role does the actor's intent play in affecting the evaluation of his action by others? In this paper we will focus on intention in moral judgment—upon the theoretical role of intent in Piaget's conception of subjective responsibility, upon theoretical parameters of intent in moral judgment, and upon some methodological and substantive issues in the assessment and interpretation of purpose as related to evaluation. This paper is not meant to be an exhaustive review of the literature in this area; rather, it is a selective view of some of the more important issues.

The distinction between subjective and objective responsibility involves two distinct aspects of an act—its intent and its consequence—as these relate to the evaluation of the act. Piaget typically presented two kinds of acts to his child-subjects, the first featuring an act whose intent is good, but whose consequences are quite negative (I + C—), the second an act whose intent is bad but whose consequences are less damaging (I − C—). If acts are assessed by the observer in terms of *objective* responsibility, he or she considers the I + C— act the naughtier because of the highly negative consequences (the C— component) despite the mitigating good intent. If acts are considered in terms of *subjective* responsibility, the observer will rate the I − C— act more negatively, since

300

the intent was bad, despite the relatively minor impact of the damaging behavior (C–), compared to the far more hurtful I + C— situation. In a typical pair of stories used by Piaget and other investigators, one child is described as breaking 15 cups accidentally while opening a door to come to dinner (I + C—, good motive, severe damage.) This child is to be compared for naughtiness with another child who climbs up in the kitchen, while mother is out, to get a cookie, but accidentally breaks one cup (I – C–, bad intent, minor damage.) Piaget found that by the age of 10, children have generally moved from an objective to a subjective sense of responsibility, basing their evaluations more on intent than on consequence.

The relation between method and concept, because of Piaget's choice of assessment technique, is an interesting one. The child is presented with two stimulus arrays, one containing an I + C— pattern, the other an I – C– structure. If, as an objectivist, the child selects I + C— as more naughty, a number of interpretive possibilities arise.

1) The young subject is ignoring the intention and concentrating on the consequences. Since the I + C— pattern contains more damaging outcomes than the I – C– pattern, the child's judgment seems determined by the action's harmful results rather than by its positive intent. Empirically we would expect both age by intent and age by consequence interactions in analysis of variance designs with independent manipulation of positiveness of intent and severity of damage. Thus consequence cues would be used more by younger children, causing them to choose as worse the I + C— over the I – C– pattern, while the older children, with their greater reliance upon intent information, would select as more culpable the I – C– rather than the I + C— actions. Several studies' results conform to this statistical patterning (e.g., Hebble, 1971; Weiner & Peter, 1973).

2) The younger subject uses intent cues in his judgments at a level comparable to that of the older child. He sees and uses these cues, assigning blame to more negative intent, credit to more positive intent. However, the younger subject weights consequence data more heavily than the older observer, hence a naughtiness preference on the part of the younger child for I + C— despite the good intention. Statistical findings supporting such an interpretation would yield no intent by age interaction (intent differences are comparable at both ages), but a significant age by consequence interaction (the consequence differences are greater for the younger children). Indeed, the results of Nummedal and Bass (1976) and Rule and Duker (1973) support this interpretation of the Piagetian effect.

3) Still another possibility is that the younger child is particularly sensitive to some combination of intent and consequence. Thus, it may be that the younger child can see the importance of good and bad intentions when the consequence is of mild severity. However, once heavy damage is perpetrated by the act, even if accidentally, the extenuating power of the positive intention is of little avail in the young child's moral assessment. This supposition would be supported by an appropriate age by intention by consequence interaction, with a sharpening of age differences in the use of intent in the heavy damage context (or, in other words, a developmental lag in the use of positive intent when outcome is severe) but minimal age differences when damage is light. Several investigators have reported findings of this nature (Armsby, 1971; Hebble, 1971; Costanzo et al., 1973).

4) Still another interpretation would cast a dubious methodological eye upon the whole Piagetian effect and upon interpretations which stress a different psychology of intents and consequences for young and older children. Such views would point to the rather special conditions posed by the traditional Piagetian format and how these may lead to an underestimation of the young child's competence in handling intent material. In Piaget's experiment the stories were originally presented in a paired form, posing a rather complex comparison task. Berg-Cross (1975) presented the stories one at a time with separate ratings for each story and found intention-based responses shifting from 35% in the paired story format to 60% in the simplified single-story mode of presentation. Other investigators, who have varied the relative saliency of intention and consequence and ease of story recall, have also found increases in intention-based judgments (Armsby, 1971; Chandler et al., 1973; Feldman et al., 1976; Nummedal & Bass, 1976). Some of these studies will be discussed in more detail below.

The above discussion perhaps does a disservice to Piaget's treatment of subjective responsibility on at least two counts. From a methodological viewpoint, it has ignored Piaget's "clinical interview" method which was designed to probe into the child's reasons for his answers, thereby avoiding artifacts of memory, attention, understanding of directions, and the like. A more serious omission is a neglect to locate subjective and objective responsibility in Piaget's theoretical scheme; thus much of the complexity of his early thinking on the subject is lost. A presentation of this theory is therefore in order.

THE THEORETICAL BACKGROUND

The objective-subjective sequence, for Piaget, is rooted in the concept of the young child's moral realism. Indeed, objective responsibility is but one of three components of moral realism, the other two being heteronomy and literalness. By heteronomy, Piaget means strict conformity to a rule or to an authority figure with the automatic judgment of an act as bad if it is not rule-conforming. Literalness denotes obedience to the letter rather than to the spirit of the law or rule. Although heteronomy and literalness have a synonymous ring, they are at least logically separable. One can be heteronomous—the rule must be obeyed—but the interpretation need not necessarily have literal punctiliousness.

Piaget sees moral realism and its three components as emerging from the interaction between environmental influence and two prior mental structures. The first of these more pervasive structures is egocentricity, the tendency of the child to see things from his own perspective, with an inability to take the viewpoint of the other. Such tendencies would interfere with the perception of the other's intentions, thereby contributing to the objective responsibility component of moral realism. A second factor is the general realism of the child, his readiness to see as objective, external, tangible that which emerges from consciousness and mind. Thus such mental products as names and dreams are perceived by the realistic child as having an objective, reified existence independent of their subjective underpinning. The rules and regulations of authority are also given this realistic cast and contribute to the heteronomy and literalness in the moral realism realm.

Over and above the cognitive structures of egocentricity and realism are environmental influences which interact with these structures to produce moral realism. These environmental factors involve the actual adult constraints upon the child, with attendant anticipations of unilateral respect flowing from child to adult. Therefore, moral realism for Piaget, as its name implies, has a) a realistic structure rooted in and supported by the egocentric-realistic nature of the child, and b) a moral content mediated by external encounters with adult strictures, sanctions, and expectations regarding the rules and obligations in which the action of children is set.

In the course of development between 7 and 10 years, still according to Piaget, there occurs a decline in moral realism and its correlated objective responsibility. This change occurs because the younger child's egocentricity is replaced by a "perspectivism," an ability to see the viewpoints of the other, and his realism is replaced by an appreciation of the degree to which "externals" represent consensus and convention rather than intrinsic absolutes. This weakening of egocentricity and realism is not an autonomous event, but combines with new environmental encounters to affect the decline of moral realism. These new experiences are marked by cooperation, mutual respect, and reciprocity characteristic of the peer group and of parental attitudes toward an older child. With the sloughing off of moral realism because of the interaction of internal-structural and external-relationship factors, subjective responsibility with its centering on other's viewpoints and intents replaces objective responsibility with its stress upon the act's breaking of the rule with its adverse consequences.

Several other features of Piaget's early conception might be mentioned. Piaget has noted instances of the child manifesting subjective responsibility in actual interaction with others but responding according to objective responsibility in the story situations. Therefore, the formulation of subjective responsibility in observation of actions of others lags behind its appearance in self-action. A second point deals with the role of intention in moral judgment. Piaget holds that the child has a grasp of intention but that his difficulty, reflected in objective responsibility, is in his lack of ability to give adequate weight to intention in the evaluational context. "It is not from lack of psychological penetration that they evaluated lies according to the criterion of objective responsibility, it is because intention does not seem to them to count from the point of view of morality itself" (Piaget, 1962, p. 155). Still another aspect of Piaget's formulation notes that objective and subjective responsibility might better be conceived as two developmentally related processes rather than as successive stages, since the same child may sometimes judge objectively, sometimes subjectively. There is also the implication that the two processes may coexist in different admixtures, with a preponderance of subjectivity in the older and a predominance of objectivity in the younger children. The stage conception has a pervasive connotation which is belied by Piaget's observations that the same child may veer from one type of judgment to another. In keeping with the notion of coexisting processes rather than sequential stages, Piaget has noted that very young children of three or four may in the course of their own activity make judgments reflecting awareness of the intentionality, or lack of it, of an act.

SOME RESEARCH RELATED TO THE THEORY

Research findings relevant to the theory will be presented in the following sequence: a) the cognitive structure of subjective responsibility, b) environmental influences, c) the role of intent in subjective and objective responsibility, d) methodological aspects.

The Cognitive Structure of Subjective Responsibility

An immediate issue is the notion of moral realism. Is there a moral realism disposition (whether conceived as structure, stage, process) with enough generality to encompass heteronomy, literalness, and objective responsibility? An adequate test of such a conception involves the construction of items tapping each of the three components and exploring evidence of a functional unity within age levels. This has not been done. However, Macrae (1954) explored the relation between intentionality items and a set of items tapping perspective-taking, which reflects a non-egocentric orientation, in a group of boys aged 5-14. When age was controlled, the intentionality items were all significantly related among themselves, but none was significantly related to any of the perspective items. Costanzo et al. (1973) also presented evidence tending to negate the importance of a relation between perspective-taking and intentionality. These investigators found that kindergarten children's evaluations of an act with positive consequences were affected by intention. Better evaluations were given to the more positively intended actions. However, the kindergarten children had difficulty assuming the viewpoint of a third person presented as ignorant of the actor's intention. Since the children were able to use intention information at a time when they could not assume the other's viewpoint, it seems that intentionality precedes social perspective-taking rather than being caused by it. In this connection, it would be interesting to use an independently derived measure of egocentricity to study relations with subjective and objective responsibility. For example, Rubin (1973) has recently demonstrated an underlying factorial structure in several measures of egocentricity. These measures are themselves operationally independent of intentionality but tap social, spatial, and communicative role-taking. The relation between an index composed of marker variables of a factorially derived egocentricity and a measure of subjective responsibility is worth exploring.

A study by Selman (1971), though not dealing directly with subjective responsibility, is also relevant in this context. Selman found a significant relation between role-taking skills and Kohlberg's (1963) moral judgment measure. The latter involves intentionality since one of the criteria differentiating the earlier preconventional from the later conventional stages is objective versus subjective responsibility. Selman used two tasks to tap role-taking skills. The first was a game situation in which the child had to anticipate the other's perception of the child's own motive. This done, the child could then counteract the other's probable move. The second situation was similar to the one used by Costanzo et al. (1973) in that the subject had to suppress his own knowledge of an actor's motivation as he took the viewpoint of a naive observer. Controlling for age and intelligence, Selman found that success in either of these role-taking situations was related to the more advanced conventional judgment. Extremely important was Selman's follow-up of a group of children who had scored low on both the role-taking and moral judgment tasks. Only if children moved into the more advanced role-taking stage did they move from preconventional to conventional levels, suggesting the significance of role-taking as a necessary condition for the development of more advanced levels of moral judgment, though it is difficult to say how much of the intentionality component of the complex moral judgment measure shared in this advance. However, Ambron and Irwin (1975) have recently reported significant relations between cognitive role-taking and subjective responsibility.

Another approach to the problem of the relation between moral realism and subjective responsibility is reflected in the work of Boehm (1962), Boehm and Nass (1962), and Nass (1964). Their approach was to construct three categories varying in degree of moral realism, with each category including a number of dimensions theoretically relevant to Piaget's position. Thus the two extreme levels, morality of constraint and morality of cooperation, were distinguished along such dimensions as relative emphasis upon automatic obedience to rules and adults versus cooperation and respect for peers, emphasis upon fear of punishment versus moral behavior for its own sake, and a dimension related to our immediate concern—an approach showing a lack of consideration of intention versus the evaluation of motive rather than outcome alone. These investigators' results are in accord with Piaget's notion of processes rather than stages. For example, Boehm and Nass (1962) found that responses were quite situation-specific. Nass (1964) reported that among a group of 6 8-year-olds, 4 of them scored in the highest category of moral judgment on one subjective responsibility situation, but none of them was in this category in a second subjective responsibility item. Similarly, Berndt and Berndt (1975) found low relations between the more advanced form of Piagetian moral judgment within groups of preschoolers, second, and fifth graders.

Environmental Influences

Let us look at some of the findings relevant to the environmental aspects of the theory. Reasoning from Piaget's theory, Peterson, Peterson and Finley (1974) hypothesized that increased subjective responsibility should result if the actor in the I + C—— pattern is an adult compared to the contrasting (I − C— case where the actor is a child. If the child-subject is dominated by a morality of unilateral adult respect, then the presence of the adult in the I + C—— case should offset the serious damage cue and lead to more positive judgments. For a group of second graders, there was indeed an increase in intention-based responses in this child-adult comparison (45%) whereas the standard child-child story combination yielded only 20%. However, the finding is tenuous since it was not replicated by Rybash, Sewall, Roodin, and Sullivan (1975). These authors suggest that their use of a one-story-at-a-time format may have attenuated the contrast between child and adult actors. Macrae's approach (1954) involved the construction of indices tapping the strictness of parental control and the child's willingness to accede to parental demands. The theoretical expectation that those answering at the adult constraint end of these dimensions would be more objective was not borne out. A third index, Violation of Norms, measured the tolerance for violation of moral injunctions when these interfered with the demands of friends, group membership, or personal need. This index is theoretically interesting from a cognitive-structural viewpoint since it comes closest to assessing an anti-heteronomous, anti-literal orientation to rules and regulations, two important components of moral realism, and should therefore have related to subjective intentionality. It did not. However, there may have been a suppressor variable masking such a relationship. Social class, in Macrae's study, correlated positively with subjective responsibility but negatively with Violation of Norms, thereby attenuating the relationship between the two latter variables. The higher social class children were more intentional but less tolerant of deviance. The statistical control of social class might have revealed a significant positive relationship in support of Piaget's position.

The importance of peer influence in mediating subjective responsibility was studied by Whiteman and Kosier (1964). They reasoned that combined-grade instruction, with its exposure of the child to older peers, should increase intentionality. The findings bear out the supposition, with their 7-8-year-old group in regular classes offering 40% intention-based responses as compared to the 62% responses of those children in the combined grade situation. Nevertheless, Kugelmass and Breznitz (1967), in their study of city and kibbutz adolescents, found little support for the importance of peer group participation in intentionality judgments.

A study by Kersey (1977) breaks new ground in varying the actor from self to other in order to follow up Piaget's observations regarding intentionality occurring earlier in the child's own real-life environmental encounters as compared to a task requiring observation and description of others. In the self-condition, the child was told to pretend he or she was the actor in the story. The kindergarten children in the self condition scored significantly higher in the subjective responsibility direction than did the children in the standard other-actor condition, attesting to the sensitivity of intentionality to situational context.

The Role of Intent in Subjective and Objective Responsibility

What is the role of intent? Is the young child's difficulty his lesser ability to grasp motivation, or is he able to see the motive but discounts it in the evaluation process?

A recent study by Bearison and Isaacs (1975) has bearing on Piaget's point that the young child understands the motive but does not give it much weight in his moral evaluation. These investigators have posed the issue in terms of whether the objective responsibility child has a production deficiency, i.e., is unable to grasp the motive, or a mediational deficiency, i.e., is aware of the intention but cannot or will not apply it to the evaluation situation. Working with six- and seven-year-olds, they formed two experimental groups: 1) an intention-explicit group for whom positive and negative motives were explicitly presented to the children; and 2) an intention-asked group in which the children were asked if the actor meant to do a bad thing, without the motives being explicitly presented. A third group comprised a control group and was given the stories in the usual fashion, with the motive to be inferred from the action. The results indicated significant differences between experimental groups and the control group, but not between the two experimental groups. The implication is that once the intention is highlighted either directly or indirectly, the children are capable of using it in their evaluations. Whereas only 7% of the control children gave subjective responsibility responses to two situations, 53% of the intention-explicit children manifested intentionality on both items. Findings by Whiteman (1970, 1976) are also consistent with the production deficiency hypothesis. Whiteman found a significant relation between subjective responsibility and the ability to infer motivation, even with controls on age and intelligence. The presented situations tapped the child's ability to grasp the motivation of an actor manifesting such defense mechanisms as displacement, rationalization, and projection. Assuming that ease in producing motive for defensive behavior is conducive to ease of producing or inferring intention in the moral judgment situation, the association between the two kinds of motivational measures is understandable.

The effectiveness of alleviating production deficiency in motivational perception, as exemplified in the Bearison and Isaacs (1975) study, is consistent with the results of Chandler et al. (1973). The latter attempted

to increase the saliency of intention relative to consequence by presenting the stories by videotape. The intentions of the actor were therefore
brought into sharper focus, presumably easing the production deficiency.
Thus a bad boy was seen as having left his younger sibling, entrusted
to him, in order to run mischievously around a store. Under such conditions of heightened motivational saliency, some 80% of seven-year-
olds offered intention-based moral judgments, as compared to 40% who
had experienced the same stories in the usual verbal form. It is interesting to note that Chandler et al. have based their theoretical argument on later Piaget (1950) with his stress upon the preoperational
child's inability to decenter from a perceptually salient dimension. Any
procedure that highlights the perceptual salience of consequence will
underestimate the young child's ability to use intention as compared to a
presentation format such as a specially devised video script which under-
scores intention. Also interesting in the Chandler et al. study is a set
effect induced when the verbal presentation (with its salient consequences) precedes the video presentation (with its salient intention).
Under these conditions, the subjective responsibility response to the
video presentation diminishd to 53% as compared to 80% when the
response was to a video presentation not preceded by verbal items. Presumably the salient consequences of the prior verbal presentation had
interfered with the salient intentionality of the video presentation. A
comparison with older children would be interesting in order to assess
whether their intentionality structure would be similarly affected by a
consequentiality set. An alternative interpretation of the video-verbal
difference in intentionality response is offered by Rybash et al. (1975).
The latter suggest that the video experience, with its realistic, vivid
quality, stimulates a more action-oriented intelligence, which, as Piaget
(1962) has hypothesized, is conducive to intentionality judgments even
in very young children.

Berndt and Berndt (1975) found that even preschoolers were able to
grasp the distinction between accidental and intentional harm. There
was a significant number of 5-year-olds who were able to identify correctly whether or not an intentionally aggressive act and an inadver-
tently hurting one were done "on purpose." However, the preschoolers
were not able to use this intent knowledge to assign differential evaluations to the two kinds of behavior. These young children were able to
identify correctly a simple motive, such as wanting an airplane, and
were able to offer more positive evaluations for good motives (actor
offers another child a toy) as compared to bad motives (grabbing a
toy for himself). That these children were able to grasp the intentional-

accidental distinction but were unable to use it in evaluation does not necessarily contradict the Bearison and Isaacs hypothesis. The grasp of intentionality was perhaps not as strong as the awareness of motive since the correct differentiation between purpose and accident occurred only in a film situation but not when presented verbally. The motive comprehension, however, was obtained for both film and verbal presentations. In line with this interpretation is King's (1971) finding that preschoolers only have a limited understanding of intentionality as compared to kindergarten and third grade children. Also pertinent are Imamoglu's (1975) results which show that though 5-year-old children did not differentiate between intentional and accidental acts in their evaluational responses, their response latencies did make the distinction, with faster reactions to the intentional evaluation. The preschoolers also expressed more dislike for the person who had caused intentional as compared to accidental harm. These more primitive responses—reactive or affective—suggest that a more refined understanding of intentionality may be necessary for its integration into an evaluative reaction.

Methodological Aspects

In reviewing studies bearing on methodological aspects, we shall center on investigations of the order in which intention and consequence are presented. Other methodologically oriented studies have been noted above, i.e., Berg-Cross' variation of one versus two story formats, and Chandler et al.'s manipulation of verbal and film modes of presentation.

In the original Piaget stories, the intentions, or the actions portraying the intentions, were presented before the consequences. Several investigators have raised the question of whether there is an age by order interaction, such that the younger children use intent less and consequence more in their judgments when the order of presentation is intent first, consequence second (IC), as in the standard Piagetian form. However, if intent rather than consequence is favored by recency of presentation (CI), the intent may be used more and consequence less. A study by Feldman et al. (1976) was designed to test this hypothesis. These investigators found that indeed their youngest group showed poorer recall for the event presented first, whether intent or outcome. Further, when intent was presented first, these 4-5-year-olds made significantly less intention-based judgments when compared to older 8-9-year-olds. But when intent was presented last, their intention-based judgments did not differ significantly from those of the older children. Presumably the salience of the intent information with a CI order had made it easier for the younger children to bring purpose into their evaluations. Furthermore, when only successfully recalled information was used, the younger children made use of intent cues at a level comparable to that of the older children even in the IC order.

How important is this order effect? More specifically, is there greater sensitivity to consequence differences when order enhances the saliency of consequence, and correspondingly, a greater awareness of intention when intention is rendered salient by the order? Table 1 extrapolates from several studies those findings which bear upon the problem. It can be seen that the order effect is quite powerful with the youngest children. Thus for the 4-5-year-olds, the kindergarten group, and the 6-7-year-olds, intent is more potent in producing evaluational differences than outcome in the intent-salient order (CI). In the consequence-salient order (IC), consequence becomes more powerful than intent in contributing to evaluational differences. For the 8-9-year-olds, the results are mixed. In one of the studies (Nummedal and Bass, 1976), the order effects are similar to those of the younger children. In the other study of 8-9-year-olds (Feldman et al., 1976), the evaluational differences associated with intent are stronger than those attributable to consequence even in the consequence-salient order, and this potency of intent over consequence is maintained among the 10-11-year-olds. These results indicate that the younger child's evaluation is not necessarily based on outcome but may shift readily to intent if the latter is more salient. The younger child's evaluation is neither objective nor subjective but salient-bound. The older child is better able to utilize intent differences even in the face of an inimical consequence-salient order.

There is also the suggestion that among the younger children, the negative quality of intent combines with recency of presentation to produce more negative evaluations. Thus the kindergarten children in the Parsons et al. study were particularly prone to see negative intent as downgrading a positive consequence. However, their results indicate that this effect occurs when the negative intent is made salient by its recency of presentation. The children show less concern with positive intent cues. The latter cues, even if salient because of the CI order, do not show a parallel offsetting of a bad consequence. That young children have a disinclination to use the extenuating power of good intent against a bad consequence has also been noted by Feldman et al. (1976) and Costanzo et al. (1973).

In these studies of order, a perplexing question is the meaning of an order manipulation. Feldman et al. conceive of it as affecting memory— intention being more difficult to remember in the IC order and easier

TABLE 1

Evaluational Differences as a Function of Intent and
Consequence Differences and Order of Presentation—
Findings from Three Studies

Group	Intent Differences	Consequence Differences
4-5 yrs. (a)		
IC	.51	4.27
CI	6.07	.77
"Kindergarten" (b)		
IC	3.94	5.41
CI	4.15	1.63
6-7 yrs. (c)		
IC	1.6	3.8
CI	5.3	1.0
8-9 yrs. (c)		
IC	1.4	4.0
CI	5.5	1.1
8-9 yrs. (a)		
IC	3.86	2.58
CI	6.42	2.00
10-11 yrs. (c)		
IC	3.4	2.4
CI	5.9	.9

Note. IC— intention presented first, consequence second; CI— consequence first, intention second.
a) Feldman et al. (1976).
b) Parsons et al. (1976). Consequence differences derived from pooled means of moral judgment and achievement situations which did not interact significantly with order and consequence.
c) Nummedal and Bass (1976).

to remember in the CI order because of recency variation. But Nummedal and Bass (1976) seem to think of order as tapping attentional and perceptual functions; they speak more of saliency and do not mention memory, though they probably do not mean to exclude this factor. It is, of course, possible that both memory and perception-attention factors are at work in an order manipulation. Indeed, in the Feldman et al.

study, there was an intent by order interaction even with control on memory, perhaps because of the enhanced vividness of the intent material when it is presented in the CI order. At any rate, it would be desirable to ferret out and hence be in a position to control separately the effects of attentional vividness and memorial retrieval upon the use of intent and consequence in moral judgment. Complicating the matter is that recall difficulties need not have a selective effect on the young child's performance. Shantz and Voydanoff (1973) found that in the recall condition (where the subject tells a story and is corrected), intention cues were used more for children of all ages studied. There was no intention by age by method interaction.

Some Conclusions from the Research

Several conclusions emerge from this literature review.

1) The role of subjective responsibility in Piaget's moral judgment theory has not been addressed thoroughly or systematically. It is not at all clear what the empirical relation is between subjective responsibility and the two other components of moral realism—heteronomy and literalness. Perhaps MacRae's Violation of Norms index comes closest to tapping the heteronomy and literalness dimensions since it purports to separate the "sticklers" to a moral order from those who place more weight on mitigating circumstances. However, we have seen from MacRae's study that the interrelationships between moral intentionality and this index of mitigation is disappointingly low.

The theoretical relation between egocentricity and intentionality fares somewhat better. At least the work of Selman, and Ambron and Irwin indicate interrelationships between perspectivism—the antithesis of egocentrism—and maturity in moral judgment. Selman's study moves furthest in this direction since his longitudinal data are consistent with the Piagetian notion that a decline in egocentricity should lead to greater intentionality in moral judgment.

2) The environmental studies do not lend convincing support to the idea that factors involved in adult constraint and peer group reciprocity are strong contributors to growth in subjective responsibility. Perhaps the emphasis is wrong. Piaget's theory stresses that moral realism and its component, objective responsibility, are products of cognitive structures (egocentricity and a more general realism) *and* environmental constraint. The theory therefore suggests that objective-subjective responsibility be studied in connection with the interaction (in the analysis of variance sense) between inner structural tendencies and outer con-

straining forces. Thus one would predict that subjective responsibility would be high in those children showing signs of theoretically appropriate cognitive development (high in perspectivism and low in general realism) *and* having the requisite environmental support (more mutual respect with parents, peer group interaction). There are apparently no studies which conjoin the inner and outer factors, as the theory demands.

3) Piaget seems to be right in conceptualizing subjective and objective responsibility as separate processes, with increasing ascendancy of subjectivity over objectivity as a developmental trend. The alternative is a stage conception resting upon the notion of a relatively fixed sequence. That the same child can be subjectivist in one story situation, objectivist in another, subjectivist as a participant, objectivist as an onlooker, subjectivist in some early encounters, objectivist in later childhood, subjectivist with minor damage, objectivist with serious damage, subjectivist when intent is salient, objectivist with more salient consequence, subjectivist in one-story presentations, objectivist in the paired story mode—all these fluctuations are consistent with a conception of a shifting balance of objectivist and subjectivist tendencies rather than one stressing an unfolding of discrete stages. It should be mentioned that this literature review has omitted discussion of studies in which experimental interventions have been applied to intentionality, since this is a complex area in itself. (Some of these studies have been discussed previously—cf. Whiteman, 1970.) However, their collective import would be in keeping with a shifting process rather than with a stage formulation for objectivist-subjectivist development.

4) Subjective responsibility, at least theoretically, is a two phase process: (a) the actor's intent is grasped, (b) the intent is integrated within an evaluational framework. The evidence is consistent with the importance of the first phase—intent grasp—and the lesser significance of the second phase—intent integration. Such a conception makes one uneasy. Intent integration involves judgments of whether an intent or an action meets certain standards, adheres to the observer's internalized norms, fulfills inner criteria of worth, accords with societal needs and functions. Surely the developmental picture must take account of growth in these evaluational interpretations and of their progressive integration with the sheer cognition of an intent. In the case of harmful, antisocial, or egocentric behavior, an important factor may be the observing child's set of expectations about the controls he believes the actor should have over such behaviors. The greater the violation of such expectations, the greater the devaluation. This factor will be discussed more fully in the next section.

INTENT QUALITY, INTENTIONALITY, AND EXPECTED CONTROL

In discussing the role of intention in subjective and objective responsibility, it is useful to distinguish two aspects of purpose. The first is its quality, its variation along a positive-negative dimension. The second aspect, partially independent of the first, is the relation between intent and the action's consequence. The latter relation may be intentional or inadvertent. These two aspects of intention, its quality and intentionality, have by no means been clearly delineated in the literature (but see Berndt and Berndt, 1975).

Piaget's original story pairs show considerable variation in the quality and intentionality of the delineated purposes. Consider the intentionality aspect first. The cups stories compare a good child coming to dinner with a bad child who is climbing up to get some jam. In both stories, the relation between intent and consequence is inadvertence—the motives of dinner preparation or jam desire were not related to the accidental breaking of the cups. In the stealing series, a child steals something valuable to help a poor boy. The comparison is with a child who steals something of less value for herself. In both stories, the relation between intent and consequence is intentionality—the loss by theft is deliberate in both cases. Finally, a combination of inadvertence and intentionality is exemplified by still another story pair, the one comparing the child who mistakenly misdirects someone with the child who deliberately does so.

Turning to variation in intent quality, it can be noted that there were three ways in which such variation was secured in the original Piaget stories: 1) action variation; 2) motive specification; 3) intentionality contrast. The cups pair cited above illustrates how intent quality is varied by differing actions—coming to dinner versus climbing for jam. The subject must infer the differing intent quality from the details of the behavior. The subject is assumed to infer correctly that coming to dinner bespeaks a more positive motive than climbing for jam, possibly a safer assumption for older or more intelligent or less venturesome subjects. This interpretive demand of contrasting motives by action variation has been noted by some investigators. For example, note the differences in explicitness of motivational delineation in the original Piaget story and Grinder's (1964) adaptation which emphasizes awareness of wrong-doing and egocentric focus.

> Piaget: "One day when his mother was out, he tried to get some jam out of the cupboard. He climbed up on a chair and stretched out his arm."

Grinder: "Paul knows that he is not to reach across the table for the jam but Paul wants the jam for himself. He leans and reaches across the table."

In motive specification, there is explicit mention of altruistic, egocentric or harmful intents, e.g., stealing for needy other vs. stealing for oneself. Piaget's stealing stories show a clear delineation of intent quality by means of motive specification. Intentionality contrast, the third mode of manipulating intent quality, does not specify a positive or negative motive but a clearly damaging or helpful behavior, i.e., an act whose consequence is some clear harm or benefit. Intentionality is then invoked to vary the intent quality. If the act is damaging and intentional it reflects a more negative motive than the same harmful consequences produced accidentally. Thus the child who is giving wrong directions in another Piaget story pair has bad intent if he is misdirecting deliberately, good intent if the damaging consequences are prompted by unwitting error. However, this story pair is complex since motive specification is also used to contrast good and bad intent; the purposely misdirecting child "wants to play him a trick."

Researchers subsequent to Piaget have used various ways of manipulating intent quality. Thus Feldman et al. (1976) manipulated motive quality by contrasting action—the child who cleans up his room versus the child who messes up his room. Rule and Duker (1973) and Hewitt (1975) have used motive specification to vary the intent quality. An aggressive act is presented as more positive when the explicit motive is to teach the other a lesson, less positive when the goal is to hurt the other. Garrett and Libby (1973) have induced different levels of intent quality by varying the intentionality of behavior. Over- and under-rewarders in a choice condition, where their intention can be realized, were evaluated most and least positively, respectively, by the recipients of the rewards. Rewarding behavior that was attributable to chance factors averaged medium ratings.

The use of motive in evaluation is contingent upon grasp of motive. If certain ways of varying intent quality require more inference than others and therefore interfere with motivational understanding, they may underestimate the young child's ability for subjective responsibility. Action variation and intentionality contrast seem to demand more motivational inference than the more explicit motive specification. Therefore, studies of subjective responsibility designed to explore the young child's competence might rely upon motive specification as the method of choice in intent variation.

TABLE 2

Types of Acts, Motives, and Consequents as Related to
Intent Quality (I + vs. I —), Severity of Consequence
(C—, C——), and Relation Between Intention
and Consequence

Intent Quality and Consequence		Intentional Intention-Consequence Relation	
Severity	Intrinsic	Instrumental	Accidental
I + C—	*	Does C— to realize I+	I+ effort, but accidental C—
I + C—	*	Does C— to realize I+	I+ effort, but accidental C—
I — C—	Does bad C- for its own sake	Does C— to realize I—	I— effort but accidental C—
I — C—	Does bad C— for its own sake	Does C— to realize I—	I— effort but accidental C—

* No entry since positive motive would not have intrinsic desire to harm.

It may also be pointed out that there are distinctions within the broad intentional category that may have implications for subjective responsibility. Thus an act may be damaging intentionally in two senses. The act may have an intrinsic intent. The actor harms the other, produces the act's negative consequence, as an end in itself. The harmful act was performed, in one of Rule and Duker's vignettes, to hurt the other boy. The act, however, may have an instrumental intent—to teach the provoker a lesson. In both cases there is intentionality, but the latter instance draws more upon the child's capacity to see the act and its consequence as means to further ends. The greater difficulty that young children have with motives ranging beyond the more immediate action consequences has been noted by a number of investigators (Berndt & Berndt, 1975; Collins et al., 1974; Whiteman, 1967). However, there has been little systematic investigation of the role of intrinsic and instrumental intentionality on children's developing moral judgments. The distinction has operational significance since the manipulation of intent quality via motive specification may take various forms.

Table 2 shows how the combination of intent quality and intentionality relation generates the various kinds of vignettes used in subjective responsibility studies. Here are some examples:

I + C—— (accidental): Child accidentally producing heavy damage by breaking 15 cups, as compared to breaking one cup (Piaget, 1962; Armsby, 1971).

I + C— (instrumental): Child hits other to make her give back candy to rightful owner (Rule et al., 1974).

I — C— (intrinsic): Child hits other to hurt him (Rule and Duker, 1973).

I — C— (instrumental): Child steals minor articles for himself (Piaget, 1962; Grinder, 1964).

I — C— (accidental): Child wants to get toy for himself, accidentally knocks over other child (Berndt and Berndt, 1975).

There are some advantages to be derived from the possibilities sketched out in Table 2. One can control for type of action since it is possible to fit one action, e.g., breaking cups, or stealing or aggressing, to any of the 10 possibilities in Table 1, thereby controlling for the different moral and emotional connotations of these behaviors. One can compare intent-consequent combinations by controlling for specific values of the intentionality dimension. Thus the classical Piagetian dilemma of 1 + C—— versus I — C— can be looked at within the *instrumental* column and within the *accidental* column. Psychologically the two kinds of story pairs are quite different. The instrumental stories involve questions of means-end relations. The actor is aware of costs, potential damage, and necessary evil, but still acts in order to realize some ultimate end, worthy as contrasted to unworthy. In the accidental stories the consequences are by definition unanticipated and not part of the actor's decision processes. Therefore, the older child, because of the relatively complex means-end necessary condition implications may see the rationale and justification of actions more clearly than the younger *in the instrumental series*. The comparison of intrinsic and instrumental intention, holding an intent-consequence combination constant, e.g., I — C—, is also meaningful since the younger child would be relatively sensitive to the more direct relation between motive and act in the case of the intrinsic motive than in the case of the more sophisticated cognition required for the instrumental intent (Whiteman, Brook, & Gordon, 1977).

Still another aspect of intent in moral judgment may be noted. An important distinction has been made by such theorists as Heider (1958) and Jones and Davis (1965) with regard to locus of control—whether the action is externally induced by threat or provocation or motivated by inner-directed self-interest or intrinsic pleasure. Perhaps more pertinent in the moral judgment context than locus of control is the degree of expected control of actor over his behavior. Thus if conditions obtain in which it is impossible to maintain control over one's behavior, the latter's harmful consequences are seen in a less dismal light. If, however, the harmful behavior is in a context in which control can be expected, the act will suffer devaluation. Table 3 is an attempt to capture some of the conditions producing variation in this control dimension and therefore theoretically exerting influence upon the observer's assessments.

Within the sphere of intentional behavior, if there has been coercion, whether due to external threat or inner unconscious need, the damaging action should appear less blameworthy than harmful behavior which has been spontaneously and freely selected. One of Berg-Cross' (1975) motivational categories, *"obedience,"* is exemplified by stories in which a child causes damage because of actions demanded of him by powerful others, a good illustration of instrumental behavior under duress. Inspection of her results indicates that first graders tend to view such actions less negatively than behavior which is more freely chosen. The extenuating effect in the case of the constrained action is particularly strong, not unexpectedly, when the damage is minimal. However, these suppositions need statistical testing, and it would be pertinent to compare these data with those derived from an older sample for developmental trends.

Table 3 also indicates that intentionally harmful behavior which has been provoked should occasion less expectation of control and therefore less severe devaluation than unprovoked harmful acts. Hewitt (1975) has found that 12-year-olds react more positively to severely than to mildly provoked aggression. The 8-year-olds, however, rate even a highly provoked, well-intentioned aggressive act quite negatively. The possible explanations of this finding attest to the complexity of these phenomena.

TABLE 3

Conditions Producing Variation in Expected Control of
Actor over Own Harmful Behavior

Intentional Behavior				Accidental Behavior	
		External Pressure			
Actor's Need Consciousness		Threat, Provocation	Free Choice	Unpreventable Consequence	Preventable Consequence
Unconscious	Conscious				
Less expected control	More expected control	Less expected control	More expected control	Less expected control	More expected control

Hewitt suggests that the younger subjects, because of the high provocation of the actor, assumed the latter's bad intention, despite the experimenter's attesting to his good intention, and therefore rated negatively. One might argue, too, that the good intention in the face of high provocation pointed to the feasibility of the actor's control over his behavior, so that aggression was seen as inappropriate and therefore devalued.

Table 3 also suggests that the actor's unconscious intentions may also serve to extenuate damaging consequences, since, by definition, one's unconscious needs are not under conscious control. Berndt and Berndt (1975) found that fifth graders understand the intentions depicted in a displaced aggression story better than younger children (preschoolers and second graders). However, this understanding did not carry more weight in extenuating the actor's aggressiveness than in the case where the actor exhibited consciously motivated aggression. It may be therefore that the utilization of unconscious motivation in moral judgment lags behind the ability to understand unconscious intent. The situation therefore may differ from the case of external pressure where both a less negative evaluation and a grasp of external duress may both develop relatively early, as the Berg-Cross data cited above suggest.

Turning to the *accidental* heading of Table 3, we see that the expected control should be influenced by the preventability of the accidental damage. If the damage wrought is purely accidental and could not have been prevented, there can be no expected control and little culpability. When preventive control is expected, even accidentally damaging behaviors will carry a freight of devaluation—"careless," "sloppy," "should've known better," "it was a potentially dangerous situation," and the like. In this regard, Kugelmass and Breznitz (1968) have placed *carelessness* and *insanity* at the inadvertent end of their intentionality continuum. Presumably insanity has the connotation of more sharply limited control by the actor of his behavior than carelessness and therefore possesses greater extenuating power in the case of harmful acts. The use of such relatively refined perceptions of control is presumably a late appearing developmental process, and Kugelmass and Breznitz have used such control conceptions in their studies of adolescent intentionality. However, Lukoff (1977) has observed that 8-9-year-olds (but not her 6-7-year-old group) spontaneously cite carelessness as a reason for assigning blame in accidental damage. It would seem that study of the various conditions affecting level of expected control and, particularly, their interactions with intent quality and outcome seriousness would contribute an important dimension to the understanding of the development of subjective responsibility.

REFERENCES

AMBRON, S. R. and IRWIN, D. M. Role taking and moral judgment in five- and seven-year olds. *Developmental Psychology*, 1975, 11, 102.

ARMSBY, R. E. A reexamination of the development of moral judgments in children. *Child Development*, 1971, 42, 1241-1248.

BEARISON, D. J. and ISAACS, L. Production deficiency in children's moral judgments. *Developmental Psychology*, 1975, 6, 732-737.

BERG-CROSS, L. G. Intentionality, degree of damage, and moral judgments. *Child Development*, 1975, 46, 970-974.

BERNDT, T. J. and BERNDT, E. G. Children's use of motives and intentionality in person perception and moral judgment. *Child Development*, 1975, 46, 904-912.

BOEHM, L. Development of conscience: A comparison of different mental and socioeconomic levels. *Child Development*, 1962, 33, 575-590.

BOEHM, L. and NASS, M. L. Social class differences in conscience development. *Child Development*, 1962, 33, 565-574.

CHANDLER, M. J., GREENSPAN, S., and BARENBOIM, C. Judgments of intentionality in response to videotapes and verbally presented moral dilemmas: The medium is the message. *Child Development*, 1973, 44, 315-320.

COLLINS, W. A., BERNDT, T. J., and HESS, V. L. Observational learning of motives and consequences for television aggression: A developmental study. *Child Development*, 1974, 45, 799-802.

COSTANZO, P. R., COIE, J. D., GRUMET, J. F., and FARNHILL, D. A reexamination of the effects of intent and consequence on children's moral judgments. *Child Development*, 1973, 44, 154-161.

FELDMAN, N. S., KLOSSON, E. C., PARSONS, J. E., RHOLES, W. S., and RUBLE, D. N. Order of information presentation and children's moral judgments. *Child Development*, 1976, 47, 556-559.

GARRETT, J. and LIBBY, W. L. Role of intentionality in mediating responses to inequity in the dyad. *Journal of Personality and Social Psychology*, 1973, 28, 21-27.

GRINDER, R. E. Relations between behavioral and cognitive dimensions of conscience in middle childhood. *Child Development*, 1964, 35, 881-891.

HEBBLE, P. W. The development of elementary school children's judgment of intent. *Child Development*, 1971, 42, 1203-1215.

HEIDER, F. *The Psychology of Interpersonal Relations*. New York: Wiley, 1958.

HEWITT, L. J. The effect of provocation, intentions, and consequences on children's moral judgments. *Child Development*, 1975, 46, 540-544.

IMAMOGLU, E. O. Children's awareness and usage of intention cues. *Child Development*, 1975, 46, 39-45.

JONES, E. E. and DAVIS, K. E. From acts to dispositions: The attribution process in person perception. In: L. Berkowitz (Ed.), *Advances in Experimental Social Psychology*. New York: Academic Press, 1965.

KERSEY, C. B. Young children's attribution of intentionality to themselves and others. *Child Development*, 1977, 48, 261-264.

KING, M. The development of some intention concepts in young children. *Child Development*, 1971, 42, 1145-1152.

KOHLBERG, L. The development of children's orientations toward a moral order: I. Sequence in the development of moral thought. *Vita Humana*, 1963, 6, 11-33.

KUGELMASS, S. and BREZNITZ, S. The development of intentionality in moral judgment in city and kibbutz adolescents. *Journal of Genetic Psychology*, 1967, 11, 103-111.

KUGELMASS, S. and BREZNITZ, S. Intentionality in moral judgments: Adolescent Development. *Child Development*, 1968, 39, 249-256.

LUKOFF, J. Personal distance, race, grade, and moral judgment. Unpublished doctoral dissertation. Teachers College, Columbia University, 1977.

MacRae, D. A test of Piaget's theories of moral development. *Journal of Abnormal and Social Psychology,* 1954, 1, 14-18.

Nass, M. Development of conscience: A comparison of the moral judgments of deaf and hearing children. *Child Development,* 1964, 35, 1073-1080.

Nummedal, S. G. and Bass, S. C. Effects of salience of intention and consequence on children's moral judgments. *Developmental Psychology,* 1976, 12, 475-576.

Parsons, J. E., Ruble, D. N., Klosson, E. C., Feldman, N. S., and Rholes, W. S. Order effects on children's moral and achievement behaviors. *Developmental Psychology,* 1976, 12, 357-358.

Peterson, C., Peterson, J., and Finley, N. Conflict and moral judgment. *Developmental Psychology,* 1974, 10, 65-69.

Piaget, J. *The Psychology of Intelligence.* New York: Harcourt, Brace, 1950.

Piaget, J. *The Moral Judgment of the Child.* New York: Collier Books, 1962.

Rubin, K. H. Egocentrism in childhood; a unitary construct? *Child Development,* 1973, 44, 102-110.

Rule, B. G. and Duker, P. Effects of intentions and consequences on children's evaluations of aggressors. *Journal of Personality and Social Psychology,* 1973, 27, 184-189.

Rule, B. G., Nesdale, A. R., and McAra, M. J. Children's reactions to information about the intentions underlying an aggressive act. *Child Development,* 1974, 45, 794-798.

Rybash, J. M., Sewall, M. B., Roodin, P. A., and Sullivan, L. Effects of age of transgressor, damage, and type of presentation on kindergarten children's moral judgments. *Developmental Psychology,* 1975, 11, 874.

Selman, R. L. The relation of role taking to the development of moral judgment in children. *Children Development,* 1971, 42, 79-91.

Shantz, D. W. and Voydanoff, D. A. Situational effects on retaliatory aggression at three age levels. *Child Development,* 1973, 44, 149-153.

Weiner, B. and Peter, N. A cognitive-developmental analysis of achievement and moral judgments. *Developmental Psychology,* 1973, 9, 290-309.

Whiteman, P. H. and Kosier, K. P. Development of children's moralistic judgments: Age, sex, IQ, and certain personal-experiential variables. *Child Development,* 1964, 35, 843-850.

Whiteman, M. Children's conceptions of psychological causality. *Child Development,* 1967, 38, 143-156.

Whiteman, M. The development of conceptions of psychological causality. In: J. Hellmuth (Ed.), *Cognitive Studies,* Vol. 1. New York: Brunner/Mazel, 1970.

Whiteman, M. Children's conceptions of psychological causality as related to subjective responsibility, conservation, and language. *Journal of Genetic Psychology,* 1976, 128, 215-226.

Whiteman, M., Brook, J., and Gordon, A. S. Perceived intention and behavioral incongruity. *Child Development,* 1977, 48, 1133-1136.

Appendix: Publications of
Herbert G. Birch, M.D., Ph.D.

Articles and Chapters

1. BIRCH, H. G. Psychological differences as among races? *Science*, 101, 173-174, 1945.
2. BIRCH, H. G. The effect of socially disapproved labeling upon a well-structured attitude. *J. Abn. Soc. Psychol.*, 40, 301-310, 1945.
3. BIRCH, H. G. The role of motivational factors in insightful problem-solving. *J. Comp. Psychol.*, 38, 295-317, 1945.
4. BIRCH, H. G. The relation of previous experience to insightful problem-solving. *J. Comp. Psychol.*, 38, 367-383, 1945.
5. CLARK, G. and BIRCH, H. G. Hormonal modifications of social behavior: Part I. The effect of sex-hormone administration on the social status of a male-castrate chimpanzee. *Psychosom. Med.*, 7, 321-329, 1945.
6. BIRCH, H. G. and CLARK, G. Hormonal modifications of social behavior: Part II. The effect of sex-hormone administration on the social dominance status of the female-castrate chimpanzee. *Psychosom. Med.*, 8, 320-331, 1946.
7. CLARK, G. and BIRCH, H. G. Hormonal modifications of social behavior: Part III. The effects of stilbesterol therapy on social dominance in the female-castrate chimpanzee. *Bull. Canad. Psychol. Assn.*, 6, 1-3, 1946.
8. CLARK, G. and BIRCH, H. G. Hormonal modifications of social behavior: Part I. The effect of sex-hormone administration on the social status of a male-castrate chimpanzee. *Yrbk. of Phys. Anthrop.*, 17-25, 1964.
9. FENSTERHEIM, H. and BIRCH, H. G. The influence of group ideology on individual behavior. *Amer. Psychologist*, 2, 317, 1947.
10. BIRCH, H. G. Review of "Sexual behavior in the human male." A. C. Kinsey, *Child Study*, 25, 51-52, 1948.
11. CLARK, G. and BIRCH, H. G. Observations of the sex skin and sex cycle in the chimpanzee. *Endocrinol.*, 43, 218-231, 1948.
12. BIRCH, H. G. and BITTERMAN, M. E. Reinforcement and learning: The process of sensory integration. *Psychol. Rev.*, 56, 292-308, 1949.
13. RIESS, B. F., ROSS, S., LYERLY, S. B., and BIRCH, H. G. The behavior of two captive specimens of lowland gorilla, (Savage and Wyman), *Zoologica*, 34, 111-117, 1949.
14. FENSTERHEIM, H. and BIRCH, H. G. A case study of group ideology and individual adjustment. *J. Abn. Soc. Psychol.*, 45, 710-720, 1950.
15. BIRCH, H. G. and CLARK, G. Hormonal modification of social behavior: Part IV. The mechanism of estrogen-induced dominance in chimpanzees. *J. Comp. Physiol. Psychol.*, 43, 181-193, 1950.

324   *Cognitive Growth and Development*

16. BIRCH, H. G. and RABINOWITZ, H. S. The negative effect of previous experience on productive thinking. *J. Exp. Psychol.*, 41, 121-125, 1951.
17. BELMONT, L. and BIRCH, H. G. Re-individualizing the repression hypothesis. *J. Abn. Soc. Psychol.*, 46, 226-235, 1951.
18. BIRCH, H. G. and BITTERMAN, M. E. Sensory integration and cognitive theory. *Psychol. Rev.*, 58, 355-361, 1951.
19. BIRCH, H. G. Communication between animals. Proceedings of the 8th Cybernetics Conference, 134-172, May 15-16, 1951.
20. BIRCH, H. G. Psychosurgery. In: D. Brower and L. Apt. (Eds.), *Progress in Clinical Psychology.* Chapter XXXVII, 493-499. New York: Grune & Stratton, 1952.
21. BIRCH, H. G. Psychology and culture. In: J. Wortis (Ed.), *Basic Problems in Psychiatry*, 90-106. New York: Grune & Stratton, 1953.
22. BIRCH, H. G. Comparative psychology. In: F. Marcuse (Ed.), *Areas of Psychology.* Chapter XII, 446-477. New York: Harper & Brothers, 1954.
23. BIRCH, H. G. How children begin to learn. In: S. Gruenberg (Ed.), *Encycl. of Child Care and Guidance.* Chapter V, 717-725. New York: Doubleday, 1954.
24. GRUENBERG, E. M. and BIRCH, H. G. Reading skills and school entrance age. *Milbank Mem. Fund. Quart.*, 33, 333-340, 1955.
25. BIRCH, H. G. and LEE, J. Cortical inhibition in expressive aphasia. *Arch. Neurol. & Psychiat.*, 74, 514-517, 1955.
26. BIRCH, H. G. Theoretical aspects of psychological behavior in the brain damaged. Psychological Services for the Cerebral Palsied. United Cerebral Palsy Association, New York, 48-61, 1956.
27. BIRCH, H. G. The evaluation and treatment of the mentally retarded child in clinics. Problems in the differential diagnosis of mental retardation: Psychological aspects. Proc. Training Institute of N.Y. Medical College and NARC. National Assn. for Retarded Children, New York, 40, 40-49, 1956.
28. BIRCH, H. G. Sources of order in the maternal behavior of animals. *Amer. J. Orthopsychiat.*, 26, 279-284, 1956.
29. BIRCH, H. G. Experimental investigations in expressive aphasia. *N.Y. J. of Med.*, 56, 3849-3852, 1956.
30. BIRCH, H. G. and KORN, S. J. Place-learning, cognitive maps ,and parsimony. *J. Gen. Psychol.*, 58, 17-35, 1958.
31. BIRCH, H. G. Introduction to E. Haeussermann, *Developmental Potential of Preschool Children*, ix-xii. New York: Grune & Stratton, 1958.
32. HALPERN, A., SHAFTEL, N., SELMAN, D., and BIRCH, H. G. The cardiovascular dynamics of bowel function. *Angiology*, 9, 99-111, 1958.
33. BIRCH, H. G. and DILLER, L. Rorschach signs of "organicity": A physiological basis for perceptual disturbances. *J. Proj. Tech.*, 23, 184-197, 1959.
34. CHESS, S., THOMAS, A., and BIRCH, H. G. Characteristics of the individual child's behavioral responses to the environment. *Amer. J. Orthopsychiat.*, 29, 791-802, 1959.
35. BIRCH, H. G. Summary of Conference. (Methodologic problems in research in mental deficiency: Woods School Conference). *Amer. J. Ment. Defic.*, 64, 410-420, 1959.
36. BIRCH, H. G. and DEMB, H. The formation and extinction of conditioned reflexes in "brain-damaged" and mongoloid children. *J. Nerv. Ment. Dis.*, 129, 162-170, 1959.
37. BELMONT, L. and BIRCH, H. G. The relation of time of life to behavioral consequence in brain damage: I. The performance of brain-injured adults on the marble board test. *J. Nerv. Ment. Dis.*, 130, 91-97, 1960.
38. BIRCH, H. G. and BELMONT, L. The relation of time of life to behavioral consequence in brain damage: II. The organization of tactual form experience in brain-injured adults. *J. Nerv. Ment. Dis.*, 131, 489-494, 1960.

39. THOMAS, A., CHESS, S., BIRCH, H., and HERTZIG, M. E. A longitudinal study of primary reaction patterns in children. *Compr. Psychiat.*, 1, 103-112, 1960.

40. HALPERN, A., SHAFTEL, N., SELMAN, D., SHAFTEL, H. E., KUHN, P. H., SAMUELS, S. S., and BIRCH, H. G. The straining forces of bowel function. *Angiology*, 11, 426-436, 1960.

41. BERMAN, A. J., HALPERN, A., SHAFTEL, N., SELMAN, D., SHAFTEL, H. E., KUHN, P. H., SAMUELS, S. S., and BIRCH, H. G. The cerebrovascular dynamics of bowel function. *Angiology*, 11, 437-442, 1960.

42. HALPERN, A., SHAFTEL, N., SELMAN, D., SHAFTEL, H. E., KUHN, P. H., SAMUELS, S. S., BIRCH, H. G. The cardiopulmonary dynamics of bowel function. *Angiology*, 11, 448-459, 1960.

43. HALPERN, A., SELMAN, D., SHAFTEL, N., SHAFTEL, H. E., KUHN, P. H., SAMUELS, S. S., and BIRCH, H. G. The peripheral vascular dynamics of bowel function. *Angiology*, 11, 460-479, 1960.

44. CHESS, S., THOMAS, A., BIRCH, H. G., HERTZIG, M. Implications of a longitudinal study of child development for child psychiatry. *Amer. J. Psychiat.*, 117, 434-441, 1960.

45. BORTNER, M., and BIRCH, H. G. Perceptual and perceptual-motor dissociation in brain-damaged patients. *J. Nerv. Ment. Dis.*, 130, 49-53, 1960.

46. BIRCH, H. G., PROCTOR, F., BORTNER, M., and LOWENTHAL, M. Perception in hemiplegia: I. Judgment of vertical and horizontal by hemiplegic patients. *Arch. of Phys. Med. & Rehab.*, 41, 19-27, 1960.

47. BIRCH, H. G., PROCTOR, F., BORTNER, M., and LOWENTHAL, M. Perception in hemiplegia: II. Judgment of the median plane. *Arch. Phys. Med. & Rehab.*, 41, 71-75, 1960.

48. HALPERN, A., KUHN, P. H., SHAFTEL, H. E., SAMUELS, S. S., SHAFTEL, N., SELMAN, D., and BIRCH, H. G. Raynaud's disease, Raynaud's phenomenon, and serotonin. *Angiology*, 11, 151-167, 1960.

49. BELMONT, I. and BIRCH, H.G. Personality and situational factors in the production of rigidity. *J. Gen. Psychol.*, 62, 3-17, 1960.

50. BIRCH, H. G. and BELMONT, I. Functional levels of disturbance manifested by brain-damaged (hemiplegic) patients as revealed in Rorschach responses. *J. Nerv. & Ment. Dis.*, 132, 410-416, 1961.

51. THOMAS, A., BIRCH, H. G., CHESS, S., and ROBBINS, L. Individuality in responses of children to similar environmental situations. *Amer. J. Psychiat.*, 117, 798-803, 1961.

52. BIRCH, H. G., PROCTOR, F., and BORTNER, M. Perception in hemiplegia: III. The judgment of relative distance in the visual field. *Arch. of Phys. Med. & Rehab.*, 42, 639-643, 1961.

53. BIRCH, H. G., PROCTOR, F., and BORTNER, M. Perception in hemiplegia: IV. Body surface localization in hemiplegic patients. *J. Nerv. & Ment. Dis.*, 133, 192-202, 1961.

54. BIRCH, H. G. and BELMONT, L. The problem of comparing home rearing versus foster-home rearing in defective children. *Pediatrics*, 28, 956-961, 1961.

55. BIRCH, H. G., BELMONT, I., REILLY, T., and BELMONT, L. Visual verticality in hemiplegia. *Arch. of Neurol.*, 5, 444-453, 1961.

56. BIRCH, H. G. Comment on article "Minimal brain damage in children." *Children*, 8, 239-240, 1961.

57. BIRCH, H. G. The concept of brain damage. Proceedings of Conference on Psychological Problems in the Habilitation of the Mentally Retarded. The Vineland Training School, New Jersey, 25-32, 1961.

58. BIRCH, H. G., BELMONT, I., REILLY, T., and BELMONT, L. Somesthetic influences on perception of visual verticality in hemiplegia. *Arch. of Phys. Med. & Rehab.*, 43, 556-560, 1962.

326   Cognitive Growth and Development

59. BORTNER, M. and BIRCH, H. G. Perceptual and perceptual-motor dissociation in cerebral palsied children. *J. Nerv. & Ment. Dis.*, 134, 103-108, 1962.

60. BIRCH, H. G. and STEINBERG, R. Changes in autonomic functioning in hemiplegia. *Arch. of Phys. Med. & Rehab.*, 43, 518-524, 1962.

61. BELMONT, I. and BIRCH, H. G. "Productivity" and mode of function in the Rorschach responses of brain-damaged patients. *J. Nerv. & Ment. Dis.*, 134, 456-462, 1961.

62. BIRCH, H. G. Dyslexia and the maturation of visual function. Chap. in J. Money (Ed.), *Reading Disability: Progress and Research Needs in Dyslexia.* New York: Johns Hopkins Press, 161-169, 1962.

63. BIRCH, H. G., THOMAS, A., CHESS, S., and HERTZIG, M. E. Individuality in the development of children. *Developm. Med. & Child Neurol.*, 4, 370-379, 1962.

64. CHESS, S., HERTZIG, M. E., BIRCH, H. G., and THOMAS, A. Methodology of a study of adaptive functions of the preschool child. *J. Amer. Acad. of Child Psychiat.*, 1, 236-245, 1962.

65. BIRCH, H. G. Letter to editor: Reply to comment by Dr. Hersher. *Pediatrics*, 30, 1008-1010, 1962.

66. THOMAS, A., BIRCH, H. G., CHESS, S., and HERTZIG, M. E. The developmental dynamics of primary reaction characteristics in children. Proceedings of the Third World Congress of Psychiatry. Canada, 722-726, 1962.

67. BELMONT, L. and BIRCH, H. G. Lateral dominance and right-left awareness in normal children. *Child Developm.*, 34, 257-270, 1963.

68. CHESS, S., THOMAS, A., RUTTER, M., and BIRCH, H. G. Interaction of temperament and environment in the production of behavioral disturbances in children. *Amer. J. Psychiat.*, 120, 142-147, 1963.

69. RUTTER, M., KORN, S., and BIRCH, H. G. Genetic and environmental factors in the development of 'primary reaction patterns.' *Brit. J. Soc. Clin. Psychol.*, 2, 161-173, 1963.

70. BIRCH, H. G. The problem of "brain damage" in children. In H. G. Birch (Ed.), *Brain Damage in Children: Biological and Social Aspects.* Baltimore: Williams and Wilkins, 1964, pp. 5-12.

71. BIRCH, H. G. and LEFFORD, A. Two strategies for studying perception in "brain-damaged" children. In H. G. Birch (Ed.), *Brain Damage in Children: Biological and Social Aspects.* Baltimore: Williams and Wilkins, 1964, pp. 46-60.

72. BIRCH, H. G. Brain injured children: A definition of the problem. *Rehab. Lit.*, 25, 34-39, 1964.

73. BELMONT, I., BIRCH, H. G., KLEIN, D. F., and POLLACK, M. Perceptual evidence of CNS dysfunction in schizophrenia. *Arch. of Gen. Psychiat.*, 10, 395-408, 1964.

74. BIRCH, H. G. Introducing the American Orthopsychiatric Association's President for 1964-65. *Amer. J. Orthopsychiat.*, 34, 611-612, 1964.

75. BIRCH, H. G. A review in N. Ellis (Ed.), *Handbook of Mental Deficiency.* Behavioral Science Book Service, 1964.

76. BIRCH, H. G. and BELMONT, I. Perceptual analysis and sensory integration in brain-damaged persons. *J. Genet. Psychol.*, 105, 173-179, 1964.

77. RUTTER, M., BIRCH, H. G., THOMAS, A., and CHESS, S. Temperamental characteristics in infancy and the later development of behavioral disorders. *Brit. J. Psychiat.*, 110, 651-661, 1964.

78. BIRCH, H. G., BELMONT, I., and KARP, E. The relation of single stimulus threshold to extinction in double simultaneous stimulation. *Cortex*, 1, 19-39, 1964.

79. BIRCH, H. G. and BELMONT, L. Auditory-visual integration in normal and retarded readers. *Amer. J. Orthopsychiat.*, 34, 852-861, 1964.

80. BIRCH, H. G., THOMAS, A., and CHESS, S. Behavioral development in brain-

damaged children: Three case studies. *Arch. of Gen. Psychiat.*, 11, 596-603, 1964.

81. BIRCH, H. G. and BELMONT, L. Auditory-visual integration, intelligence and reading ability in school children. *Percept. Mot. Skills*, 20, 295-305, 1965.

82. BIRCH, H. G., BELMONT, I., and KARP, E. Excitation-inhibition balance in brain-damaged patients. *J. Nerv. & Ment. Dis.*, 139, 537-544, 1965.

83. BIRCH, H. G., BELMONT, L., and KARP, E. Social differences in auditory perception. *Percept. Mot. Skills*, 20, 861-870, 1965.

84. BIRCH, H. G. and BELMONT, L. Auditory-visual integration in brain-damaged and normal children. *Developm. Med. Child Neurol.*, 7:135-144, 1965.

85. TURKEWITZ, G., GORDON, E. W., and BIRCH, H. G. Directed head-turning in the human neonate: The effect of prandial condition and lateral preferences. *J. Comp. Physiol. Psychol.*, 59, 189-192, 1965.

86. BELMONT, L. and BIRCH, H. G. Lateral dominance, lateral awareness and reading disability. *Child Developm.*, 36, 57-71, 1965.

87. TURKEWITZ, G., GORDON, E. W., and BIRCH, H. G. Head turning in the human neonate: Spontaneous patterns. *J. Genet. Psychol.*, 107, 143-158, 1965.

88. BIRCH, H. G., BELMONT, I., and KARP, E. The prolongation of inhibition in brain-damaged patients. *Cortex*, 1, 397-409, 1965.

89. BELMONT, I., BIRCH, H. G., and KARP, E. The disordering of intersensory and intrasensory integration by brain-damage. *J. Nerv. & Ment. Dis.*, 141, 410-418, 1965.

90. BIRCH, H. G. and WALKER, H. A. Perceptual and perceptual-motor dissociation in schizophrenic and brain-damaged patients. *Arch. of Gen. Psychiat.*, 14, 113-118, 1966.

91. BIRCH, H. G. Research needs and opportunities in Latin America for studying deprivation in psychobiological development. PAHO, WHO Scientific Pub. #134, 77-84, 1966.

92. CHESS, S., THOMAS, A., and BIRCH, H. G. Distortions in developmental reporting made by parents of behaviorally disturbed children. *J. Child Psychiat.*, 5, 226-234, 1966.

93. BELMONT, L. and BIRCH, H. G. The intellectual profile of retarded readers. *Percept. Mot. Skills, Monogr. Suppl.*, 6, 22, 787-816, 1966.

94. TURKEWITZ, G., BIRCH, H. G., MOREAU, T., LEVY, L., and CORNWELL, A. C. Effect of intensity of auditory stimulation on directional eye movements in the human neonate. *Anim. Behav.*, 14, 93-101, 1966.

95. RUTTER, M., GRAHAM, P., and BIRCH, H. G. Inter-relations between the choreiform syndrome, reading disability and psychiatric disorder in eight to eleven year old children. *Developm. Med. Child Neurol.*, 8, 149-159, 1966.

96. TURKEWITZ, G., FLEISCHER, S., MOREAU, T., BIRCH, H. G., and LEVY, L. The relationship between feeding condition and organization of flexor-extensor movements in the human neonate. *J. Comp. Physiol. Psychol.*, 61, 461-463, 1966.

97. BIRCH, H. G. and BELMONT, L. Reply to Sterritt and Rudnick. *Percept. Mot. Skills*, 23, 314, 1966.

98. TURKEWITZ, G., MOREAU, T., and BIRCH, H. G. Head position and receptor organization in the human neonate. *J. Exper. Child Psychol.*, 4 (2), 169-177, 1966.

99. BIRCH, H. G. and TURKEWITZ, G. Research perspectives in studying the perceptual world of infants. *Inst. Juv. Research*, 24-43, 1966.

100. BIRCH, H. G. and BORTNER, M. Stimulus competition and category usage in normal children. *J. Genet. Psychol.*, 109, 195-204, 1966.

101. HERTZIG, M. E. and BIRCH, H. G. Neurologic organization in psychiatrically disturbed adolescent girls. *Arch. of Gen. Psychiat.*, 15 (6), 590-599, 1966.

102. BIRCH, H. G. and BELMONT, L. Development and disturbance in auditory-visual integration. *E.E.N.T. Digest*, 28, 47-63, 1966.

103. KLAPPER, Z. S. and BIRCH, H. G. The relation of childhood characteristics of outcome in young adult cerebral palsied patients. *Developm. Med. Child Neurol.*, 8, 645-656, 1966.

104. BIRCH, H. G. Scientific investigation: The problem of relevance to the issue under consideration. Proceedings of Conference on Mechanisms in Restitution of Function after Brain Damage. NINDB, 165-167, 1966.

105. BIRCH, H. G. and TIZARD, J. The dietary treatment of Phenylketonuria: Not proven? *Developm. Med. Child Neurol.*, 9, 9-12, 1967.

106. CRAVIOTO, J., BIRCH, H. G., DELICARDIE, E. R., and ROSALES, L. The ecology of infant weight gain in a pre-industrial society. *Acta Paediatrica*, 56, 71-84, 1967.

107. KLAPPER, Z. S. and BIRCH, H. G. A fourteen-year follow-up study of cerebral palsy: Intellectual change and stability. *Amer. J. of Orthopsychiat.*, 37, 540-547, 1967.

108. BIRCH, H. G., BELMONT, I., and KARP, E. Delayed information processing and extinction following cerebral damage. *Brain*, 90, 113-130, 1967.

109. BELMONT, I., BIRCH, H. G., and BELMONT, L. The organization of intelligence test performance in educable mentally subnormal children. *Amer. J. Ment. Def.*, 71, 969-976, 1967.

110. COHEN, H. J., TAFT, L. T., MAHADEVIAH, M. S., and BIRCH, H. G. Developmental changes in "overflow" in normal and aberrantly functioning children. *J. Pediatrics*, 71, 39-47, 1967.

111. CHESS, S., THOMAS, A., and BIRCH, H. G. Behavior problems revisited. *J. Am. Acad. Ch. Psychiat.*, 6, 321-331, 1967.

112. GITTELMAN, M. and BIRCH, H. G. Intellect, neurologic status, perinatal risk and family pathology in schizophrenic children. *Arch. Gen. Psychiat.*, 17, 16-25, 1967.

113. BORTNER, M. and BIRCH, H. G. Stimulus competition and concept utilization in brain-damaged children. *Developm. Med. Ch. Neurol.*, 9, 402-410, 1967.

114. BIRCH, H. G., BELMONT, I., BELMONT, L., and TAFT, L. T. Brain damage and intelligence in educable mentally subnormal children. *J. Nerv. & Ment. Dis.*, 144, 247-257, 1967.

115. BIRCH, H. G. Health and the education of socially disadvantaged children. Proc. Conf. Biosocial factors in the development of learning of disadvantaged children. Syracuse, April 1967.

116. BIRCH, H. G. Bright rats and dull rats—race and behavior. A symposium, The Columbia University Forum, 10, 30-31, 1967.

117. BIRCH, H. G. and BORTNER, M. Brain damage: An educational category? Chap. in M. Bortner (Ed.), *Evaluation and Education of Children with Brain Damage*. Springfield, Ill.: Charles C Thomas, 3-11, 1967.

118. TURKEWITZ, G., MOREAU, T., BIRCH, H. G., and CRYSTAL, D. Relationship between prior head position and lateral differences in somesthetic stimulation in the human neonate. *J. Exper. Ch. Psych.*, 5, 548-561, 1967.

119. CRAVIOTO, J., GAONA, C. E., and BIRCH, H. G. Early malnutrition and auditory-visual integration in school age children. *J. Spec. Educ.*, 2, 75-82, 1967.

120. BIRCH, H. G. and HERTZIG, M. E. Etiology of schizophrenia: An overview of the relation of development to atypical behavior. Chap. in J. Romano (Ed.), *The Origins of Schizophrenia*. Proceedings of First Rochester International Conference, March, 1967. Excerpta Medical International Congress Series No. 151, Amsterdam, Excerpta Medical Foundation, 92-110, 1968.

121. BIRCH, H. G. and CRAVIOTO, J. Infection, nutrition and environment in mental development. Chap. in H. F. Eichenwald (Ed.), *The Prevention of Mental Retardation Through Control of Infectious Diseases*. Public Health Service Publication No. 1692, U.S. Government Printing Office, Washington, D. C., 1968. (Proceedings of Conference on Prevention of Mental Retardation through Control of Infectious Diseases), pp. 227-248.

122. CRAVIOTO, J., DELICARDIE, E. R., MONTIEL, R., and BIRCH, H. G. Motor and adaptive development of premature infants from a preindustrial setting during the first year of life. *Biol. Neonat.*, 11, 151-158, 1967.

123. BIRCH, H. G. and TAFT, L. T. Mental subnormality (Mongolism). Chapter in Robert E. Cooke (Ed.), *Biologic Basis of Pediatric Practice*. New York: McGraw-Hill, pp. 1289-1299, 1968.

124. BIRCH, H. G. Boldness and judgment in behavior genetics. Chap. in M. Mead, T. Dobzhansky, E. Tobach, and R. E. Light (Eds.), *Science and the Concept of Race*. New York: Columbia University Press, pp. 49-58, 1968.

125. KAHN, D. and BIRCH, H. G. Development of auditory-visual integration and reading achievement. *Percept. Motor Skills*, 27, 459-468, 1968.

126. TURKEWITZ, G., MOREAU, T., and BIRCH, H. G. Relation between birth condition and neuro-behavioral organization in the neonate. *Pediat. Res.*, 2, 243-249, 1968.

127. BELMONT, I., BIRCH, H. G., and KARP, E. The sequence of errors made to double simultaneous stimulation in older persons. *Cortex*, 4(3), 280-287, 1968.

128. BIRCH, H. G. Health and the education of socially disadvantaged children. *Develop. Med. Child Neurol.*, 10, 580-599, 1968.

129. HERTZIG, M. E. and BIRCH, H. G. Neurologic organization in psychiatrically disturbed adolescents. A comparative consideration of sex differences. *Arch. Gen. Psychiatry*, 19(5), 528-537, 1968.

130. BIRCH, H. G. Problems inherent in population studies of nutrition and mental subnormality. Chap. in G. A. Jervis (Ed.), *Expanding Concepts in Mental Retardation. A Symposium*. From the Joseph P. Kennedy, Jr. Foundation. Springfield, Ill.: Charles C Thomas, pp. 57-62, 1968.

131. CRAVIOTO, J., BIRCH, H. G., and DELICARDIE, E. R. Influencia de la desnutricion sobre la capacidad de aprendizaje del nino escolar. *Boletin Medico del Hospital Infantil de Mexico*, XXIV: Marzo-Abril (2), 217-233, 1968.

132. BIRCH, H. G. Field measurements in nutrition, learning and behavior. Chap. in N. S. Scrimshaw and J. E. Gordon (Eds.), *Malnutrition, Learning and Behavior*. Cambridge, Mass.: MIT Press, 497-508, 1968.

133. BELMONT, L., BIRCH, H. G., and BELMONT, I. Auditory-visual intersensory processing and verbal mediation. *J. Nerv. Ment Dis.*, 147, 562-569, 1968.

134. KARP, E., BELMONT, I., and BIRCH, H. G. Unilateral hearing loss in hemiplegic patients. *J. Nerv. Ment. Dis.*, 148, 83-86, 1969.

135. HERTZIG, M. E., BORTNER, M., and BIRCH, H. G. Neurologic findings in children educationally designated as "brain-damaged." *Amer. J. Orthopsychiat.*, 39(3), 437-446, 1969.

136. ROSENBERG, Z. K. and BIRCH, H. G. Age effects of irrelevant stimulus changes on a discrimination in children. *Percept. Motor Skills*, 28, 467-475, 1969.

137. BELMONT, I., BELMONT, L., and BIRCH, H. H. The perceptual organization of complex arrays by educable mentally subnormal children. *J. Nerv. Ment. Dis.*, 149(3), 241-253, 1969.

138. KARP, E. and BIRCH, H. G. Hemispheric differences in reaction time to verbal and non-verbal stimuli. *Percept. Motor Skills*, 29, 475-480, 1969.

139. KLAPPER, Z. S. and BIRCH, H. G. Perceptual and action equivalence of objects and photographs in children. *Percept. Motor Skills*, 29, 763-771, 1969.

140. TURKEWITZ, G. and BIRCH, H. G. Comparative psychology. Chap. in J. Wortis (Ed.), *Mental Retardation*, Vol. 1. New York: Grune & Stratton, Inc., 14-27, 1969.

141. BIRCH, H. G. Research issues in child health. IV: Some philosophic and methodologic issues. In *Critical Issues in Research Related to Disadvantaged Children*. Proceedings of Head Start Research Seminars held in Wash., D.C., Nov. 1968. Princeton, N.J. Educational Testing Service, 1969.

142. CORNWELL, A. C. and BIRCH, H. G. Psychological and social development in

home-reared children with Down's syndrome (Mongolism). *Amer. J. Ment. Def.*, 74 (3) , 341-350, 1969.

143. TURKEWITZ, G., MOREAU, T., DAVIS, L., and BIRCH, H. G. Factors affecting lateral differentiation in the human newborn. *J. Exper. Ch. Psych.*, 8, 483-493, 1969.

144. COHEN, H. J., BIRCH, H. G., and TAFT, L. T. Some considerations for evaluating the Doman-Delacato "Patterning" method. *Pediatrics*, 45 (2), 302-314, 1970.

145. BORTNER, M. and BIRCH, H. G. Patterns of intellectual abiilty in emotionally disturbed and brain-damaged children. *J. Spec. Ed.*, 3 (4) , 351-369, 1970.

146. MOREAU, T., BIRCH, H. G., and TURKEWITZ, G. Ease of habituation to repeated auditory and somesthetic stimulation in the human neonate. *J. Exp. Child Psychol.*, 9, 193-207, 1970.

147. BIRCH, H. G. Research issues in child health. IV. Some philosophic and methodologic issues. *Pediatrics*, 45 (5) , 874-883, 1970.

148. BORTNER, M. and BIRCH, H. G. Cognitive capacity and cognitive competence. *Amer. J. Ment. Def.*, 74, 735-744, 1970.

149. THOMAS, A., CHESS, S., and BIRCH, H. G. The origin of personality. *Scientific Amer.*, 223 (2) , 102-109, 1970.

150. WALKER, H. and BIRCH, H. G., Neurointegrative deficiency in schizophrenic children. *J. Nerv. Ment. Dis.*, 151 (2), 104-113, 1970.

151. BIRCH, H. G. Introductory remarks. Symposium: nutrition, growth and mental development. Eightieth Annual Meeting of the American Pediatric Society. Atlantic City, April 29, 1970. *Amer. J. Dis. Child.*, 120, 395-397, 1970.

152. WALKER, H. A. and BIRCH, H. G. Lateral preference and right left awareness in schizophrenic children. *J. Nerv. Ment. Dis.*, 151, 341-351, 1970.

153. BIRCH, H. G. Preface—*A Neuropsychiatric Study in Childhood*. Clinics in Developmental Medicine Nos. 35/36. M. Rutter, P. Graham, and W. Yule. London, Spastics International Medical Publications, 1970, pp. 1-11.

154. TURKEWITZ, G., MOREAU, T., BIRCH, H. G., and DAVIS, L. Relationships among responses in the human newborns: The non-association and non-equivalence among different indicators of responsiveness. *Psychophysiology*, 7 (2) , 233-247, 1971.

155. BIRCH, H. G. Functional effects of fetal malnutrition. *Hospital Practice*, 6 (3), 134-148, March, 1971.

156. TURKEWITZ, G. and BIRCH, H. G. Neurobehavioral organization of the human newborn. Chap. in J. Hellmuth (Ed.) , *Exceptional Infant. Studies in Abnormalities*, Vol. 2. New York: Brunner/Mazel, Inc., 24-40, 1971.

157. KLAPPER, Z. S. and BIRCH, H. G. Developmental course of temporal patterning in vision and audition. *Percept. Mot. Skills*, 32, 547-555, 1971.

158. HERTZIG, M. E. and BIRCH, H. G. Longitudinal course of measured intelligence in preschool children of different social and ethnic backgrounds. *Amer. J. Orthopsychiat.*, 4 (3), 416-426, 1971.

159. BIRCH, H. G. Malnutrition and early development. In E. Grotberg (Ed.), *Day Care: Resources for Decisions*. Office of Economic Opportunity, Office of Planning, Research and Evaluation: Experimental Research Division, 340-372, 1971.

160. BELMONT, I., KARP, E., and BIRCH, H. G. Hemispheric inco-ordination in hemiplegia. *Brain*, 94, Part II, 337-348, 1971.

161. DeLICARDIE, E. R., VEGA, L., BIRCH, H. G., and CRAVIOTO, J. The effect of weight loss from birth to fifteen days on growth and development in the first year. *Biol. Neonate*, 17, 249-259, 1971.

162. BIRCH, H. G. Malnutricion Y desarrollo Mental. III. Seminario Regional Interamericano Sobre El Nino Con Retardo Mental. Lima, Peru, Dec. 1970. U.S. Department of Health, Education and Welfare, Secretary's Committee on Mental Retardation. Washington, D.C., 1971.

163. BIRCH, H. G. Levels, categories, and methodological assumptions in the study of

behavioral development. Chap. in E. Tobach, L. R. Aronson, and E. Shaw (Eds.), *The Biopsychology of Development*. New York: Academic Press, 1971.

164. CRAVIOTO, J., LINDORE, M., and BIRCH, H. G. Sex differences in I.Q. pattern of children with congenital heart defects. *Science*, 174, No. 4013, 1042-1043, Dec. 1971.

165. BIRCH, H. G., PIÑEIRO, C., ALCALDE, E., TOCA, T., and CRAVIOTO, J. Relation of kwashiorkor in early childhood and intelligence at school age. *Pediat. Res.*, 5, 579-585, 1971.

166. KARP, E., BELMONT, I., and BIRCH, H. G. Delayed sensory-motor processing following cerebral damage. *Cortex*, 7 (4), 419-425, 1971.

167. TURKEWITZ, G., BIRCH, H. G., and COOPER, K. K. Responsiveness to simple and complex auditory stimuli in the human newborn. *Develop. Psychobiol.*, 5 (1), 7-19, 1972.

168. BIRCH, H. G. Malnutrition, learning and intelligence. *Amer. J. Public Health*, 62 (6), 773-784, 1972.

169. HERTZIG, M. E., BIRCH, H. G., RICHARDSON, S. A., and TIZARD, J. Intellectual levels of school children severely malnourished during the first two years of life. *Pediatrics*, 49 (6), 814-824, 1972.

170. TURKEWITZ, G., BIRCH, H. G., and COOPER, K. K. Patterns of response to different auditory stimuli in the human newborn. *Develop. Med. Child Neurol.*, 14 (4), 487-491, 1972.

171. RICHARDSON, S. A., BIRCH, H. G., GRABIE, E., and YODER, K. The behavior of children in school who were severely malnourished in the first two years of life. *J. Health & Social Behavior*, 13, 276-284, 1972.

172. BELMONT, L. and BIRCH, H. G. The intellectual profile of retarded readers with normal IQs. Chap. in L. M. Schell and P. C. Burns (Eds.), *Remedial Reading: Classroom and Clinic*. Boston: Allyn & Bacon, Inc., 96-109, 1972.

173. BIRCH, H. G. and RICHARDSON, S. A. The functioning of Jamaican school children severely malnourished during the first two years of life. In *Nutrition, the Nervous System and Behavior*. Proc. Seminar on Malnutrition in Early Life and Subsequent Mental Development. Mona, Jamaica, Jan. 10-14, 1972. Pan American Health Org. WHO, Scientific Publ. #251, pp. 64-72, 1972.

174. BIRCH, H. G. Issues of design and method in studying the effects of malnutrition on mental development. In *Nutrition, the Nervous System and Behavior*. Proc. Seminar on Malnutrition in Early Life and Subsequent Mental Development. Mona, Jamaica. Jan. 10-14, 1972. PAHO, WHO, Scientific Publ. #251, pp. 115-128, 1972.

175. BIRCH, H. G. Summary of Session I. Malnutrition and the nervous systems in animals and man. PAHO Seminar on Malnturition in Early Life and Subsequent Mental Development. In *Nutrition, the Nervous System and Behavior*. PAHO, WHO Scientific Publ. #251, pp. 38-40, 1972.

176. BIRCH, H. G. Summary of Session V. Future research directions. Seminar on Malnutrition in Early Life and Subsequent Mental Development. Mona, Jamaica, Jan. 10-14, 1972. In *Nutrition, the Nervous System and Behavior*. PAHO, WHO Scientific Pub. #251, pp. 133-135, 1972.

177. BELMONT, I., FLEGENHEIMER, H., and BIRCH, H. G. Comparison of perceptual training and remedial instruction for poor beginning readers. *J. Learning Disabilities* 6 (4), 230-235, 1973.

178. BORTNER, M., HERTZIG, M., and BIRCH, H. G. Neurological signs and intelligence in brain damaged children. *J. Spec. Ed.*, 6 (4), 325-333, 1972.

179. RICHARDSON, S. A., BIRCH, H. G., and HERTZIG, M. E. School perfrmance of children who were severely malnourished in infancy. *Amer. J. Ment. Defic.*, 77 (5), 623-632, 1973.

180. BIRCH, H. G. Two views on cognitive and intellectual development: Discussant's

Comments. In David J. Kallen (Ed.), *Nutrition, Development and Social Behavior*. Proc. Conference on the Assessment of Tests of Behavior from Studies of Nutrition in the Western Hemisphere. NICHD and PAHO. Mayaguez, Peurto Rico, Oct. 1970, U.S. Dept. of Health, Education and Welfare. DHEW Publ. No. NIH 73-242, pp. 191-196, 1973.

181. KAUFMAN, J., BELMONT, I., BIRCH, H. G., and ZACH, L. J. Tactile and visual sense system interactions: A developmental study using reaction time models. *Develop. Psychobiol.*, 6 (2), 165-176, 1973.

182. BELMONT, I. and BIRCH, H. G. The effect of supplemental intervention on children with low reading readiness scores. *J. Spec. Ed.*, 8 (1), 81-89, 1974.

183. BIRCH, H. G. Introduction: Session IV. Development of cognitive functions. In D. P. Purpura and G. P. Reaser (Eds.), *Methodological Approaches to the Study of Brain Maturation and Its Abnormalities*. (NICHD Mental Retardation Centers Series). Baltimore, Md.: University Park Press, 115-120, 1974.

184. BIRCH, H. G. Methodological issues in the longitudinal study of malnutrition. In D. Ricks, A. Thomas, and R. Roff (Eds.), *Life History Research in Psychopathology*, Vol. 3. Minneapolis: Univ. of Minnesota Press, pp. 3-24, 1974.

185. RUFF, H. A. and BIRCH, H. G. Infant visual fixation: The effect of concentricity, curvilinearity and number of direction. *J. Experimental Child Psychology*, 17, 460-473, 1974.

186. LEFFORD, A., BIRCH, H. G., and GREEN, G. The perceptual and cognitive bases for finger localization and selective finger movement in preschool children. *Child Development*, 45, 335-343, 1974.

187. TURKEWITZ, G., GILBERT, M., and BIRCH, H. G. Early restriction of tactile stimulation and visual functioning in the kitten. *Developmental Psychobiology*, 7 (3), 243-248, 1974.

188. WALKER, H. A. and BIRCH, H. G. Intellectual patterning in schizophrenic children. *Journal of Autism and Childhood Schizophrenia*, 4, 143-161, 1974.

189. MOREAU, T. and BIRCH, H. G. Relationship between obstetrical general anesthesia and rate of neonatal habituation to repeated stimulation. *Developmental Medicine and Child Neurology*, 16, 612-618, 1974.

190. BIRCH, H. G. Some ways of viewing studies in behavioral development. In Proceedings of the International Conference on Pre- and Post-natal Development of the Human Brain. Josiah Macy, Jr. Foundation and the International Children's Center of Paris, France, Dec. 11-13, 1972. Basel, Switzerland, S. Karger AG, pp. 320-330, 1974.

Monographs

1. BIRCH, H. G. and LEFFORD, A. *Intersensory Development in Children*. Monogr. Soc for Res. in Child Develop. Ser. 89, 28 (5). 1-48, 1963.

2. BELMONT, L. and BIRCH, H. G. *The Intellectual Profile of Retarded Readers*. Percept. Mot. Skills, Monogr. Supplement 6, 22, 787-816, 1966.

3. CRAVIOTO, J., DELICARDIE, E. R., and BIRCH, H. G. *Nutrition, Growth and Neurointegrative Development: An Experimental and Ecologic Study*. Supplement to Pediatrics, *The Journal of the American Academy of Pediatrics*, 38, 319-372, No. 2, Part II, 1966.

4. BIRCH, H. G. and LEFFORD, A. *Visual Differentiation, Intersensory Integration, and Voluntary Motor Control*. Monogr. Soc. for Res. in Child Develop. Ser. 110, 32 (2), 1-87, 1967.

5. HERTZIG, M. E., BIRCH, H. G., THOMAS, A., and MENDEZ, O. A. *Class and Ethnic Differences in the Responsiveness of Preschool Children to Cognitive Demands.* Monogr. Soc. for Res. in Child Develop. Ser. 117, 33 (1), 1-69, 1968.

6. CRAVIOTO, J., BIRCH, H. G., DELICARDIE, E., ROSALES, L., and VEGA, L. *The Ecology of Growth and Development in a Mexican Preindustrial Community. Report 1: Method and Findings from Birth to One Month of Age.* Monogr. Soc. for Res. in Child Develop. Ser. 129, 34 (5), 1-76, 1969.

Books

1. THOMAS, A., BIRCH, H. G., CHESS, S., HERTZIG, M. E., and KORN, S. *Behavioral Individuality in Early Childhood.* New York: New York University Press, 1963.

2. BIRCH, H. G. (Ed.). *Brain Damage in Children: Biological and Social Aspects.* Baltimore: Williams & Wilkins, 1964.

3. CHESS, S., THOMAS, A., and BIRCH, H. G. *Your Child is A Person. A Psychological Approach to Parenthood Without Guilt.* New York: Viking Press, 1965.

4. THOMAS, A., CHESS, S., and BIRCH, H. G. *Temperament and Behavior Disorders in Children.* New York: New York University Press, 1968.

5. BIRCH, H. G. and GUSSOW, J. D. *Disadvantaged Children: Health, Nutrition and School Failure.* New York: Harcourt, Brace & World and Grune & Stratton, 1970.

6. BIRCH, H. G., RICHARDSON, S. A., BAIRD, D., HOROBIN, G., and ILLSLEY, R. *Mental Subnormality in the Community—A Clinical and Epidemiologic Study.* Baltimore: The Williams & Wilkins Co., 1970.

Name Index

Subject Index